# ANCIENT

# CHAMORRO

# SOCIETY

by Lawrence J. Cunningham

To Robin!
Thank you for
your help and advice
on this book in 1980
and in 1986.
Best Wishes
Lawrence J. Cunningham
Aug. F, 1995
P.S. see page iv

The Bess Press
P. O. Box 22388
Honolulu, HI 96823

Dedicated to the Chamorros of the 21st Century

Cover art: **Noe Pegarido**

Cover design: **Paula Newcomb**

Index: **Kathy Cannallo**

Library of Congress Catalog No.: 91-78031

Cunningham, Lawrence J.
   Ancient Chamorro Society
   Honolulu, Hawaii: The Bess Press, Inc.

ISBN: Hardcover:  1-880188-05-8
        Paperback:  1-880188-06-6

Printed in the United States of America

# TABLE OF CONTENTS

# ACKNOWLEDGMENTS

**Students (hundreds) but especially the following:**

Kim Thai Cunningham
Annie Tyquingco

Mary M. Penafiel
Clyde Valdez

Mary Rose Tigulo

## Teachers

Geronimo T. Anderson - Inarajan High School
George Borja - George Washington High School
Julie C. Caguioa - Sanchez High School
Roque B. Eustaquio - John F. Kennedy High School
Madlynn Kirkland - Oceanview High School
Elizabeth LG Meilicke - Inarajan High School
Patricia Rankin - Oceanview High School
Martha C. Salas - Inarajan Jr. High School
Richard Selnikoff - Inarajan High School

Lani Bordallo - George Washington High School
Judy Bothmer - George Washington High School
Hilda Duenas - Sanchez High School
James N. Kessler - Oceanview High School
Rosita Lorenzo - Oceanview High School
Tomas Pangelinan - Oceanview High School
Frances Sablan - CNMI Department of Education

## Artists

Lyndon Asuncion - Student
Rogelio Faustino - Guam Department of Education
Judy Flores - Council of Arts and Humanities
Herman Pablo - Student
Joey Quintanilla - Student

Laura Butler - Student
Ramon Flesvig - Oceanview High School
Victor Lobdell - Student
Noe Pegarido - Student
Carla Thompson - Student

## Linguistic and/or Cultural Acceptability

Balbino and Patricia Aguigui - Agat
Josefina P. Barcinas - Guam Department of Education
Clotilde C. Gould - Guam Department of Education
Rosa Palomo - University of Guam
Illuminada S. Perez - Guam Department of Education
Vicky Flores Ritter - Santa Rita
Jose S. Rivera - Guam Department of Education
Albert Topasna - Mayor of Umatac
Raymond Yamashita - Agat

Antonio C. Babauta - Mayor of Agat
Bernadita Camacho-Dungca - University of Guam
Juan Nededog - Guam Commercial Port
William M. Paulino - Guam Department of Education
Joaquin Reyes - Guam Department of Education
Ana Maria T. Rivera - Guam Department of Education
Nerissa B. Shafer - Guam Department of Education
Robert Underwood - University of Guam

## Anthropologists

Richard Chaney - University of Oregon
Laura Maria Torres Souder - University of Guam

Jane Jennison-Nolan - University of Guam

## Archaeologists

Victoriano April - Guam Territorial Archaeologist
Michael A. Fleming - CNM Archaeologist

Richard D. Davis - Historic Preservation Officer
Hiro Kurashina - University of Guam

## Ethnohistorian and Translator

Marjorie G. Driver - Micronesian Area Research Center

## Curriculum and Instruction

Robin Butterfield - NWREL
Gary Ferrington - University of Oregon
Ray Hull - University of Oregon
Phill Mendel - Guam Department of Education
Leslie Peckens - NWREL
Ione M. Wolf - Guam Department of Education

Joseph Coburn - NWREL
M.D. Gall - University of Oregon
Larry Lawcock - Guam Community College
Steven R. Nelson - NWREL
William G. Savard - NWREL
Aline Yamashita - Guam Department of Education

## Sex Bias

Marcia K. Hartsock - Guam Senator

Frank Lizama - Guam Department of Education

## Technical Support

Kathy Cannallo - Honolulu
Susie C. Duenas - Fast Copy Service
Faye E. Mata - Guam Department of Education
Ann Rayson - University of Hawaii
Barry D. Smith - University of Guam

Cheryl N. Cunningham - Agat
Margaret Leon Guerrero - Oceanview High School
Faye F. Panganiban - Guam Department of Education
Revé Shapard - Bess Press
Steve Spencer - Guam Department of Education

# LIST OF ILLUSTRATIONS

# Chapter 1
# Origin

## INTRODUCTION

**Chamorros** are the **aborigines** of the Mariana Islands and their descendants. Where did the word "Chamorro" come from? The most commonly held theory is that the Spanish gave this name to the people of the Mariana Islands. Chamorro, an old Spanish term for "shaven head," was used to describe the high caste (*chamorri*) who shaved their heads. The statue of Chief Quipuha at the Paseo de Susanna in Agaña, Guam, shows this hair style. Quipuha's head is shaved except for a short finger-length of hair at the crown.

However, the word "Chamorro" may have come from *Chamurre*, an **indigenous** word, not an adaptation of the Spanish word "chamorro." In reports by Gonzalo de Vigo (1564), Chamurres was used in reference to the people of the Mariana Islands. The fact that Chamorro men shaved their heads was not reported until after 1668.

Don Luis de Torres in the early 1800s said that Chamorro came into usage as the result of a misunderstanding. When the Chamorros' canoes came close to the Spanish ships, the chiefs cried, "*Tcha-mo ulin*," which meant, "Don't use the rudder any more." The Spanish took these words pronounced "*chamulin*" or "*tchamorin* " as the name of the country or people.

Generally, the Spanish called the people in newly discovered areas Indios. The Spanish first referred to the Indios of the Mariana Islands as Ladrones. Magellan gave this name to the people and the Mariana Islands. This name means "thieves." Padre Sanvitores (1668), the first priest to establish a permanent mission on Guam, did not want the honest people of our archipelago to be called thieves, so he changed the name of the islands to Mariana Islands. He called the people Marianos.

English-speaking Americans gave the people of the Mariana Islands the name Guamanians, Rotanese, Tinianese, and Saipanese. **Guamanians** are Chamorros from Guam (**Guahan** -"we have").

**Rotanese** are Chamorros from Rota (Luta). **Tinianese** are Chamorros from Tinian, and **Saipanese** are Chamorros from Saipan.

Since the **ancient Chamorros'** history was oral and not written, most of it has been forgotten over the years. The information we will study has been collected by anthropologists, ethnologists, archaeologists, historians, and linguists. Some information about the ancient Chamorros can be learned by observing modern Chamorros because a few **ancient** customs are still practiced today

**Anthropology** is the study of humankind. Primarily anthropologists are concerned with culture. Anthropologists are also concerned with people in relation to where they are found (distribution); where different groups of people came from (origin); putting labels on different groups of people (classification); in what ways people look different (physical characteristics); how people adapt to their environment; and how people get along (social relations). The most famous anthropologist who studied Guam is Laura Thompson. Her most comprehensive book is *Guam and Its People*, 1947.

Since anthropology covers such a wide field, there are many specialties: ethnology and archaeology, for example. **Ethnology** is the science that deals with the division of mankind into ethnic groups, and their origin, distribution, and characteristics. **Archaeology** is also a specialized field of anthropology. It is the scientific study of the material remains, such as fossil relics, artifacts, and monuments, of past life and activities. Archaeologists study people by digging up their past. The most famous archaeologists to study the Chamorros are Alexander Spoehr, Fred Reinman, and Hiro Kurashina. Spoehr did his work on Saipan, Tinian, and Rota. Reinman did his work on Guam. Kurashina is continuing to study Guam's past.

**History** is a chronological (in order of time) record and interpretation of the past. The most famous historians to study Guam are Paul Carano and Pedro Sanchez, who jointly wrote *The Complete History of Guam*, 1964. For information on **prehistoric** times, historians rely on reports of the first European explorers and priests who visited the Mariana Islands.

**Linguistics** is the study of human language. Linguists can classify languages into families. They can determine which languages are related to each other. They can tell the origin of a language.

# THEORIES

Where did the aborigines of the Mariana Islands come from? Many theories are offered to answer this question. Some accounts claim the first people of the Marianas, as well as those of other parts of **Oceania**, came from the lost Pacific continent of Mu. Others claim that the Pacific peoples came from South America. Most experts agree that the Chamorros, along with most other Pacific peoples, have their origin in Southeast Asia.

We have defined the Chamorros as the aborigines of the Mariana Islands. Is this true? It may be more correct to claim that the aborigines of the Marianas became a group of people we have come to call Chamorros. Look at these facts: (1) People were in the Mariana Islands long before Chamorros built *latte* stone house supports. (2) High **caste** people in the Mariana Islands were big, healthy, and light brown in skin color. (3) Low caste people in the Mariana Islands were smaller, less healthy, and darker in skin color than the high caste.

Two popular theories have been derived from these facts. The first theory is that the aborigines of the Marianas were conquered by a big, healthy, light brown, *latte*-building people, who have come to be called Chamorros. The conquerors made the aborigines the low caste. The second theory is that the original people of the Mariana Islands were a people we call Chamorros. Either they came to the Marianas with a caste system or developed it in the Mariana Islands, as land fell into the hands of an elite group. The high caste people were healthier and bigger than the low caste because their caste position allowed them to eat better. The high caste was lighter in skin color because they spent less time in the sun than the low caste. Since *latte* stones are not found in any other part of the world, the Chamorros must have invented the *latte* stone in the Marianas.

## Settlement of Oceania

| AREA | DATE SETTLED | GROUP | PHYSICAL FEATURES | CULTURAL FEATURES |
|---|---|---|---|---|
| Melanesia (Black Islands) | 25,000 B.C. in New Guinea | Negritos and other dark-skinned peoples from Southeast Asia | Dark skin, frizzy black to blonde hair; short in height | Deep-pit cooking<br>Bow and arrow<br>Hunters and food gatherers<br>Some Melanesians were farmers; made pottery; chewed betel nut; and had men's houses. |
| Micronesia (Small Islands) | Between 3,000 and 2,000 B.C. | Malayo-Polynesians or Indonesians from Southeast Asia, but departed from Island Asia, Indonesia, Philippines, Taiwan or Malaysia. Based on linguistics. Some departed from Vanuatu (New Hebrides) | Brown skin, black hair, medium height | Deep-pit cooking<br>Slingstones<br>Pottery (art lost by some)<br>Farmers<br>Some areas had betel nut.<br>Men's houses<br>Navigators |
| Polynesia (Many Islands) | In Tonga and Samoa by 1,000 B.C.<br>In Marquesas, Tokelaus, Ellice Island by A.D. 1.<br>In Hawai'i and New Zealand by A.D. 500<br>In Kapingamarangi and Nukuoro for the last 1,000 years | Polynesians out of Southeast Asia, but departed from Fiji | Brown skin, black hair, tall | Deep-pit cooking<br>Slingstones<br>Pottery (lost)<br>Farmers<br>Kava<br>Navigators |

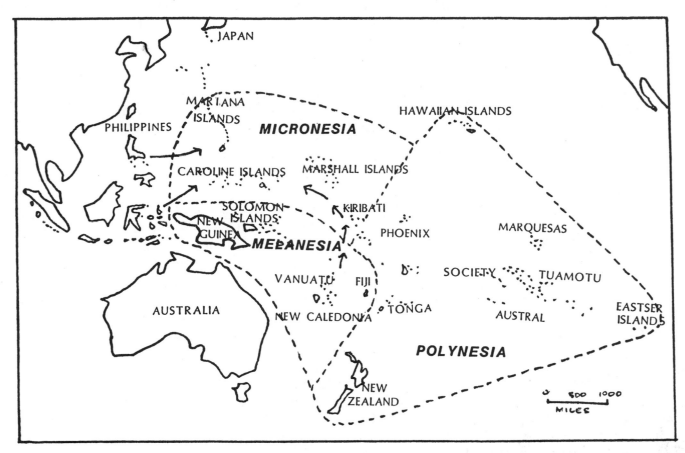

1.1 **Pacific Migration Map:** Adapted from *Atlas of Micronesia*, by Bruce G. Karolle, Guam Publications Inc., 1988.

# Mythology

According to Chamorro **mythology**, in the beginning there was nothing but space. Without parents, a brother and a sister were born of this nothingness. **Puntan**, the man, decided to die so a universe could be created for people. He instructed his sister, **Fu'uña**, to take the parts of his body to make the universe. One eye became the sun; one eye became the moon. His stomach became **Mt. Tuyan** (Barrigada Hill). His penis became

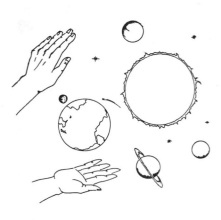

1.2 **Fu'uña Creates the Universe**

**Laso de Fua** (the rock pillar found near **Fouha Bay**). His eyebrows became rainbows.

After the universe was created, there were *ante* or spirits inhabiting the world at **Mt. Sasalaguan**. A devil named **Chaife**, who lived there, controlled the winds, waves, and fire. Chaife tortured souls inside the volcano of Mt. Sasalaguan. An escaped soul created humans at Fouha Bay. He made men and women from the red earth and the heat of the sun.

1.3 **Chaife's souls escape.** Adapted from *Chamorro Legends on the Island of Guam* , by Mavis Warner Van Peenen, Micronesian Area Research Center Publication No. 4, 1974.

3

The Spanish asked about the origin of the Chamorros, and usually got this unbelievable answer. The ancient Chamorros' **ethnocentric** view was that all the peoples of the world were descended from the first people created at Fouha Bay. Since the Spaniards were separated from the Marianas a long time, they had forgotten how to speak Chamorro. The Spanish did not believe this; they had ethnocentric views, too. The Spanish were sure man and woman first appeared in the Garden of Eden. They felt their God had created mankind and the universe.

There are other Spanish records that claim that the Chamorros said they came from the South and had the same origins as the Tagalogs who are from the Philippines. This report was made in *Mission in the Marianas*, an account about Padre Diego Luis de Sanvitores. Sanvitores established a permanent Roman Catholic settlement on Guam in 1668. In this same book, experts in the late 1600s felt the Chamorros came from Egypt or Japan. In other reports about Sanvitores, Francisco Garcia says that the Chamorros came from the south and west.

Today, we know humans were not created on Guam, because there is no evidence of humans in the Mariana Islands prior to 2000 B.C. In many other parts of the world, older evidence of humans has been discovered. At present, the earliest evidence of humans is found in Africa.

We must conclude that the Chamorros were not the first humans on Earth. Nevertheless, the Chamorros were in the Marianas for a long time. So long, in fact, that since they did not have a written language, their origins were forgotten and replaced by a myth. Perhaps the Chamorros' creation myth is an old one. Perhaps every new place they traveled the myth was changed to fit their new home. Could the escaping soul in the myth be symbolic of a group of people escaping from a volcanic eruption in another part of the world?

# Southeast Asian Origins

## Cultural and Physical Change

Since we cannot find the origin of the Chamorros from the historical record, we must look for similarities between the Chamorros and other peoples. This is a very difficult problem because of cultural and physical changes.

People are always changing their customs. Chamorros of the present drive cars, watch television, and work in a modern technological society. Social change, today, is very rapid. In the past, social change took place, but at a much slower pace.

All things do not change at the same speed. Language changes at a slower pace than dress. Chamorros still speak Chamorro, as they did seven years ago, one hundred years ago, or even five hundred years ago. The Chamorro language has changed over the years, but it is still Chamorro. Chamorros have added new words and dropped old words. Chamorros have chosen to add many Spanish, English, Filipino, and Japanese words to their language, but they still speak Chamorro. The speakers of all languages borrow words and all languages change. These cultural changes make it difficult to compare ancient peoples.

Physical changes can take place in a people. A people's looks can change rapidly, if there are many mixed marriages. Even if a people are isolated, evolutionary changes take place. It is difficult to compare ancient peoples because of these changes, and because we have limited descriptions of various ancient peoples.

Individuals and groups of people are always changing. They are always becoming something new, but what they are becoming has its roots in the past. The Chamorros became and are continuing to become a distinct ethnic group with their language and customs in the Mariana Islands. People who strongly resist cultural change, whether it is internal or external, tend to die out. On the other hand, people who blindly accept social changes find the results equally disastrous. Cultural changes should be the result of rational decisions made by the individuals and groups involved. People should avoid forced changes in their culture.

Now we are aware that people are always changing, and we can begin the difficult task of finding similarities between Chamorros and other peoples throughout the world. We can assume that Chamorros are related to the people they look like, eat like, act like, and speak like.

## Physical Similarities

The ancient Chamorros have been described as brown, tall, heavy, straight-eyed people with black hair. They were a bold and strong-limbed people.

A typical adult male was five feet six inches tall. This was tall in comparison to the Spanish colonists, who were typically around five feet tall. Early accounts say the men wore their hair long. Some Chamorro men tied their hair in a single knot; others tied it in a double knot. By the time of Padre Sanvitores, some men were shaving their head, but leaving a finger length of hair at the crown. Several early accounts state that the women had flaxen or light brown hair. Nevertheless, most accounts say the Chamorro women had long, black hair.

The inhabitants of the world are divided into races, because certain groups have similar bodily characteristics. Anthropologists identify four main races: **Negroid, Caucasoid, Australoid,** and **Mongoloid.** Chamorros are not black, not white, and not yellow. They are brown. The Chamorros, along with millions of other people, do not fit neatly into these standard categories. If they must be categorized as one of these four groups, the Chamorros are classified as Mongoloid. It is believed that the peoples of **Micronesia** and **Polynesia** are from Mongoloid stock. Some of them mixed with the Australoid people of **Melanesia** prior to making their grand voyages into the Pacific. Since many people do not fit neatly into one of these four major races, experts have divided the peoples of the Earth into as many as thirty races, and still the Chamorros do not fit neatly into any of the categories.

Indeed, if we were to line all the people in the world up by color from the darkest black to the lightest white, we would have billions of different shades of color. In addition, we would have the environmental problem of how much sun a person had been exposed to. Where would you place the albino Negroid? Race involves more than skin color. It involves hair, shape of nose, lips, and other physical characteristics. The peoples of the world have been intermarrying for so long it is difficult to categorize millions of people by race. For this reason some anthropologists believe that the concept of race is not very useful.

Again we have

1.4 Ancient Chamorros looked similar to the people of Southeast Asia.

the problem of physical change. Chamorros today do not necessarily look like Chamorros of five hundred years ago, or two thousand years ago. Five hundred years ago there were no Latin Americans; today there are millions of them. This large group of brown-skinned people came about because Europeans, especially Spanish, married American Indians. The physical appearance of the peoples of Southeast Asia today is greatly different from what it was two thousand years ago, because of additional migrations of Chinese into that area.

The people of the Mariana Islands, too, have mixed, and are continuing to mix with other racial groups. The Chamorros have intermarried with Spanish, other peoples of European descent, Filipinos, Carolinian Islanders, Japanese, Chinese, Mexicans, American Indians, and others.

A people's physical appearance can also change drastically without intermarriage. Mutations can take place. These changes in the genes can be beneficial as well as harmful. This is especially true if a small population is isolated for a long period of time. **Natural selection** and **genetic drift** probably created the differences we see in human beings today.

A people's cultural preferences can change their physical appearance. For example, if men and women prefer big-boned mates, then small-boned people tend to die out. Diet can also change a people's appearance. Japan is noted for having a short population. Since World War II, however, the Japanese people have eaten a diet with more protein, and the average height of the Japanese people has increased dramatically as a result of this change in diet.

Physical anthropologists can categorize people by inner and outer differences. Instead of dividing people by color, they can be divided by blood type. Instead of black, white, or yellow, we have type A, B, AB, or O blood. Physical anthropologists also divide people into those with wet or dry ear wax.

After taking all these inner and outer differences into consideration, and the fact that physical appearance is always changing because of intermarriage, genetic drift, and natural selection, physical anthropologists conclude that the Chamorros are most like the people of Southeast Asia. Since evidence of man in the Mariana Islands is much later than evidence of man in Southeast Asia, anthropologists assume the Chamorros must have migrated to the Marianas from islands in Southeast Asia.

# Cultural Similarities

Another way to learn where the Chamorros originated is to find cultural similarities between them and other peoples of the world. **Culture** is the total pattern of human behavior, the thought, speech, action, and artifacts of a people. Culture includes the customary beliefs, social forms, and material traits of a people. Unlike race, culture is not inherited; it is acquired. Culture, therefore, depends on man's capacity for learning and teaching future generations.

Many feel "culture is thicker than blood." By this they mean that what you are is more dependent on culture than race. Each human being regardless of race is born without a culture. A child regardless of race can learn to speak French, eat French foods, and appreciate French music. A human being is taught his or her culture. A child learns to be a Frenchman, a German, or an American. Black and white Americans have more in common than black Americans and black Nigerians, because the former share American culture.

## Artifacts

Where can we find people with artifacts similar to the ancient Chamorros? **Artifacts** are the

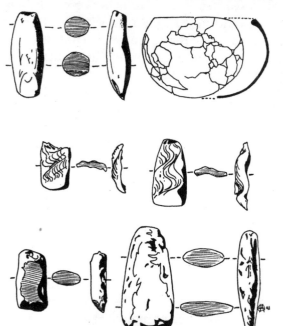

**1.5 Ancient Chamorro artifacts are of the same type found in coastal areas of Southeast Asia.** Illustrations adapted from *An Archaeological Survey and Preliminary Test Excavations on the Island of Guam, Mariana Islands, 1965-1966*, by Fred R. Reinman.

material culture or things people use. Probably ninety percent of the ancient Chamorros' material culture has been destroyed by time. However, their shell, bone, and stone tools and pottery have been studied by archaeologists. We have written accounts of their outrigger canoes and pole-and-thatch-style homes. Some ancient Micronesian artifacts are similar to Polynesian, Melanesian, and Micronesian artifacts, but the roots of all these artifacts are in the coastal areas of Southeast Asia. Of particular importance is Lapita pottery, which archaeologists find throughout the islands of Southeast Asia and in the Mariana Islands as well.

## Plants Introduced to the Mariana Islands by the Ancient Chamorros

Where do we find plants similar to those introduced to the Mariana Islands by the ancient Chamorros? **Ethnobotanists** are able to determine which plants existed in the Marianas before the islands were inhabited. Such plants are called indigenous. Ethnobotanists can also tell us which plants were brought to Guam by the ancient Chamorros. These plants are called **native**. A few important plants introduced by the ancient Chamorros are *lemmai* (breadfruit), *suni* (taro), *fa'i* (rice in the field; cooked rice is *hineksa'*), *tupu* (sugarcane), *mangga* (mangoes), *gaddo'* (yam), *pugua'* (betel nut). After examining this list, botanists agree that the only place all these plants are found is the tropical Southeast Asian area.

A good way to learn these plants is to have an ancient Chamorro cookout. Foods like chickens, pigs, corn, and potatoes should not be allowed, because they were introduced by the Spanish.

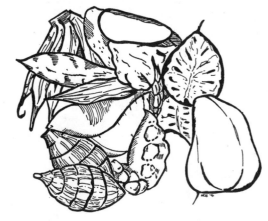

**1.6 Ancient Chamorro foods are of the same type found in Southeast Asia.**

6

Two of the most interesting plants introduced by the Chamorros are rice and betel nut. The Chamorros were the only people of Melanesia, Micronesia, and Polynesia to cultivate rice. The cultivation of rice began in Southeast Asia. At first, people considered rice a weed in the swamp taro (starchy root crop) patch. People got tired of weeding, or perhaps they were unable to weed their taro patch because of a war. Whatever the reason, they began to eat rice. Later, around 6,000 B.C., people began to cultivate rice. Early European explorers claimed that the Chamorros cultivated rice. Linguists found that *fa'i*, the Chamorro word for rice (growing in the field), is very similar to the Indonesian word for rice. Even with this evidence, few anthropologists were willing to accept the idea that the Chamorros grew rice, because no other peoples in Melanesia, Polynesia or Micronesia did so.

In 1971, a Japanese archaeologist studying the ancient Chamorros on Rota discovered the impression of a grain of rice in a piece of pottery. The archaeologist was able to date the pottery as a type made long before Europeans came to the Marianas.

This new evidence supports the historical accounts and linguistic evidence for the existence of rice in the Mariana Islands. Even so, some anthropologists do not accept the ancient Chamorros' cultivation of rice as a fact. Early reports state that rice was not a staple food for the Chamorros; rice was reserved for special occasions.

Betel nut (*pugua'* ), like tobacco, is not a food, but is an addictive substance. It has been estimated that more than thirty million people presently use betel nut in Southeast Asia, India, Indonesia, Melanesia, and Micronesia. Betel nuts are generally not used in Polynesia. Chewing betel nuts is a social custom and chewers consider it a courtesy to offer another person betel nut. This ancient Chamorro custom is still practiced today.

Ancient Chamorros chewed betel nut with quicklime (*åfok*, or chemically, calcium hydroxide). They produced quicklime by heating coral limestone until it converted into a white powder. Chamorros say that the quicklime "cooks" the betel nut and makes it stronger. Calcium is an important mineral the body must have to remain healthy. The Chamorros had only a few sources of calcium, like the infant rabbit fish (*mañahak*). Since *mañahak* is seasonal, the Chamorros needed a regular source of calcium to maintain their good health. When ancient Chamorros chewed betel nut with *åfok*, this important dietary need was satisfied.

The betel pepper leaf (*pupulu*) gives a person's breath a fragrant smell, and eliminates bad breath. *Pugua'*, *åfok* and *pupulu* are often chewed together and called **mama'on**. **Mama'on** chewing stains the teeth a dark brown and turns the saliva red. Many Pacific Island people consider stained teeth beautiful. This stain also serves as a protective coating on the betel nut user's teeth. When people chew betel nut, it kills their stomach worms and other intestinal parasites. In addition, people use the betel nut husk as a toothbrush.

On the other hand, scientists have found that people who chew betel nut are more likely to develop mouth cancer than those who do not chew it.

## Language

The study of language is one of the best ways ethnologists can find a people's origin. Usually, an area of many related languages indicates an area that many people have migrated from. By examining the languages of the world, we can see if any are similar to Chamorro. If we find languages similar to Chamorro, we will find additional clues to help us answer the question, where did the Chamorros come from?

People's languages, like their cultures, are always changing. Some theorists believe language is culture, and culture is language. People add new words to and drop old words from their language. They add new words by inventing them or by borrowing them. For example, the English word "typhoon" was borrowed from Chinese. "Tai" means supreme and "fun" means wind. "Television" is a word that was invented to describe a new product. In Chamorro the word "*ma'estro*" or "*ma'estra*," borrowed from Spanish, means teacher. In Chamorro "*chigando'*" traditionally has been used to describe a thumb sucker. After tobacco was introduced to the Mariana Islands, it came to mean a smoking pipe.

Over long periods of time the changes in a language can become so great that there is no longer just a difference in accent, or dialect, but a separate language. Nevertheless, the new language will still reveal its roots in the old language it came from. French, Spanish, Italian, and Portuguese are referred to as Latin languages, because they came from Latin. Latin is a "dead" language because we do not find any people who use it in normal everyday activities. Latin is still used by Roman Catholic priests for special purposes. Scientists give plant and animal species Latin names.

Since we can find similarities in languages, languages can be categorized on the basis of their degree of relationship. In our families, we do the same thing. An extended family includes brothers, sisters, parents, grandparents, aunts, uncles, first cousins, and second cousins.

Of course some relatives are closer than others, and so it is with languages. In the animal kingdom we know that lions and house cats are quite different, but they are all cats. **Zoologists** group a type of animal into a particular species. Related species are grouped to form a genus. A number of related genera make up a family. Families are grouped into orders, orders into classes, and classes into phyla (plural of the Latin word phylum). For example, humans are members of the species sapien; genus Homo; family Hominidae; order Primate; subclass Eutheria; class mammalia; subphylum Vertebrata; phylum Chordata.

Linguists have not standardized their classification to the degree that botanists and zoologists have. They usually classify languages by group, branch and phylum; or by branch, subfamily, family, and phylum. Spanish is in the Latin group; which is in the Italic branch; which is in the Indo-European phylum. The Indo-European phylum includes most of the languages of Europe, the Middle East, and India. Indo-European languages include the Germanic languages like Norwegian, German, and English; Latin languages like Portuguese, Spanish, French, and Italian; Greek languages like Bulgarian, Macedonian, Polish, and Russian; Iranian languages like Persian and Kurdish; and Indic languages like Hindi and Nepali.

Chamorro is in the Austronesian language phylum. This language includes languages from Madagascar eastward through the Malay peninsula and archipelago, as far north as Formosa and Hawai'i, as far east as Easter Island, and as far south as New Zealand. Austronesian languages include all the traditional languages of Indonesia, Melanesia, Micronesia, the Philippines, and Polynesia; except Papuan, Negrito languages, and the languages of the Australian aborigines.

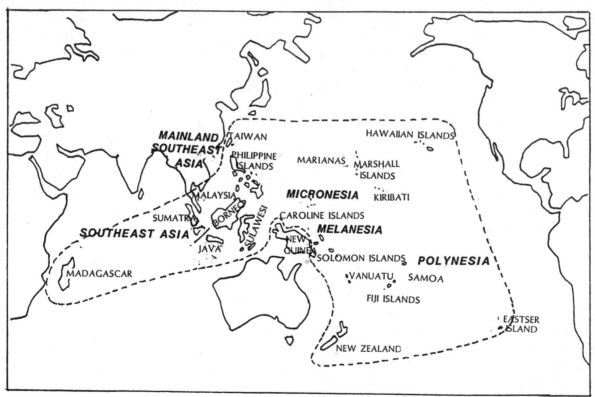

**1.7 Distribution of Austronesian Languages:** adapted from *Man's Conquest of the Pacific: The Prehistory of Southeast Asia and Oceania*, by Peter Bellwood. New York: Oxford University Press, 1979.

Ethnologists, who specialize in the study of languages, have selected hundreds of key words from thousands of different languages. The key words chosen were the ones they felt would be least likely to change. By using computers they found the degree of correlation between languages. Languages that were similar had a high degree of correlation. Even before computers it was known that the language of the Mariana Islands was similar to the languages spoken in Indonesia. In 1521 Magellan's Moluccan slave, Enrique, talked with the Chamorros.

The Austronesian phylum is composed of many separate language families. Chamorro is in the Malayo-Polynesian Family.

# MALAYO-POLYNESIAN FAMILY

| SUBFAMILY | BRANCH | SUBBRANCH or CLUSTER | LANGUAGE |
|---|---|---|---|
| Heonesian | Vanuatu (New Hebrides) | | |
| | Fijian | | |
| | Rotuman | | |
| | Polynesian | E. Polynesia | |
| | | Maori | |
| | | W. Polynesia | |
| | | Nukuoro | |
| | | Kapingamarangi | |
| | Mota | | |
| | Kiribatian (Gilbertese) | | |
| | Carolinian | Kosraean | |
| | | Marshallese | |
| | | Pohnpei (Ponapean) | |
| | | Chuukese (Trukese) | Chuukese |
| | | | Woleaian |
| | S. Solomons | | |
| | W. Melanesian | | |
| | Motuan | | |
| Chamorro | | | |
| Belauan (Palauan) | | | |
| Hesperonesian | Sulawesi (Celebes) | Bareic or Toradja | |
| | | Bugic | |
| | Totemboan | | |
| | Sangir | | |
| | Northwest | Gorontalic | |
| | | Ilongot | |
| | | Philippine* | |
| | Sentah of Borneo | | |
| | Malagasy | | |
| | W. Indonesian | Sundic | Dayak |
| | | | Balinese |
| | | | Sasak |
| | | | Javo Sumatra |
| | | | Gayo of Sumatra |
| | | Batak | |
| | | Cru of Vietnam | |
| Formosa | Central | | |
| | Atayalic | | |
| Moluccan | 10 Branches | | |

* All the languages of the Philippines except Ilogot, plus the following languages of northern Borneo: Dusun, Kalabit, Kayan, Kenya, and Murut

Compiled from George P. Murdock's *Genetic Classification of the Austronesian Languages*, 1968.

# MICRONESIAN LANGUAGES

| PHYLUM | FAMILY | BRANCH | CLUSTER | LANGUAGE |
|---|---|---|---|---|
| AUSTRONESIAN | | | | |
| | EARLY INDONESIAN | | | |
| | | CHAMORRO | CHAMORRO | CHAMORRO |
| | | PHILIPPINE INDONESIAN | | |
| | | BELAUAN (PALAUAN) | BELAUAN (PALAUAN) | BELAUAN (PALAUAN) |
| | YAPESE | YAPESE | YAPESE | YAPESE |
| | EARLY OCEANIC | | | |
| | | POLYNESIAN SOME NEW GUINEA LANGUAGES MELANESIAN MICRONESIAN | | |
| | | | CHUUKESE (TRUKESE) | CHUUKESE (TRUKESE) ULITHIAN WOLEAIAN SATAWALESE |
| | | | POHNPEIAN (PONAPEAN) | POHNPEIAN (PONAPEAN) PINGILAPESE MOKILESE NGATIKESE |
| | | | KOSRAEAN | KOSRAEAN |
| | | | NAURUAN | NAURUAN |
| | | | MARSHALLESE KIRIBATIAN (GILBERTESE) | MARSHALLESE KIRIBATIAN (GILBERTESE) |

Compiled from Francis X. Hezel's and Charles Reafsnyder's *Micronesia through the Years*, n.d.

# CHAMORRO, INDONESIAN, AND FILIPINO LANGUAGE SIMILARITIES

| ENGLISH | CHAMORRO | INDONESIAN | TAGALOG | VISAYAN |
|---|---|---|---|---|
| and | yan | dan | at | kag |
| breast/milk | susu (breast) | susu (milk) | gatas | gatas |
| dead(to die) | matai | mati | patay | patay |
| ear | talanga | telinga | tenga | dulungan |
| eye | mata | mata | mata | mata |
| female | palao'an | perawan | babae | babayi |
| fish | guihan | ikan | isda | isda |
| five | lima | lima | lima | lima |
| here | guini | ini | dito | diri |
| land | tano | tanah | lupa | duta |
| louse | hutu | kutu | kuto | kuto |
| laughter | chalek | gelak | tawa | kadlaw |
| man | lahi | laki | tao | tawo |
| me | guaku | aku | ako | ako |
| moon | pulan | bulan | buwan | bulan |
| more | lage | lagi | maramit | madamo |
| pig | babui | babi | babui | babui |
| rain | uchan | hujan | ulan | ulan |
| road | chalan | jalan | daan | dalan |
| roof | atof | atap | bubumgam | atup |
| sky | langet | langit | langit | langit |
| sweet | mames | manis | matamis | tamis |
| we | hami | kami | namin | kami |
| what | hafa | apa | ano | ano |
| you | hamyu | ikaw | ikaw | ikaw |

Compiled from Steven S. Amesbury's *Whether Pigs Have Wings*, 1988, and personal interviews with Mary M. Penafiel and Mary Rose Tigulo.

Linguists have found that Chamorro does not correlate closely enough to any other language to be part of a subbranch or even a branch. Therefore, Chamorro stands as a unique subfamily (see the Malayo-Polynesian Family Chart). The Chamorro language is like a person with relatives, but no close living relatives. Chamorro's closest relative is a "distant cousin" Bareic, a Hesperonesian Subfamily member (see the Malayo-Polynesian Family Chart). Bareic or Toradja Cluster, outside of the Hesperonesian Subfamily, is most closely related to Philippine Ivatan, Palauan (Belauan) and finally Chamorro. Almost every language of the Philippines is in the Hesperonesian subfamily.

Similarities between languages can be measured by their degree of correlation. According to these measurements Chamorro is most similar to Indonesian languages.

## Customs

Where do we find people with customs similar to the ancient Chamorros? The original inhabitants of the Mariana Islands had a social structure, including castes, **matrilineal clans**, men's houses, marriage customs, and government by headman leadership and decision making by consensus, that points to a Southeast Asian origin. Even their style of deep-pit cooking, funerals, strategy in war, reciprocal gift-giving (*chenchule'* ) and sports seem to have Southeast Asian origins.

# Lost Pacific Continent Theory

There is growing evidence to support a lost Pacific continent, according to the latest geological plate tectonics theory.

The Maya of Mexico and the Hare Krishna of India have written of a lost continent of Mu. These people are separated by the Pacific and both have a symbol for God shown in the diagram below:

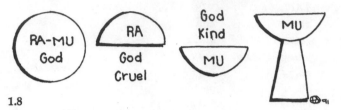

1.8

The kinder parts of God represented in this diagram closely resemble the capstone of the *latte* stones, which were used in the Mariana Islands as foundations for important buildings. Hare Krishna converts can be seen in most large U.S. cities today. The men shave their heads, but leave a small finger length of hair at the crown, just as the *Chamorri* (high caste) of ancient times did in the Mariana Islands.

The chief problem with this theory is that the geologists claim the Pacific continent sank over 100 million years ago, while Maya writings claim this event took place twelve thousand years ago.

# Lost Tribe of Israel

The lost tribe of Israel theory is supported by the evidence that waves of Caucasoid people migrated into Southeast Asia and mixed with the original inhabitants. Dates are again a major obstacle in accepting this theory. The Bible suggests dates later than this migration.

Another problem with this theory is racism. Some ethnocentric people believe that only Caucasians could have had the ability to discover and people the Pacific Islands. They believe that only Caucasians could have erected the large stone structures found in Oceania. These people find it hard to recognize the accomplishments of people of races other than their own.

# Outer Space

Those who claim that Oceania was settled by or aided by people from outer space usually base their belief on the assumption that "primitive" humans could not have built the large stone structures found in Oceania and developed the sophisticated knowledge of navigation found in Oceania. They argue that primitive man could not

have built the *latte* stones (house foundations) of the Marianas, Nan Madol (a stone city) in Pohnpei (Ponape), nor the large stone monuments of Easter Island. There is no evidence to support Oceania's settlement from outer space.

# South American Origins

The theory that the Chamorros migrated from South America was popular a few decades ago. This theory is based on casual observations that Patagonians (aborigines from Argentina) look like Chamorros and the belief that the ancient Chamorros grew the sweet potato before the Spanish arrived. The ancient Chamorros may have looked similar to the Patagonians of old, but that is not enough evidence to support this theory. They should look similar because Native Americans and ancient Chamorros have Asian origins.

Many Pacific peoples grew the South American sweet potato, even as a staple, before Western contact, but not the Chamorros. Most archaeologists believe that Polynesians did go to South America and returned with the sweet potato, which they spread through much of Oceania. Others theorize that a few South Americans drifted into Polynesia and introduced the sweet potato.

Thor Heyerdahl's popular books *Kon Tiki* and *Aku Aku* state that Polynesia was peopled from South America. Most anthropologists consider Heyerdahl a great adventurer and a poor ethnologist. We can learn from his mistakes. He examined some evidence, created a theory, and then collected only evidence to support his theory. He ignored all evidence in conflict with his theory. Linguistically, the people of the Pacific Islands are not like South American people. Most of their plants are from Asia and not South America.

# SUMMARY

Where did the ancient Chamorros come from? Examining the common theories is like trying to put together a puzzle from which many of the pieces are missing; the picture we get is not as clear as we would like. We have looked for similarities between Chamorros and other people of the world. You should have an opinion by now. You should know that most evidence points to Southeast Asia as the origin of the people we have come to call Chamorros.

# Chapter 2
# Migration

## PEOPLING OF THE PACIFIC

As early as one to two million years ago, people first appeared in what are now the islands of Southeast Asia. The remains of *Homo erectus* have been found in central and eastern Java, which at that time was connected to the mainland of Southeast Asia.

The first ocean voyagers were Australoid *Homo sapiens*. About 40,000 years ago these **hunter-gatherers** somehow crossed deep water to settle empty Australia and New Guinea. The descendants of these **Australoid** peoples are found today in Australia and the highlands of New Guinea. Also, the Negritos of Malaysia and the Philippines are descendants of these people.

About 6,000 years ago **Mongoloid** people from eastern Asia migrated to the islands of Southeast Asia. Later they passed through **Melanesia** and settled the empty islands of **Micronesia** and **Polynesia**. These people spoke **Austronesian** (also called Malayo-Polynesian) languages. Do not confuse Austronesian with Australoid. Australoids do not speak Austronesian languages.

Austronesian languages can be traced to the island of Formosa (Taiwan). They may also be related to the Thai family of languages on the mainland of Asia. It is believed that these Austronesians came from the area of China south of the Yangtze River. There are only archaeological traces of their existence in mainland China. Ta-p'en-k'eng, Lungshanoid, and Yuan-shan are the earliest mainland cultures associated with the Austronesian family of languages.

These early Austronesians were a **Neolithic** people. They cultivated rice and millet and may have grown yam, taro and sugarcane. They had domesticated animals like pigs, dogs, and perhaps chickens. As these people moved into the islands to the south, they added tropical crops like breadfruit, banana, sago, and coconut. Sago is a palm tree whose mature trunk can be pounded to yield starch. It is often used to make a type of pancake.

The Austronesian speakers made pottery, were good fishermen, and, most importantly, built seagoing canoes of the outrigger design.

Since they used a slash-and-burn method of agriculture, they were always in search of new land. Probably for this reason they used their advanced outrigger canoe technology to settle the thinly populated islands to the south. The hunter-gatherer **Paleolithic** people in those areas were easily overcome by the more advanced Neolithic farmer-sailors. The only exception to this seems to be some Australoids in New Guinea who had independently become **horticulturists**.

About 5,500 to 4,500 years ago the simple flaked stone tools in island Southeast Asia began to be replaced by stone tools shaped by grinding. Also, plain and red-slipped pottery were introduced. These events coincide with the evidence that an Austronesian language was introduced into those areas at the same time.

As these people moved into the tropical areas, they often dropped their cereal crops like rice in favor of tree fruits such as breadfruit, banana, coconut, and sago-palms. Their dogs, pigs, and chickens seem to have done well in the southern environment.

In some areas they mixed with the Australoid peoples in island Southeast Asia. This probably accounts for the great diversity of peoples in Melanesia.

One active group of trading and seafaring people were the **Nusantao**. Less than 4,000 years ago, these Austronesian speakers moved into western Micronesia from eastern Indonesia or the Philippines. At about the same time, they moved from island Melanesia into eastern Micronesia and western Polynesia. The languages of eastern Micronesia show influences from Vanuatu (the New Hebrides). The languages of Polynesia are linked to Fiji, whereas the Chamorro language is related to eastern Indonesia and the Philippines. The closest language to Chamorro is Bareic in Sulawesi (Celebes). Most of this colonization was characterized by a distinctive **Lapita pottery**,

**2.1 Lapita Pottery:** Adapted from *Oceanic Prehistory* by Richard Shutler, Jr., and Mary Elizabeth Shutler. Published 1975 by Cummings Publishing Company.

frequently made from red clay and tempered with shell particles or sa

Finally, after the birth of Christ, the Polynesians settled the Pacific all the way to Easter Island, the Hawaiian Islands, and New Zealand. Some Austronesian-speaking peoples from western Indonesia settled the island of Madagascar near Africa.

The main elements of these cultures were as follows: They

- spoke an Austronesian language
- made Lapita pottery (where they had the raw materials)
- practiced horticulture
- caught fish
- navigated and built outrigger canoes (skilled mariners)
- were capable of settling uninhabited islands

**2.2 Southeast Asia & Oceania and the Distribution of Lapita Pottery Sites:** Adapted from *Oceanic Prehistory*, by Richard Shutler, Jr., and Mary Elizabeth Shutler. Published 1975 by Cummings Publishing Company.

# POSSIBLE ANCESTORS OF THE MICRONESIANS & POLYNESIANS

## The Change from Paleolithic to Neolithic Cultures

Thirty thousand years ago, in the Southeast Asian area including the Sunda Shelf, which is Thailand, Laos, Cambodia, Vietnam, Malaysia, Sumatra, and Java, there lived a people with similar lifestyles. We call these people the Hoabinhians.

Their homeland, even in the Ice Age, was tropical. Their lowlands of open grasslands were full of big game. The highlands were densely forested. The **Hoabinhians** were brown-skinned people who roamed this land in small groups of two hundred to four hundred people. They did not farm, because they did not need to. Each group had about as many square miles of land to roam as people in their group. With so much land, there was plenty of food.

14

All of this changed when the polar ice caps melted as the earth warmed up. As the ice became water, it raised the level of the ocean 300 to 700 feet. The lowlands, so rich in big game and food just for the picking, gradually were flooded. The Hoabinhians gradually had to change their lifestyle. One half of their land was gone, and it was their best land. To support their population they had to use the land more efficiently, so they became farmers.

The people did not do this immediately; it was a slow process over 11,000 years. At first they planted some food and then wandered around in their old nomadic way, just making sure they returned for the harvest of the planted crops. But as land got more scarce, they chose the best farm land and settled on it. By this time some Hoabinhians were building something they had never needed before, permanent houses. These houses were pole-and-thatch structures.

Some Hoabinhians hated giving up their old life of wandering around hunting and food gathering. As the lowlands full of big game shrank and there was less food to gather, they became hungry. These remaining nomads began to resent the Hoabinhians who had become farmers and lived in permanent settlements. The nomads began to attack the settlers and steal their food.

As the settlers became more skilled in farming, they found they could release more men for defending the community. This is how their warrior class or military started. This was just the beginning of specialization. As people became better farmers, they needed fewer full-time farmers, so the extra people became tool makers, entertainers, and leisured noblemen. (Today the United States has progressed to the extent that one percent of the population can grow enough to feed the remaining 99% of the population. This allows the remainder of the population of the United States to perform jobs other than raising food.)

As if the Hoabinhians did not have enough problems, a new one developed. Other people began to migrate into their area of the world. Also, the population density was increased by their increased agricultural production. Because of the crowded conditions, wars began. Some Hoabinhians intermarried with the newcomers, some retreated to the mountains, and some set out on exploratory voyages for new land.

Descendants of the Hoabinhians built the outrigger canoe and developed the navigational skills that made it possible to sail out of the sight of land. With problems brewing from within and without, these people began a search for a better life that took them over a large area of the world. Over a long period of time and in small groups they settled as far east as Easter Island, as far west as Madagascar, as far north as Hawai'i, and as far south as New Zealand. The Chamorros were one of the first groups to make it to an open ocean island. They probably settled the Mariana Islands 4,000 years ago.

The ancestors of the Micronesians and the Polynesians could have been the Hoabinhians or a group similar to them. Because of population pressures they were forced into developing the technology of the outrigger canoe and a system of navigation. With these skills they became great explorers. They settled, over a long period of time and in small groups, from Madagascar to Easter Island and from Hawai'i to New Zealand. The first group to reach open ocean islands were the people who became known as the Chamorros. They became Chamorro and distinctively different in the Marianas. We can see this best through their language. The Micronesians and the Polynesians learned the skills for island living in their migrations through Indonesia and Melanesia.

# WHY DID THE CHAMORROS MIGRATE TO THE MARIANAS?

**Ethnologists** will probably never know exactly why the Chamorros migrated to the Mariana Islands. The best ethnologists can do is offer some hypotheses to explain the migration. They suggest the following reasons for migrations: overpopulation, famine, war, quarrels among leaders, accident, adventure, or a natural catastrophe. Let us examine a few of these educated guesses.

Overpopulation is a likely cause for migration. Overpopulation is related to many of the other reasons for migration. **Overpopulation** means that there are too many people for the resources and technology available in a given area. People will starve if there is not enough food available. Famine is the lack of enough food in a place. It can be caused by too many people competing for the food that can be produced. Famine can be caused by drought. It can also be caused by a plant disease or insects that destroy food.

Perhaps the Chamorros migrated to the Mariana Islands to avoid starvation because of overpopulation or famine. The slash-and-burn method of agriculture demands a constant supply of virgin land. When the fertility of the land was exhausted, the Chamorros might have migrated to an area of fresh land.

Overpopulation and famine often lead to war. Starving people go to war against the people who have food. Wars, of course, can have other causes. For example, wars can be caused by a quarrel over land, ethnic prejudice, religious prejudice, or even a difference of opinion among the same people. Frequently, war is caused by a desire for power and control.

Perhaps the Chamorros migrated to the Mariana Islands because they were conquered in war. Maybe the Chamorros moved to the Mariana Islands to avoid a senseless war or because they were exiled.

The Chamorros could have settled the Mariana Islands by accident. If men and women were on a fishing trip or a trading mission and were blown off course, they may have discovered the Mariana Islands. Rather than risk a dangerous voyage back to their homeland, they may have decided to stay in the Marianas. Perhaps some Chamorros discovered the Mariana Islands by accident and returned to their homeland. Later on, when they decided they needed a new home, they could have returned. On this second trip they would have brought their families and the food plants they needed.

Adventure could have played an important role in the settlement of the Mariana Islands. Human beings like to know what is beyond the horizon. Humans are curious by nature. This desire to know burns very strongly in some people. Chamorro explorers may have ventured out on long voyages simply for the pleasure of visiting new places. They could have been on a raiding voyage or simply a trading mission. After finding the Mariana Islands, they might have decided to settle them.

The Chamorros could have been forced to migrate to the Mariana Islands because of a natural catastrophe. Perhaps a volcano erupted, covering their land with ashes and lava. An earthquake, flood, or **tsunami** could have forced the survivors to move.

One important point is that there probably was not one migration to the Mariana Islands, but many small migrations over a long period of time. There is some **linguistic** evidence that Chamorro is a fusion of two, as yet unidentified, languages. Some archaeologists theorize that there was an invasion of *latte*-stone (house supports) building, rice growing, and slingstone throwing people around A.D. 845. People spread the cultivation of rice and the manufacturing of slingstones throughout East Asia at the same time. Others see the introduction of slingstones and *latte* stones as a gradual process over a period of about 300 years.

In conclusion, we do not know why the Chamorros migrated to the Mariana Islands. There are several hypotheses: overpopulation, famine, war, quarrels among leaders, accident, adventure, or a natural catastrophe. Perhaps they moved to the Marianas for one or a combination of these reasons. It is generally believed that at first there was probably some return voyaging to their point of origin.

# ANCIENT CHAMORRO MIGRATION TO THE MARIANA ISLANDS

The Chamorros' migration to the Mariana Islands was a grand achievement by a brave and daring people. Thousands of years before Europeans dared sail out of sight of land the Chamorros sailed the open seas in search of a better life. Europeans viewed nature as a foe to be conquered and thought the earth was flat. The ocean in their view was a fearful enemy they had to overcome. In contrast, the Chamorros felt a part of nature. Although aware of the dangers, they felt at home on the sea.

The migration to the Mariana Islands was a series of short migrations by small groups of people over many generations. The first people of the Marianas did not leave Southeast Asia and head directly to the Mariana Islands. They may have settled in Malaysia, Borneo, Sulawesi (the Celebes), or even New Guinea first. They may have settled in all of them. Along the way they were changing their customs, language, and physical appearance. In this way they were becoming the distinct ethnic group we have come to call Chamorros. It seems likely that they departed from the Philippines, with perhaps stops in Belau (Palau) and Yap, before finding the Mariana Islands. Once in the Mariana Islands they may have continued contact with their last homeland, but not for long. After many generations, their origins were forgotten and replaced by a creation myth.

Only extensive work in archaeology and linguistics will allow researchers to trace the migration route of the Chamorros more closely. Perhaps we can find traces of their ancestors who were left behind to go their own way or who were **assimilated** into the dominant population of that area.

After the Chamorros reached the Marianas, they stopped migrating for thousands of years. The Mariana Islands provided them with the better life they were searching for. There seems to have been no significant migration of Chamorros until after the Spanish-Chamorros Wars in the late 17th Century. At that time some Chamorros migrated to the Caroline Islands to escape Spanish rule. Since World War II many Chamorros have migrated to the "States."

# Migration Requirements

In order to migrate, the ancient Chamorros needed a means of transportation. It was not the little reef canoe we call a *galaide'* but rather a *sakman*. The *sakman* was an oceangoing outrigger canoe. It was not a simple dugout. The sides were planks from the *dokdok* tree, sewn together with **sennit** and caulked with *lemmai* gum. The canoe, over forty feet long, was lashed to an outrigger for stability. The *sakman* was powered by the wind, which was caught by an *akgak* woven sail. The canoe was steered by a paddle-like rudder.

For its day, the *sakman* was the fastest and safest means of transportation available. The outrigger canoe with its **lateen** sail is a technological wonder that Europeans did not fully understand until the invention of the airplane. Why? The triangular sail creates a vacuum in front of the sail that allows the craft to be pulled as well as pushed by the wind. It allows the craft to sail closer to the wind, which is very important when your destination is to the windward. This vacuum, caused by air flowing over the sail, is similar to the vacuum above an airplane wing that provides lift and allows a plane to fly.

**2.3 The *sakman* made oceangoing travel possible.**

The ancient Chamorros were willing to take risks. Their migrating ancestors had always found land before. If unsuccessful in their search for land, they could always use their knowledge of navigation to return home. Their navigation was based on a knowledge of wind, waves, birds, and the stars. It worked.

The Chamorros trusted nature. The spirits of their ancestors were their "backers." **Animistic** beliefs probably assured the Chamorros that their *sakman*, the sea, and the land they sought had spirits. The ancient Chamorros believed that if they treated those spirits, and especially the *ante* of their ancestors, with respect, everything would turn out right.

If the people they met were friendly, fine; if not, they could fight or move on. If they found an uninhabited land, they were prepared with the skills and supplies necessary to settle it.

The Chamorros had to carefully prepare food for their journey. They probably brought preserved pandanus, breadfruit, yams, taro, sugarcane, bananas, arrowroot flour, coconuts and dried fish. For drinking they brought water in gourds or pots made of pottery and plenty of green coconuts.

The large *sakman* probably did not average over four **knots**. They sailed at a little over 500 miles a week. It seems likely that the Chamorros could have remained at sea as long as one month in their search for a new homeland. Modern travelers would find the hardships of the voyage nearly unbearable.

2.4 Food for a long ocean voyage

It must have been a glorious day when the Mariana Islands came into view. When they landed, the Chamorros were ready. If enemies approached, they had weapons with which to defend themselves, like the *sapblasos* and *fisga*. If the enemy proved too strong, no one could catch them in their "getaway" *sakman*. If friends approached, they were ready with gifts (*chenchule'*) to show their goodwill.

As it turned out, the islands were uninhabited and they were ready with their skills in island living and had plants to set out. The Chamorros either brought with them or returned to their past home for the following food plants: breadfruit, yams, taro, coconuts, bananas, and perhaps rice. The Chamorros had to wait for a long time before these plants began to produce. In the meantime they exploited the resources of the sea and probably collected edible land plants.

# When Did the Chamorros Land in the Mariana Islands?

The Chamorros probably landed in the Marianas as early as 2000 B.C. Through **radiocarbon dating**, archaeologists have proved there were people living at Chalan Piao in Saipan by 1527 B.C., at Nomna Bay near Inarajan by 1320 B.C., and at Tarague Beach by 1485 B.C. **Midden** is soil that contains refuse, artifacts, and other evidence of human inhabitation. On Saipan there is four feet of midden below the point where the 1527 B.C. date was found. Although it is not generally accepted, some experts have speculated that the Marianas were settled as early as 3000 B.C.

We measure time before and after the birth of Christ. At this writing it has been almost 2,000 years since the birth of Christ. If you went back those 2,000 years and that far again, the date would be 2000 B.C. That would be a total of 2,000 + 2,000, or 4,000 years ago. Chamorros have likely been in the Mariana Islands for those 4,000 years. If a **generation** is 20 years on the average, then that is 200 generations ago.

**Radiocarbon dating** is based on the fact that all living cells contain radioactive carbon 14. When a living organism dies, it no longer absorbs carbon 14 from the atmosphere. Instead it loses carbon 14 at a known rate through a process called radioactive decay. Radioactive decay is measured in half-lives. After so many years, the organism loses half of the carbon 14 that is left, and so on, forever. It can never lose all of its carbon 14, because no matter how small the amount left, you can always take half of it.

Radiocarbon dating can be compared to a man walking along with a hole in his pocket. We know that he started his walk with 64 pennies (or units of carbon 14) in his pocket, and that every step (or 200 years) he will lose half of his money (or carbon 14). After one step he has 32 pennies. After two steps he will have 16 pennies and so on. If you found the man had only 8 pennies, how many steps had he taken? Of course, three steps is the answer. How many years did this take if one step is 300 years? That is right, 900 years. The real half-life of radiocarbon is 5,730 plus or minus 40 years. The half-life of radioactive potassium, used in potassium-argon dating, is 1.3 billion years.

# SUMMARY

The Chamorros, a Mongoloid people from Southeast Asia, migrated to the Mariana Islands about 4,000 years ago. They were motivated to explore the Pacific Ocean because they were searching for a better life. The Chamorros spoke an Austronesian language. Chamorro, like most languages in the Philippines, is related to Indonesian. The Chamorros had a Neolithic culture. They made Lapita-style pottery, practiced horticulture, lived in villages, and had an advanced fishing technology. Most importantly, they were able to navigate and build oceangoing outrigger canoes. Chamorro mariners were capable of finding and settling the uninhabited islands of the Marianas thousands of years before Europeans were capable of such feats.

# Chapter 3
# Food

## INTRODUCTION

Human beings must have food to survive. We are an **omnivorous** (eaters of plants and animals) species. The protein, carbohydrates, fats, minerals, and vitamins in food are essential for growth, repair, and energy in the body. Life cannot continue long without food. The natural environment of the Mariana Islands provides many opportunities for satisfying this basic need. Guahan, the original name for Guam, may refer to the abundance of food on Guam. *Guahan* means "we have."

In the days before transworld transportation networks, a person's environment limited his or her food choices. Eskimos had to rely almost completely on meat and fish because few plants grow in the Arctic. In the time before Columbus discovered America, some Indians raised corn as a **staple**. Europeans, however, did not eat corn or potatoes until those crops were discovered in America and taken back to Europe. These limitations of the types of foods we eat are determined by our environment.

The foods we eat are further limited by our **culture**. There are foods in our environment that contain adequate nutrients, but we refuse to eat them because our culture discourages it. How would you like a sea cucumber (*balate'*) for supper tonight? You probably wouldn't. But some Chinese consider this a delicacy. Perhaps you would like a protein-rich meal of barbecued German Shepherd. No? Some people in Micronesia, New Guinea, Korea, the Philippines, and China do enjoy eating dog. Many people in the Mariana Islands like fruit bat (*fanihi*) and raw fish (*sa'sime'*), while other people are disgusted by these fine foods. Fray Antonio del los Angeles (1596) was amazed that the Chamorros ate raw, ungutted fish and were still very healthy. We tend to eat the foods that are accepted in our culture. Our choices of foods are limited by our environment and our culture.

Clyde Kluckholm, an authority on human behavior, told an interesting story that demonstrates just how strongly our culture determines the foods we choose to eat. He once knew a lady who loved playing cultural tricks on visitors. She served delicious meat sandwiches. Some guests would argue that it was chicken, while others insisted that it was tuna. While her guests ate, the hostess would not answer any of their questions. However, after the meal was over, she explained that the delicious meat they had just eaten and enjoyed so much was the rich white flesh of freshly killed rattlesnake. Often her guests' reaction was violent vomiting. Why would someone throw up something that they just had said tasted good?

Our culture is so powerful in determining the foods we consider fit to eat that some people would starve to death before breaking the rules of their society. Muslims and Jews will not eat pork. Hindus do not eat beef. Some Buddhists are **vegetarians** and won't eat any meat. Low class ancient Chamorros (*manachang*) could eat freshwater eels, whereas eels were **taboo** (forbidden) for the upper caste (*chamorri*). The *chamorri* caste was divided into the higher ranking *matao* and their helpers, called the *acha'ot*.

The foods of the ancient Chamorros represent cultural choices from their natural environment in the Mariana Islands and from their Malaysian origins. Chamorros divide foods into several categories. *Aggon* are starchy foods such as rice, taro, and breadfruit. *Totche* are protein foods like fish and meat. *Na'yan nengkanno'* are foods used in making sauces. *Fruta* are all fruits that are eaten raw. *Postre* are desserts like cakes, rolls or even ice cream. *Gimen* includes all drinks except alcoholic drinks, which are called *maneska*. The ancient Chamorros did not consume *maneska*. Tuba, fermented coconut palm sap, was introduced to the Mariana Islands from the Philippines.

Early human beings relied completely on the animals (including fish) they could catch and the plants they could collect. People who obtain their food by hunting, fishing, and collecting wild plants are called **food gatherers**. So long as there is a great deal of land and few people, this often **nomadic** method of obtaining food is completely adequate.

Most people, however, due to overpopulation, have been forced to **cultivate** gardens and **domesticate** animals. This type of economy in which food is not just collected but produced is called **agricultural**. Some people cultivate gardens by hand and do not keep domesticated animals. They are **horticulturists**. Others do not cultivate gardens but do raise domesticated animals. They are herders and have a pastoral **economy**.

The preparation of food is largely a cultural affair. In the Mariana Islands today, many cultures have contributed to our cooking, giving us a rich variety in our diet. Humans must eat to live, and some of us live to eat. Some people tend to put all their food in one pot and serve it in a bowl like Hungarian goulash. Others, like the Japanese, tend to cook and serve each food in a separate container. Some people serve food in courses. For example, first they serve soup or a salad, then the main course, and finally a dessert. Some foods we eat raw; others we cook. Cooking can be done with heat or chemically as in the case of *kelaguen*.

If we use heat to cook our food, we can roast, bake, or fry. We can use an open flame or an electrical burner to cook. There is almost an endless variety of ways we can cook, utensils we can use, and seasonings we can choose. The world's population can be divided into thirds on the basis of the ways by which they eat food. One-third of the world's population eat with their hands, one-third use knives, forks and spoons, and one-third use chopsticks.

One early account claims that the ancient Chamorros served all the food at the same time rather than in separate courses. Spanish accounts say that the ancient Chamorros did not talk much while they ate. These sources state that the Chamorros ate a great deal of food, and they ate it very quickly. Other sources claim that the Chamorros ate moderately. The ancient Chamorros valued the sharing of food, according to all existing records.

A great variety of foods satisfied the cultural tastes and biological needs of the ancient Chamorros. It is helpful to examine these foods in two major categories. The foods the Chamorros found in the Mariana Islands are **indigenous foods**; the foods they introduced from Malaysia and the islands of Southeast Asia are called **native foods**. Some foods have become so completely a part of Chamorro culture today that it is difficult not to consider them the foods of the aborigines of the Mariana Islands. For this reason, a list of some of the more important foods introduced by the Spanish will be included.

The more important plant and animal foods will be listed with their Chamorro, English, and scientific names. The scientific name is in Latin. The Latin name allows biologists all over the world to know exactly what plant or animal is being discussed, regardless of the language they speak. The scientific name has two parts. The first name is the **genus**; the second is the **species**.

# INDIGENOUS FOODS

## Food Plants

For a complete list of the indigenous plants of Guam, see "Plants Endemic to Guam," *Savanna, Old Fields, Roadsides*, by Margie Cushing Falanruw, pp. 66-68. For a complete list of all of Guam's plants see the *Flora of Guam*, by Benjamin C. Stone.

**3.1** *Dokdok* - **wild or seeded breadfruit tree and fruit**, *Artocarpus mariannensis*

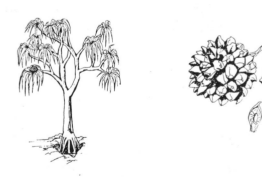

**3.2** *Kaffo'* - **pandanus tree and fruit**, *Pandanus fragrans*

**3.3** *Pahong* - **pandanus tree and fruit**, *Pandanus dubius*

Adapted from Guam Department of Education illustrations.

20

**3.4** *Fadang* - Federico palm and nuts, *Cycas circinalis*: *Fadang* was not eaten by the ancient Chamorros. Until the 1800s it was believed to be inedible. Unfortunately, it became an important food on Guam. This plant has been linked to *litiku* (amyotropic lateral sclerosis) and *boddek* (Parkinsonian dementia). The first cases of these afflictions began in the mid 1800s.

# Land Animals

There is little evidence about which land animals the Chamorros ate. Some historical accounts indicate that they did not eat land animals. Nevertheless, there is archaeological evidence that the Chamorros ate *fanihi* (fruit bat) and some birds.

**3.5** *Fanihi* - fruit bat, *Pteropus mariannus* and *Pteropus tokudae*: The latter is probably extinct in the Mariana Islands.

**3.6** *Nganga'* - duck, Mariana Mallard, *Anas oustaleti*

**3.7** *Sasengat* - Micronesian Megapode, *Megapodius laperouse*: This bird, the size of a chicken, became extinct on Guam prior to 1800, but it is still found in the Northern Mariana Islands.

**3.8** *Ko'ko'* - Guam Rail, *Rallus owstoni*: The *ko'ko'* is unique to Guam. The *ko'ko'* is not found naturally on the other islands in the Marianas. It was probably not an important food.

**3.9** *Totot* - Marianas Fruit Dove, *Ptilinopus roseicapilla*: Even though the *totot* was eaten, it was also kept as a pet. The *totot* is the official bird of Guam.

# Freshwater and Seafoods

The aborigines of the Mariana Islands relied on freshwater foods and seafoods as a major source of protein. There is evidence that the Chamorros ate **crustaceans** (crabs, lobster, and shrimp); **mollusks** or shellfish (clams, top shells, conch shells, squid, octopus), and fish. There are 25,000 species of crustacea, and 80,000 species of mollusks, and almost countless species of fish in the world. Many of these species live in the waters around the Mariana Islands. It would be impossible to list all of them. In Topping, Ogo, and Dungca's *Chamorro-English Dictionary*, there are over one hundred types of fish listed. In this section only some of the more common types of freshwater foods and seafoods will be listed.

## Freshwater Foods

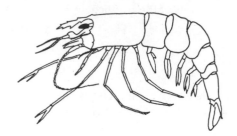

3.10 *Uhang* - freshwater shrimp

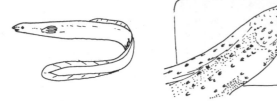

3.11 *Asuli* - freshwater eels, *Anguilla marmorata*: It was **taboo** for high-caste Chamorros to eat eels.

# Seafoods

## Crustaceans

**Crustaceans** include crabs, lobsters and shrimp. There are 600 kinds of crustaceans in the Mariana Islands. A few of the best-tasting crustaceans are listed.

*Pangla* - **crabs.** Land and sea crabs are included as seafoods because all crabs must lay their eggs in the sea.

*Ayuyu* - coconut crab, *Birgus latro*
*Panglao tano'* - land crab, *Cardisoma* (common on roads during a full moon)
*Panglao oro* - golden crab or 7-11 crab, *Carpilius maculatus*
*Akmangao* - mangrove crab, *Scylla serrata*

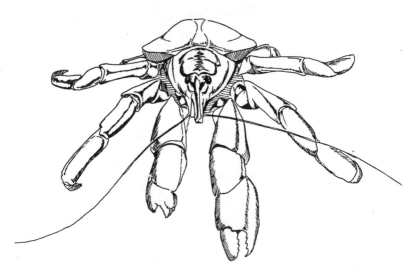

3.12 *Ayuyu* - coconut crab, *Birgus latro*

## *Mahongan* - Lobsters

*Mahongan* - langouste or spiny lobster, *Panulirus pencilliatus*
*Papangpang* - slipper lobster, *Parribacus antarcticus*

## *Uhang* - Shrimp

*Uhang tasi* - various marine shrimp

## Mollusks or Shellfish

*Gamson* - octopus: The *Cepthalopoda* class has several representatives in the Mariana Islands.

*Nosnos* - squid: The *Cepthalopoda* class has several representatives in the Mariana Islands.

*Alileng* - top shells, Trochidae Family: The most common top shell on Guam today, the commercial top shell (*Trochus niloticus*) was not eaten by the ancient Chamorros. This shell was introduced to the Mariana Islands from either Yap or Palau (Belau) in this century by the Japanese. The ancient Chamorros ate *Tectus pyramis*.

*Pulan* - turban shells, Turbinidae Family: *Turbo argyrostomus* and *Turbosetosus*. The turban shells were also used to make scraper tools.

*Pedis* - nerite snails, Neritidae Family

*Toru* - spider conchs, Strombidae Family: The spider conch (Common Spider Conch - *Lambis lambis* and the Giant Pacific Spider Conch - (*Lambis truncata*) are still eaten today. Another conch, the horned helmet (*Cassis cornata*), is not eaten on Guam today, but since other Pacific Islanders eat them, the ancient Chamorros probably did too.

*Do'gas Dankolo* - Blood-mouthed conch, *Strombus luhuanus*

*Do'gas* - Humped Conch, *Strombus gibberulus*

*Kulo'* - triton trumpet, *Charonia trinonis*: Although this shell is not eaten today, it may have been eaten by the ancient Chamorros. Many other Pacific Islanders eat the meat of this shell. We know the ancient Chamorros used this shell as a horn.

Vase shells - *Vasum turbinellus* and *Vasum ceramicum*

*Tapon* or Clams - Class *Pelecypods* or *Lamellibr* Tapon is a general name for small clams or oysters (Family Ostreidae).

*Amsong* - small white sand clams or baby clams:

*Pahgang* or *Pa'gang* - large clams in general

*Palos* - large clams with oblong shells

*Hima* - giant clam, *Tridacna maxima* and *Tridacna squamosa*: These clams were eaten in ancient times and are still eaten today. The *hima* shells were used by the ancient Chamorros to make tools.

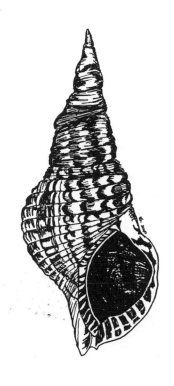

3.13 *Kulo'* - triton trumpet, *Charonia trinonis*

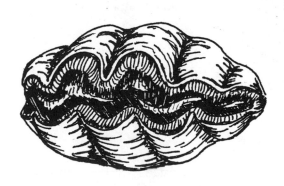

3.14 *Hima* - giant clam, *Tridacna maxima* and *Tridacna squamosa*

# Echinoderms

Echinoderms are sea urchins, starfish, and sea cucumbers. Today, most Chamorros do not eat sea urchins. However since most Pacific Islanders consider them a delicacy, it seems likely that they were eaten by the ancient Chamorros. On the other hand, some Spaniards do eat sea urchins. The famous painter Pablo Picasso loved to eat sea urchins. *La'on* (short-spined sea urchin, *Tripneustes gratilla*, and short-hard-spined pink sea urchin, *Echinometra mathaei*) are edible.

## *Haggan* - Turtles

*Haggan* - Green Turtle, *Chelonia mydas*
*Haggan Karai* - Hawksbill, *Eremtmochelys imbricata*

## *Guihan* - Fish

Surgeon Fish - Acanthruidae Family
    Examples: *guasa', hamottan, hangon, hiyok odda', tataga', patgon hugupao, kichu, hugupao, patgon tataga', satan a'paka'* or *dadalak-ña hamoktan,* and *sata*

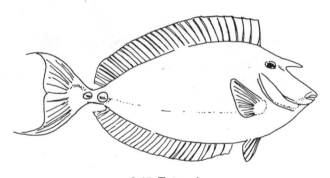

3.15 *Tataga'*

Cardinal Fish - Apogonidae Family
    Examples: *lange, satmoneti,* and *lanse*
Trigger Fish - Balistidae Family
Examples: *pulonnon, pulonnon lagu, pulonnon sasadu,* and *pulonnon attilong*
Needle Fish - Belonidae Family
Examples: *pulos* and *palo*
Flounders - Bothidae Family
    Example: *tampat*
Jackfish - Carangidae Family
    Examples: *i 'e'* - baby jackfish; *tarakitiyu* - small jackfish; *tarakitu* - medium jackfish; and *mamulan* - large (15-100 lbs.) jackfish

Butterfly Fish - Chaetodontidae Family
    Examples: *ababang, guihan ababang* and *ababang amariyu*
Hawkfish - Cirrhitidae Family
    Examples: *aluda* and *gadao knotra kosta*
Dolphins or Mahimahi - Coryphaenidae Family
    Examples: *botague* (this word is no longer in used) *dofen* or *tunio*
Flying Fish - Exocuetidae Family
    Example: *gaga* or *gahga*

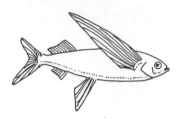

3.16 *Gaga*

Squirrel Fish - Holocentridae Family
    Examples: *saksak, saksak sumulo', saksak fetda, essok cha'lak, sisi'ok,* and *sag'milon*
Rudderfish - Kyphosidae Family
    Examples: *guili* and *guilen puengi*
Wrasses - Labridae Family
    Examples: *lasaga', a'aga, ga'das* or *gatdas, palakse'* (also used for parrotfish), *tangison, lalacha' mamati* or *lalacha' mate*
Snappers - Lutjanidae Family
    Examples: *bu'a, funai, kaka'ka', mafute', matan hagon, saligai, sihik, tagafen saddok, tagafe, fafa'et, guatafi,* and *buninas*

3.17 *Mafute'*

Mullets - Mugilidae Family
    Examples: *Aguas* is a general name; *pi'os;* from baby size to large size they are as follows: *pegge', aguas, dahong,* and *laigu.*
Goatfish - Mullidae Family
    Examples: *ti'ao* (baby goatfish), *satmoneti, satmoneten acho', satmoneten le'ao, satmoneten maninen,* and *batbasbas*

24

Damselfish - Pomacentridae Family
Examples: *doddo*, *fohmo'*, and *gadudok*
Parrotfish - Scaridae Family
Examples: *palakse'*, *dalfa* (blue *palakse'*), *laggua* (big *palakse'*), *foge'* (small *laggua*), *ha'yan*, and *tangison* (also used for some wrasses)
Stonefish - Scorpanenidae Family
Example: *nufo'* or *ñufo'*
Tuna - Scrombridae Family
Examples: *diabang* (large tuna), *to'sang*, *kacho'* (blue tuna), *kacho'* or *binitu* (white tuna), *maguro'* (yellow-fin tuna) *atulai* or *hatulai* or *haiteng* (mackerel), and *uahu* (wahoo)

Barracuda - Sphyraenidae Family.
Examples: *alu* and *alon laiguan*
Marlins - Sailfish - Istiophoridae.
Example: *batto* (this word is no longer in use)
Sharks - Chodrichthyes. Sharks were caught when trolling but not on purpose. They were the enemy of fishermen.
Examples: *halu' u* and *ulon mattiyu na halu'u*

**Seaweeds or Algae**

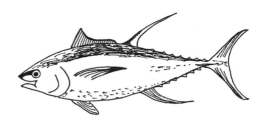

3.18 *Maguro'*

Groupers or Sea Basses - Serranidae Family.
Examples: *gadao*, and *gadao mama'te*
Rabbitfish - Siganidae Family.
Examples from baby to large adult: *mañahak*, *lesso'*, *dagge'*, and *sesyon* or *hiteng*

3.21 *Addo'* - Green Alga, *Caulerpa racemosa*

3.19 *Mañahak*

3.22 *Chaiguan* - Red alga, *Gracilaria edulis*
*Chaiguan* can be poisonous at times.

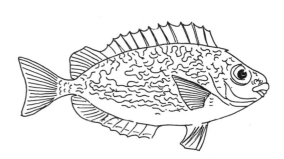

3.20 *Sesyon*

# NATIVE PLANT FOODS
## (Introduced by the Ancient Chamorros)

1. **Lemmai** - breadfruit
   *Artocarpus incisus*

2. **Pi'ao Palao'an** - bamboo
   *Bambusa vulgaris*

3. **Lemon** - Lime
   *Citrus aurantifolia*

4. **Niyok** - Coconut
   *Cocos nucifera*

5. **Suni** - taro
   *Colocasia esculenta*

6. **Mango'** - orange ginger or turmeric
   *Curcuma domestica*

7. **Baba'** - giant swamp taro
   *Cyrtosperma chamissonis*

8. **Dagu** or **Dagon A'paka'** - winged
   yam, *Dioscorea alata*

9. **Gaddo'** - wild yam
   *Dioscorea esculenta*

10. **Chotda** - banana
    *Musa paradisiaca* and *sapientum*

11. **Fa'i** - rice
    *Oryza sativa*

12. **Tupu** - sugarcane
    *Saccharum officinarum*

13. **Hasngot-** white ginger
    *Zingiber zerumbet*

14. **Mangga** - mango
    *Mangifera indica*

15. **Gapgap** - arrowroot
    *Tacca leontopetaloides*

16. **Rau'al or lasret-** football fruit
    *Pangium edule*

17. **Maronggai or kutdes** -
    horseradish tree, *Moringa oleifera*

18. **Atmagosu** - bitter melon
    *Momordica charantia*

19. **Loofah, patola** - vegetable
    sponge, *Luffa acutangula*

20. **Kangkong** - duck weed
    *Ipomonea aquatica*

21. **Buoy** - Tahitian or Yapese
    chestnut, *Inocarpus edulis*

The ancient Chamorros also introduced plants that, although eaten, are not really food. For example, they brought *pugua'* (betel nut) - *Areca catechu* and *pupulu* (betel pepper) - *Piper betle* to the Mariana Islands. They even brought a saucer leaf, *platitos - Polyscias scutellaria* to use as a plate. For a complete list of all of the plants introduced by the ancient Chamorros or other islanders, see "Pre-European Introductions," in *Life on Guam: Savanna, Old Fields, Roadsides*, by Margie Cushing Falanruw, pp. 68-69.

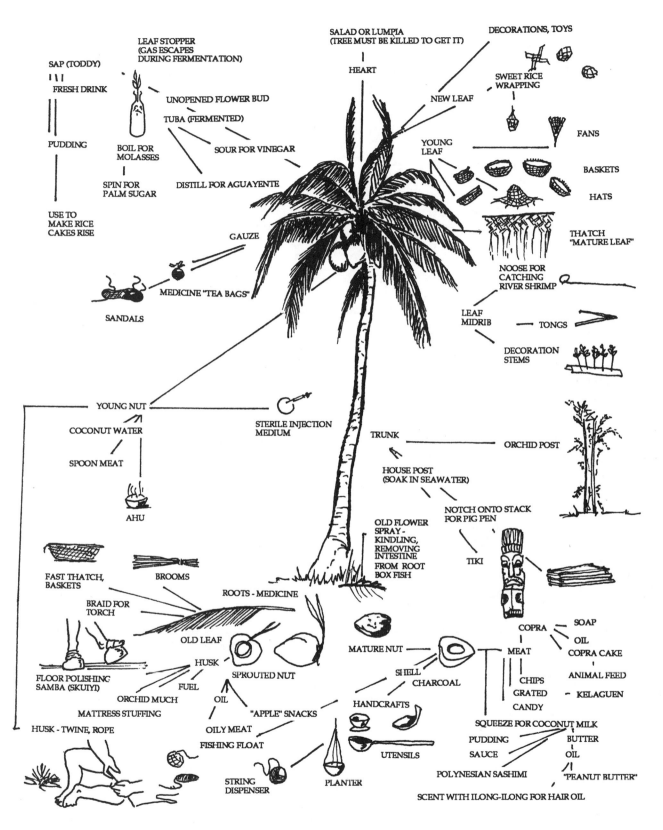

SAP (TODDY)

FRESH DRINK

PUDDING

USE TO MAKE RICE CAKES RISE

LEAF STOPPER (GAS ESCAPES DURING FERMENTATION)

UNOPENED FLOWER BUD

TUBA (FERMENTED)

SOUR FOR VINEGAR

BOIL FOR MOLASSES

SPIN FOR PALM SUGAR

DISTILL FOR AGUAYENTE

GAUZE

MEDICINE "TEA BAGS"

SANDALS

SALAD OR LUMPIA (TREE MUST BE KILLED TO GET IT)

HEART

NEW LEAF

YOUNG LEAF

DECORATIONS, TOYS

SWEET RICE WRAPPING

FANS

BASKETS

HATS

THATCH "MATURE LEAF"

NOOSE FOR CATCHING RIVER SHRIMP

LEAF MIDRIB

TONGS

DECORATION STEMS

YOUNG NUT

COCONUT WATER

SPOON MEAT

AHU

STERILE INJECTION MEDIUM

TRUNK

ORCHID POST

HOUSE POST (SOAK IN SEAWATER)

NOTCH ONTO STACK FOR PIG PEN

TIKI

OLD FLOWER SPRAY - KINDLING, REMOVING INTESTINE FROM ROOT BOX FISH

FAST THATCH, BASKETS

BROOMS

BRAID FOR TORCH

FLOOR POLISHING SAMBA (SKUTYI)

ORCHID MUCH

MATTRESS STUFFING

HUSK - TWINE, ROPE

ROOTS - MEDICINE

OLD LEAF

HUSK

FUEL

SPROUTED NUT

OIL

"APPLE" SNACKS

OILY MEAT

FISHING FLOAT

STRING DISPENSER

PLANTER

MATURE NUT

SHELL

CHARCOAL

HANDCRAFTS

UTENSILS

COPRA

MEAT

SOAP

OIL

COPRA CAKE

ANIMAL FEED

CHIPS

GRATED

CANDY

KELAGUEN

SQUEEZE FOR COCONUT MILK

PUDDING

SAUCE

POLYNESIAN SASHIMI

BUTTER

OIL

"PEANUT BUTTER"

SCENT WITH ILONG-ILONG FOR HAIR OIL

**3.23** *Niyok* - **Coconut,** *Cocos nucifera:* Adapted from Ruth Hembekides' *Coconut: Wonder Tree of the Pacific.* Nutrition Division, Department of Public Health and Welfare. Agaña, Guam, n.d.

3.24 *Suni* - taro, *Colocasia esculenta*

# NATIVE ANIMAL FOOD
## (Introduced by the Ancient Chamorros)

There is little evidence of domesticated animals in the Mariana Islands prior to the Spanish. The ancient Chamorros may have introduced a jungle fowl (similar to a chicken) and pigs, but there is little evidence to support this conclusion.

Jungle fowl were reported in the northern Mariana Islands by William Safford around 1900. Pigafetta, who was with Magellan, said the Chamorros ate birds. Reports from the Nassau Fleet (1625) claim birds were found in the Mariana Islands.

Some early reports state that eggs were available on Guam. Others claim the Chamorros did not eat meat. Loaisa, a Spanish explorer (1526) who stayed on Guam longer than most explorers, claimed there were only little doves. None of the explorers mentions a domesticated bird except the Marianas fruit dove. This green bird with a rose crown is called *totot*. They were domesticated and taught to speak, according to one account, but were they eaten?

There is some linguistic evidence to support the existence of a domesticated jungle fowl in the Mariana Islands. The Chamorros called the chicken the Spanish introduced a *mannok*. *Mannok* is a Chamorro word. This Austronesian word is also used by the remote Tasaday of Mindinao for chicken. Usually when an unknown animal is introduced, the people also borrow the name. It seems possible that the aborigines of the Mariana Islands had a domesticated fowl similar to the chicken.

There was no evidence of pigs in the Mariana Islands when early explorers from Europe arrived. That does not mean pigs could not have been there before. Perhaps a disease wiped out the pig population. This seems to have been the case in Belau (Palau). The Chamorro word for pig, *babui*, is not a European word. It is very similar to the Indonesian and Filipino words for pig. This evidence could mean that the Chamorros knew of pigs prior to their introduction by Europeans. If the ancient Chamorros had pigs, archaeologists should be able to find their bones. At Fouha Bay a fragment of a bone was found. Fred Reinman, the archaeologist who found it, thinks that it could be a part of a pig's nasal bone. He is not sure. He dated this bone fragment at about 1000 A.D. If there were pigs in the Marianas prior to European contact, they would have been descended from an Asian swine (*Sus cristatus*). Unless more evidence is found, we must conclude that the ancient Chamorros did not introduce pigs to the Mariana Islands.

# SPANISH-INTRODUCED
## PLANT FOODS

1. *Piña* - pineapple
   *Ananas comosus*

2. *Laguana* - soursop
   *Annona muricata*

3. *Anonas* - custard apple
   *Annona peticulata*

4. *Ates* - sweetsop
   *Annona squamosa*

5. *Donne'* - chili pepper
   *Capsicum annuum*

6. *Papaya* - papaya or pawpaw
   *Carica papaya*

7. *Kamuti* - sweet potato
   *Ipomoea batatas*

8. *Tumates* - tomato
   *Lycopersicon esculentum*

9. *Mendioka, cassava* - tapioca
   *Manihot esculenta*

10. *Alageta* - avocado
    *Persea americana*

11. *Abas* - guava
    *Psidium guajava*

12. *Sunen Honolulu, yautia*  taro
    *Xanthosoma spp.*

13. *Mai'es* - maize, corn
    *Zea mays*

For a complete list of the plants introduced by the Spanish, see "Crops Introduced from the Americas by the Spaniards," in *Life on Guam: Savanna, Old Fields, Roadsides*, by Margie Cushing Falanruw, p. 70.

# SPANISH-INTRODUCED
## ANIMAL FOODS

1. *Karabao* - Carabao, water buffalo
   *Babalus bubalis*

2. *Binadu* - deer
   *Cervus nigricans*

3. *Mannok* - chicken

4. *Babuen halom tano'* or *Babuen machalek* - European  Wild Hog
   *Sus scrofa*

5. *Babui* - domesticated pig
   *Sus scrofa*

6. *Baka*  or *Guaka* - Cow (*Bos* sp.)

7. *Chiba* - goat (*Capra hircus*)

8. *Nganga'* - duck (*Anas* sp.)

# METHODS OF OBTAINING FOOD

The ancient Chamorros gathered food from their natural environment and were horticulturists and fisherpersons. Gathering food may seem like a simple matter. Nevertheless, one does not just go out and collect the foods that are available. There are always cultural restrictions. For the aborigines of the Mariana Islands it was taboo to take more from nature than was needed. This is still a Chamorro custom today. Westerners (people of western European origin) have a tendency to exploit nature. That practice is catching up with the world today. Many natural resources are almost used up. Many plants and animals are extinct or about to become extinct. We have polluted our environment, too. The world would do well to follow the conservation principle of the Chamorros. Individuals should take only what their families need.

For the most part, food gathering was done by women rather than by men. The ancient Chamorro culture divided people by **castes**. This affected their methods of obtaining food. The upper caste controlled the land and the sea. The lower caste (*manachang*) had to ask the upper caste (*chamorri*) for permission to use the land. They were never granted permission to use the sea. This old custom is seen today when Chamorros ask the permission of the *taotaomo'na* for land use privileges. The old upper caste people are no longer around, so people ask their spirits. Before the Spanish came to the Mariana Islands and killed most of the people, it was not necessary to ask permission from the *taotaomo'na*. A person in need could simply ask the landowner.

Generally, the lower caste women gathered foods from the land, while the lower caste men farmed the land. The upper caste women gathered seafoods from the reef, while upper caste men did the fishing. This was not a strict division of labor. Upper caste men could and did do some farming. Nevertheless, lower caste men and women could not fish.

The ancient Chamorros' food gathering, horticultural, and fishing economy was based on reciprocal kinship and caste exchanges. These exchanges are called *ayudu* (helping) and are part of a complex system of reciprocal gift giving called *chenchule'* -ika--ayudu. Basically, the *ayudu*

system meant that relatives shared the products of their labor. Perhaps the castes shared, too. The lower caste was obligated to share the foods they gathered and raised with the upper caste because the upper caste gave the lower caste land use privileges. The upper caste probably shared their extra fish with the lower caste. If the Chamorro caste system was similar to the Yapese caste system, the upper caste treated the *manachang* not as slaves but in much the same way that parents treat their children.

Since these exchanges were along kinship and caste lines, there was no need for money except for ceremonial purposes.

# Horticulture

The aborigines of the Mariana Islands raised *suni* (taro), *tupu* (sugarcane), *chotda* (bananas), *lemmai* (breadfruit), *niyok* (coconuts), *dagu* (yams), *mangga* (mango), and lemons. Some experts believe that the ancient Chamorros also grew *fa'i* (rice; cooked rice is *hineksa'*; jungle rice is *cha'guan agaga'* ).

The tree crops required little effort. For many trees the land was simply cleared and seeds planted. In the case of the *chotda* and *lemmai*, this procedure was complicated by a lack of seeds. A shoot had to be cut and rooted first. The breadfruit shoots were planted only when there was a crescent moon. The tree crops, once planted, generally required little care. Nevertheless, in the case of *mangga*, a greater production of fruit could be assured by smoking the trees and slashing the trunks. The smoking drives away insects. The slashing encourages the sap to go to the fruit instead of the leaves. These practices are used today, and it seems likely they were used in ancient times.

Crops like *fa' i* and *suni* had to be cultivated. The ancient Chamorros used the **swidden agriculture** method. In order to clear the land for planting, they cut down the natural vegetation, allowed it to dry, and then burned it. This slash and burn method not only clears the land, but also enriches the soil. The ashes contain a great deal of potassium.

Swamp rice produced a larger yield than the dry ground variety. However, it took five and a half months to reach full growth. It was planted at the end of October. The dry ground variety was ready in four months. It was planted in July,

August or September. *Nika* (yam or *Dioscorea esculenta*) provided food all year. *Suni* was pulled in December, regardless of when it was planted. *Dagu* (yam or *Dioscorea alata)* ripened between November and January. *Gapgap* ripened between December and January.

In order to further prepare the land for planting, the aborigines of the Mariana Islands used a thrust hoe. This tool was a long, hard wood stick with a blade-like end. It was used to break up the soil. It was thrust into the ground and leaned on to overturn the soil.

The ancient Chamorros had three types of thrust hoes. The *dagao* was made of *mangle* (mangrove tree) or *gagu* (ironwood tree). It was about four and one-half feet long. The *tanum*, a similar tool of the same size, was used for planting *suni* and for opening coconuts. The *akao* was a spade with a stone blade. The handle was five feet long; the blade was three inches wide and one and one-half inches thick. It was attached to the handle with coconut fiber sennit. Today we call this same tool with a metal blade a *fusiños*.

After the soil preparation, the ancient Chamorro farmer used a digging stick (*dagao, tanum,* or *bonga*) to prepare a hole to plant seeds or young plant starts. As the plants grew, they were weeded with the above tools and by hand. When the plants reached maturity, they were harvested. Of course, the first of the harvest went to the high caste.

Planting swamp taro and rice was different from the general planting method. These crops had to be planted in muddy ground. The natural vegetation in the area was uprooted and buried in the mud. Those plants decayed and enriched the soil. The rice or taro plants were planted by hand or with the help of the *tanum*. The October moon was named *Fa'gualo*, "planting time," because this is when the ancient Chamorros planted rice. As the plants matured, they were weeded by hand. The rice was harvested with a sharp bamboo knife. The other swamp crop, taro, was harvested with the *tanum* digging stick.

The ancient Chamorros did not raise rice by the paddy method. That is, they did not build dikes and flood the land. They relied on the natural environment to provide the necessary muddy areas. River valleys like the Geus and Talofofo were excellent natural areas for growing rice.

The ancient Chamorros were the only open-ocean island people of Oceania who grew rice in prehistoric times. They did not grow as much rice as they would have liked. Therefore, they kept rice for special festivities.

The ancient Chamorros were horticulturists. They had a knowledge of agriculture we may find surprising today. They enriched the soil with ashes and **humus** (decaying plants). They knew, by practical application, that a tree's heart sap goes to the fruit and the sap near the bark of a tree goes to the leaves. This is why the slashing of a mango tree's trunk is so effective.

Rice-grain impressions have been found in ancient Chamorro pottery, indicating that the ancient Chamorros cultivated rice. Early explorers also report that the Chamorros cultivated rice. If so, they were the only Micronesian, Melanesian or Polynesian people to cultivate rice prior to European discovery, and for this reason, some investigators doubt that the ancient Chamorros cultivated rice.

# Fishing

The ancient Chamorros relied heavily on the resources of the sea for their subsistence. They had a great variety of fishing equipment and many methods of catching fish. Some of the fishing methods are unique to the aborigines of the Mariana Islands. Juan Pobre de Zamora (1602), a Spanish priest, described the Chamorros as "the most skilled fishermen ever to have been discovered."

## Customs

The ancient Chamorros denied fishing rights to the *manachang* (lower caste). The *manachang* were not even allowed to touch the sea. The upper castes thought that the *manachang* would spoil the fishing. The lower caste could catch *asuli* (freshwater eels) because eels were taboo for the *matao* and *acha'ot*. The *manachang* could not use nets or a hook-and-line to catch the *asuli*. They had to rely on their quick hands, a club, or a spear.

Returning deep-sea fishermen flew pandanus mat banners of different designs on their mast to let the people on shore know what kind of fish they had caught. Children who helped carry the catch ashore would receive the entrails as a reward. As the fishermen cut up the fish, they gave slices to their neighbors and salted the rest.

Fishing privileges within the upper caste were divided by sex. The women generally gathered the mollusks or shellfish, crabs, and lobsters. The men did the deep-sea fishing and were assisted by the women in the net and hook-and-line fishing.

The upper castes were not free to fish just anywhere. The fishing grounds on the reef and just offshore were owned. It seems likely that the open ocean fishing **banks** were owned, too. A bank is the relatively shallow waters over submerged mountains. Banks are excellent fishing grounds. Many fish live on banks because of the mineral-rich waters that are forced to the surface from the surrounding deep waters. These minerals from the ocean depths and the sunlight that filters through the shallow water create a good environment for **plankton**. All fish are either directly or indirectly dependent on this lower plant and animal life for existence. Even migrating fish will stop by a bank to feed.

Ancient Chamorro fishing grounds had names and were owned by **clans** or **matrilineages** (see the "Social Structure" chapter for details). The "Guam Fishing Grounds" illustration shows where Guam's major fishing areas are located.

The ancient Chamorro law of the sea was very different from that of Westerners (people of western European origin) until recently. Traditionally, the international community has maintained freedom of the seas, beyond a three-mile or twelve-mile limit. The United Nations is currently working on a new law of the sea. Most countries are claiming at least a 200-mile economic zone beyond their shores. Underdeveloped countries are demanding that the world powers exploit the resources of the sea for their benefit. They argue that this is only fair. Most of their land resources were exploited for the benefit of their colonizers. If the sea resources are developed for the benefit of the exploited nations, this would help repay them for past damages. In 1978, an important United Nations Law of the Sea Conference was held on Guam.

The aborigines of the Mariana Islands had very definite laws of the sea. *Manachang* were not allowed to "pollute" the ocean by their touch. The matrilineages or clans owned reef areas and banks offshore. Violators of these rules were punished by death. There were wars fought over fishing rights.

Today, in the Mariana Islands the United States federal government controls the reef and the offshore areas up to 200 miles for economic purposes. Citizens are generally free to exploit the wealth of the sea. There are some restrictions. Endangered species cannot be harvested. Dynamite and poison cannot be used to catch fish. The federal government also controls the inland streams and rivers.

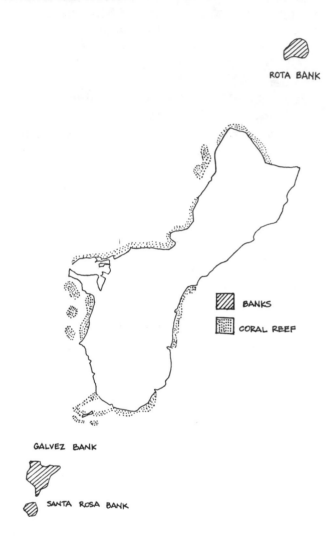

ROTA BANK

BANKS

CORAL REEF

GALVEZ BANK

SANTA ROSA BANK

**3.25 Guam's Fishing Grounds**

In ancient times, there were restrictions, rituals and customs governing fishing. No one could refuse to help another person during the *mañahak* season. Any catch was always shared with the lower caste. Fishermen the world over are superstitious. The aborigines of the Mariana Islands probably observed some rituals before important fishing expeditions. Elsewhere in Micronesia, men abstain from sexual intercourse before a big fishing trip. The Chamorros sought help from their *ante* (ancestral spirits) for good fishing. Since *makahnas* were experts in dealing with the spirit world, they were asked for help to insure successful fishing.

Even the Chamorro calendar, which is based on the thirteen moons of the year, was influenced by fishing seasons. *Umatalaf*, or March, means to go catch *guatafi*. *Umagahaf* is the thirteenth moon of the year. It is translated as the time to go crayfishing.

## Fishing Seasons

| MONTHS | FISH | METHODS |
|---|---|---|
| | *sesyon* | |
| February - April | *ti'ao* | |
| | *satmoneti* | |
| | | |
| May - June | *ti'ao* | various net |
| | *mañahak* | methods |
| | | |
| | *i'e'* | |
| July - September | *ti'ao* | |
| | *tarakitu* | |
| | | |
| July - October | *atulai* | |
| | *achuman* | |
| | | |
| November - | *mafute'* | spear and |
| December | *guili* | torch method |
| and into January | *palakse'* | |

# Implements

## Fishing Lines
### (*Gugat, Katgat, and Kotdet*)

The aborigines of the Mariana Islands used coconut fiber and *pagu* (wild hibiscus tree) fiber fishing lines. In order to obtain coconut fiber lines, the Chamorros soaked coconut husks in seawater. This process separated the fibers. An ancient Chamorro twisted the fibers into line by rubbing the fibers together on his or her thigh. Several lines formed in that way were then wound together to form a heavier line or even a rope. This coconut line or rope is called sennit today. It is extremely strong, and is slow to rot, even in seawater. The lines are fuzzy, with small fibers sticking out all over. The stray fibers keep knots tied in the line tight. *Pokse'* is made by stripping the bark from the *pagu* tree and twisting it into lines. Fishing lines of *pokse'* have been tested by archaeologists and found to have the strength of sixty-pound test line.

In later years, the Spanish introduced *piña* (pineapple) fiber for fishing lines.

## Nets

Several types of nets were used by the ancient Chamorros. They made large drag nets (*chenchulu*), gill nets (*tekken*), and small hand nets (*lagua'*). They did not have casting nets (*talåya*). The *talåya* was introduced into Micronesia and Polynesia by the Japanese. The Chamorro fish nets were made from *pokse'*. After the Spanish introduced *piña* (pineapple), its fiber was used. Sinkers for the nets were made from rocks, and floats for the nets were made from *puteng* (*Barringtonia asiatica*) seeds.

## Mortar and Pestle

The *lusong* (mortar) and *lommok* (pestle) were used to crush the *puteng* to make poison. Sometimes a large wooden pestle called a *fayao* was used. The mortar and pestle were usually made of *alutong* or basalt (volcanic rock), although sometimes *acho'* or limestone (coral rock) was used. The crushed pulp from the *puteng* was then put in a sack or mixed with sand and sprinkled in tidal pools. This poison stuns the fish and they float to the surface. It is illegal to fish by this method today.

## Spear (*Fisga*)

Wooden spears were used in fishing. Barbs were either carved in the wood or bones were added for spear tips. After the Spanish came to the Mariana Islands, metal spear tips replaced the bone. Today even the shaft of the spear is metal.

## Knife and Scraper
### (*Se'se' yan Guesgues*)

A knife (*se'se'*) was used to scale, gut, and cut up fish. Knives were made from bamboo, stone, and shell. A stone or shell scraper (*guesgues*) was used to scale fish.

## Fishhook (*Haguet*)

Fishhooks were made from tortoise- and pearl-shell (oyster - *Isognomon*) and sometimes fish bones. The hooks were of two basic types: J-shape and L-shape. The J-shaped hooks were very similar to modern metal hooks and operated the same way. The L-shaped hooks were gorge hooks. The fish had to swallow the entire hook for it to be effective. A few hooks had coral shanks. There were notches on the shank to attach the lines to the hooks.

*Gaga* (flying fish) were caught by a special hook of fish bone. Lures with a tortoise-shell hook were used for deep-sea fishing. The lures were decorated with *pokse'* (*pagu* bark fibers) or feathers. Squid lures were made from a sinker and shell blade covered with pieces of tiger cowrie shell.

3.26 **Fishhooks:** Adapted from *Archaeology of the Marianas Island*, by Laura Maud Thompson. Published as Bernice P. Bishop Museum Bulletin 100 in 1932 by Bishop Museum Press.

## Sinker (*Katgaderu*)

Sinkers were used to weight fishing lines and nets. There were several types of sinkers made from stone. Spherical sinkers were called *poio*. Grooved sinkers from a conical to a spherical shape were called **talac**. Slingstones were often grooved or perforated and used as sinkers.

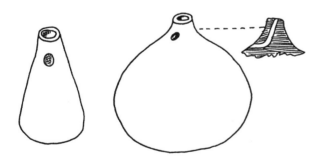

3.27 **Sinkers:** Adapted from *Archaeology of the Marianas Islands*, by Laura Maud Thompson. Published as Bernice P. Bishop Museum Bulletin 100 in 1932 by Bishop Museum Press.

## Creel (*Guagua'* or *Guagua' tumalaya*)

*Guagua'* are baskets used to hold fish. They are usually made of woven coconut leaves.

# Fishing Methods

### Maño'cho'

Some parrotfish and wrasses can be caught by hand (*maño'cho'*). The *lachon* (*Leptoscarus vaigiensis*) hides in the seagrass. At low tide they can be run down and caught. A *tatanum* (*Novaculichthys taeniourus*) leaves a pile of coral rocks in the sand above its hiding place in the sand. Usually women reached in the sand under the fish and grabbed it.

### Lalagu

*Lalagu*, or tickling the fish, was a method used primarily by women in ancient times. Feeling among the crevices in the rocks on the reef, the fisherwoman caught the fish by hand. Then she quickly bit the fish's head to kill it, and placed it in her *guagua'* (creel). This method is often used today to catch freshwater shrimp. There is always a danger that an eel will bite the person who uses this fishing method. The trick here is not to prevent the bite, but to lessen the damage of the bite. If an eel bites, you do not pull your hand away. The eel's angled and pointed teeth will tear the flesh away. Instead, you must wait patiently until the eel opens its mouth to get a better hold. If you are very still, the eel's mouth will open. At that instant you can safely withdraw your finger. Using this method, you can come away with only minor puncture wounds, instead of severe lacerations. The *lalagu* method is not for the fainthearted.

### Umefohmo'

Another similar method often used by women was to place rocks in a large basket, then put the basket near a group of rocks or coral where fish were hiding. As the fisherwoman removed the rocks one by one, the fish often would hide among the rocks in the basket. When enough fish had been fooled, the woman took the basket full of rocks and fish from the water.

## Ka'tokcha'

Fishing with a *fisga* (spear) is called *ka'tokcha'*. The aborigines of the Mariana Islands used barbed fishing spears in a variety of ways. Standing in shallow water or on a rock above the water, they threw a spear at a fish. This takes considerable skill because of light refraction. If you throw directly where the fish appears to be, you are sure to miss. The light waves move at different speeds in water and air. In order to hit the fish, you must aim below its apparent position. It takes practice to become good at this type of fishing.

3.28 *Ka'tokcha'* or Spearfishing

### Peskan Sumulo'

*Sulo'*, or torch fishing, was used in ancient times. A torch was made from a bundle of dried coconut leaves. The torch served two purposes. First, it allowed the fisherman to see at night. Second, the light from the torch attracted the fish. Today a similar method called *tahu* is used to catch crabs at night with the aid of a flashlight. *Sulo'* fisherman today use a lantern and a three-pronged metal spear.

Spear- and torch-fishing methods were used from August to December to catch parrotfish. At low tide during the time of the new moon, this method was very effective. A canoe was paddled along the edge of the reef. With the light from the *sulo'*, the sleeping parrotfish, wrapped in their mucous-like "pajamas," were easy to see and to spear. Can you guess why parrotfish are called *palakse'*?

## Etokcha'

*Etokcha'* is spear fishing while skin diving. Today we use goggles or masks when using this method. The ancient Chamorros had to open their eyes underwater. After this type of fishing, they needed medication for their eyes. The Chamorros probably used *nanasu* (half-flower tree). This small tree grows near the beach and in the savanna plant communities in the Mariana Islands. The small, round white fruits are squeezed so that the juice drops in the fisherperson's eye. Chemically, this fluid is almost identical to natural tears. Other Micronesians use this method today for red eyes. Perhaps we should call *nanasu* "Marine Murine."

The ancient Chamorros did not have a rubber-powered spear gun. They had to spear a fish with an underhand thrusting motion. In the case of larger fish, they used an overhand method.

## Guasa'

*Guasa'* was a method of fishing by poisoning or stupefying the fish. The round seed taken from the pyramid-shaped husk of the *puteng* or *Barringtonia asiatica* was ground with a *putot* (small mortar and pestle). The pulp was mixed with sand and sprinkled in a tidal pool. The fish floated helplessly to the surface after about five to ten minutes. This method is illegal today, but is much preferable to bleach, which kills everything. A similar method was used by scraping the skin of the *atilong na balate'* (black sea cucumber) to obtain poison.

## Gigao

The *gigao* was a wedge-shaped barrier on the reef made of rocks by the ancient Chamorros. It served as a fish trap or fish weir. As the tide went out, some water was held behind the stone barrier. The fish in that area did not realize the tide was going out until the water was so low that they had no means of escape. When the tide was at its lowest level, the fisherpersons went out on the reef and collected the trapped fish. A *ngagsan* was used for a fish pond near the shore. It helped in preserving fish until they were needed as fresh food or bait. (See illustration, next page.)

The Chamorros of the 1800s used bamboo fish weirs of two basic designs. Chamorros today use wire fish weirs.

3.29 *Gigao* (left) and *Ngagsan* (right)

A bamboo tube trap called *okkodon panglao* is used to catch crabs today. A similar trap was probably used in ancient times.

Today, the use of the *nasa* (shrimp trap) is popular. It is made from split bamboo and baited with coconut meat. The *nasa* is used in freshwater streams. The ancient Chamorros probably used similar traps in the ocean as well as in fresh water.

## Net Fishing

*Manhalla*, or *managgam*, is a method of blocking a school of fish with a net. This method has several variations, but always a *chenchulu* (large net) is used. The *chenchulu* is formed into a hemisphere, and the fish are driven toward the shore.

If a school of *atulai* is spotted coming into a channel, the opening is blocked to trap the fish. At night this is done blindly to catch a variety of fish.

*Ma mongle*, or *chumenchulu*, is a method of surrounding fish with a net. About midway between the reef's margin and the beach, the fisherperson stacks rocks. The pile of rocks is called *guma'* (house) because it forms a house for the fish. At about four in the morning, the *guma'* is encircled by a net. As the tide goes out, the fish hide in the rocks. The fisherpersons tear down the *guma'* and spear the fish. The net prevents fish from escaping.

This method is more commonly used without building the *guma'*. The fish are chased into the net by swimmers splashing the water. Once a large number of fish are surrounded by the net, spears or poison from the *balate'* are used to catch them, or the fish are just scooped up.

3.30 *Manhalla*

3.31 *Ma Mongle* or *Chumenchulu*

*Lagua'* is a small net with a handle. Fish, especially *atulai*, are scooped up with the net. *Lagua'* is also used to describe a section of a larger net. The *lagua'* was also used on land to catch *fanihi* (fruit bat).

36

*Gadi* is a type of fishing using palm leaves or a long net. The *tekken* (gill net) is used today. The net is positioned between two vertical poles on the reef. The fish are either chased into the net or are captured as they swim for deep water as the tide goes out.

In ancient times palm fronds were used instead of a net. The palm frond was cut from the tree and split into two halves. The halves were twisted and tied end to end. A group of people then used the line of palm fronds to chase the fish into a net or up on the beach. Also, the halves were twisted and supported between poles on the reef. The fish were afraid to pass the palm leaves and had to remain on the reef. When the tide went out, the fish were easy to find hiding among the rocks and were speared.

The *talåya*, or casting net, was not used in ancient times. Today, it is used to catch *mañahak*, *ti'ao* and other small fish. In the past, these fish were caught by a large group using a fine-meshed net. The *talåya* was probably introduced into Micronesia and Polynesia by the Spanish, who call it the *tarraya*. Some authorities, nevertheless, claim that it was introduced by the Japanese.

Corte, a Spanish governor of Guam (1855-1866), reported a circular fishing net attached to a ring. Three lines were attached to the ring and used to pull the net up. He claimed that with this type of net a ton of fish could be caught in one day. He also said that this was an old Chamorro method of fishing.

## Ma Batsalla or Batangga

*Ma batsalla* (trolling) is an ancient fishing method. A lure was towed behind a sailing canoe. The aborigines of the Mariana Islands used this method to catch a variety of fish. The favorite fish caught by this method were *bunitu*, *gaga* (flying fish), *batto* (marlin), and mahimahi. One early priest reported that the Chamorros were the most skilled deep-water fishermen yet discovered.

## Edipok

*Edipok* is a type of fishing in a tidal pool. This word, though still used in the Northern Mariana Islands, is not common on Guam. *Edipok* can also refer to fishing in a tidal pool from a cliff.

## Lulai

*Lulai* is the practice of fishing on a moonlit night with a hook and line. Usually a *pisao* (fishing pole) was used, too. Fishing by either hooks or with nets often involved chumming. This is the practice of throwing chopped bait into the sea to attract fish.

3.32 *Ma Batsalla*

3.33 *Edipok*

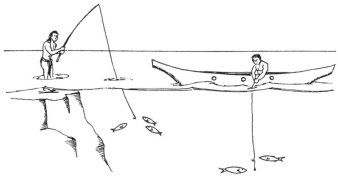

3.34 **Fishing with a Hook and Line**

37

# Special Chamorro Fishing Methods

There are several fishing methods that seem to be unique to the Chamorros. As a variation of the *gadi* method, the Chamorros substituted split *pahong* (pandanus) roots for coconut leaves. These white strips of wood were weighted and placed in a line up to 100 feet long parallel to the reef's edge. This "white line" was placed at high tide midway between the reef's edge and the beach. When the tide went out, the fish were afraid to cross the line. Some fish would go around the visible barrier, but most would hide in tidal pools and among the rocks. At low tide these fish could easily be caught by hand or with a short, barbed spear.

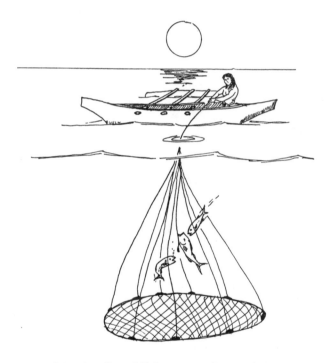

**3.35 A tethered fish was used to catch *laggua*.**

In order to catch *laggua* (big parrotfish) Chamorros used a decoy method of fishing. This daytime method of fishing may be unique to the Mariana Islands. A net was weighted and dropped into the sea. A *laggua* was tethered by the lower jaw to a fishing line. To further restrain the fish, a sinker was attached. The weighted fish was played over the net. Other fish took advantage of the bait fish's helpless condition. They attacked the tethered fish or attempted to bite the cord. The bait fish and the attacking fish were played up and down in the water. When the fish were no longer suspicious, they were lured near the surface. The weighted net was then brought up, catching the tethered fish and the attacking fish. Next, a freshly caught fish was tethered and the process continued. The last fish caught was kept alive in a fish pond (*ngagsan*) near shore for the next day's fishing.

Perhaps the cleverest fishing method in the world was a Chamorro technique using an *acho' achuman*. This method does not seem to be used anywhere else in the world. It trained fish to come to the fisherperson. The fish caught by this method were *achuman* (or *hachuman* or *opelu*, *Decapterus*), a small tuna-like fish. Nevertheless, this word is used for salted herring today.

During June and July (some accounts claim the fish were trained beginning in August and were harvested in October), every day at the same time and place, the fish were fed with an *acho' achuman*. Once the fish were trained, they were easily caught.

The *acho' achuman* was made from a large *poio* (spherical stone sinker) tied to an inverted half-empty *ha'iguas* (coconut shell). The fisherperson chewed coconut meat and forced it from his or her mouth into an opening in the coconut shell. This feeding apparatus was then lowered from a canoe into ten fathoms (60 feet) of water. The fisherperson shook the line. The resulting noise and escaping coconut mash attracted the fish. Each day the fisherperson would feed the fish a few feet closer to the surface. Finally, when the fish were feeding about six feet below the surface, they were caught with a net. The conical-shaped net was about nine feet in diameter.

This reminds us of Pavlov, the famous Russian scientist, who trained dogs to salivate by ringing a

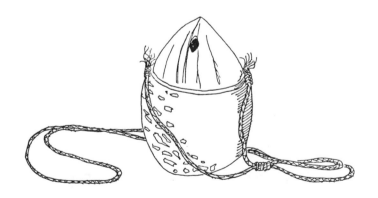

**3.36 *Acho' Achuman***

bell before he fed them. Behavioral psychologists like B. F. Skinner have even trained pigeons to play Ping Pong with their beaks. They do this by rewarding correct behavior. The Chamorros had a practical application to their experiments in behavioral animal psychology. They caught fish.

The ancient Chamorros used a great variety of fishing methods. Some methods took great skill and some demonstrated a knowledge of animal psychology. Some methods were dangerous. Fray Juan Pobre de Zamorra (1602) reported that the ancient Chamorros would actually jump in the water and fight sharks away from their marlin catches. You might like to try *lalagu*, but watch out for the eels. If you try *ka'tokcha'*, remember your science lessons on the refraction of light. Try *sulo'* and see that fish are attracted to light just as termites are. If you try *etokcha'* with a thrust spear, you will appreciate modern spear guns. You might consider taking your sweetheart *lulai* fishing by moonlight. If you are interested in behavioral psychology, use the *acho' achuman* method of fishing. *Katna* (Good Fishing).

# COOKING

The aborigines of the Mariana Islands used a variety of methods and implements in preparing their food. It is impossible to give exact recipes from ancient times. Nevertheless, by relying on the accounts of early European explorers and missionaries and by looking at the rest of Micronesia and even the Malaysian area, we can draw a few conclusions. Archaeologists and linguists have contributed some knowledge in the area of ancient Chamorro cooking, too. We can also learn something about the past from observing surviving customs.

## Cooking Methods

### Tunu

*Tunu* is roasting food over embers. Early accounts refer to this method as *pehu*. This word is used differently today. Since the ancient Chamorros did not have metal grills, they probably supported their food over the fire with sticks. Breadfruit, with its thick skin, can be placed directly on the embers.

3.37 *Tunu*

### Na'lagu

*Na'lagu* is a general word for cooking in a pot. *Saibok* is to boil starchy foods. *Changkocha* is to boil protein foods. In this method the Chamorros used clay pots and probably green bamboo. Green bamboo is used by the Dyak of Borneo for boiling food. The rice is wrapped in banana leaves and placed into a green bamboo tube full of water. The bamboo tube is placed over a low fire. The rice will cook before the green bamboo catches on fire. Boiling in clay pots was the way most ancient Chamorro food was cooked.

### Chahan

*Chahan* is a method of cooking in a deep pit (*hoyo*). A pit was dug, lined with rocks, filled with firewood, and burned. Rocks were placed on the fire, too. Once the fire was out, the food was placed among the hot rocks. The food was wrapped in banana leaves and tied with *akgak* (pandanus). The food was covered with more hot rocks, leaves, dirt and still more leaves. The hot rocks were moved with large tongs made from the partially split trunks of small trees. Periodically, water was poured from a *bongbong* (bamboo tube) on the *chahan* to produce steam. This sped up the cooking. The food cooked by this method was called *chinahan*. The village of Sinajana on Guam gets its name from food cooked in a *chahan*. This type of cooking, done by men, was used for special feasts. (See illustration, next page.)

### Kelaguen

Some foods were "cooked" without fire. Meats can be "cooked" chemically, as in the case of

**3.38  Chahan or Deep-Pit Cooking**

*kelaguen*.  The acid in the lemon juice and salt mixture does the marinating.

## Preserving Food

The ancient Chamorros had several procedures for preserving food.  Foods were dried in the sun.  Some foods were salted.  Fish were kept alive in fish ponds until needed.  Other foods, especially breadfruit and yams, were soaked in the ocean for hours and then buried in an underground pit.  Food stored in this manner is preserved by the process of **fermentation**.

## A Few Important Foods

Fish and shellfish were eaten dry or salted, and almost always raw.  Sometimes they were put in brine instead of being salted.  One early account states that only women in labor ate cooked fish.  This was probably an exaggeration.  Other accounts report that baked flying fish were served to a sick person.  An average family liked to store 34 liters of *mañahak* (rabbit fish or *Siganidae*) for a year's supply.

Turtle was an important food.  It was also

important for its shell, which was used for money. Bat and a small number of birds were eaten, but they were not major foods. The birds were wild ducks, doves, martins, and megapodes. The later is found only in the Mariana Islands; in Chamorro it is called *sasengat*. Today this bird is extinct in all but the northernmost Mariana Islands. The Mariana Mallard (*Anas oustaleti*) is extinct on Guam and is threatened in the rest of the Mariana Islands. Turtle, bat, and fowl were roasted in an earth oven, cooked with an open flame, or boiled in earthenware pots.

Rice was the ancient Chamorros' preferred starch. In ancient times *hineksa'* was the Chamorro name for rice cakes. These cakes were cooked in water and used for bread. This was different from boiled rice, which was called *alagan*. Today, *hineksa'* is the word for cooked rice. The ancient Chamorros probably had rice before Europeans came to the Mariana Islands. The early explorers reported this fact. Also, rice-grain impressions have been found in ancient Chamorro pottery by archaeologists. Nevertheless, some experts believe rice was introduced after the Mariana Islands were discovered by Europeans. It is doubtful that rice was cultivated by the earliest settlers in the Mariana Islands.

Rice was harvested with the valve of a mussel shell. The stem of the plant was pressed against the cutting edge with the thumb. The falling grains were caught in a basket. Rice in the field was called *fa'i*.

*Lemmai* was fixed in five ways. *Lemmai chinahan* was like a sea biscuit. It was cut in round slices and baked. It would last a long time if kept dry. When cooked whole under a blanket of hot ashes and then flattened by hand, it was called *mapanes*. Sometimes it was picked before it was ripe. The breadfruit was allowed to soften for a few days in the shade; then it was baked and eaten with coconuts. More often the rough skin was removed and it was crushed in a mortar with coconut sap until it was the consistency of a thin pap. This was called *laulau lemmai*.

Preserved breadfruit was made by picking and quartering the fruit. A hole was dug in the ground and lined with banana leaves. The fruit was soaked in sea water for five hours and then placed in the hole. When the hole was full, it was covered with leaves and earth. After four or five days, the worms were removed. The fruit was then packed down to form a compact mass, more leaves were added, and it was covered again. After four or five days the fermented breadfruit was removed. This smelly mass was then kneaded and molded into fist-sized balls. After these were dried in the shade, they would last for months. This food was called *bulao*. It was an important food for long canoe trips.

The fifth method of preparing breadfruit was related to the one above. The seeds and meat were mashed up for *bulao*. People took the fermented breadfruit and mixed it with grated coconut. Then they made little pellets and baked them. This was called *apighighi lemmai*. These recipes can be used with *dokdok* (seeded wild breadfruit) as well. Normally the seeds were baked separately and called *hutu*. It is interesting to note that breadfruit shoots were planted only when there was a crescent moon.

*Gapgap* (arrowroot) could be prepared in a manner similar to *bulao*.

*Fadang* (federico palm) was considered inedible by the ancient Chamorros. The ancient Chamorros baked these and other root crops: *dagu* (winged yam), *suni* (taro), *gaddo'* (wild yam). *Chotda* (banana), *tupu* (sugarcane), and *niyok* (coconut) were also important foods.

# Implements Used in Cooking

The Chamorros used a wide variety of implements in the preparation and serving of food. Big-mouth gourds called *sumag* were used to hold water. When used to hold fish, they were called *tagua*. The smallest kind, which were used for buckets, were called *linghig*. (See illustration, next page.)

# SUMMARY

The ancient Chamorros took advantage of their rich natural environment to satisfy their nutritional needs. They used a variety of methods to obtain their food. They farmed, fished, and gathered their food. Some of their food was found naturally in the Mariana Islands. These are the indigenous foods. They brought other food plants with them when they settled the Mariana Islands. Food and the sharing of food continues to be very important parts of Chamorro culture.

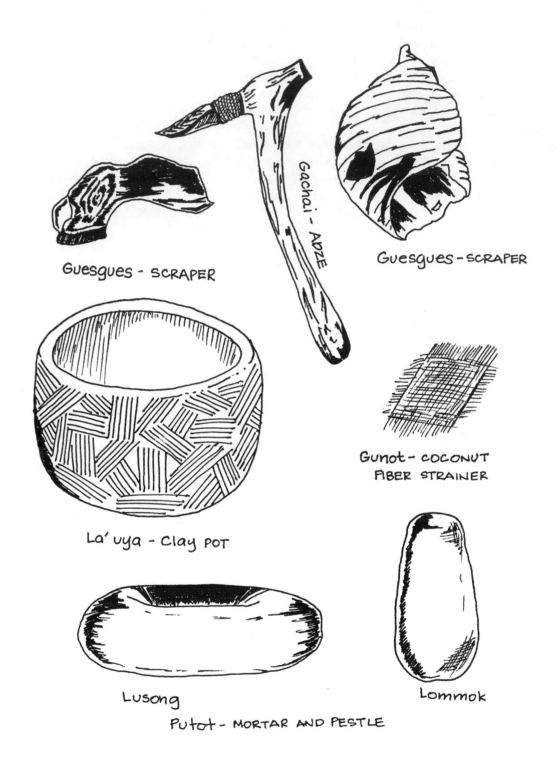

Guesgues - SCRAPER

Gachai - ADZE

Guesgues - SCRAPER

Gunot - COCONUT FIBER STRAINER

La' uya - Clay POT

Lusong

Lommok

Putot - MORTAR AND PESTLE

3.39 Cooking Implements

42

# Chapter 4
# Clothing

## INTRODUCTION

Clothing has two major functions. First, clothing is used for protection from the environment. Eskimos in the past wore animal skins to protect them from the extreme cold of the Arctic. Cowboys wear chaps over their trousers to protect their legs from cactus thorns and other underbrush. The second function of clothing is not determined by the physical environment. Clothing reflects culture. People the world over use clothing as a means of individual expression. People almost always dress within the limits set by their culture. When an individual's choice in clothes deviates too far from what **society** expects, **sanctions** will be placed on the individual.

Ancient Chamorros had few restrictions from their natural and cultural environment on the clothing they wore. The tropical climate was comfortable. Most of their clothing was for decoration. Modesty in most cultures demands that the genitals be covered. This sense of shame in the human body is sometimes extended to other parts of the body. Frequently, a Muslim woman covers her entire body and even veils her face. Modesty varies with different cultures. In Yap, women must always cover their thighs, but go topless. In American culture today, we are just the opposite. American women wear shorts, which show their legs, but usually are careful to cover their breasts. Men and women the world over generally cover their genitals. The ancient Chamorros were unusual in that they had few of these common restrictions of modesty. They seem to have been proud rather than ashamed of the natural human form.

## ENVIRONMENTAL PROTECTION

Ancient Chamorros wore pandanus hats, called *batya,* to protect them from the sun and rain. Sunlight can cause sunburn, heatstroke, or even skin cancer. When working in the sun, a person can see better and is more comfortable if wearing a hat. At times a piece of gourd was used as a skull cap.

The ancient Chamorros normally went barefoot. Nevertheless, when walking on jagged rocks of the reef, they wore protective palm-leaf sandals.

Most people use clothing designed to protect them from their physical environment in a decorative way. The ancient Chamorros were no exception. To protect the skin from the sun, seawater, a cold rain shower, and skin infections, the aborigines of the Mariana Islands anointed themselves with coconut oil. Although this is not clothing, it does have a protective function and is also decorative. An oiled body glistens with a sparkling, glowing radiance. Coconut oil smells good, too.

## MEN'S DRESS

Most historical accounts agree that ancient Chamorro men went naked. Unless we include the hats and sandals previously mentioned, this seems to be true. Besides the historical evidence, there is also evidence from Guam's folklore. In the legend of Maria del Camarin, the fisherman cannot pick up the statue of Mary until he properly clothes himself.

Even with all of this evidence, we must be wary. Early explorers are noted for exaggerating. There are other cultures in the world where men do not cover their genitals, but this custom is extremely rare. We know that in the Americas, where Spanish records state that the people went completely naked, the men did cover their genitals. Early illustrations that depict Chamorro men without any clothing were drawn in Europe and were based on written accounts. We know that in other areas of Micronesia, men wrapped *pokse'* (pagu fibers) around their waist and between their legs. It seems likely that ancient Chamorro men wore similar clothes. During battles and while on the ocean, men wore a pandanus-mat sleeveless vest called a *ngufa' guafak.*

The ancient Chamorro bachelors carried a *tunas.* The *tunas* was a long stick decorated with distinctive geometric carvings. It had an 18-inch tassel of *pokse'.* The *tunas* was colored with orange from the *mango'* root. *Mango'* is the turmeric or ginger used in *eskabeche* (a fish and vegetables dish).

The purpose of the *tunas* is not given in historical record. Nevertheless, history does give us one strong hint. Only bachelors carried the *tunas*. In Truk, the nearest island group to the east of the Mariana Islands, the young men carried a carved stick, too. Their stick was much shorter and lacked streamers attached to the top. Each unmarried man carved a distinctive design on his stick. Each young man made sure that the girl he liked saw his carved stick. At night he would sneak to the girl's house. He would push his stick through the thatch of her house. The young suitor would entwine the stick in her hair, or poke her with it until she woke up. Feeling the distinctive carving, the girl could tell who was outside. If she did not like the young man, she pushed the stick away. If she wished to join him outside, she tugged on the stick. If she desired that the bachelor sneak into the house, she would pull the stick inside. This communication without making sound was important. They did not want her parents to know what they were up to.

Based on this comparative cultural evidence, it seems likely that the ancient Chamorro *tunas* was used as a "love stick." In addition, the *tunas* could have been used as a walking stick, an insect swatter, or a weapon. It was also used to hold a banner. During festivals, the young people paraded with these banners.

Ancient Chamorro men had various hairstyles. Just as hairstyles change today, they did in ancient times, too. In 1521 the men wore their hair long. In 1526 it was reported that men wore their hair to the waist. In 1565, the men bleached their hair yellow. This was done with a water and *åfok* (quicklime) solution. At this time, the men wore their hair long and loose or tied it up behind the head in one or two knots.

A man's hair style could have been an indication of caste. Over one hundred years later, high-caste chiefs called *chamorri* shaved their heads, leaving only a small topknot at the back of the head. Sanvitores, who made this report, did not say if the men still bleached their hair. Since he said the women did, we must assume that the men did not bleach their hair in 1668.

The most valuable ornament worn by men was the *guinahan famagu'on*. It was given as a reward for someone who saved a child's life. For a full description, see the chapter on "Money."

**4.1 Ancient Chamorro Clothing**

# WOMEN'S DRESS

Ancient Chamorro women wore a small triangular apron called a *tifi*, or a skirt of grass or leaves suspended from a belt. The *tifi* may have been made from *gunot*. *Gunot* is the fiber found on coconut trees where the leaves sprout from the trunk. Fray Juan Pobre de Zamora reported that by the age of 8 to 10 girls began to wear a leaf or a plate of turtle shell to cover themselves. This was their everyday clothing.

On special occasions women wore grass skirts with a pandanus belt strung with *daddek* (baby coconuts). These belts had precious shells and little carved immature coconuts on them. Some women wore waistbands of shell money like the necklaces described below. They wore wreaths of flowers in their hair. These are called **"marmars"** in most areas of Micronesia today. At times they decorated their forehead with a piece of tortoise-shell.

At festivities, Chamorro women wore *guini* and *lukao hugua* necklaces. These were *ålas* (tortoiseshell money). For details on *ålas*, see the chapter on "Money." Rich women wore a tortoise-shell plaque. It was fastened around the hips with a double cord and worn as an apron. It was polished on both sides and was called a *maku dudu*. The women adorned their foreheads with pendants, which were fashioned of tortoise-shell, rare shells or beads, and flowers.

The most prized shell ornament for women was a red spondylus shell necklace. This pink oyster shell has many spines on it and is very fragile. Harry Smith, at the University of Guam Marine Laboratory, reports that this shell could exist on Guam today, but no one has found any. Archaeologists have found these perforated shells. Perhaps they no longer exist in the Mariana Islands. Even in ancient times they may have been imported. The shell is found in the Ryukyu Islands to the northwest of the Mariana Islands. Perhaps this shell had great value because it could only be obtained by a hazardous trading voyage. Of course, traders could have brought it here, or it could just be extremely rare on the reefs in the Mariana Islands.

4.2 **The Manufacture of a Spondylus Shell Necklace:** Adapted from B.A.L. Cranstone, *Melanesia: A Short Ethnography*, London 1961.

In eastern New Guinea fine spondylus-shell necklaces are made that are similar to ones found in the Mariana Islands. In New Guinea they break the shell into pieces by pounding it with a rock. The broken pieces are fitted one at a time into the end of a stick. So held by the stick, a piece of shell is rubbed on a stone block until the side is smooth and level. First one side is done and then the other side. The smooth discs are then pierced by a pump drill. The pierced discs are then threaded on a thin stick and rubbed again on a stone. This makes them smooth and of uniform size. Finally, they are strung on fiber strands and made into necklaces. The ancient Chamorros probably made their necklaces in a similar way.

The women's hairstyles changed over time. Magellan (1521) found the women wearing their hair long. Five years later, it was reported that the women wore their hair almost to the ground. Legazpi (1565) reported that the women bleached their hair yellow. Sanvitores (1668) reported that the women bleached their hair white. They tied it in the back in a bun. Women of the nobility divided their hair into two parts and tied each part into a separate bun.

Women wore a special pandanus mat skirt for childbirth. During childbirth they were expected to maintain control and not cry out.

# DECORATIVE DRESS

There is a long period of Chamorro history in the Mariana Islands for which we have no written accounts. This time is called **prehistory**. What were the hairstyles like in the year A.D. 1000 or in 1500 B.C.? We will never know. Nevertheless, archaeologists do find many ornaments that are not mentioned by the early explorers or missionaries. The ancient Chamorros wore **"puka"** - shell necklaces. "Puka" shells are the ends of cone shells. They can be found on many tropical beaches. Each button-shaped shell has a natural hole in its center. In addition, the ancient Chamorros wore finely carved shell-bead necklaces and pendants. Pottery pendants have been found too.

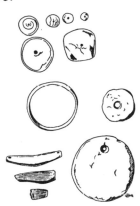

4.3 **Decorative Shell Beads and a Bracelet, and Stone and Pottery Pendants:** Adapted from *Marianas Prehistory: Archaeological Survey and Excavations on Saipan, Tinian and Rota*, by Alexander Spoehr. Published as Fieldiana: Anthropology Vol. 48 in 1957.

Another decoration that ancient Chamorro men and women used resulted from their habit of chewing betel nut. *Pugua'* (betel nut), *pupulu* (pepper leaf), and *åfok* (quicklime) when chewed together stain the teeth a dark brown and the lips red. The quicklime was not strong enough to be immediately dangerous. Nevertheless, it does irritate the tissues in a person's mouth. Some ancient Chamorro teeth seemed to have been purposely stained black with something other than betel nut juice. Archaeologists have found stained teeth with hatch marks scratched on them. Some of the teeth had diamond-shaped etching. Others had diagonal lines carved into the teeth.

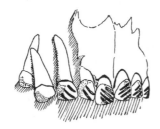

**4.4 Incised Decorations on Teeth**

**4.5 Shell Quicklime Container:** Adapted from *Marianas Prehistory: Archaeological Survey and Excavations on Saipan, Tinian and Rota,* by Alexander Spoehr. Published as Fieldiana: Anthropology Vol. 48 in 1957.

Men and women carried baskets for their *pugua'*, *pupulu*, and *åfok*. The *åfok* was kept in a *ha'iguas* (coconut shell), bamboo, or sea-shell container.

Some historical accounts of the ancient Chamorros claim that they pierced and elongated their ears and wore long fingernails. These accounts are not true. They are based on a case of mistaken identity. Sir Francis Drake (1579) visited a group of islands and described the people, as stated above. He called their home the Island of Thieves. Since the Mariana Islands were known as Islas de los Ladrones (Island of Thieves), many researchers naturally assumed he referred to the Chamorros. Drake's Island of Thieves was actually Belau (Palau). This error by historians has a good lesson for us. We must be very careful to evaluate what we read.

## SUMMARY

Early historical accounts, archaeological evidence, and even folklore give us some understanding of how the ancient Chamorros dressed. Unfortunately, we will never know the complete story. Sometimes we have to make hypotheses to explain what an artifact may have been. These educated guesses are often based on evidence from other areas in Micronesia.

# Chapter 5
# Shelter

## INTRODUCTION

Miguel Lopez de Legazpi, who landed at Umatac in 1565, described the houses of the Chamorros as "high, neatly made, and better constructed than those of any aboriginal race hitherto discovered in the the Indies . . . ."

As students of the early people of the Mariana Islands, we are concerned about all ancient Chamorro shelters. If we were studying the shelters of Guam today, we would have to include not only a description of houses, churches, hospitals, and office buildings, but also the bomb shelter at the Government House. By looking at shelters today we can tell a lot about ourselves. The churches tell us about our religion. The hospitals tell us about our medical care. The bomb shelter tells us that we are concerned with protecting our leaders. By studying Chamorro shelters, we can learn about ancient life in the Mariana Islands.

Other Micronesians require **rituals** through all stages of the construction process. We can assume that the ancient Chamorros had construction rituals too. None of these customs have survived.

As we look at the record of the past, there is more information about the *latte* house than any other ancient Chamorro shelter. There are several reasons for this. First, parts of *latte* houses still stand. Second, the *latte* houses were the most impressive type of ancient Chamorro house, so more is written about them. Third, they are more recent than other ancient structures. Most importantly, though, the *latte* house was unique to the Mariana Islands.

The high-caste people (*chamorri*) lived in *latte* houses. The *latte* houses were also used as boat-houses, and possibly men's houses (*uritao*). Historians always record more information about the upper classes. This is a common problem for students of culture. We are interested in all the people in ancient Chamorro society.

Even though we have more information about the *latte* house, there is little firsthand information available. There is not one firsthand drawing of the most impressive architectural accomplishment of the ancient Chamorros. There are drawings of *latte* stones, but not with a house on them. The written accounts are often not clear. We will look at the historical accounts and the archaeological record and attempt to get a clear idea about all the shelters of the ancient Chamorros.

## TYPES OF ANCIENT CHAMORRO SHELTERS

The ancient Chamorros used caves, rock overhangs, and various pole-and-thatch structures for shelters. There is abundant evidence of the use of caves in the Mariana Islands for shelters. Most cave floors are littered with pottery fragments called **potsherds**. Closer examination reveals that fires were built in caves. There is charcoal in the soil on the floor of caves, and the walls are often blackened by soot.

Most of the time, caves were used only for a temporary shelter or in conjunction with a nearby dwelling. At Talofofo Caves there are *lusong* (mortars) cut in the bedrock in front of caves. There is evidence of *suni* (taro) patches near these caves. This seems to indicate a more permanent type of inhabitation. Nevertheless, at no time in the prehistory of the Mariana Islands were caves the most important type of Chamorro shelter.

The ancient Chamorros built several types of pole-and-thatch shelters. For emergency use or as a temporary shelter, they built a small grass thatched hut on a pole frame. *Nette* (swordgrass) is still used in this way. For dwellings they built A-frame pole-and-thatch buildings on the ground. In order to protect themselves from the muddy ground, the ancient Chamorros spread coral gravel on their floors, yards, and village grounds. This type of house was recorded by early explorers and missionaries. This is also the type of house that the ancient Chamorros less frequently placed on stone supports called *latte* stones.

## *Latte* Houses

*Latte* stones were used as foundations for large structures built by the ancient Chamorros. The Chamorros have inhabited the Mariana Islands since 2000 B.C. The *latte* stones were first built around A.D. 845. However, some experts see them as a general development of huge stone construction found throughout the Pacific around 1000 - 1100 A.D. Some experts regard them as a natural development of the Chamorros' culture. Others think that the *latte* stones were the work of a conquering people and think that slingstones and rice were introduced to the Mariana Islands at the same time.

A *latte* stone looks like a toadstool with the cap inverted. Each *latte* stone is composed of a trapezoidal stone pillar called a *haligi* and is topped with a hemispherical cap called a *tasa*. The *latte* stones were placed by the ancient Chamorros in two parallel rows of three to seven stones as pilings for a pole-and-thatch structure. Generally the houses were long and narrow. A typical latte house might be 11 feet by 33 feet or 12 feet by 48 feet. A typical *latte* house was usually from four to seven feet off the ground. Rarely, additional supports were placed on each side of the parallel rows of *latte* to form a house in the shape of a cross. About eighty percent of the *latte* structures have a total of eight supports.

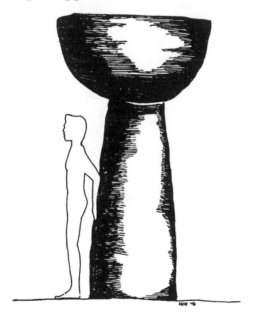

5.1 *Latte* stones had two parts, the *tasa* and the *haligi*.

*Latte* stones are found extensively throughout the islands of Guam, Rota, Tinian, and Saipan. On Guam there are over 138 villages with *latte* house remains. It is not unusual to find an ancient village of at least eight houses with ten stones to each house. Usually the *latte* house was placed parallel to a natural physical feature like the sea, a cliff, or a river, or simply placed to take advantage of the trade winds.

5.2 **Houses were often built parallel to a river in southern Guam.**

The *latte* stones vary in size with age. The beach sites, which are the oldest, have *latte* about four feet high. Some *latte* stones built just prior to Western discovery (Magellan, 1521) are over sixteen feet high. The largest latte stones on Guam and Luta (Rota) are located in interior areas. The As Nieves *latte* **quarry** on Luta reveals incomplete *latte* stones as large as single stones in the pyramids of Egypt. Some of the *haligi* are approximately 16 feet by seven feet by four feet and weigh nearly 35 tons. Perhaps Spanish conquest interrupted the completion of these *latte* stones. Nevertheless, on Saipan an iron tool was found under a *latte* stone, leading investigators to conclude that it was erected after the arrival of the Spanish. The Spanish missionaries referred to the *latte* as "casa de los antiguos."

The A-frame houses constructed on the *latte* stones in times past were not for the common folk. These large structures were used to house the *Chamorri* (high caste - *matao* and *acha'ot*). They were also used as men's houses. The men's house was a bachelors' quarters and meeting place for men. The men's house was called the *uritao*. Some *latte* houses were used for sheltering and building oceangoing outrigger canoes. Oftentimes the men's house and the canoe house may have been the same building. These buildings were probably the largest structures in the village.

There is considerable controversy over *latte* houses. The best compilation of the historical record on *latte* stones is by Felicia Plaza. Her article

"The Lattes of the Marianas" describes the *latte* house as more than a simple A-frame. The historical evidence states that the *latte* house was a framed rectangular house with a steep, pitched roof supported by stone pillars. This description is very similar to the style of men's houses still found in Yap and Palau. In Yap and Palau, the houses are built on stone platforms rather than *latte*-stone pillars.

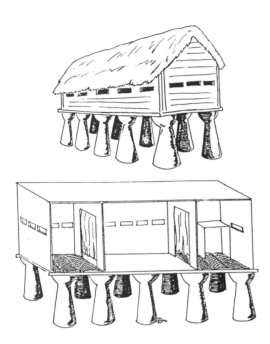

**5.3 Professor Pauline C. Harvey's Interpretation of a *Latte* House:** Adapted from Felicia Plaza's "The *Lattes* of the Marianas" in the January - March 1973 issue of the *Guam Recorder*, pp. 7 & 8.

The doors and walls of the houses were mats. Mats were also used to cover the bamboo floor and for blankets and mattresses. Movable screens were probably used inside instead of walls. Some accounts report that the ancient Chamorros used carved wooden blocks for pillows. There was a storage room and a sleeping room in the house.

Some accounts claim there were kitchens in the *latte* house, too. This does not seem practical because of the danger of fire. A separate pole-and-thatch structure was probably built for a kitchen. In other parts of Micronesia, a fire pit in the cook house is often used to help illuminate the house at night. Since ancient Chamorro houses were on pillars above the ground level, they must have had some other means of illuminating their houses. Perhaps they had some type of oil lamp. Oil lamps were definitely used during and after contact with the Spanish explorers.

Underneath the house, boats could be built and stored. Some accounts tell of a storage area like an attic. A basket with ancestral skulls was one of the things stored in that area.

Alejandro Lizama presents one archaeologist's view of *latte* houses. He envisions a simple A-frame on the *latte* stone supports. He believes that this type of structure would have been more stable and better able to withstand earthquakes and typhoons than the house described by Plaza. William N. Morgan, another archaeologist, makes a strong argument for the type of *latte* house described by Felicia Plaza. His conclusions are based on the historical record, the archaeological evidence, and the comparison of Chamorro structures to other structures in Micronesia.

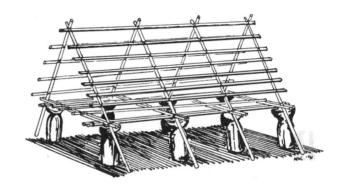

**5.4 Archaeologist Alejandro Lizama's Interpretation of a *Latte* House:** Adapted from Archaeologist Alejandro Lizama's interpretation of a *Latte* house, in "Advanced Technology of the Ancients," in the *Pacific Daily News*, May 16, 1976.

**5.5 Tinian *Latte* House:** Adapted from *Prehistoric Architecture in Micronesia*, by William N. Morgan, Austin: University of Texas Press, 1988.

**5.6 Tinian *Latte* House Interior:** Adapted from *Prehistoric Architecture in Micronesia*, by William N. Morgan, Austin: University of Texas Press, 1988.

Why did the Chamorros choose to build their houses on such substantial stone pillars? Archaeologists have theorized many possibilities. The frequent earth tremors and periodic typhoons of the Mariana Islands made the ball-and-socket joint between the cap and pillar an invaluable shock absorber. The cap extending up and outward from the pillar prevented rodents and crabs from paying an unwelcome visit to the inhabitants. Stone was used as the building material because wooden pillars soon rot in the Marianas' climate. The raised structure allowed for increased ventilation, protection from the mud, and perhaps some protection from attack.

Despite these practical reasons, the extra work involved in quarrying rock with stone tools can hardly be justified in the *latte's* later stages of gigantism. Perhaps the colossal *latte* stand as a monument to competitiveness and desire to outdo our neighbors. There is a plan to build a 400 foot "*Latte* of Freedom" on Guam to house a museum. In summary, a *latte* house offered these advantages: a long lasting structure, protection, ventilation, and prestige.

Sculpture by fire was one of the methods the Chamorros used to quarry *latte* stones for over a thousand years. The first step in this process was to locate an area of land that had faultless

limestone, plenty of hot-burning firewood, and proximity to the building site. The area was cleared of vegetation and the firewood stacked to season. Next, the area was laid out into rectangular shapes for *haligi* and round shapes for the *tasa*. On the margins of these outlines, fires were started. The limestone under the fire was converted to calcium hydroxide (quicklime or *åfok*) and rubble, which could easily be scraped out by hand and broken with **basalt** hammers. This technique was well known to the Chamorros prior to their arrival in the Mariana islands. It is still used among betel nut chewers the world over to obtain quicklime for chewing with betel nut (*pugua'*).

Successive firings and scrapings formed a trench around the outlines of the *latte* stones. Once the desired depth was reached, the difficult undercutting began and continued until only a narrow keel was left supporting the *latte* stones. As the keel was chipped away, the *latte* stone was shored up with rocks to prevent it from falling on the pyro-sculptors.

**5.7 *Latte* stones were quarried with fire.**

50

**5.8 Ancient Chamorros carve out a *tasa*.**

After the *latte* stone was free of the bedrock, the *latte* had to be moved from its pit-like grave. Smaller trenches were cut to allow levers to be placed under the *latte*. With a great deal of force, many men pushed down on the lever. As the *latte* was forced upward, other workers quickly filled the space under it with rocks. The levers were moved to another side and the filling continued until the *latte* rested on ground level over its former pit, which had been completely filled with loose rocks. The final shaping of the *latte* was done with basalt chisels and **adzes**.

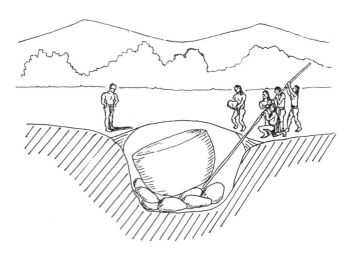

**5.9 Ancient Chamorros lever a *latte*-stone cap out of its pit.**

According to legend, superhuman ghosts called *taotaomo'nas* then hefted the stones and carried them to the building sites. Often such work was relegated to mere boys of four or five years old. Actually a bipod was the tool that allowed many people to move these monoliths to the building site. The trunks of two large trees were lashed together near the top. A rope was attached to the *latte* and secured to the apex of the bipod, which had been positioned so it leaned slightly toward the *latte* stone. From the apex, the secured rope continued to the workers, who pulled the *latte* stone forward. As they pulled, the front end of the *latte* lifted from the ground, reducing the friction to the back edge. As they pulled still more, the *latte* stone moved forward to a position in which the bipod straddled the *latte*. Each leg of the bipod was then pulled forward, dropping the *latte* to the ground again. With great effort another pull on the apex of the bipod brought the *latte* up and sliding forward a few more feet. By this slow process, it is theorized, the *latte* were "walked" to the building site.

**5.10 Ancient Chamorros move a *latte* stone by using the leverage of a bipod.**

At the building site a shallow hole was dug in the sand, into which the *haligi* was placed. After the *haligi* was placed in an upright position, its base was surrounded by supportive rocks and covered with sand. The *tasa* could have been swung into place by a large bipod or simply rolled up a temporary earthen ramp to the top of the *haligi*. In the early phases of *latte* building, the *tasa* was a hemispherical brain-coral head, which could have been lashed to poles and lifted into place.

5.11 Ancient Chamorros erect a *latte* stone using a bipod.

5.12 Ancient Chamorros erect a *latte* stone using an inclined plane.

5.13 Ancient Chamorros place the *tasa* on a *haligi*.

After parallel rows of three to seven *latte* were in place, the timbers were lashed to them with sennit to form an A-frame structure, which was thatched with woven coconut leaves. Time has taken its toll on the *latte* houses, but the stark, silent, stone *latte* remain as a testimonial to human ingenuity, and in the later stages of gigantism, to human competitiveness.

5.14 Thatching a *Latte* House

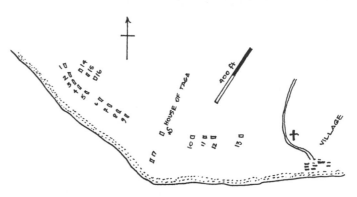

5.15 Map of Taga Site, as it was in 1924. Each box represents a separate *latte* house. Adapted from *Marianas Prehistory: Archaeological Survey and Excavations on Saipan, Tinian and Rota*, by Alexander Spoehr. Published as Fieldiana: Anthropology Vol. 48 in 1957.

Today, with Janice J. Beaty's *Discovering Guam* or Alexander Spoehr's *Mariana Prehistory* as a guide, the curious can trek to numerous remote areas of the Mariana Islands and experience the exhilaration of discovering the *latte* relics. For the less adventurous, Guam's *Latte* Stone Park or Tinian's House of Taga allow viewing with less physical exertion but, sadly, without the thrill of discovery. Out of respect for past generations and future generations, no souvenirs should be taken from a *latte* site.

As a sign that Guam's people are increasingly aware of the importance of their past, *latte* stones are a featured part of the construction of Guam's Won Pat International Airport. A field of blue, a gray *latte* stone, and a lone star make up the flag of the Commonwealth of the Northern Mariana Islands, the first district of the United Nations' Trust Territory of the Pacific to decide its political future. The lone star on the flag stands for the new American ties of the Commonwealth. The field of blue represents the vast reaches of the Pacific Ocean. The future must be built on the foundation of the past and the Marianas; *latte* stone is an impressive foundation.

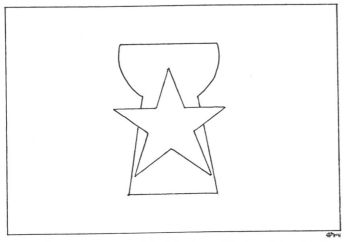

5.16 Commonwealth of the Northern Mariana Islands' Flag

# CULTURAL FACTORS

Ancient Chamorro houses were built for extended families and in some cases for the community. Despite descriptive accounts by Spanish Jesuit priests Gaspar and Grijalva and British Commodore George Anson, the *latte* have been surrounded by an aura of mystery. Nothing has encouraged this more than the ancient Chamorro custom of burying their esteemed dead under their houses between the rows of *latte*. The ancient Chamorros housed the skulls of their ancestors in baskets, which they kept in their attics.

Perhaps the *latte* house had a spiritual function, too. Anson reported that the *latte* houses on Tinian were for those who had taken a special vow. Young men might have taken a vow when they moved from their parents' home to live in the men's house.

Shelters varied for members of different classes. *Latte* houses were designed, built, and lived in by the upper caste (*chamorri*). The lower caste, called *manachang*, could not build *latte* houses and were forbidden to learn advanced skills in architecture. The lower-caste people lived in small A-frame pole-and-thatch shelters. They had raised platforms for sleeping off the ground.

Cooperation was the key to getting a house built. Relatives and friends helped in house building. The custom of *ayudu* (helping) survives today. An extended family today rarely builds a

house, but they still contribute money for having the house built. On Luta (Rota) families still build houses, even concrete houses. *Palapålas* (huts, shacks, or pavilions) are still built in the old way by kin and friends. Having received help, a person is obligated to help others when they are in need.

Cleanliness is a Chamorro cultural value. The ancient Chamorro houses were described as the cleanest found among the colonies of Spain in reports by Padre Garcia. This cleanliness still survives today.

Chamorro villages usually had from 20-150 houses, although there are some reports of villages of 1,000 houses. Remember that these were large houses for an extended family. Most of the houses were probably not *latte* houses.

The most prized locations for building a house were along the coast near sources of fresh water, good farm land, and ocean resources. In ancient times, over three-fourths of the villages were in southern Guam. Today, more than three-fourths of the people live in northern Guam because that is where most of the jobs are, and because it is easier to build houses in that area.

Guam's population has been estimated as high as 60,000 people during the 1600s. Recent estimates by archaeologists suggest that Guam's population was probably not more than 30,000 during that time. In a 1709 report Governor Pimentel estimated the population of the Marianas Islands to be 24,000 in 1668. A map showing the distribution of ancient Chamorro settlements is in the chapter on "Artifacts."

Rivers, wells, and springs were the best sources of fresh water. The largest *latte* house was often near a spring, well, or river. River banks were considered desirable locations for villages. Villages in the interior of the island were generally smaller than beach villages. Nevertheless, on Guam, interior villages had the largest *latte* stones. The *latte* stones displayed in Agaña Park are from the ancient village of Meppo' near present-day Fena Lake (this lake did not exist in ancient times).

Villages were located in areas where the people could take advantage of a variety of natural environmental zones. It was an advantage to have a village near the sea and good farm land. Each village had to have a fresh water supply.

Ancient Chamorro villages were ranked. Hagatña (Agaña) is generally recorded as the most respected village. Even today, people tend to divide themselves by village. The high class on

Guam today are known as *manggi Hagatña*. All others are called *manggi sengsong*. The people of each village have a great deal of pride in their village. People still like to do things to increase the prestige of their village. For example, we take pride in our sports teams, in our fiestas, and in the floats we build for parades. In the past the Mariana Islands were probably ranked in order of importance.

People were meant to be impressed by *latte* stones. The *latte* stones at the House of Taga on Tinian stand 16 feet high. The *latte* stones at As Nieves quarry on Luta (Rota) were never erected. The *haligi* weigh as much as 68,860 pounds. The largest *tasa* weighs 43,726 pounds. The villagers gained status by building many *latte* houses and very large *latte* houses.

Each village had a *uritao*, or men's house. This was a community house for men. The *uritao* probably occupied a central location in a village and was the largest structure in the village. Under this *latte* house large oceangoing canoes were built, stored, and repaired. Often, but not always, *latte* houses formed a line parallel to the sea or a river. Nevertheless, *latte* houses on northern Guam were perpendicular to the sea. Perhaps the ancient Chamorros situated them to catch the prevailing breeze. Often there were approximately an equal number of *latte* houses on either side of the main *latte* house. It is assumed that ordinary dwellings were scattered around these major structures.

# BUILDING MATERIALS

The ancient Chamorros used materials from their natural environment to build their shelters. They needed materials for roofing, a structural framework, and a means of binding them all together into a functional shelter. The Mariana Islands provided thatch, lashing, poles, and stone to satisfy these needs.

## Thatch

Historical records state that the ancient Chamorros used palm thatch. Today coconut leaves are still the first choice for thatch. *Higai* (coconut leaves) are readily available. Their only disadvantage is that they do not usually last more than one or two years. The *higai* are split and woven into shingles.

Nipa (*nipa*) and swordgrass (*nette*) are sewed onto strips of bamboo for thatch, too. Awls used for sewing have been found in archaeological digs. This method is called *tagon nipa* or *tagon nette*. Nipa lasts a long time, but it is a fire hazard. Nipa is not as readily available as coconut leaves as it grows in the brackish (slightly salty) water near river mouths.

Pandanus is still used on Guam for long-lasting thatch and it can last as long as eight years. Pandanus is sewed onto strips of bamboo to form shingles. There are three major types of pandanus in the Mariana Islands: *kaffo'*, *pahong*, and *akgak*. *Akgak* was used in recent and ancient times to make sleeping mats. In ancient times *akgak* was used to make the sails for sea-going canoes. You are lucky indeed if you own something woven from *akgak*, because it is a beautiful and durable material for weaving.

The ancient Chamorros made lashing from coconut fibers and *pagu* (wild hibiscus) bark. To obtain coconut fiber, coconut husks were soaked in seawater. This separates the fibers. Rubbing the fibers on the thigh forms a line. Several lines twisted together make a heavier line. These in turn can be wound together to make rope. Coconut fiber sennit is extremely strong and slow to rot. This sennit is fuzzy, with small fibers sticking out all over that help to make knots stay tight. Since the ancient Chamorros did not use nails or pegs in their construction, tightness was a very important quality in rope.

*Pokse'* is made by stripping the bark from the *pagu* tree. It, too, can be twisted into lines or rope.

If we are to judge by lashings in other areas of Micronesia, the Chamorros' lashings were not only a functional means of tying the house poles together, but were also wound in beautiful, artistic designs. Lashings have an advantage over nail or peg construction. Lashings can give in a strong wind, whereas more rigid joints break.

## Poles

Three types of wood for shelters are in the historical record. *Niyok* (coconut palm), *da'ok* (Maria or *palu maria*), and *pi'ao* (bamboo) were used in house building. Today, in Palau, coconut logs are still sometimes used in construction. First, the logs are made strong and rot resistant. A tree is felled and then one end is burned. This drives the sap out the other end. Next, the trunk is tethered in the ocean. Since the sap has been removed, the tree trunk soaks up seawater. This makes the wood hard, termite proof, and rot resistant.

*Da'ok (calophyllum inophylum)* is an excellent hardwood. *Da'ok* trees are planted along Marine Drive in Agaña. The leaves are dark green and shiny. They have an inedible fruit that is about the size of a golf ball. *Da'ok* has a beautiful grain and may have contributed greatly to the neat, handsome appearance of the ancient Chamorro houses.

*Pi'ao* was probably used in a variety of ways. For small structures it was used for poles. In larger *latte* houses, it was split for flooring. Bamboo can be split into flooring by cutting each *gao* (node) vertically every quarter of an inch or so. This weakens the bamboo and makes it flexible. Next, it is split from end to end on one side only. Then the pole-like cylinder is opened and flattened into a bamboo board. Bamboo was probably bundled together to make long, strong ridge poles. Using this technique you can make a timber as long and as strong as you like.

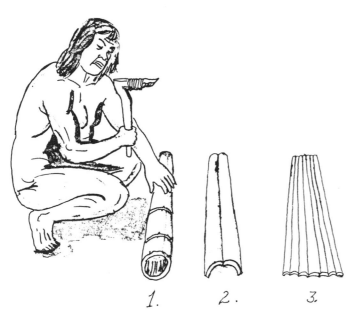

5.17 Split bamboo was used for flooring.

# Stone

*Latte* stones were made from *acho'* (limestone and natural coral heads), *alutong* (basalt or volcanic rock), and a composite sedimentary rock that looks a lot like concrete. Limestone converted by fire to *åfok* (quicklime) was mixed with dirt and coconut oil to caulk between timbers. This also

served as a varnish. The ancient Chamorros had knowledge of paint, but did not paint their houses, only their canoes.

The quarrying of limestone by fire has already been explained. Basalt rocks were probably found naturally and simply shaped with an adze (*guaddukon*) or hammer and chisel. Composite sedimentary rocks are soft enough to be quarried by basalt stone tools.

# CARPENTRY TOOLS

The ancient Chamorros used several basic tools in carpentry. They used the adze (*guaddukon*) and the axe for cutting, splitting, and planing. Both the axe and the adze are called *gachai* today. An archaic word for adze is *eskoplo*. These tools were used in quarrying, too, but hammerstones (*mattiyu*), mauls (*acha*), and chisels (*asuela*) were probably more important.

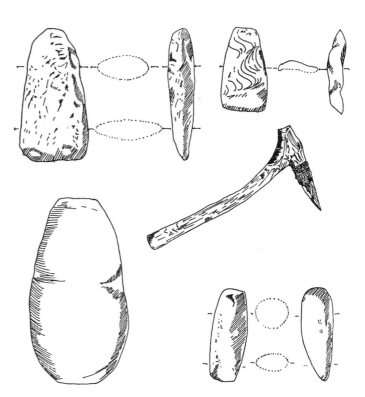

5.18 Ancient Chamorro Carpentry Tools: Adapted from *An Archaeological Survey and Preliminary Test Excavations on the Island of Guam, Mariana Islands, 1965-1966,* by Fred R. Reinman.

All the tools were usually made of hard basalt rock except for the adze. Adzes were made of basalt and also shell. The *hima* (tridacna clam) shell was most frequently used for adzes. The hafted (with handle) tools probably had handles made of *lemon dichina* (Limeberry - *Triphasia trifolia*). This tree is used for tool handles today. *Lemon dichina* has a small, cherry-sized fruit and was introduced to the Mariana Islands by the ancient Chamorros.

# SUMMARY

The ancient Chamorros built A-frame pole-and-thatch shelters. The structures were fashioned with adzes, hammerstones, and chisels, and were probably erected with bipods. Coconut fiber and pagu fiber ropes were used for lashing. The roofs of these structures were thatched with coconut, nipa, or pandanus leaves. Many of their shelters were raised on posts. The floors were built of split bamboo. The area under the floor served as a sheltered work area. Their yards were covered with coral pebbles. The ancient Chamorros built houses, kitchens, canoe sheds, and temporary structures called *palapålas*. The latter were used for celebrations.

The most impressive shelters were built on stone pillars called *latte* stones. The *latte* stones still stand today. Each *latte* stone is composed of a trapezoidal *haligi* (pillar) and a hemispherical cap (*tasas*). The *latte* structures were used for houses of the most influential members of the high caste and for a men's house (*uritao*). Boats were kept under many of the *latte* structures.

Villages were built near a source of fresh water and close to a variety of environmental zones. Early explorers and priests describe the ancient Chamorro structures as clean, neat, and well constructed.

# Chapter 6
# Artifacts

## INTRODUCTION

You can learn a great deal about the ancient Chamorros by studying their **artifacts**. Artifacts are things fashioned by humans. Tools, ornaments, and pottery are artifacts. The ancient Chamorros did not leave us written records, so we are studying **prehistory**. As a student of the first people of the Mariana Islands, you must examine the things they left behind. This type of study is called **archaeology**. Archaeology is the scientific study of the material remains (artifacts, monuments, and fossils) of past human life and activities. The material remains are not so important in themselves. The important thing is what the artifacts can tell us about the people of long ago.

Archaeologists want to know how important the Mariana Islands were in the conquest and settlement of the Pacific Ocean. They want to know if there were cultural changes over time. They want to know what caused cultural changes. Were there gradual changes in the lifestyles of the first people who settled the Mariana Islands? Were the changes caused by visiting peoples? Were the changes the result of warlike invasions? How involved was Guam in inter-island trade? How was Guam colonized? Who colonized Guam? Where did they come from? When were the Mariana Islands first settled?

The artifacts of the Mariana Islands suggest that the **aborigines** (original people) came from Southeast Asia. Most of the people in the Pacific came from this area. This common origin has led to a similarity between the tools of the peoples of Oceania. Even so, there are some differences between Micronesian, Melanesian, and Polynesian artifacts. There are further variations in the tools within each of these geographic regions. Differences in the styles of tools were caused by environmental and cultural factors. The structure of a tool is limited by the materials available. The ancient Chamorros used shell, stone, bone, and clay to make various artifacts.

The function of a tool in a particular environment will cause variations in style. The special fishhook that worked so well in one location may not be as effective in another area with slightly different fish. Contact with other people spreads new ideas. These new ideas can change the kinds of tools people make. Sometimes a person gets a new idea without outside help. This can lead to better tools. It can mean a new tool or a better way of making an old tool. Within the Mariana Islands the artifacts of the ancient Chamorros are very similar. This indicates that the people were probably of one culture. This does not mean that artifacts within the Mariana Islands were always the same. They changed over time.

6.1 **Archaeological Excavation**

Basically, the artifacts are divided into two major divisions. These divisions are the **Pre-*latte* Period** (20th Century B.C. to the 9th Century A.D.) and the ***Latte* Period** (9th Century A.D. - 17th Century A.D.). The most obvious difference gives these periods their names. Before the 800s there were no *latte* **stones**. *Latte* stones are two-part stone pillars. The ancient Chamorros built houses on them. A *latte* stone looks like a toadstool with the cap upside down. Each *latte* stone is composed of a stone pillar called a *haligi* and is topped with a hemispherical cap called a *tasa*.

Another difference is that **slingstones** are a product of the *Latte* Period. They were not used in the Pre-*latte* Period.

The differences in pottery between these two divisions are not rigid. Generally, the thickness of the pottery decreased through time. *Latte* Period pottery is better fired. Firing makes the clay hard. Some *Latte* Period pots were probably used for

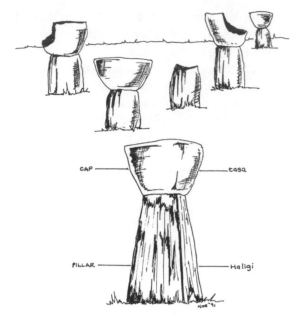

**6.2 *Latte* Stones**

cooking rice. Rice was not grown in the Pre-*latte* Period.

The *Latte* Period ended during the late 1600s and early 1700s. The Spanish introduced metal tools, which replaced most stone and shell tools. Nevertheless, the Spanish did introduce one stone tool, the *mitati*, from western Mexico. The Indians in Mexico first made this tool. The *mitati* is still used to grind corn. Both corn and the *mitati* were brought to Guam probably during the 1700s.

**6.3 The *mitati* is still used for grinding corn. It is an Indian grindstone from Mexico. It was introduced to Guam by the Spanish.**

To study ancient Chamorro tools and pottery, we will divide them into categories and base the categories on the type of material used to make the tool. In other chapters on the ancient Chamorros, tools and their uses are described under headings like "Fishing," "Cooking," "Farming," "Shelter," and "Weapons." Here the tools are listed under the following headings: stone, bone, shell, and

pottery. Tools made of these materials have not been destroyed over time.

Archaeologists estimate that 90% of the material culture of the ancient Chamorros has not survived. For example, historical reports tell of beautiful woven articles of pandanus (*akgak*). These articles rotted away long ago. We can get some idea of what they looked like by observing articles woven today. A few people still make pandanus mats and baskets in the Mariana Islands. Although the ancient articles did not survive, the skills needed to produce those articles did survive.

It may be of some help to examine the woven products of other Micronesians, too. We may know more some day. Archaeologists could find impressions of mats left in clay, or they might find burned pieces of woven material. Partly burned pieces would not rot.

# HISTORICAL PRESERVATION

As you travel around the Mariana Islands, you cannot avoid finding ancient artifacts. People have lived here for 4,000 years. DO NOT DISTURB ARTIFACTS! We owe it to the ancient Chamorros and ourselves to let the past be examined by trained archaeologists. It is a violation of present law to disturb ancient artifacts. It is also a violation of traditional custom to disturb these artifacts. If you find an area that may be of historical interest, report it to the Territorial Archaeologist. This person works for the Government of Guam in the Parks and Recreation Department.

Why is protecting artifacts so important? The objects found can only tell us a little bit about the ancient Chamorro people. What is more important is where an artifact is found, what other artifacts are nearby, and how deep in the soil each artifact is located. Position and order are more important than the tool itself.

For example, suppose you found a simple pile of sea shells. Would it hurt to disturb them? Let us suppose you decide not to bother them. But instead you report them to the Territorial Archaeologist. This officer could examine the shells. The archaeologist could tell you what kind they are. You could find out if the animal that once lived inside the shell was good to eat.

The government officials may decide to excavate (systematically dig) the entire area in which you found the artifact. In doing so, they may find that there are other piles of sea shells arranged in the order of the four points of the compass. One pile of shells indicates north. Other piles indicate south, east, and west. If you had disturbed the shells or not reported them to an archaeologist, this information would have been lost. We would not have physical evidence that the ancient people had knowledge of the cardinal directions (N, S, E and W).

Perhaps the piles of sea shells over the area diagramed a constellation of stars. They could have made the outline of a human figure. You can see that the shells themselves are not so important, but their arrangement could be very important.

Many artifacts are in very poor condition. If you remove an old pot or skull, it could very easily break. A trained archaeologist could remove it with minimum damage.

Ancient artifacts are treasures of the past and they belong to all the people. These artifacts should be placed in a museum for all to see. Then the public can enjoy them. Then everyone who visits the museum can learn from them. The pot you remove without expert assistance will end up in the garbage can. It will not end up on a museum shelf. No one would learn anything new from it. On the other hand, if you report the pot to the Territorial Archaeologist, things will be very different. It may prove valuable enough to be placed in the museum. Your name would be put on the artifact. Then museum visitors would know who discovered it and who donated it.

# CULTURAL SEQUENCE AND RADIOCARBON DATING

Archaeologists have found that the Mariana Islands were settled by people from Southeast Asia about 4,000 years ago. Why do they think the ancient Chamorros came from Southeast Asia? Because there are strong similarities between the artifacts in the Mariana Islands and the Philippines, Indonesia, and mainland Southeast Asia. There are also similarities in the skeletal remains of the ancient Chamorros and the human skeletal remains in Southeast Asia.

Archaeologists are supported in these claims by the research of botanists. They find similar plants in both areas. Linguists find that the Chamorro language comes from Southeast Asia, too. In addition, many of the past customs of these two areas are similar.

How do archaeologists know that the ancient Chamorros settled the Marianas 4,000 years ago? They **radiocarbon date** pieces of bone, shell, or charcoal. All living things have some **radiocarbon (C14)**. After an organism dies, the C14 will decay into nitrogen (N14). Half of the C14 will decay in 5,730 years. This is not exact. The 5,730 years is plus or minus 40 years. Half of the remaining C14 will disappear in another 5,730 years and so on.

Scientists can measure the amount of C14 in a sample of something that once lived. Since the half-life for radiocarbon is known, they can then tell how old it is. This method is good for objects as much as 70,000 years old.

Generally, the deeper the artifacts are in the ground the older they are. There are many different **strata** deposited on the limestone bedrock. These layers formed as sand, dust, and the debris from human inhabitation were deposited. The layers are separated by deposits that formed when a village was abandoned or when storms washed sand over a village site. Sand Layer I in the "Stratigraphic Sequence at Tarague Beach" illustration (on the next page) is the latest. Layer II is older. Layer VIII is very old.

Layer I contains modern objects like beer bottles and cans. Spanish pottery is also found in this layer. The top layer also contains ancient Chamorro *latte* stones, pottery fragments, shell and stone tools, slingstones, and fishhooks. Toward the bottom of Layer I, the pottery style changes a little. This is probably a period of change between *latte* style pottery and the earlier Pre-*latte* Period pottery.

Charcoal samples from Layer I show that the artifacts go back over one thousand years to the 800s. Everything from the 800s to the Spanish settlement of the Mariana Islands in the late 1600s is called the *Latte* Period. The human occupation of the Mariana Islands before the 800s is referred to as the Pre-*Latte* Period.

Most of the Pre-*latte* Period artifacts of the ancient Chamorros are found in Layers II through VIII. A few artifacts from this period have been found at the lowest level of Layer I. As more is learned about the Pre-*latte* Period, each layer will probably be given a special name. Objects from Layer V have been dated from about 120 B.C. Layer VII goes back to 1100 B.C.

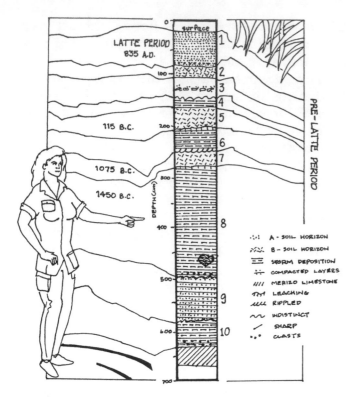

**6.4 Stratigraphic Sequence at Tarague Beach:** Adapted from Hiro Kurashina's and R. N. Clayshulte's "Site Formation Processes and Cultural Sequence at Tarague, Guam."

Layers II, IV, and VI do not have many artifacts. They are mostly beach sand. Why? Because these layers are the result of super-typhoons. During a storm huge amounts of sand and pieces of the reef were washed ashore. This sand was deposited on the strand. The strand is the area between the beach and the cliffline.

Evidence was found that humans lived on Guam when Layer VIII was formed. That layer was formed about 1485 B.C. Just imagine! The ancient Chamorros were living on Guam 1,485 years before Christ was born.

# SETTLEMENT PATTERNS ON GUAM

Archaeologists excavate an area where they think people once lived. They look for artifacts and other clues that will help them learn about the people who once lived in that area. On Guam there have been many such excavations. Some of the most important archaeological sites on Guam are at Asan, Ipao (Ypao), Talagi (Tarague), Pagat, Talo'fo'fo' (Talofofo) Bay, Nomña (Nomna) Bay, Urunao (Uruno), Faifai, Meppo' (Mepo), and

Toguan Bay. About 150 different village sites have been found.

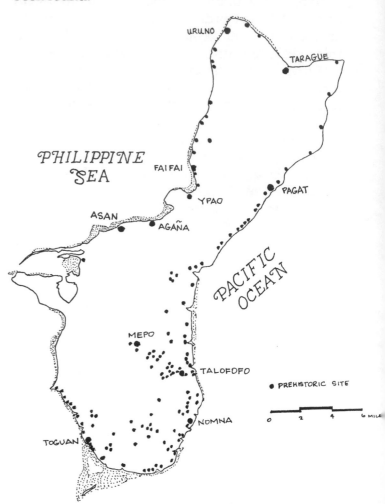

**6.5 Ancient Chamorro Village Settlements on Guam:** adapted from Kurashina, Hiro, *Prehistoric Settlement Patterns on Guam.* Paper presented at the meeting of the Society for American Archaeology, New Orleans, Louisiana (April 23-26), 1986.

Where archaeologists find artifacts can tell us a great deal. For example, many artifacts show us where the ancient Chamorros settled. Generally, they settled near the beach. Why? Because they could take advantage of the land and sea resources there. Near a wide reef or a river was a really choice location for a village.

During the *Latte* Period, new settlements moved in two directions. Because of a sea-level change, the ancient Chamorros moved seaward towards the new beach. Because the population increased, some people moved inland.

The inland villages took advantage of the environment. First, water had to be available. Usually, they settled where one or more environmental zones came together. For example, a settlement would be built where a limestone and a savanna plant community bordered one another. A limestone plant community is a thick jungle. It grows on soil formed from an old coral reef. A savanna plant community is a grassland with scattered trees. It grows on soil formed from volcanic rock.

The huge typhoon that formed Layer II in the "Stratigraphic Sequence at Tarague Beach" illustration was probably very hard on the people of Guam. It seems that there was a large population at that time. The typhoon really disturbed the way that the people provided for themselves. After the super-typhoon there was not enough food for everyone. Normal food resources were disrupted. So some ancient Chamorros settled inland areas. The reef, disturbed by the storm, could no longer provide enough fish. The population had grown too large, so the ancient Chamorros began to do more deep-sea fishing.

At about this same time there seems to have been an increase in trade and communication throughout the Pacific area. It seems likely that rice was introduced into the Mariana Islands at that time. The ancient Chamorros were desperate to feed their growing population. Rice is a good food source. A farmer can produce a lot of rice on a small piece of land. Rice is grown on swampy land. Swampy areas near Hagåtña (Agaña), Hagat (Agat), Talo'fo'fo' (Talofofo) Bay, and Malesso' (Merizo) are the best areas on Guam for growing rice. This valuable land for growing rice might have led to the increase in warfare, which took place at that time.

Archaeologists know there was warfare, because slingstones, which are used in fighting, began to be produced at this time too. Chamorros are noted for sharing food. If the growing population fought over scarce resources, it was probably because the fighting was thought to be necessary for survival.

The building of huge stone monuments increased throughout the Pacific at this time. The knowledge necessary for creating large stone objects spread from island to island. People traveled by oceangoing sailing canoes. With many of the larger trees destroyed by the super-typhoon mentioned earlier, the ancient Chamorros might have put this new stone technology to work. The ancient Chamorros turned to the use of stone for house supports.

Was this the only reason for *latte* stones? Why did the ancient Chamorros choose to build their houses on such substantial stone pillars? Archaeologists have theorized many possible reasons for *latte* stones.

1. The frequent earth tremors and typhoons of the Mariana Islands made the ball-and-socket-like joint between the cap and pillar a valuable shock absorber.

2. The cap, extending up and outward from the pillar, prevented rodents and crabs from paying an unwelcome visit.

3. Stone was used as the building material because wooden pillars soon rot in the Mariana Islands' climate.

4. The raised structure allowed for a breeze to pass under the house. It protected the people from the muddy ground. It may have been some protection from attack. The height of the *latte* stones would have been a military advantage. Also, who would want to bother a village strong enough to build huge *latte* stones?

The above reasons are practical. But do they justify the extra work involved in quarrying rock with stone tools? This would have been a big job. This is especially true of some of the giant *latte* stones. Perhaps the huge *latte* stand as a monument to human competitiveness. The tallest standing *latte* stones are on Tinian. They are 16 feet high. On Rota there are some even bigger *latte* stones. They were never finished. But some of these *latte* stones weigh over 34 tons. Were people just trying to out-do their neighbors?

In summary, a *latte* house offered these advantages: a long-lasting structure, protection, ventilation, and prestige.

In this chapter, we will examine the stone, bone, shell, and pottery artifacts that have been found in the Mariana Islands. Particular tools and their uses are found in the sections titled Stone, Bone, Shell, and Pottery. As you study these tools, think about the similar tools we have today. You will find that we still have many of these tools. But our tools are not handmade. We use metal and plastic today, and our tools are made in factories.

# STONE ARTIFACTS

Stone was the hardest material in the Mariana Islands. It was used for making tools. **Basalt** and other volcanic rocks were used for tool making. Coral and limestone were also used. Some grinding tools were made from volcanic **pumice**. A pink marble-like rock was used to make some tools.

The simplest tools were **flaked**. A hard rock was struck against another one in order to break off pieces with sharp cutting or scraping edges. This method could also be used to obtain the general shape of a tool.

Next, the stone tool was chipped and pecked with a hard rock to obtain the final shape. Finally, some tools were ground with pumice or sanded to a smooth, polished finish.

As you look at the pictures of the tools, ask yourself some questions. How did the ancient Chamorros use these tools? Why did they use these tools? Do we have similar tools today?

**6.6 Scrapers or *Guesgues***

**6.7 Ancient and Modern Drills and Perforators**

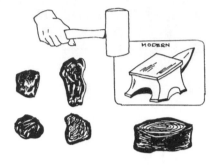

**6.8 Hammerstones (*Mattiyu*), Mauls (*Acha*), and an Anvil (*Acha'on*)**

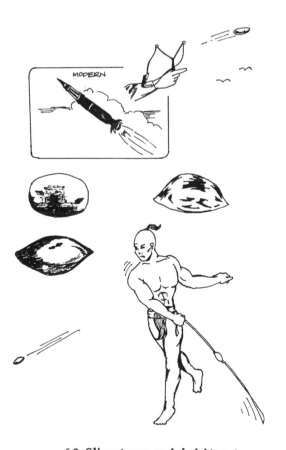

**6.9 Slingstones or *Acho' Atupat***

**6.10 Mortar and Pestle or *Lusong* and *Lommok***

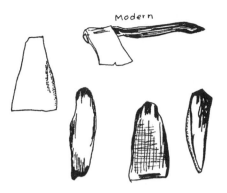

**6.11 Adzes and Axes (*Gachai* or *Guaddukon*) and a Hoe or *Akao***

**6.12 Sinkers or *Katgaderu***

**6.13 Stone Chisels or *Asuela***

**6.14 Ancient Chamorro Stone Pendant or *Kalang***

**6.15 Grindstone or *Guasa'on***

**6.16 Stone Knives or *Se'se'* or *Chachachak***

63

# BONE TOOLS

With shell and stone tools the ancient Chamorros fashioned artifacts from fish and human bones. The human tibia, or shin bone, was used for spear points. Fish bones were used as parts of octopus and squid lures. Sometimes bones were used for sewing needles. **Awls**, pointed tools for piercing holes, were sometimes made of bone.

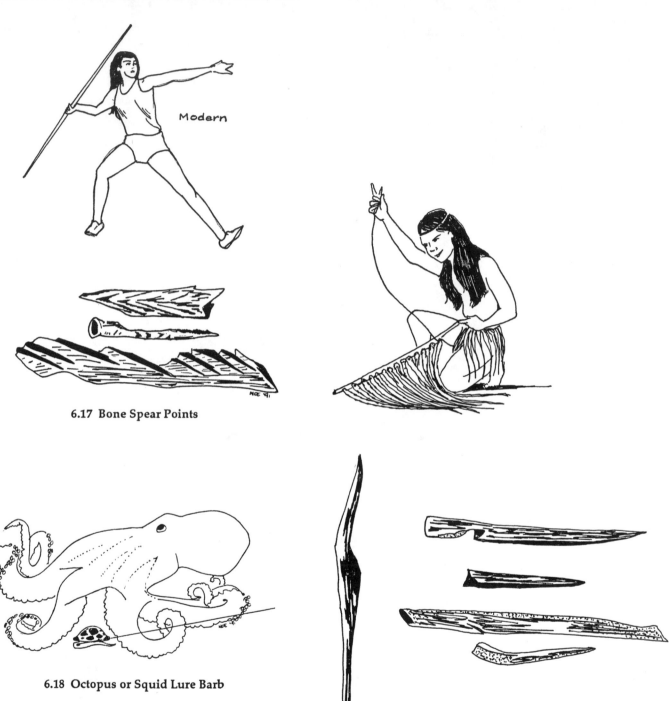

Modern

6.17 Bone Spear Points

6.18 Octopus or Squid Lure Barb

6.19 Awls or Thatching Needles

Ancient Chamorro skeletons can tell us a lot about the ancient Chamorros. We know that the ancient Chamorros were **Mongoloids** by examining their skeletons. Mongoloids are one of the four major racial divisions of human beings. Mongoloids originated in Asia and migrated into Southeast Asia.

In the drawing below, **a shovel incisor** is compared with an incisor with no shoveling The ancient Chamorros often had shovel incisors. This is an indication that the ancient Chamorros were not **Caucasoids, Australoids,** or **Negroids.** Those races do not usually have shovel incisors. Since Mongoloids usually have shovel incisors, it seems likely that the ancient Chamorros were Mongoloids.

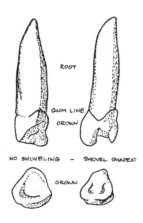

6.20 **Shovel incisors indicate a skeleton is Mongoloid.** Adapted from the *World Book Encyclopedia*, Volume 16, 1978.

The skeletal remains of the ancient Chamorros are thick. The places where the muscles were attached are large. This indicates that the Chamorros were generally a stocky, muscular people. The skeletal remains indicate that the ancient Chamorros were taller than most of the Spanish explorers.

There was no one pattern for ancient Chamorro burials. Some people were buried under and around *latte* houses. Others were buried in large urns called *sahayan* or even in caves. Archaeologists at Talagi (Tarague) Beach in northern Guam found mostly female skeletons. This may be just an unusual sample. Perhaps more care was taken in burying females; perhaps males were cremated. To cremate means to burn someone to ashes. There are still many questions to be answered about ancient Chamorro prehistory.

# SHELL TOOLS

There were plenty of shells in the Mariana Islands. The people used them to make tools. Shells come from animals called **mollusks** (snails or clams). Shells have the advantages of being relatively hard and easily worked with stone tools.

One common ancient Chamorro tool was the **adze**. It had a handle and looked like an axe with the blade turned sideways. The blade was made from the *hima* clam shell. This **hafted** tool was used to plane wood and to open green coconuts. Some people in Micronesia still use adzes.

The triton trumpet shell was used to make noise. A hole was drilled in one end. If you blow it like a trumpet, you produce a loud sound. Some Pacific peoples still use this kind of shell to signal one another.

Shells were used to carry *åfok* (quicklime), which was chewed with betel nut.

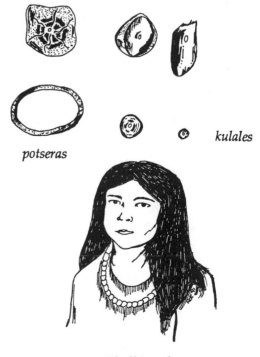

*potseras*

*kulales*

6.21 Shell Jewelry

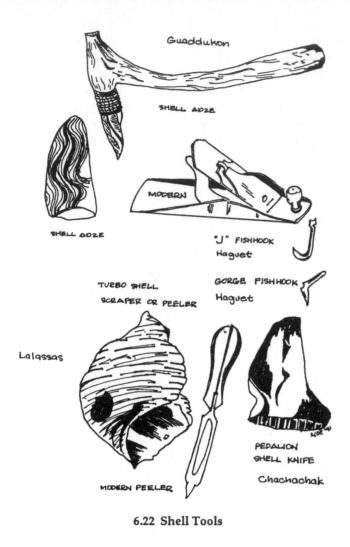

Guaddukon

SHELL ADZE

SHELL ADZE

MODERN

"J" FISHHOOK
Haguet

TURBO SHELL
SCRAPER OR PEELER

GORGE FISHHOOK
Haguet

Lalassas

PEDALION
SHELL KNIFE

MODERN PEELER

Chachachak

**6.22 Shell Tools**

# POTTERY ARTIFACTS

In this section we will compare the pottery from the *Latte* Period and the Pre-*latte* Period. These eras are the major divisions of the prehistory of the Mariana Islands. **Potsherds** (pieces of pottery) make up 98% of the ancient artifacts found in the Mariana Islands. Pottery must have been important in ancient times.

The pottery of the ancient Chamorros has changed over time. Its uses have changed and the way pottery was made has changed. The designs on the pottery have changed. Finally, imported pottery has replaced the locally produced pottery.

In the earlier Pre-*latte* Period, the pottery was generally wide mouthed, shallow, and flattened. This pottery was probably used for serving food. In general the Pre-*latte* Period pottery is smaller and more artistically decorated than the *Latte* Period pottery. The lack of big storage containers in the Pre-*latte* Period suggests that food was rarely

scarce. The *Latte* Period pottery is very different. This pottery often had round or cone-shaped bottoms, instead of flat bottoms. These pots were globe shaped. The mouths of the pots were small. Such a design helps the pot retain heat. Therefore, these pots were probably used for cooking. Some large pots were probably used to store food and water.

The *Latte* Period pottery was generally better fired than the earlier pottery. The designs on the pots seem more for making them less easy to slip out of the user's hands than for decoration.

How was the pottery made? First, you needed clay. Clay deposits are found in the Mariana Islands. If the clay was simply shaped and baked, it would crack. To prevent this, temper was mixed with the clay before firing. **Temper** is various types of sand mixed with clay to make pottery. The firing makes the clay hard. By mixing temper with the clay, it became easier to shape. Temper also allowed the clay to expand without breaking during the firing.

During the Pre-*latte* Period, coral sand temper was most frequently used. In the *Latte* Period, volcanic sand temper was primarily used. If you cannot determine the period a piece of pottery comes from by its design, you can do so by checking the temper. Using a magnifying glass or microscope, you can examine the interior of a piece of pottery (potsherd). If the temper is generally white, it is coral sand and therefore Pre-*latte* Period pottery. If the temper is dark, it is volcanic sand, and therefore *Latte* Period pottery.

Sometimes the temper found in the pottery is a mixture. It is not presently known if this was a transition period between Pre-*latte* and *Latte* pottery. If it was, this suggests a change within a people. But what if there was no transition period? That would suggest that the change was the work of a conquering people. The new people might have had a different way of making pottery.

There are other theories for the changes in pottery styles. The changes could have been caused by the exhaustion of the natural supply of high-quality clay in the Mariana Islands. If so, this can serve as a lesson for us today. Can you think of any resources we might completely use up? What can we do to prevent this?

The ancient Chamorros worked the clay by hand into the desired shape. They probably also used a paddle to shape the pottery. The potter's wheel was not used by the ancient Chamorros.

**6.24** *Latte* **Period Pottery:** Adapted from Fabiola Calkins' May 15, 1976, *Pacific Daily News* article "Prehistoric Pottery."

**6.23** **Pre-***latte* **Period Pottery:** Adapted from Fabiola Calkins' May 15, 1976, *Pacific Daily News* article "Prehistoric Pottery."

There are some examples of the coil method of making pottery. In this method, clay was rolled into snake-like rolls. This "snake" of clay was then coiled into the shape desired. Next, with hand or paddle, the shaping continued. This type of pottery breaks horizontally in straight lines. Vertical breaks are irregular. Irregular breaks are expected vertically and horizontally in pottery not formed by the coil method.

With their fingers, coconut husks, and impressing tools, the ancient Chamorros placed designs on their pottery. In the Pre-*latte* Period, these designs were very artistic. There were many interesting decorations. During the *Latte* Period, the designs were less artistic and more functional. The later designs gave the pot a textured finish, which made the large pots easier to hold on to. Why did the large, ancient Chamorro pots need this textured surface? Because the huge pots did not have handles.

A **slip** was put on some pots before decorations were added. Water was rubbed on the pot, or a smooth layer of wet clay was added to the pot before firing. The resulting smooth finish is called slipped pottery.

In the Pre-*latte* Period, some impressions on pottery were filled with lime. In Chamorro this lime is called *åfok*. Until recently, these pots were thought to be items the Chamorros got from some other people. A similar pottery was produced in the central Philippines. About 1000 B.C., there was probably frequent contact between the Marianas and the Philippines. Today this frequent contact with the Philippines continues.

At first, archaeologists thought the lime-filled impressed pottery was a trade item. Why? Because they found very few of these potsherds. Recently, archaeologists on Guam have found many of these lime-filled impressed potsherds. Therefore, they no longer think of these potsherds as a trade item. This lime-filled impressed pottery is thought to be the highest achievement of the Pre-*latte* Period potters.

Archaeologists are not sure how the pottery was fired. It was not fired in a **kiln** (oven). Probably, the open fire method or pit-firing method was used. These methods have been used by some Pacific people in modern times.

In the open fire method the pottery is placed in the flames of a fire. The fire is usually made with

**6.25 Ancient Chamorro Pottery Designs:** Adapted from *Archaeology of the Marianas Islands,* by Laura Maud Thompson. Published as Bernice P. Bishop Museum Bulletin 100 in 1932 by Bishop Museum Press.

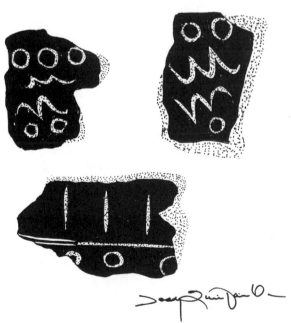

**6.26 Lime-filled Impressed Potsherds:** Adapted from *Marianas Prehistory: Archaeological Survey and Excavations on Saipan, Tinian and Rota,* by Alexander Spoehr. Published as Fieldiana: Anthropology Vol. 48 in 1957.

dry coconut leaves. The pit-firing method is similar to the open fire method. It is also similar to the kiln method. In the pit-firing method the fire is placed in a depression in the side of a bank.

Pottery was used by the ancient Chamorros for serving and storing food and water. Some pottery may have been used for cooking. One flat type looks perfect for making pancakes. There is evidence that some were used to hold charcoal. Hot coals were moved on these trays to start another fire.

Because the *Latte* Period pottery is better fired, it could have been used for cooking. Rice was introduced into the Mariana Islands during the *Latte* Period. The globular pots with a small opening at the top would have been good for cooking rice. The small mouth of the pot would help to retain heat. The round or conical bottom would allow the rice to be heated through the sides of the pot as well as from the bottom.

The most unusual use of pottery by the ancient Chamorros was in burials. A large pot (*sahayan*) was placed over the deceased, after the body had been put in a sitting position in the grave. Only a few Chamorros were buried this way. This custom is similar to the burial urns of Indonesia, Southeast Asia, and China. For further details on burial, see the chapter on "Customs."

After the Spanish-Chamorro Wars (1672-1695), pottery making died out. This skill, believed to have been performed by women, was no longer needed. The Spanish introduced kiln-fired vessels called *hara*, *tebbot*, *butati*, and *tinaha*. Some jars were used to salt fish and some to collect and store *tuba* (fermented coconut palm tree sap).

In modern times, most pottery has been replaced by china, metal, plastic, and glass containers and pots. Nevertheless, people prize the old Spanish and Okinawan pottery still found on Guam.

Before World War II, the Department of Corrections tried to revive pottery making at Lebougon in Barrigada, Guam. There is good clay in the area, but the project was discontinued.

Local potters in the Mariana Islands today are for the most part immigrants from the United States. Their pottery is usually more artistic than useful. Generally, they do not use local clays and tempers.

Chamorros no longer make much pottery. They use other things for containers. But pottery was once an important part of Chamorro culture.

It is interesting to imagine what life must have been like in those days. Perhaps that will be easier someday when archaeologists find unbroken pots. Could that be archaeological work you will do someday? It might help if experts made pots like the ancient Chamorro pots. Then we could get a better idea of what they looked like.

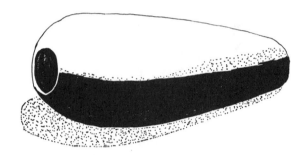

**6.27 Pottery used after the Spanish colonized the Mariana Islands.** Adapted from Fabiola Calkins' May 15, 1976, *Pacific Daily News* article "Prehistoric Pottery."

# SUMMARY

The first people of the Mariana Islands were the Chamorros. Archaeologists systematically have examined their prehistoric settlements. The objects they made of bone, stone, shell, and clay have not rotted away. These artifacts tell us about the way the ancient Chamorros lived. Their tools and pottery are similar to the artifacts of the ancient people of Southeast Asia and the surrounding islands. An examination of the ancient Chamorros' skeletons suggest that they were originally from that area too.

The Chamorros probably came to the Marianas Islands as many as 4,000 years ago. The oldest generally accepted date of human occupation is

1485 B.C. This date was determined by radiocarbon dating.

The long occupation of the Mariana Islands can be divided into two major periods: the *Latte* Period and the Pre-*latte* Period.

During the *Latte* Period, the population was relatively large (24,000-40,000 for the entire Mariana Islands). Since resources were scarce, some people had to move inland. Rice, a new source of food, may have been introduced at this time. During this period there seems to have been more competition. Villagers probably tried to make bigger *latte* stone supports for their houses than other villages had. The slingstone seems to have been introduced during this time. The pottery of the *Latte* Period was better fired; it could have been used for cooking. Big pottery jars seem to have been used for storing food and water. There was probably a lot of inter-island trade and communication during this time. There was more deep-sea fishing, too.

The *Latte* Period lasted from the 800s to the late 1600s, when Spanish missionaries and soldiers formed permanent settlements.

The Pre-*latte* Period may go back to 2000 B.C. Less is known about this period. Most of the people lived near the sea during this time. In this way they could take advantage of two very different environments: the land and the ocean. There was less deep-sea fishing during this time. Since the population was small, all the fish they needed could be found on or near the reef. There was less fighting, too. Resources were not scarce. There seems to have been plenty for all.

It is important to protect the remains of ancient Chamorro village settlements. This shows respect for the ancient Chamorros. Archaeologists know how to excavate artifacts properly. Through their work, we will learn more and more about the ancient Chamorros. The most important of their discoveries will be placed in a museum for all to see and learn from.

# Chapter 7
# Weapons

## INTRODUCTION

The ancient Chamorros did not use the bow and arrow or swords in combat. They used the lance or spear and the sling and **slingstones**. It seems likely that they used clubs, but this claim has limited historical evidence to support it. The ancient Chamorro spear (*fisga*) was made of wood. The tip was fire hardened, or bones were attached to it. In some cases, fish bones were used as spearheads. Human bones, especially the tibia (shin bone), were also used for spearheads. The tibia was a deadly spear point. Even a slight wound was usually fatal. The brittle bone broke off easily upon contact. In an age before antibiotics, infection would set in and the victim would eventually die. The Spanish thought that the Chamorro spears were poisoned. No poison was placed on the spears. It was not necessary, for the bacteria present was capable of killing in time, if the wound was not deep enough to do so immediately.

**7.1 Warriors Carry Lances with Human Tibia Spearheads**

The spears were eight feet long, two inches in diameter, and sometimes had human bones at each end. Barbed harpoons called *pulos*, which had notched human bones or wood on the end, were not used in battle by an ancient Chamorro, unless a person was trapped and had no other means of escape. It was a point of honor not to use a *pulos* in battle. In order to parry the lance thrusts, the ancient Chamorros had a *fudfud*. It was a stick three inches in diameter and five and a half feet long adorned with palm leaves at one end.

Fire-tipped spears were hurled at enemy thatched houses. Dry plant fibers like *pokse'* (bark of *pagu* tree) were probably soaked in coconut oil and used on spearheads.

Slingstones were introduced to the Mariana Islands just prior to the *Latte* Period. They were surely present by A.D. 845 and were used continuously through the Spanish-Chamorro Wars, which ended in 1695.

Slingstones are football shaped and were made from various volcanic rocks, coral and, in a few cases, clay. Slingstones are referred to as *jijuk pato* or *djiukpatu* in early accounts; today they are called **acho' atupat** in Chamorro. They varied in size from that of a pigeon egg to that of an ostrich egg. Most slingstones are pointed on the ends; nevertheless, some are more rounded.

An *atupat* (sling) was used to throw slingstones. The sling was made of **coir** (coconut fiber sennit or rope) or pandanus. The pandanus slings were less prized. Other areas of Micronesia use *pokse'* from the pagu tree to make slings, and it was probably used in the Mariana Islands, too. The slingstones were carried in a bag called a **balakbak**. The slinger wore this at his side, hanging from his shoulder on a long strap.

The *atupat* was used in David-and-Goliath fashion. The slingstone was placed in a pouch, which was located midway between the ends of the sling. The ends of the *atupat* were held in one hand. The pouch cradled the slingstone. The sling and stone were swung around and around over the warrior's head. This added a great deal of centrifugal force to the warrior's normal throwing power. One end of the sling was released and the slingstone sped in spiral fashion toward its intended target.

The aerodynamic football shape and symmetry helped maintain accuracy. The pointed end, which struck the target, greatly increased the missile's penetrating power and the pounds per square inch

71

of force applied. A karate fighter is well aware of the latter principle. Martial artists rarely strike with their fist. The area is too great, and reduces the effectiveness of the punch. Instead, a martial artist uses the side of his or her hand or the extended fingers. Women who wear high heels are aware of this principle, too. In a normal shoe, a woman's weight is distributed over several square inches when her heel hits the ground. When she wears high heels, her entire weight is concentrated on a very small area. Many tile floors have been damaged in this way. The extra centrifugal force, aerodynamic qualities, and pointed ends greatly increased the weapon's effectiveness. With this in mind, we can see that historical accounts of slingstones penetrating coconut trees do not sound so farfetched. Obviously, they could crack the enemy's skull and this, not hunting animals, was the purpose for which slingstones were designed.

The ancient Chamorros did not wear armor, but one historical account claims that they used shields. Unfortunately, the Legazpi Expedition (1565) accounts do not describe the shields.

The ancient Chamorros tended to rely on agility for protection from spears and slingstones. They wore a pandanus vest for protection against cold when at war and when on the sea. They also had pandanus baskets to carry supplies. Some baskets had straps and were worn on the back. Others were carried at the hip and had a shoulder strap.

There is no documented evidence of formal training in the martial arts by ancient Chamorros. Nevertheless, recent work in Micronesia by anthropologists reveals a very sophisticated form of hand-to-hand combat training. These methods stress systematic self-defense. Young men were trained to disarm an enemy. They were trained to take the enemy's weapon and use it against him. Today, on a less formal level, young men in the Carolines south of Guam must learn some self-defense before fathers allow them to live in the men's house.

Historical records about the Mariana Islands state that there was competition in the martial arts. Slingstone and spear throwing, running, jumping, and wrestling were practiced around the men's house. Young children played with slings and spears. Demonstrations of spear throwing and wrestling ability were common at village feasts. Young men could actually catch spears that were thrown at them.

**7.2 Warrior Hurls Slingstone**

# STRATEGY AND TACTICS

The ancient Chamorros did not build extensive fortifications. They relied on agility to dodge spears and slingstones for defense. The major strategy was to watch the movements of the enemy and to try to make them fall into a trap or ambush. They fought individually. A man would move forward to strike and put himself at risk. This was his choice. There were no specific orders in the heat of battle. The troops rallied at the sound of the conch shell. It was used to signal withdrawals and other movements. They marched under a banner called *babao*. They used hidden obstacles such as thorns, sharp fish bones, and piles of brush to block the enemy or force them to a path not to the enemy's advantage. The ancient Chamorros used camouflaged deep pits lined with bamboo stakes to catch the unsuspecting enemy. This Malaysian custom was used in the Vietnam War.

When fighting the Spanish, the ancient Chamorros took advantage of all the accidents of the terrain. They built tree and stone barricades and made trenches. Perhaps the Chamorros learned the latter technique from the Spanish. W. C. Repetti, S.J., wrote an article on the Chamorro uprising in 1684. By that time the Chamorros were using swords, as well as traditional weapons.

Outrigger canoes were used for the transport of troops. Chamorros also fought from outrigger canoes. The prime ingredient in a successful attack was surprise. Often this was accomplished by an ambush at sea.

# CULTURAL FACTORS

Land and the right to use land were very important to the ancient Chamorros. War was used to settle land disputes. The *manachang* were not allowed to participate actively in warfare. They had no right to land. The *manachang* were used to carry slingstones, spears, food and water for the warriors of the upper caste (*chamorri - matao* and *acha'ot*). Territorial disputes included violations of fishing rights.

The concept of reciprocal exchange applied to gifts and grief. For example, if you give me a gift, I am obligated to give you a gift in return at some later date. If I do you a favor, you are obligated to do me a favor, too. For every action, there must be a reaction. This custom was carried over into warfare. If there was a real or even imagined insult, it had to be avenged. If an interior village diverted or cut off a stream, this could cause a war. For example, if your family does my family harm,

my family is obligated to harm your family. If you attack me, you are attacking my family and my village. This custom of getting even or revenge is called *emmok*. Much of this can be seen today, when there are fights at school. This is a surviving custom. It is a custom found all over the world.

Ancient Chamorro warfare was more of a sport than warfare is today. It demanded a great deal of physical skill. Those of you who have participated in sports such as surfing, mountain climbing, or motorcycle racing know the great thrill of overcoming your fear. The wars of the ancient Chamorros were not long and drawn out like modern wars. They were short. A few days were spent planning the attack. A few hours were spent playing a deadly game. There was a great deal of shouting and bragging during the game. We shout and brag at sporting events today. We do this to "psyche-up" ourselves and to "psyche-out" the opposition.

After two or three men were killed, the game

**7.3 Camouflage and ambush were common strategies.**

73

was over. The losers sued for peace. The ancient Chamorros would present the victors with tortoiseshell money. The winners would accept the gift and end the hostilities by blowing a triton trumpet shell (*kulo'*). The victory was celebrated with song, dance, and food. The losers would bury their dead. They would probably blame the loss on supernatural forces. Ancestors' skulls, which were taken into battle for help, would be promised revenge. They were now obligated to pay the enemy back. Probably the ancient Chamorros began to train and plan for a new fight, in circumstances that would be more to their advantage.

Some accounts hold that to die a violent death led to everlasting torment for the soul. This did not seem to restrain men from fighting. Perhaps the torment was believed to end when the death was avenged. It was believed that a person's ancestral spirits would protect him or her against a violent death. All people who who met their family obligations were believed to be protected by their ancestral spirits. Warfare was a family affair. Village fought village, but several villages did not usually unite to fight a common enemy. The failure to make village alliances, along with inferior weapons and strategy, were the prime reasons for the Chamorros' defeat at the hands of the Spanish. Valor they did not lack, and they fought beyond the hope of winning for their way of life.

# SUMMARY

The main ancient Chamorro weapons were spears and slingstones. They did not build extensive fortifications. They relied on agility and camouflage. Only the high caste could participate in warfare. Battles were fought over violations of land and fishing rights. Insults to the *maga'lahi* (chief) were also a cause for war. Battles ended after one or two people were killed. Tortoiseshell money was used to sue for peace.

# Chapter 8
# Money

## INTRODUCTION

Money is anything that the members of a community are willing to accept in payment for goods, services, or debts. Societies without money must barter goods and services if they desire to exchange. For example, I'll give you two medium-sized fish for two breadfruits. If you repair my canoe, I'll give you six pounds of taro. Bartering becomes difficult when you want something from another person, but do not have anything he or she desires to offer in exchange. For example, if I want to have a house built, but can only pay for it in rice, and if the house builder already has more rice than he or she needs, I've got a problem. Can you imagine how long you would stand in line at the grocery store, if we still bartered to make exchanges of goods and services? Money solves this type of problem. Money facilitates exchange.

Modern Guam has a market economy, an economy in which most of the output is produced for exchange rather than for use by the immediate producers. In a market economy people must depend on others to produce most of the things they need.

Today we use paper money and metal coins. We also use checks and credit cards. Yes, they are money, too, because the members of our community are willing to accept them in payment for goods, services, and debts. Paper money began as a convenient substitute for metal currency. Banks in the past issued paper money on the basis of the gold or silver in their vaults. Today, paper money is issued by all countries. Its value fluctuates (goes up and down) on the world market.

Coins made of metal are commonly used for money. Metal is used to make money because it is durable, rare, and can be fashioned into art objects or articles for personal decoration.

Paper and metal money are not the only things that have been used for money. Many people have used cloth, beads, standard units of foods, and shells for money. In Japan, before modern times, a standard-sized basket of rice was used as money. A person's wealth was determined by the amount of rice he had stored. Taxes were paid to the government in units of rice. The Masai of East Africa used livestock for money. They paid their bride price in so many cows or goats. U.S. prisoners of war have used cigarettes for money, but the most unusual money in the world is Yapese money.

The Yapese, our neighbors to the southwest of Guam, created from stone the largest money in the world. They carved most of these large stone disks from the Rock Islands in Belau (also called Palau). They carved some stone money on Guam. Chamorros call crypto-crystalline silica, the rock used to make Yapese money, acho' Yap. It is very beautiful and takes a fine polish. Pieces of stone money twelve inches in diameter were made by the Yapese from this Guam rock. Since these types of rocks are found on Guam and in Belau, but are not found in Yap, the stone was very valuable to the Yapese. There is a story on Guam that the Yapese quarried some large pieces of stone money on Guam. As the Yapese were transporting the money to their canoes they stumbled and fell. The precious money, which took days to carve, broke. One elderly resident of Guam remembers this incident because it caused grown men to cry. The broken stone money is supposed to be in the Camp Covington area.

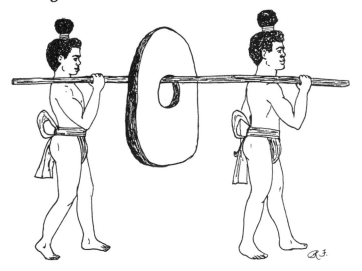

**8.1 Yap Stone Money**

In order to make them easy to carry, Yapese stone money disks have a hole in the center. Even so, the largest piece of stone money was twelve feet in diameter, and must have taken many men to lift. This piece of stone money is on Rumung Island.

The people of Rumung do not allow many outsiders to see it. They will not let anyone take a photograph of this piece of stone money. In Yap they are not bothered by bank robbers.

The value of Yapese stone money depends on how difficult it was to obtain. Larger pieces are heavier and generally worth more, but size is not the only factor. *Acho' Yap* is a rare rock. Even small pieces of it are of great value. The Yapese had to travel over 200 miles to Belau or 500 miles to Guam to quarry the stone. In Belau, they sometimes had to fight for the right to take the rock. The Yapese quarried the rock with tools and sailed it back to Yap on rafts. If the trip was difficult and they barely survived a storm, this increased the value of the stone money.

Once a returning raft overturned in Yap's main harbor, Chamorro Bay. The bay got its name from the many Chamorros who lived there before World War II. These Chamorros were **copra** (dried meat of the coconut) traders and shopkeepers. They controlled most business in Yap during the late 1800s. Most of these Chamorros returned to the Marianas Islands after World War II. In order to obtain land on Yap to build a navigational radio tower, the U.S. Navy relocated all the Chamorros willing to leave Yap to Tinian. A few Chamorro families remained in Yap despite the offer of free land on Tinian. The piece of stone money that rests at the bottom of Chamorro Bay can still be used as money. The Yapese do not care where the money is located. The important thing is that they know the stone money exists. In Yap, money does not have to be physically in your possession to be owned or spent. If you buy some land from Falan, he may not bother to move the heavy money. Everyone in the community knows that the stone money in front of your door belongs to Falan.

Each piece of stone money has a history. Knowledgeable Yapese can tell you how the money was obtained and all the people who have owned it. A piece of stone money with an interesting history has a higher value, just as a diamond once owned by Queen Elizabeth or a

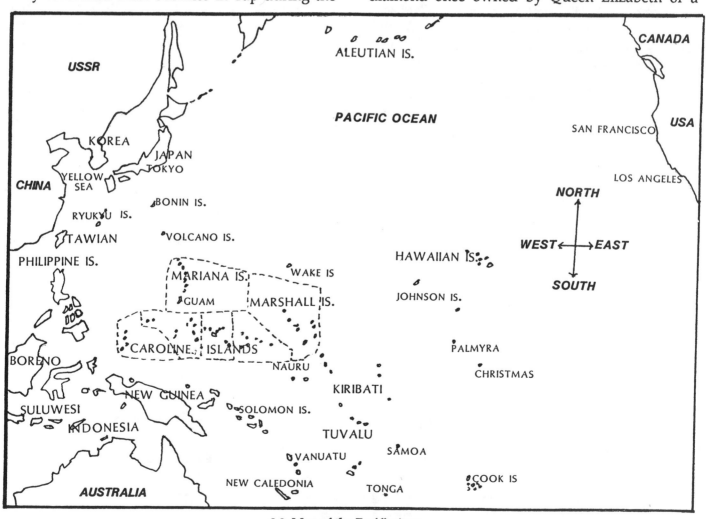

**8.2 Map of the Pacific Area**

famous movie star like Elizabeth Taylor increases in value.

Much of what has been said about Yapese money applies to ancient Chamorro money. Valuable pieces of money had a history of their own. The value of money was determined by how difficult it was to obtain. Today, the Yapese use the same money we do, U.S. currency. Nevertheless, stone money is still used for special purposes. The Yapese also have traditional oyster shell money.

Peoples all over the world have used shell money. Like metal money, it is durable, it can be used for objects of adornment, and it is fairly difficult to obtain. Native Americans (American Indians) used **wampum** for money. Wampum is beads of polished shells strung in strands, belts, or sashes. Some Africans used cowrie shells for money. We can find these money cowries on the reefs of Guam. In the past, 100,000 money cowries equalled one ivory elephant tusk. The ancient Chamorros, like others, used shell money.

# ANCIENT CHAMORRO MONEY

The general name for Chamorro shell money was *ålas*. The aborigines of the Mariana Islands used the red spondylus shell and the **tortoiseshell** for money. Today, the red spondylus **mollusk** is not found on the reefs of Guam. Perhaps it never was found in the Mariana Islands. This could account for its great value. The shell is found in other areas of the Western Pacific, especially the Ryukyu Islands between Taiwan and Japan. Okinawa is the best known of the Ryukyu Islands. It is possible that the Chamorros had contact with the people of these islands in prehistoric times.

The red spondylus has many spikes on the top surface. The spikes were removed and cut into disks. These disks were strung as a necklace. Chamorro women wore these necklaces on special occasions in ancient times. Historical

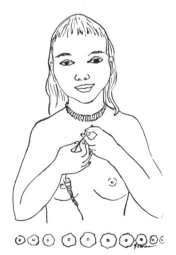

**8.3 Shell Necklace**

accounts use the Spanish term for money to describe the necklace. Chamorros have borrowed this word and spell it *salape'*. Archaeologists have found a few of these red spondylus disks. They have also found many other perforated shells, and polished shell beads, which could have been used for money as well as ornaments.

Chamorro tortoiseshell money is described in historical records. It has not been found by archaeologists. Unlike other shells, tortoiseshell rots away in time. There is another reason we do not find tortoiseshell money today. A great deal of it was collected during Spanish times and sold to the Chinese. The Chinese use tortoiseshell to make ornaments. Perhaps some of the Chamorro tortoiseshell money was traded to the Carolinian Islanders, who visited Guam during Spanish times. They still use tortoiseshell belts as ceremonial money. Their belts of tortoiseshell disks are very similar to the description of ancient Chamorro tortoiseshell money.

Turtles are difficult to catch and fairly rare, and the shell is durable and beautiful and can be used to make nice ornaments. For these reasons, tortoiseshell is a perfect material for making into money. In ancient times, when a fisherperson caught a turtle, he or she took it to the chief. Only certain chiefs had the privilege of manufacturing money. In order to determine the value of the turtle shell, the chief asked the fisherperson how the turtle was caught. If the turtle was found sleeping on the surface, or on the beach, it was not given a high value. If more than one person helped catch the turtle, its value went down. If a person made a dive deep into a submarine cave, almost

**8.4 Catching a Turtle**

drowned, but still caught the turtle, it was very valuable.

The value of the turtle shell was indicated by the number of holes the chief cut into it. Once the chief heard the story, he legally placed the proper number of holes in it. The plain plates of tortoiseshell called *lailai* were punctured with neat round holes. The more holes in the plate the more valuable it became. Large holes were placed in the middle of each plate and smaller holes were placed around the edges. Once the holes were made, the *lailai* was called *pinipu*. The *pinipu* was given to the person who caught the turtle.

8.5 *Pinipu* worn by an ancient Chamorro woman.

Other accounts explain this process differently. If a group caught a turtle, the thirteen plates in the shell were divided among them. They passed them to their closest female relative, who in turn did the same. When it reached the highest ranking female relative of each man, it was then divided among all who had passed it along. Since a group captured the turtle, no holes were allowed to be cut in it. Had a man captured the turtle by himself, the highest ranking woman relative would have given it to the chief to cut holes in it. Then she would distribute the shares to all the women who had passed it to her. When a man captured a turtle by himself, he followed the same procedure, but holes, which increased its value, were put in each plate. The first time he caught a turtle, only one big hole was put in each plate. The next time he caught a turtle by himself, one big hole and one small hole were cut in it. The third time, three holes and so on. For a more detailed account of this sharing process, see the chapter on "Customs."

These plates of tortoiseshell were sometimes worn on the forehead as an ornament by women. These pendants were fashioned of tortoiseshell, rare shells or beads, and flowers. Rich women wore a tortoiseshell plaque. It was fastened around the hips with a double cord and worn as an apron. It was polished on both sides and was called a *maku dudu*.

It is not stated in the historical record, but it seems likely that the tortoiseshell removed from the *lailai* to make a *pinipu* were kept by the chief. Perhaps he used these pieces to make *guini* and *lukao hugua.* These were two types of tortoiseshell necklaces. They were used for money. These necklaces were formed of thousands of thin, button-like, perforated disks of tortoise-shell. They were strung on **coir** (coconut fiber sennit). This is still done in the Caroline Islands for belts. The disks are perfectly round and exactly the same size. When strung together they make a cylinder of tortoiseshell. Some early accounts mention waistbands of shell money, too.

One account claims that a village on Tinian, called Fanutugan-ålas, had the exclusive right to string *ålas*. Other accounts claim that this was the exclusive privilege of some chiefs.

The *guini* was made from disks the diameter of a little finger. Perhaps these pieces came from the smaller holes in the *pinipu*. The *guini* was a long necklace. It reached the waist, after having been wound around the neck twice. The *lukao hugua* was probably made from the shell pieces removed from the center of the *pinipu*. These pieces, the diameter of the thumb, were strung on coir. The *lukao hugua* necklace reached the hips, after passing around the neck once.

The word *guini* was probably introduced by the Spanish. Guinea is a province in Africa. This is where the gold for English coins supposedly came from, in those days. *Lukao hugua* is a Chamorro term. It may mean "a real necklace worn in a procession." *Lukao* means "a religious procession " today. *Huguan*, today, means "really," or "it is true."

We know that a dollar equals four quarters, and that ten, ten-dollar bills equal a hundred dollar bill. The relative value of Chamorro money was also fixed. The chart below shows how much *lailai, pinipu, guini,* and *lukao hugua* were worth in the terms of Chamorro *ålas*.

3 *lailai* = 1 *pinipu* (1 hole)
6 *lailai* = 1 *pinipu* (2 holes) = 1 *guini*
9 *lailai* = 1 *pinipu* (3 holes)
12 *lailai* = 1 *pinipu* (4 holes) = 2 *guini*
15 *lailai* = 1 *pinipu* (5 holes)
18 *lailai* = 1 *pinipu* (6 holes) = 3 *guini*
21 *lailai* = 1 *pinipu* (7 holes)
24 *lailai* = 1 *pinipu* (8 holes) = 4 *guini*
= 1 *lukao hugua*

8.6 Money Necklaces

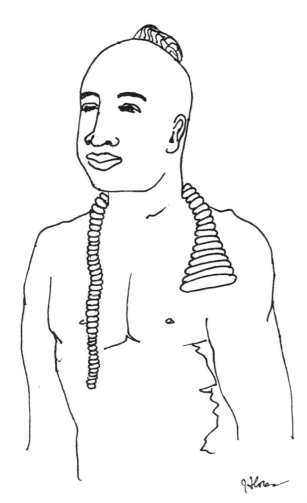

8.7 *Guinahan Famagu'on* - Child's Wealth

Sections of *guini* or *lukao hugua* necklace were also used as money. A *ghintos* was part of a *lukao hugua*. It was worth less than one *guini* but more than one *lailai*.

One type of Chamorro *ålas* was extremely valuable. The *guinahan famagu'on* was practically priceless. The type of shell used to make it is not in the historical literature. Archaeologists have not yet found anything like it. Perhaps in years to come a better description can be given. For now all we know is that it was a string of shell disks. At one end these shell disks were about one inch in diameter. They were gradually larger so that at the other end they were six inches in diameter. The shells were not polished on the edges, and the shell disks were of varying thicknesses. The *guinahan famagu'on* was worn by men on very special occasions. It was worn draped around the neck.

# USES OF ANCIENT CHAMORRO MONEY

The ancient Chamorros used money, as we do today, to pay for goods and services and to pay debts. Nevertheless, in their fishing and farming economy, it was not necessary to buy food. Food was raised or collected and shared with relatives. The ancient Chamorros had a **subsistence economy**. In a subsistence economy, most of the production or output is consumed by those who produce it.

The ancient Chamorros' economy provided for the essentials of life, and each community was relatively self-sufficient. They were not dependent on other villages or other groups for survival. The exchanges that were made did not require money. Money was used more as a gift to compensate others. Money was probably used to pay for special services like the building of a canoe or a house and making special tools or ornaments. Men and women acquired money in these ways, and by catching turtles and obtaining red spondylus shells. The latter were probably obtained through trade.

Money may have been used for trade with people from other islands. This seems very likely because *guini* is almost identical to the money used in the atolls of the Western Carolines. Instead of necklaces they used the strung tortoiseshell disks for belts.

Money was used to obtain land-use privileges. If a sister or female cousin presented you with *ålas*, you were obligated to give her the right to use your land, or grant her whatever favor she requested. This is very different than the way we use money today. We pay for renting land. We do not present a gift and then receive the gift of land use in return. In ancient Chamorro times prices were not fixed. First you gave a gift, and then asked for a favor. This system worked because the people involved were relatives.

The ancient Chamorros used money to pay restitution. If you harmed another person, you could compensate the person with a money gift.

Money in ancient Chamorro times was used for ceremonial reciprocal gifts. These gifts of money are still called *chenchule'*. The recipient of a gift is obligated to the giver. This custom survives among Chamorros today. Money was used as a bride price, in divorce settlements, and at funerals. At funerals the *chenchule'* given by a family was called *ika*. Some older people still use this word.

Money was used to settle wars. Losers had to present the winning side with *ålas*. The Chamorros also played a game of ceremonial capture, *hotyong songsong*. A group of men would capture a man and hold him for ransom. The ransom was paid in *ålas*. Nevertheless, once the ransom was paid, the kidnappers' gifts to the captured man's family were far greater than the amount they asked in ransom. It seems likely that money was used for ransom in less ritual capture, too.

Money was used for other political purposes. If a male *matao* (high caste person) broke a law, he was banished and reduced to the status of *acha'ot*. If his family wished to join him in exile, they had to present the chief with a money gift and a gift of food. Money could have also been used to regain the status of *matao*. In a sense this was like paying a fine.

Money was used to demonstrate status and to gain prestige. Today, some people think they can gain prestige and status by driving an expensive car, or by wearing expensive clothes and jewelry. The ancient Chamorros wore their money as ornaments at important ceremonies. The ancient Chamorros probably gained prestige by presenting another village with valuable gifts of money. This custom is practiced in Yap. It seems likely that it was practiced in the Mariana Islands, too.

Money was probably used to pay for religious

8.8 *Hotyong Songsong* - Ceremonial Capture

services. If a *makahna* (spiritual leader) helped ensure a successful fishing trip, trading voyage, or love affair, this was an obligation to be paid. It could have been paid for in food or in money. In addition, turtle shells were placed in the graves of important ancient Chamorros.

The main use of money in ancient Chamorro times was for ceremonial purposes. Their fishing and farming economy required less use of money for everyday living than our market economy today. This infrequent use of money probably led to the keeping of oral histories on important pieces of money. This was probably the case with the *guinahan famagu'on*.

*Guinahan famagu'on* literally translates as "children's wealth." If you saved a child's (remember, everyone is a child to someone regardless of age) life, his or her family was obligated to give you the *guinahan famagu'on*. Since few people had such a precious gift, the family was required to raise enough money to purchase one. The valuable shell collar was then presented to the person who rescued the child. You then had the right to accept the gift and square things, or refuse it and become a fictitious in-law. If you chose the latter, your family could ask your new in-laws for any favor and it had to be granted. This united the families, just as if a marriage had taken place. Both families were probably obligated to one another for the life of the child.

If you were of higher status than the family whose child you rescued, it would probably have been best to take the *guinahan famagu'on*. If you were of lower status or desperately needed assistance, it would have been more to your advantage to refuse the gift and gain the assistance of relatives of high status. If the parents agreed, sometimes a rescuer of high status would bestow his or her name on the child.

Today, we rarely reward a person who saves a child's life with money. We certainly do not have a special piece of money for this purpose. Also, we would not dream of making such a person an immediate in-law. Chamorros hold their children in especially high regard. The custom of *guinahan famagu'on* demonstrates this concern for children in ancient times.

Additional relatives are a valuable asset in many cultures. The *guinahan famagu'on* custom had this potential. Since children are not rescued often, there were other ways in which the *guinahan famagu'on* custom could operate. A child's family was obligated not only to their child's rescuer, but also to his benefactor. If a great gift was given to your child, you were obligated to repay it with a *guinahan famagu'on*. Such a gift could have been an education in navigation, spiritual practices, or medicine, or perhaps training in warfare.

Today, most Chamorros are still anxious to increase the number of their relatives. The Roman Catholic custom of godparents is an excellent example. Parents gain compadres (*kompaire*) and children gain a *ninu* and *nina*. Many still consider it advantageous to increase kinship alliances. Godfathers, today, throw handfuls of coins to the children at a christening party. Money still has this ceremonial purpose.

After the Spanish came to the Mariana Islands, many customs were changed or modified. The form of money changed, too. Nevertheless, many of the uses of money by the Chamorros did not change. Iron, cloth, tobacco, and pipes were used to trade with visiting Carolinians. Tobacco was used as money. Within the Mariana Islands,

Spanish currency was used, too. This money was minted in Mexico (New Spain) for the most part.

When the United States captured Guam, the money of Guam consisted of Mexican, Philippine, Chilean, and other South American coins. It seems likely that some U.S. currency was present, too. An "Exploring Guam" student found an 1851 U.S. penny in her yard in Umatac, Guam, after a heavy rain several years ago. This coin probably came from trade with U.S. whalers. It seems unlikely that this penny would have been introduced later.

Japanese money was introduced after World War I, when Japan took over all of the Mariana Islands except Guam. A large part of the business community on Guam was Japanese prior to World War II. There was probably some Japanese money on the island, even though it was not legal tender. It was probably used to pay for goods imported from Japan. Of course, during the three years that Guam was held by the Japanese (1941-1944), their money was used.

U.S. currency has been the dominant form of money in this century on Guam. Nevertheless, all kinds of money are exchanged in our banks. We have many people from China, Taiwan, Korea, and the Philippines working in the Mariana Islands. These people exchange the money they earn for their home currency and send it to their families.

Guam is becoming an important financial center for Asia. Guam has recently established banking laws that encourage foreign countries to deposit large sums of money in our banks.

During the fall of Saigon in 1975 thousands of Vietnamese refugees passed through Guam. Some of them even settled in the Mariana Islands. The Vietnamese introduced the gold tael and baht necklaces. This type of ornamental money is very reminiscent of the money of the ancient Chamorros. The gold and silver baht necklaces from Thailand, like the shell *guini* or *lukao hugua*, are durable, are ornaments, can easily be converted to other money, and can be subdivided into smaller units like the *ghintos*.

# SUMMARY

Money is used to facilitate exchanges of goods or services in a market economy. In a subsistence economy most exchanges are by bartering, and money is used for ceremonial purposes. The ancient Chamorros had tortoiseshell money, red spondylus shell money, and a special shell money called *guinahan famagu'on*. They called their shell money *ålas*. The tortoiseshell money was worn as necklaces and called *guini* or *lukao hugua*. The ancient Chamorro money was used as gifts, as rewards, as ransom, to end wars, to pay fines, and to show respect at funerals.

# Chapter 9
# Beliefs, Attitudes, and Values

## INTRODUCTION

## Culture

Human beings are social animals. Each of us was helpless at birth. As children we needed our parents to care for us. Without them we could not have survived. In turn our family needs a social group to belong to. Humans differ from other animals in their ability to learn, to use symbols, and to communicate. The greatest strength of human beings is the ability to pass on their social heritage. This ability allows us to pass on our beliefs, attitudes, values, knowledge, and customs to the next generation. All of these factors make up our culture. A **culture** is the patterns of shared, learned behavior that humans develop. Culture is language, art, music, humor, technology, beliefs, and all that is characteristic of human social life. As we study culture, we should look at culture not just as a model *of* living. We should examine culture as a model *for* living. Our culture gives meaning to our lives.

Humans live in two environments. There is the natural environment of the land, sea, air, plants, and animals, which has always been. These things were not created by people. Our other environment is the human-made or cultural environment. It consists of our tools, buildings, religion, social organization, customs, and ideas. Humans do not leave their natural environment untouched. We make shelters, prepare food, create tools, and build roads. We gather knowledge, develop a system of right and wrong behavior, establish spiritual beliefs, form economic values, set up a social organization, and create a language.

**Social organization** is the fixed way in which groups behave. A social system is governed by specific laws, customs and manners. Through our upbringing we develop a conscience. Our moral values and our sense of right and wrong are learned.

We are socialized by our group. **Socialization** is the process through which we learn to adjust to our society's norms and, as a result, become accepted members of society. A **norm** is a group-shared expectation of behavior. We develop attitudes toward the members of our group, especially our relatives. We also develop attitudes toward the material objects in our surroundings, and toward the spiritual world. An **attitude** is a predisposition to behave in a certain manner once a particular stimulus is given. It is a ready-made response toward a given person, situation, object, or idea.

The values we learn from our culture are strong. People sometimes prefer death rather than surrender their values. For example, some people have died for their religion. Our values are strong enough to cause us to prefer pain to pleasure in some cases. For example, war prisoners have endured torture rather than betray their country. Strongly held values will cause people to do without rather than satisfy their desires. Many religions forbid eating certain foods. For example, Muslims do not believe it is right to eat pork. They would rather go hungry than eat ham. We gain these cultural values over a long period of training. **Cultural values** are the assumptions shared by the members of a society as to what is right and wrong, good or bad, important or unimportant.

If you had been born in China, you would become a Chinese. You would speak their language, practice their religion, and act as they act. We are not born with our culture. We learn it. Culture is acquired.

In a rapidly changing culture, conflicting beliefs, values, and attitudes are acquired. This is confusing, and individuals feel alienated. **Alienation** is a feeling of estrangement from your society and culture. Those who do not have a strong sense of values tend to feel alienated.

## Institutions

The basic building blocks of culture are institutions. An **institution** is a system of norms that have grown up around a major social function or concern. Family, religious, political, economic, and educational concerns are found in all societies. Each of these areas is an institutional order and has a cluster of institutions associated with it. For example, the institutions of marriage, the home, and inheritances relate to the association or institutional order of family. Marriage is an institution that regulates mating and having children.

**Institutional orders** are organized systems that center on basic human needs. For example, we have schools to educate the young. We have a military to protect us. We have institutional orders for growing and distributing food. Each institutional order organizes a group of people in a cooperative task. It usually has its own set of rules, values, and specific techniques to achieve its purpose. All cultures have a system of laws, a system of knowledge, a mythology, and a religion because they satisfy basic human needs.

In order to go fishing, I am dependent upon human-made fishing gear. I am also dependent on organized cooperation. **Cooperation** is a universal social process wherein people work together toward the attainment of goals. For example, many types of net fishing require more than one person. Even if I go fishing by myself, I'm dependent on others who manufactured my fishing equipment. When I get home with the fish, my culture will determine who cleans the fish, who cooks them, and who gets the best-tasting parts. I am also dependent on a knowledge system. There are techniques for successful fishing. I also need to know which fish are safe to eat. I am dependent on economic and moral values. Do I have a right to fish in the sea? Who says so? How many fish do I have a right to catch? How will I distribute the fish when I return home? My culture determines the superstitions a fisherman should follow. My shared, learned behavior determines if I should pray for a successful fishing trip.

Whenever we cooperate, we must sacrifice our personal ends for the community good. This social constraint in the long run helps everyone. In order to ensure social constraint we develop rules and regulations. We have rules of property. For example, we might say, "This belongs to me. It would be wrong for you to take it."

Organizations develop a hierarchy. A **hierarchy** is a group of persons or things arranged in successive classes, where each class is dependent on the ones above it. For example, in the Roman Catholic church's hierarchy, there is the pope, then cardinals, archbishops, bishops, monsignors, priests, nuns, and parishioners. In a hierarchy there are ranks and leadership statuses. Human organizations develop rules to control ambition within these systems.

## Basic Institutions

The three most basic imperatives in culture are economic organization, law, and education. Religion and magic are important too. Human knowledge and planning give people some control over their natural and human-made environment. But no matter how much knowledge and control they have, there are always chance, accidents, and unforeseen natural events that can and do interfere. So, humans turn to magic rituals and to higher spiritual beings for help.

## Cultural Change

Cultures are constantly changing. They are never static. Cultures change by invention, transmission, and diffusion. **Inventions** are the adoption by a society of new ways of doing things. **Cultural transmission** is the process by which knowledge is passed from one generation to the next. Change also occurs when there is the faulty transmission of knowledge. Each generation will omit some things and put emphasis on others. **Cultural diffusion** is the process by which customs and discoveries are borrowed from other cultures. This takes place when there is contact between cultures. **Acculturation** is a process of cultural change whereby one culture takes over elements from another culture it has frequent contact with.

Cultural change does not necessarily destroy a culture. Throughout all this change there is a fundamental core of a culture, which remains. This cultural core is the most difficult to change, because it rests on the basic underlying world view of the members of the culture. This "heart and soul" of a culture rests in its values. **Values** are those concepts that the members of a culture see as desirable. What we value is worth something, important, or useful. Values stress the idea of what we ought to do.

# Core Values

Outwardly, two cultures may look alike. Nevertheless, it is the core values that give a culture its uniqueness and distinguish it from other cultures. As we saw above, cultures are always changing from within and from without. Therefore, if people wish to maintain and preserve a culture, they should focus on the fundamental values of the culture. It is not necessary to prevent change or to return to a traditional lifestyle.

People who are forced to change their culture feel sad, angry, and regretful. They blame themselves and others. For example, how could we let something as creative as traditional canoe building be lost forever? But a culture can survive without canoes. Despite the fact that important cultural traits are lost, a people can still retain a viable culture. To do so, the culture must maintain its core values. Most Chamorros see these values as the extended family, hospitality, relating to people through cooperation and consideration, and respect for leaders and elders.

A world of cultural diversity demonstrates a respect for ethnic differences and a belief in equality. Cultural change should be controlled by the members of a culture. Each culture is unique and has as much right to exist as any other culture. Cultural diversity enriches our world. Each culture has its own point of view and novel ways to solve problems. It is in every culture's interest to preserve the great human cultural diversity that we have on this planet. If we are to preserve a people's identity, then we must be able to focus on the key values of each culture. Once we are conscious of these key values, we will understand ourselves and others to a far greater degree. Then we can take steps to preserve those values and thereby preserve the culture. Some people fear that without this awareness the world will lose its diversity. Then we would have a planet with a single mass culture. It would be a world of one language, one set of customs, and no diversity. It would be a world of oppression by the dominant culture.

# Comparison of American and Chamorro Values

Let us look at the fundamental values of Chamorros and compare them with American values. **In this discussion it is important to remember that we are dealing with generalizations.** Within every culture there are variations. Some members of one culture may deviate from the norm. A person could be more like the members of another culture than his or her own. But this is not likely. Also, throughout this discussion, remember that values are a matter of degree. For example, all people value material comforts, but Americans tend to place more importance on material comforts than many other cultures. Americans value self-reliance, but we have Social Security, and cooperate in many ways with one another. Most values are common to all cultures. The distinguishing characteristics lie in the degree to which a culture emphasizes a particular value.

Americans value the individual and hold the self as supreme. Almost all Americans a hundred years ago felt the most important human activity was to gain eternal salvation. Now it seems that many view the most important human activity as "getting ahead." An old value was that you must work hard or starve. There is one thing that hasn't changed, though, and that is the emphasis on the individual person. Honesty, truthfulness, respect for person and property, accepting responsibility for your actions, and even a tolerance for others all show the American's emphasis on the individual rather than the group.

For Americans the highest good is for each of us to realize our full potential. Although Americans value helping others, it is not seen as the highest good. Many Americans believe that the ultimate authority on morals and ethics is a person's own opinion. All this implies that the individual is the most important thing in the world.

On the other hand, among the ancient Chamorros and many other traditional cultures, the constant was the interdependence of all things in nature, with a focus on the family group and not the individual. This can be seen in the practice of sharing and hospitality, the desire for harmony, in the importance of family, respect for age and authority, discipline, and the practice of good manners.

The Chamorro cultural heritage is presently endangered. It is amazing that it has withstood the acculturation of the Spanish, Americans, Germans, and Japanese. The belief that an emphasis on the extended family and not the individual brings true happiness is the core value that has not changed. Because the ancient Chamorros valued the group over self, they were interdependent rather than individualistic. The primary group in Chamorro culture is still the extended family.

Ancient Chamorro interdependence formed a network of social obligations between the human, spirit, and natural worlds. To give order to their interdependent relationships they ranked everything in order of importance. This led to respect for social position and seniority. To avoid abuses by this hierarchy, a *mamahlao* attitude and controls on *champåda* were developed to hold them in check. These concepts will be explained below. Chamorro culture still exists because these core values have been passed on to each new generation.

# CHAMORRO CORE VALUES

## Inafa'maolek - Interdependence

*Inafa'maolek*, or interdependence within the kinship group, is the key or central value in Chamorro culture. It is the soul of Chamorro culture. *Inafa'maolek* literally means "making it good for each other" or "getting along." *Inafa'maolek* depends on a spirit of cooperation. This is the armature or core that everything in Chamorro culture revolves around. It is a powerful concern for mutualism (within the family) rather than individualism and it includes the living, dead, animate, and inanimate. Rank, age, family, friendship, hospitality, ancestral spirits, religion, law, nature, social organization all revolve around this central core value of *inafa'maolek* or interdependence within the kinship group.

In American folklore, heroes are usually individualists. They are competitive rather than cooperative. In Chamorro folklore, individuals who take the liberty to act on their own usually meet misfortune. For example, when Sirena thought only of her personal happiness and her desire to swim, she was ignoring her family responsibilities. Sirena's mother told her to do some housework. Instead of doing the housework, Sirena went swimming. Because she disobeyed her mother, Sirena was punished.

Sirena's mother prayed that Sirena would turn into a fish. Sirena was turned into a mermaid and not an entire fish because the mother's selfish wish was partially counteracted by another relative, whose feelings were not being considered. Okkodu is the most selfish Chamorro character in folklore. His tricks and pranks were admired, but ultimately he was doomed to failure and suicide.

For the ancient Chamorros there was no such thing as an individual free to act as he or she pleases. *Inafa'maolek*, or interdependence, operated on the basis of reciprocity. You are obligated to others and they are obligated to you in a network of mutual responsibility. Whereas Americans teach children to be independent, the Chamorro way is to teach children to be interdependent. Instead of stressing individual achievement, Chamorros stress cooperation and group achievement. Americans are free to make their own arrangements and tend to say "I love to . . . ." Chamorros choose a network of group relations and tend to say "I owe to . . . ." Americans read the newspaper to be entertained or informed. Chamorros read the newspaper for those purposes, but they read it first to see who has died. This will tell them where they will have to go that week, and to whom they will be obligated.

Consideration of others means that confrontations are to be avoided. Americans cooperate through a democracy where there are winners and losers, because decisions are made by a majority vote. The ancient Chamorros made decisions by consensus of their village councils, which included high-ranking men and women. They did not vote, but rather discussed matters until each person agreed. **Consensus (*todu manatungo'*)** is a decision-making process by general agreement.

Americans emphasize the individual. They want freedom, progress, initiative, and independence, and tend to struggle against authority. The traditional Chamorro is more concerned with duty and privileges, security, tradition, dependence, harmony, and obedience to authority. Among Americans there is a constant pressure for change. In Chamorro culture there is a move toward equilibrium. Whereas Americans celebrate the new and up-to-date over the old, Chamorros tend to favor the traditional.

We can see the Chamorros' value of interdependence take many forms in the following example. Fray Juan Pobre de Zamora visited Luta

(Rota) in 1602. He stayed in the village of Tazga, which was located about 50 paces from the sea. He reported that the Chamorros were good to him and invited him to share whatever they had. They treated him as a family member. The chief, Sunama, and his wife, Sosanbra, treated him as a son, and the chief's children treated him as a brother.

Sancho, a Spaniard who had lived on Guam for some years, came from Pago to visit the priest on Luta. During the day Sancho had unkind words with a man named Sinaro from the neighboring village, Guaco. It seems that Sancho ridiculed Sinaro and may have even pushed him. That night Sinaro came to a shed where Sancho was sleeping and speared Sancho.

When Sunama heard about the attack, he took the wounded Sancho into his house. Tears were shed for the stranger who was in so much pain. The relatives of Sunama brought meals in the morning around 8 o'clock, and in the afternoon around 3 o'clock for the entire household. They arranged the gifts in front of the house. They waited beside their gifts until the chief or his wife went down to thank them. After this the relatives returned home, and the food was taken into the chief's house.

Since Sancho had a spear wound to the spine and was beyond hope, all that could be done was to make his suffering a little more bearable. The sick man's food was prepared first. They fixed him one or two freshly baked flying fish. The head was removed and the body scaled. Then they crumbled the fish flesh into small pieces. Grated coconut meat mixed with salt was used to garnish the fish. Next, breadfruit, sweet potatoes, and a special treat were taken to him. The latter was made from rice flour mixed with grated coconut meat. It was shaped into balls and eaten in place of bread. Sometimes it was diluted into a drink. The Chamorros did not let their mouths touch the pottery drinking vessel. They held the cup high and poured the drink into their mouth from a spout. All during the day they asked the dying man to eat. The priest and the other family members, who were great eaters, had a stew. They practiced this same generosity when there was a visitor. Again the relatives and friends all brought food.

Since Sancho could not move, they carried him when he needed to relieve himself or brought a chamber pot to him. The chamber pot was only used for the sick. Normally people evacuated (moved bowels and/or urinated) far from their houses at designated places in the jungle or on the reef.

After Sancho died they buried him halfway between the house and the beach. They asked if he were *chamorri* (high caste). The priest told them yes, so they built a little shelter over the grave and put a wood cross at the head of the grave. From the arms of the cross they attempted to hang an adze and a knife carved from wood and painted black. The priest objected because he felt that this should not be done to the cross. The Chamorros insisted because it showed that Sancho was of high social status. Later, when the priest was not around, they hung the status symbols from the cross. When the priest removed them, the Chamorros waited until he was out of sight. Then they built a tall cross. It was so high that the priest could not remove the adze and the knife from the cross.

They placed spears in the ground in front of Sancho's grave to let others know that the people of Tazga were going to avenge Sancho's death. This was a warning to the people of Guaco. When Sinaro, the man who killed Sancho, saw this warning he fled by sailing to Guam. Sinaro's family, hoping to satisfy Sunama and his wife, gave turtle-shell money, gifts of food, and other small items to compensate them for the loss of Sancho. Toca, the chief of Guaco, denounced Sinaro as a bad person. Given time, Sinaro would probably have been free to return to Luta. Nevertheless, he was careful to stay away until tempers cooled down.

The Chamorro ideal of interdependence leads to reciprocal behavior. **Reciprocity** is the continuing process by which actions toward one party are returned. Actions require reactions. Good actions require good reactions and bad actions require bad reactions. Fray Juan and Sancho were shown gracious hospitality. This was the beginning of an interdependent human relationship based on reciprocity. They were treated exactly like family. Of course, they would be expected to act like family and help out just as any family member would.

In Sancho's case, he humiliated Sinaro. Once the interdependent bond was broken, Sinaro felt obligated to reciprocate by killing Sancho. This revenge is called *emmok*. You can see how family, friends, and relatives supported Sunama by

**9.1** *Inafa'maolek* - **Interdependence:** Adapted from Freycinet's Atlas.

bringing food to help out in his time of need. They were not doing this just because Sunama was a chief. Sharing like this illustrates their interdependent relationship. Gifts of money and food were called *chenchule'* , and assistance or help was called *ayudu.*

We can even see the ancient Chamorros' interdependence in the way they drank. Cups belonged to the family and not to individuals, so when they drank, they were careful not to touch the cup with their mouth.

The people of Tazga who had taken in Sancho as a family member felt obligated to avenge his death. They wanted *emmok* (revenge) to even the score. They let others know this by placing a spear in the ground at the foot of Sancho's grave. Again, reciprocal behavior was required. An action obligated a person to a reaction.

Interdependence can also be seen in the efforts the ancient Chamorros exerted to avoid confrontation, if possible. Harmony was valued more than being right. For example, when the priest took down the symbols of high status from the cross, the people of Tazga did not openly defy their guest. Rather than argue with the priest, the

Chamorros just built a huge cross and hung the **adze** way out of the Spaniard's reach. The Chamorros were able to get their way without a direct confrontation or a fight.

Harmony was valued more than correcting a wrong. Sinaro's chief denounced him and his behavior in the hope of keeping the conflict at the family level. Sinaro's parents apologized and gave gifts to Sunama in the hopes of rebuilding a good interdependent relationship. Sinaro's self-exile to Guam and the payments of money were efforts to re-establish harmonious relationships. This was more important than getting even or justice.

Fray Juan throughout his stay describes the basically peaceful, unpretentious, interdependent nature of the ancient Chamorros. He reports that the people were kind to one another and that he never saw them quarrel. Guests received the best, even if the host had to do without. Offers of betel nut, betel pepper leaf, and quicklime were the first thing that took place when people met.

Interdependence can be seen in the friendly, noncompetitive nature of the ancient Chamorros. Survival for the Chamorro was not a "rat-race." Although ancient Chamorros competed, life was not a struggle based on competition. **Competition** is a universal social process wherein people rival one another in an effort to obtain goals. Survival depended upon humans' interdependent relations with other humans and nature. This required mutual respect and sharing. If the ancient Chamorros saw a need, they gave whatever they had. If they had a need, they felt no hesitation to ask for help. Their social obligations, which formed a network of interdependence, were central to their life.

Competition existed in dancing, singing, debating, games, and sports, but it was always friendly. Fray Juan and Padre Sanvitores, who lived in the Mariana Islands from 1668 to 1672, described contests of wrestling and spear throwing that included mockery and laughter, but were conducted peacefully and with good sportsmanship. Villages did compete to see who could build the biggest *latte* stones (stone supports for houses). Fray Juan saw the children playing war games that got pretty rough at times. Nevertheless, when the games were over, the children comforted one another. Even war was conducted in a sensible manner. There were rarely more than a few killed. The losers would sue for peace with a turtle-shell gift to end the hostilities. Even warfare was ritualized so that harmony was never upset for long.

Interdependence can be seen in the network of social obligations that the people formed. The sharing formed a reciprocal economy in which money was needed only for ceremonial purposes. In the example above, tortoiseshell money was given to compensate for a death. It was also given when suing for peace. A more common use of ceremonial money was at weddings and funerals. When there was a death, *chenchule'* was given at the funeral. *Chenchule'* is a present of money or food that is given away as a donation. The *chenchule'* given by an entire family at a funeral had a special name, *ika*. Wedding gifts from the bridegroom to the bride's family were called *a'ok*.

Gifts of *chenchule'* were social obligations. For example, if Quipuha gave my family money when my father died, then I would be obligated to give his family money when someone in his family died. The more common kind of social obligation was *ayudu*. It was any help, aid, assistance, or service that was rendered to another. It was impolite to refuse *ayudu* or *chenchule'*. After it was accepted, no one expected you to pay it back as you

would a debt. Nevertheless, it was understood that the recipient had an obligation to the donor. They were on call when the other party needed help.

*Ayudu* can be seen in the following practices. When an ancient Chamorro was sick and could not go fishing, his son would be sent to the beach to meet the returning fishermen. The fishermen would share their catch, knowing that the sick man would do the same for them if the need arose. When a house needed to be repaired or rebuilt, all of the relatives and neighbors in the village would gather the necessary materials. Then they would repair or even construct a new house. Food was also provided for the workers. The feeling was that we help because we know our friends and relatives will always help us. Assistance could not be refused even though people knew it would obligate them. Likewise, gifts could not be refused. Interdependence operated like a law and it had to be obeyed.

# Rank

To give order to the interdependent group, ancient Chamorros ranked everything in a hierarchy. People were ranked by village, social position, and age. People were linked by a superior-inferior relationship. In order to keep the ranking system harmonious and to prevent it from being oppressive, the people valued *mamahlao* behavior and had controls on excessive competition.

Villages and clans were ranked. On Guam, Agaña was accepted by all as the paramount village in most historical accounts. It did not control other villages but it was given the most respect. Most accounts translate Agaña as a "big Agat" or "big town." However, it may come from "*agad-gna* ," or deft helmsman.

Generally, villages near the beach were considered highest, according to Fray Juan. After the Spanish came, this may have changed. Some of the largest *latte* stones are at interior sites and could have been built after Spanish contact.

Within an ancient Chamorro village, people were ranked. There were the *chamorri* (high caste) and the *manachang* (low caste). *Chamorri* could not marry, nor even have a mistress among the *manachang*. If they did so, it meant death or at least banishment to another village. Within the *chamorri* there were the *matao*, who were ranked above the *acha'ot*. The *acha'ot* class were people whose *matao*

**9.2 Respect for Social Position and *Mamahlao* Behavior**

ancestors had been banished and taken in by another village.

High statuses were based on the control of land, which meant wealth. Privileged occupations like canoe builder or navigator went with the high caste. The military and fishing were reserved for the *chamorri*.

The interdependent relationships based on rank can be seen in the social obligation for the castes to serve each other. *Manachangs* were obligated to ask permission to use the land of the *chamorri*. The *chamorri* could not refuse a legitimate request from the *manachang* and would never let them do without or starve. On the other hand, the *manachang* had to show deference to the *chamorri* and were obligated to serve them. The *manachang* were not allowed to touch the sea. They were probably given fish by the *chamorri*. Of course, in return the *manachang* provided food and other services for the *chamorri*. For example, they

90

cultivated the soil, helped in the construction of large sheds for canoes, cleaned and repaired roads, carried foodstuffs and water in battle, and transported the materials used for the construction of houses. Sometimes the *acha'ot* were given presents by the *matao* when they did an outstanding job. Nevertheless, the *matao* were only obligated to provide the *acha'ot* with food. It is important to note that there was no leisure class. The *matao* fished and the *chamorri* women made their own household utensils.

## Social Position

Social position in ancient Chamorro times depended upon the ranking of your clan and village, and upon your caste. All of these were determined by birth rather than a person's ability or accomplishments. Age was also very important. Within any given clan, age was the dominant ranking factor. As an ancient Chamorro got older, he or she could expect more status and greater respect. Grandparents had more respect than parents, and the oldest child more respect than the younger children. This respect for age was carried over into the practice of ancestor worship. Respect for authority within this hierarchical pattern was instilled from birth. Each ancient Chamorro was ranked in a superior-inferior authority system and there was intense loyalty to the group. Obedience was expected. Each person had rights and obligations, which bound all the people into an interdependent network. The social sanctions that held this system together were fear of ridicule for not meeting obligations to the group and fear of upsetting ancestral spirits.

The highest rank in an ancient Chamorro society was *maga'lahi*. He was the oldest male *chamorri* in the highest-ranking lineage of the clan that controlled a village. The highest-ranking woman in the village was the *maga'haga*. Because the *maga'lahi*'s family controlled land, he had wealth and power. Succession to the position of *maga'lahi* was inherited. A man became clan head through his mother's line. A *maga'lahi* who died was succeeded by his brothers in order of birth. If there were no younger living brothers, then his eldest sister's eldest son or his mother's eldest sister's son became chief.

Since a man inherited property rights from his mother, female relatives on that side of his family were the most important. There was a definite order for their being served. In hierarchical order

from the highest to the lowest, they were ranked as follows: great-grandmother, grandmother, mother, great aunts, aunts, sisters, first cousins once removed, first cousins, nieces, and daughters.

Great respect was shown for those in a higher position, and their authority was beyond question. Since most important decisions were reached by consensus, abuses of power were avoided. Most authority figures were relatives, so obedience was the same as following the direction of a father or a mother who had your best interest at heart.

**9.3 Respect for Old Age**

## Old Age

The social consideration accorded to relatives of the same rank depended upon their age. Respect had to be shown to those who were older. The oldest person came first. The only exceptions were that a married member of the family was more important than a a single family member. This held true even though the unmarried person was related in a higher degree. So an unmarried aunt or childless widow had lower rank than a married sister, for example. Men did not consider brothers-in-law relatives because they belonged to the clans into which their sisters had married.

The *maga'lahi* was an older man of the highest lineage in a village. "*Maga*" was the term used for

91

ancestor of the family, or the eldest child (male or female) of a family. The youngest brother or sister was "sologgna." "I sologgnan inatnganan" was used to denote the youngest as related to the elder.

Respect for old age led the ancient Chamorros to the practice of ancestor worship. Perhaps veneration would be a more appropriate word than worship. Respect is still shown to older people by the custom of *nginge'* (smelling of the hand). Politicians today address a group not as ladies and gentlemen but as parents, brothers, and sisters.

The ancient Chamorros generally ranked all people, even those outside of their biological family, as *saina* (elder, parent), *che'lu* (sibling: brothers and sisters), or *patgon* (child). *Saina* are shown respect when greeted by the practice of *nginge'*.

## Mamahlao

Interdependence required clear divisions of rank. Even so, life would have been very unpleasant if people were always taking advantage of their rank. It was not polite to call attention to yourself or cause a scene. An ancient Chamorro was expected to avoid showing off, and to initially refuse offers of food or drink. Even people in high-status positions were expected to avoid being ostentatious. They were expected to be modest and not decorate themselves in too fancy a manner.

Since decisions were never individual decisions, it was not proper to express personal opinion directly. To do so would have slowed down the process of reaching an interdependent group consensus. This attitude of deference for others can be referred to as behaving in a *mamahlao* manner. It rests on the belief that we are all part of an interdependent network based on rank, which will maintain harmony. This is the reason it is not polite to correct another person, and an ancient Chamorro would never correct an older or higher status person. The ancient Chamorros valued harmony more than being right or even more than correcting a wrongdoing. The worst behavior was to ridicule another person in public. Ridicule was to be avoided at all cost. No one wanted to be shamed. *Mamahlao* behavior was expected of the ancient Chamorro so that a person would not be offensive.

## Champåda Controls

*Champåda* is the competition for rank and status. It is a Spanish word. One outlet for this type of competitiveness in ancient Chamorro times was that *matao* could establish new villages. Also, in most cultures shaman or religious leaders can come from even the lower caste. Nevertheless, competition was controlled. Interdependence required ranking, but it could not work if some people got too powerful. People were not allowed to get so much above others that they did not need anyone else. Ancient Chamorro society had many mechanisms to avoid this, because such behavior could destroy interdependence.

Statuses were given as a birthright; they were ascribed rather than acquired. Ambition was also countered by the *mamahlao* behavior described above. All ancient Chamorros, even the *matao*, worked. There was no leisure class in ancient Chamorro society. Both men and women were important and had power in ancient Chamorro society. Women had no direct political authority but greatly influenced the village councils. Actions were not taken without consulting them first. Women controlled household matters. Although men controlled land use, they inherited the right to the land through their female relatives or the matrilineage. Giving and sharing were so much a part of the culture that no ancient Chamorro could obtain and keep great amounts of wealth. It was impossible to refuse requests, especially if they came through female relatives. In order for interdependence to function in harmony it is important that no one gets too much power. Every person in the culture must remain dependent on others.

*Champåda* was controlled by a practice best described as the "crab syndrome." If a dozen crabs are put in a bucket, they will begin to climb on one another to get out. If the crabs were smart and cooperated, they could all escape. They could make a ladder of crabs. Crabs could climb out on top of each other. When all the crabs except the ones forming the ladder were out, the bottom crab could climb up and then the next one, until they had all escaped. But crabs don't do that. When one crab gets too high on the wall of the bucket, the other crabs begin to tear him down. The ancient Chamorros behaved in a similar manner. If one person was getting too powerful, and was not sufficiently dependent upon others, then he or she would be pulled down. This negative behavior was viewed as necessary to maintain the greater harmony of the interdependent whole. Abuses of power were also made tolerable through the practice of outwardly conforming to the demand of those in higher rank, while secretly pursuing other goals.

Through equality of the sexes, sharing and giving, decision making by consensus, no leisure class, *mamahlao* behavior, and controls on *champåda*, a balance was kept that limited the abuses of rank and insured that all members of an ancient Chamorro community remained interdependent. Decisions were made for the best interest of the whole community. Through these processes harmony was maintained. No ancient Chamorro person stood alone; all were an interdependent part of all others and even the cosmos. The latter can be seen in Chamorro folklore. The universe was created by **Puntan's** sister, **Fu'uña**. Puntan requested that Fu'uña take his body to form the universe and all that the universe contained.

# Family

The ancient Chamorros organized themselves into interdependent extended families. The family was the most important socializing and nurturing force in an ancient Chamorro's life. The family was more important than an individual. From birth to death, and even after death, the family was everything. The family provided the individual with personal identity, social status, and determined social obligations. The family provided a person with unconditional and unlimited support. Obedience to family authority was unquestioned. A person had no identity separate from his or her family. Whereas Americans tend to be more concerned with self, ancient Chamorros tended to be more family centered. It is important to note that the family extended to many relatives and even the whole clan. The extended family lived in close proximity.

Decision making on important matters involved the family council. Because the family was interdependent, decisions were reached by consensus. Generally, the father directed the economic activities. Nevertheless, in most matters the mother was the major decision maker about household matters. Children were reared by the entire community.

Obedience to family authority, the maintenance of family harmony, and duty to fulfill family obligations were more important than anything else to the ancient Chamorros. There was unconditional love in the family and unwavering loyalty. People lived for their families and not for themselves. All work was done voluntarily within the family without reward. Family solidarity was maintained by holding a *gupot* (party or celebration), and by always helping family members in times of need. Typical family obligations are listed below:

## *Ayudu* (Help)

Food was shared among relatives.

Relatives could not refuse a demand for help in the *mañahak* (juvenile rabbitfish, Sigunidae family) season.

Fishermen gave fish to their own family, but had to give female relatives the first catch of each kind when it came in season.

The entire family helped build and repair houses and canoes, cultivate fields, and gather the harvest.

The extended family helped in wedding celebrations, marriages, and funerals.

If a nursing mother died, the baby automatically went to the closest nursing relative.

Children were obligated to take care of older people.

Elders were obligated to nurture children, so that the children would carry on the culture's key values.

## *Chenchule'* (Donation)

*Chenchule'* was passed along by the members of the extended family.

Demands for the use of land or anything else had to be met if the request came from a female relative who offered *ålas* (tortoiseshell money).

## *Emmok* (Revenge)

Being a friend was a sacred bond; nevertheless, if the friend did anything against your interest, the friend could expect the worst from the injured person's entire family.

## *Gupot* (Party, Celebration, or Feast)

The *gupot* celebrated the cooperative spirit of the ancient Chamorro's extended family. The *gupot* was a party that celebrated success in any family enterprise. At the *gupot* the family conversed, feasted, played games, swam, raced, jumped, and danced.

The ancient Chamorros condemned the persons who neglected their family obligations. Such persons would not receive any aid when they were in need. This was the most embarrassing thing that could happen to an ancient Chamorro. It was mortifying. All family members tried to make sure they never embarrassed their family. Ancient Chamorros tried to meet all their obligations and always remain loyal to their family.

# Nature

So far we have discussed interdependence only as it relates to human beings. Most Westerners assume that the world is external to themselves and others. They see the world as physical and without a soul or spirit. This is the reason Americans and other Westerners tend to exploit the physical environment for their individual, short-term purposes. Generally, Westerners see their history as a struggle to overcome and conquer nature. They feel a need to expand into every frontier and to challenge nature.

The ancient Chamorros had a different view of nature. Humans were not unique or set apart from the rest of the living and nonliving world. Humanity and nature were intertwined. The "Religion" chapter describes examples of ancient Chamorro spirits found in nature.

Reality is based on the beliefs that the members of a culture share. These assumptions affect a people's outlook and behavior. The ancient Chamorros, like their ancestors from Southeast Asia, felt that all of nature had an essence or spirit that Westerners reserve only for humans. Consequently, the ancient Chamorros had a great concern for nature. They attempted to live in harmony with nature and to integrate their lives with all that is in nature. Humans were just another part of nature. In the ancient Chamorro world view humans and nature were interdependent.

Whereas typical middle-class Americans see themselves as individuals separate from others and the inanimate, the ancient Chamorros saw themselves as part of a whole, interdependent system, which included the animate and the inanimate. They valued harmony. So they felt it was wrong to exploit nature. The ancient Chamorros believed that people should take only what they needed from nature and leave the rest for others.

Modern ecologists are finally coming around to this point of view. The world's resources must be conserved. When we allow plants or animals to become extinct, we all lose. The tropical rain forest provides the earth with much of its oxygen. If we destroy too much of the forest, we will destroy our atmosphere. Any change to one part of the environment affects all other parts of the environment. A plant that we allow to become extinct might cost us the cure for cancer or some other disease. All of our environment should be protected, conserved, and cherished.

This harmonious relationship with nature can be seen in the design and construction of ancient Chamorro houses and canoes. The cap on the *latte* stone (house support) could wobble without breaking in an earthquake or storm. The ancient Chamorro canoes were lashed together so that they gave with the sea rather than being rigid and apt to break.

There was another aspect to the ancient Chamorros' views on nature. A person's physical attraction to the opposite sex was not viewed as something to feel guilty about. Sexual desires were considered to be part of the natural order of things.

There also was a tendency to accept fate. Whatever happened, good, bad, or indifferent, was what was supposed to happen. People should not struggle against nature and the natural order but rather adapt to it. Ifil trees are hard and strong, but coconut trees that sway in the breeze will weather the typhoon better.

# OTHER VALUED CHARACTERISTICS

In addition to believing in interdependence, rank, family, and nature, the ancient Chamorros valued humor, intelligence, physical abilities, and cleanliness.

# Humor

The ancient Chamorros were a gregarious and fun-loving people. They loved to joke and clown around. Playing pranks was appreciated. For example, they concealed rocks in the baskets of rice they traded to the Spanish and Dutch in order to increase their weight. The Europeans saw this as cheating, but the Chamorros saw it as a clever joke. When the ancient Chamorros were caught, they laughed and thought it was a good joke on the Spanish. It is interesting that the Spanish thought this was cheating, but considered trading cheap iron for good food a legitimate business practice.

Chamorros love friendly banter. They developed humor and teasing into an art form, the *chamorrita*. It is the extemporaneous creation of poetry. These four-line poems are sung to another person, who is expected to answer the poems by singing back a response. These songs required wit, voice, and a quick mind. For a full explanation of this topic, see the chapters on "Customs" and "Arts, Skills, and Education."

# Intelligence

The ancient Chamorros were quick to learn, were ingenious, and were adaptable. The speed with which they learned the ways of the Spanish was impressive. The most ingenious example of their technology was the fast-sailing proa. It enabled them to discover the Mariana Islands. It had many design features that made it the fastest sailing craft of its time. The *latte*-stone (house support) design outsmarts insects, rats, and crabs and at the same time protects the house against flooding, high winds, and earthquakes.

The ancient Chamorros' cleverness can be seen in their use of subterfuge. They used the *acho' achuman* to trick fish to come to them (see the chapter on "Food" for details). Their intelligence is revealed in their wartime strategies and verbal arts of subterfuge. Also, many of the ancient Chamorro heroic tales involve fooling adversaries rather than directly confronting them. For example, **Gadao** (see the chapter on "Folklore") hides his identity from **Malaguana**. He fools him.

This use of wit is another safety valve for the ancient Chamorro's rigid social structure. By using their wits, they could conform to the authoritarian family and social structure, and still through subterfuge pursue their own ends. You can see this in a folk tale like Juan Mala, which developed during Spanish times (1668-1898). Juan Mala frequently outsmarted the Spanish Governor. It was not seemly to openly challenge people of higher social status. Nevertheless, the ancient Chamorros found that tricks, pranks, and subterfuge were acceptable against enemies.

The ancient Chamorros valued verbal ability and trained their children as debaters. They respected people who could think quickly. The custom of *mari* (competitive debate) is discussed fully in the "Arts and Skills" chapter.

The ancient Chamorros' adaptability can be seen in their ability to survive the natural disasters of typhoons, earthquakes, and diseases that they faced. Improvisation remains a highly valued trait among Chamorros. The fact that Chamorro culture has withstood years of colonization is perhaps the best testimonial to the adaptability of the people to change.

# Physical Abilities

There are many reports in the early records about the size and strength of the ancient Chamorros. Indeed, to the short Spanish, they may have seemed like giants. One account tells of a captured Chamorro diving off a European ship. He was able to swim away despite the fact that his hands were tied behind him. Another account tells of a Chamorro who grabbed a Spaniard in each hand and lifted them off the ground. From these accounts we know that the Spanish valued strength and thought it was an important characteristic. But did the ancient Chamorros think so?

Reports claim that the ancient Chamorros had contests of strength and athletic skill. For example, the ancient Chamorros wrestled and threw spears and slingstones in order to see who was the best. However, this competition was not the most important thing in their lives. Their interest in sports does not compare with the emphasis American culture puts on sports today. It was a more relaxed and friendly type of competition. It was never an event in and of itself. It was just a part of other celebrations.

Ancient Chamorros also admired manual dexterity. The physical skill required for a man or woman to make a utensil, a mat, or a tool was valued.

# Cleanliness

Fray Antonio del los Angeles, who visited Guam in 1596-97, said, "As soon as a guest arrives, he is given hot water with which to wash . . . ." Legazpi (1565) and Padre Sanvitores reported on the cleanliness of the Chamorros. Sanvitores said, "They kept themselves clean and their houses and villages clean." He claimed that the ancient Chamorros had the cleanest houses in all of the Spanish colonies. They did not spit or eliminate near their villages. They had many sanctions that insured proper hygiene. For example, a person's human waste could be used by *makahnas* (spiritual leaders or shaman) to cast evil spells on them. Where fish were cleaned or a person had been killed, they would throw hot coals on the area to consume the blood and waste. Today, this Chamorro concern for cleanliness is still seen. Chamorros have derogatory terms for dirtiness.

# SUMMARY

In everything we study about the ancient Chamorros we will find the importance of interdependence within the extended family and village over individualism. This concept is seen over and over again in the Chamorro language, customs, and social organization - family, law, and religion. The entire Chamorro culture is permeated by this central concept. This concept expresses itself in all of the following, which were valued by the ancient Chamorros:

| | |
|---|---|
| ancestors | adaptability |
| age | banter |
| bravery | buffoonery |
| cleanliness | cleverness |
| competition (friendly) | consensus |
| cooperation | creativity |
| dexterity | discipline |
| extemporaneousness | family authority |
| friendliness | friendship |
| fun | generosity |
| harmony | hierarchy |
| hospitality | improvisation |
| intelligence | interdependence (*inafa' maolek*) |
| kindness | love (unconditional) |
| loyalty (*mamahlao*) | manners |
| mutualism | nature |
| non-confrontation | nurture |
| peace | physical skills |
| rank | reciprocal behavior (*chenchule'*, *a'ok*, *ika*, *ayudu*, and *emmok*) |
| respect | security |
| selflessness | sharing |
| social position | strength |
| trading ability | unpretentiousness |

96

# Chapter 10
# Religion

## INTRODUCTION

**Religion** is a system of beliefs in supernatural beings and worship. Through beliefs and patterns of behavior, people attempt to influence the supernatural, and the natural world that is beyond their control. Religion depends upon certain universal experiences among all humans. These include the phenomena of life and death, sleep, dreams, and unusual mental states such as trances and ecstasy. Literally, ecstasy means the soul's standing outside the body.

Religion is important in the survival of a people, because it reduces anxiety and keeps confidence high. Religion satisfies many social and psychological needs. Through religion we are able to confront and explain death and other unknowns. Through religion we are able to reinforce group rules of proper behavior or norms, and give meaning and purpose to the life of the individual and the group. Belief in the supernatural means that humans are never required to carry the entire burden of responsibility for misfortune. The belief that a higher force ultimately causes everything gives believers some relief and comfort. Religion provides an afterlife unbounded by time.

Anthony F. C. Wallace, a social scientist, defined religion as a set of rituals, explained by myth, that activate supernatural powers to help or prevent transformations in humans or in nature. **Ritual** is ceremony performed in a particular way. Ritual is religion in action. In order to influence supernatural beings and powers, humans use prayer, sacrifice, and ritual activity. Religion is based on the assumptions that supernatural beings exist, that they have an interest in human affairs, and that they can be appealed to.

New religions begin when a society's anxieties and frustrations are beyond bearing. In these cases people attempt to reduce their stress by overturning the entire social system. These are called revitalization movements, and they propose to totally reform a society. Through these efforts people hope to reconstruct a more satisfying culture. Some experts view cargo cults and even atheist Marxism in this light.

The **supernatural** usually takes the form of gods and goddesses, ancestral spirits, or nonhuman spirit beings. Ideas about spirits and souls probably came from human attempts to understand death, sleep, disease, trances, and dreams.

**Gods and goddesses** are usually viewed as remote beings who control the universe or various parts of it. **Ancestral spirits** are based on the belief that human beings are made up of two parts, a body and a spirit. Ancestral spirits are thought to maintain an active interest in the lives of their living descendants. Generally, ancestral spirits act like human beings. They can be benevolent or malevolent and they tend to be fickle. Generally, ancestral spirits are believed to protect living relatives from their enemies in this world and the spirit world, provided that the living relatives meet their family obligations. The respect and reverence shown by people to these ancestral spirits is labeled **ancestor worship**.

**Animism** is a belief that everything in nature has a spirit or conscious life. It may be a sense of awe and wonder about nature, or it may be the projections of either personal or impersonal spirits into everything in the universe. It is the belief that animals, plants, tools, or even a rock or an abstract idea has a spirit. People who believe in animism view themselves as just another part of nature and not superior to nature.

## Religious Practitioners

In every culture there are individuals who have the job of guiding and enhancing the religious practices of others. They have special abilities in contacting and influencing supernatural beings and manipulating supernatural forces. Normally they have special training, but usually they also have a personality that suits them for this job. Full-time trained religious practitioners are called priests or priestesses.

In societies that lack this degree of occupational specialization, people who acquire religious power are called shamans. A **shaman** is a religious leader who has special abilities to influence supernatural powers for his clients. He or she is a person who acquired his or her religious power through individual initiative. Frequently, shamans isolate themselves for a while in an attempt to have the supernatural powers reveal themselves to them. In doing so they are given special gifts such as the power to heal or make people sick; or the power to control the weather or see the future; and/or the power to deal with spirits. Shamans try to influence the supernatural for their clients. Whereas priests and priestesses work for the supernatural and tell people what to do, the shaman works on behalf of his clients and tries to tell the supernatural what to do.

Shamans are usually not frauds. They believe that they have been given a special power. They believe that whatever comes into their mind is a suggestion from the supernatural. Shamans, priests, and priestesses usually are paid for their services. Oftentimes shamans are paid with food. Also, shamans are given respect, high prestige, authority and social power, and an outlet for their artistic expression.

# Rituals and Ceremonies

People relate to the sacred through rituals. Rituals channel emotion and tension into socially acceptable manners. Rituals are repeated acts by which a group celebrates its myths that explain the relationship between the supernatural and natural worlds. A ritual is important because it reinforces the social bonds of a group, it relieves their tensions, and it is used to celebrate life crises.

There are rites of passage that mark important states in the lives of individuals, such as birth, puberty, marriage, parenthood, and death. Rites of passage also include rites of separation, when someone is banished from the group. In addition, there are rites of incorporation of an individual into the group, or into a new status within the group. For example, a person might become lineage head or chief, or obtain a status associated with some occupational specialization. Rites of intensification occur during a group's crisis or its fear of a potential crisis. Funerals are rites of passage and intensification. They allow the living to express how upset they are over the death and show respect to the departed.

In addition, rituals celebrate critical times like planting and harvesting. Oftentimes these ceremonies express a respect for the forces in nature upon which the group's existence depends.

# Magic and Religion

**Magic** rests on the belief that through certain actions supernatural powers can be made to act for good or evil purposes. Magic is based on the logic of association rather than the logic of cause and effect. For example, a black cat walked in front of a person, and he or she had bad luck. From this experience the person drew the false conclusion that the black cat caused the bad luck.

**Sorcery** is the craft of evil magic. Sorcery is believed to be positive magic, and taboos are negative magic. For example, sorcerers will perform certain rituals to cause certain results. If they are successful, they believe it proves their supernatural power. If they fail, it is never their fault. It is because their magic was not strong enough, or because other people or hostile forces are trying to counteract their spells.

A **sorcerer** is a person who performs evil magic. Oftentimes the sorcerer will require his or her client to do something. If the hoped-for results are not obtained, the failure is blamed on taboos that were broken or on the fact that the chants were not repeated correctly.

Broken taboos unleash negative magic, which can hurt even those who are not to blame. A **taboo** is a rule, the violation of which involves severe, automatic punishment. For example, if there is a flood, a shaman will claim that someone must have broken a taboo.

Sorcerers believe that they have supernatural powers and sometimes even the right to trick people. Often sorcerers will help their spiritual powers along with a little direct influence. Sometimes they use poison to ensure that an evil spell works. In any event, a sorcerers' one success is remembered and outweighs his or her many failures.

Magic can be sympathetic or contagious magic. Sympathetic magic is based on the principle that like produces like. For example, taking an image of someone and throwing it in the ocean so the person will go mad is an example of sympathetic magic. Contagious magic is based on the principle that anything which was once in contact with a person can be used to affect that person. For example, if a sorcerer can obtain a person's spittle, feces, fingernail clippings, or clothing, it is believed that the sorcerer can use those items to work an evil spell against that person.

Witchcraft is believed to be an inborn force of

evil. It is used to explain unwanted events. Sorcery involves the deliberate use of spiritual power to cause harm. Witchcraft is found in societies that have little way of expressing hostility. These pent-up emotions can be released using the services of a sorcerer or witch. Feelings of hostility that could not be expressed in the open can be acceptably expressed in this way. Witches are sometimes blamed for diseases and other natural calamities and are sometimes hunted down and killed.

A people's values are reflected in their religion, just as they are in their law. A people's religion serves to give them tranquillity, and their law provides peace and security. In the case of some societies, religion takes the form of totemism. **Totemism** is a belief in kinship through common clan emblem affiliation. In this case, religion restates the social organization of a group on a spiritual level. If kinship is dominant in a society, then totemism and ancestor worship can be expected.

Religion functions to give people an orderly model of the universe; it reduces their fears and anxiety by explaining the unknown. The unknown can be explained by the existence of supernatural beings and powers. These powers can be manipulated by people through sacrifice and ritual or at least appealed to through prayer. When all their efforts have been exhausted, humans appeal to the divine for aid.

Religion functions socially and psychologically. Religion tells us what is right and wrong and explains proper social conduct. If we behave ourselves, the supernatural powers will be pleased and we will be blessed. If we do not behave properly, then the supernatural powers will cause us to suffer and will punish us. This means that the supernatural is a "watch dog" for society.

Another social function of religion is the solidarity that religion brings to a group. On an individual level, if proper behavior is fixed by the supernatural, then it takes the burden of decision making on moral issues off the believer's shoulders. People find great comfort in the belief that the supernatural is responsible for everything that happens. Religious rituals help people through emotional times by celebrating the vital events in their lives. Finally, religion educates the group in ritual ceremonies and tribal lore, and thereby preserves the culture.

# ANCIENT CHAMORRO RELIGION

## Ancestor Worship

Ancient Chamorro religion is best understood if we look at it as an integral part of the Chamorros' day-to-day behavior. Ancient Chamorro religion reflects Chamorro values and social organization. The value of interdependence can be seen in the kinship system and in its extension, ancestor worship. Perhaps a better term would be ancestor veneration.

**Veneration** is looking on with great respect and reverence. The respect the ancient Chamorros had for older people naturally led them to respect their ancestors. The spirit or soul was believed to be immortal. Death did not end a family member's concern for the welfare of the whole group. Death did not end the love and honor felt toward the ancestor. Ancestor veneration was just an extension of basic human relationships from this world to the supernatural world. Just as living elders can reward or punish a person, so could the ancestral spirits. It was the prerogative of the *ante* (ancestral spirit) to cause illness if displeased or if a person was not meeting his or her kinship obligations. Nevertheless, a person's *ante* was generally thought to be constantly beside him or her and busy attending to that person's well-being.

It is important to note that ancestors were not thought of as gods, although the tremendous respect people showed their ancestors was equivalent to the respect that many people reserve for God. Although some researchers have reported **Puntan** and his sister **Fu'uña** as god and goddess, and **Chaife** as an evil god, they are better understood as remote ancestral spirits. Some researchers have stressed animism, which existed in ancient Chamorro culture, but it was not dominant. **Animism** is the belief that objects such as rocks and trees have spirits.

The ancient Chamorros venerated their ancestors by the customs of preserving ancestral skulls, burying the dead under or near their homes, and in one account of preserving their dried hands. An ancient Chamorro feared and respected his or her *ante*. The ancient Chamorros believed that these spirits cared about their descendants. Nevertheless, these spirits were forces of both good and evil. *Ante* were generally well behaved toward their descendants, as long as the living were meeting their kinship obligations. *Ante* were thought to punish those who did not behave in a proper manner. It was their prerogative to cause illness. This belief led to a more orderly society. Ancient Chamorros knew that their ancestors were always watching their behavior and depended upon the *ante* to protect them from the menacing spirits of other people's ancestors. Some accounts refer to these evil spirits or demons as *aniti*. *Ante* could be appealed to for help, and were believed often to yield to a descendant's pleas and sacrifices.

The ancient Chamorros believed that a person's character depended on the strength of his or her soul or spirit. Some people's spirits were thought to be weak. That was the reason they were lazy or cowardly. Those who were great warriors and hard workers had strong souls. Their souls could overcome the negative force of an *aniti*.

The ancient Chamorros considered women and children to be especially vulnerable to illness caused by an *ante*. Some researchers have assumed this was because their souls were not considered as strong as a man's. There is a more likely explanation. Women and children were at risk through no fault of their own. The ancient Chamorros traced descent through the female line (matrilineage). But wives moved to their husband's territory upon marriage. This meant that the children were raised on their father's land and away from their ancestral spirits. This is the reason that women and children were more vulnerable to an *ante*. When a man was away from his ancestral land, he was vulnerable, too.

Today, the term *aniti* refers to Satan. The ancient Chamorros believed that an *aniti* caused all violent deaths. The *aniti* were thought to cause a person's spirit to dwell in the jungle, caves, air, or in trees rather than near his or her home territory. Some accounts claim that an *aniti* could make a person's soul go to *sasalaguan* (a kind of volcano-like hell). The Chamorros' concept of heaven and hell was probably introduced by the Spanish. Heaven was believed to be an underground paradise, where there were good food and good things to do. *Sasalaguan* was the mountain home of Chaife (god of the wind, waves, and fire). Chaife was believed to beat a person's soul forever on a forge, which is clearly a Spanish introduction.

Some researchers have reported that the ancient Chamorros believed that the type of life a person lived had no bearing on what kind of afterlife he or she would have. Peaceful death led to paradise, and violent death led to an afterlife of torture. It seems more likely that the ancient Chamorros did believe that a person's behavior affected the person's afterlife. The ancient Chamorros probably believed that a violent death was possible only if a person's ancestral spirits removed their protection. If people died violently, it was because they had offended ancestral spirits and lost their support. The ancient Chamorros' "hell" was to reside away from their descendants and in the jungle or a cave. Such spirits were believed to be unhappy about this and became dangerous. These spirits today are referred to as the *taotaomo'na* (ghosts, demons, disembodied souls or specters). People could be protected from this lonely fate by not offending ancestral spirits. If they did not break any taboos and met family obligations, they would be protected.

When ancient Chamorros needed additional help, they sought the assistance of a shaman. Powerful enemies sometimes worked evil against a person. This could be guarded against by enlisting the help of a shaman. He or she could put ancestral spirits to work on the client's behalf. People who were protected against an *ante* could not die a violent death. When they died, their spirits were allowed to dwell near their descendants. This would have been a heaven of sorts.

Fray Juan Pobre de Zamorro (1602) reports that special ancestral places were called *sulares*. Many present-day Chamorros continue to show respect to ancestral spirits associated with the land. Chamorros in an unfamiliar area ask permission for land-use privileges. These ancestral spirits are called the *taotaomo'na* (ghosts, demons, disembodied souls or specters). Literally *taotaomo'na* translates as "people of before." *Taotaomo'na* are addressed as grandmother and grandfather. Chamorro folklore is full of references to *taotaomo'na* who are thought to dwell around *latte* stones, in the air, jungle, caves, and trees, especially *nunu* (banyan) trees.

# Practitioners, Magic and Religion

The ancient Chamorros had two kinds of religious practitioners, shamans and sorcerers. It seems likely that individual religious practitioners played both of these roles. One report claims the *makahnas* who helped people were from the the *chamorri*. This suggests that *makahnas* came from both the higher caste and the lower caste. Anthropological accounts claim that a shaman was called a *makahna* and a sorcerer was called a *kakahna*. *Makahnayi* is the act of "putting a hex" or "throwing a spell." It seems likely that ancient Chamorro leaders of this type performed magical spells and counter-magical spells. For convenience, only the term *makahna* will be used.

The historical record indicates that *makahnas* were men and that *suruhanas* (herb doctors) were women. Nevertheless, given the status of women in Chamorro society, it seems likely that some women held the position of *makahna*. This is further supported by the claim by most spiritual practitioners that they did not choose their profession but were called to it by supernatural forces.

*Makahnas* were shamans who used magic for the purpose of curing the sick and guaranteeing success in warfare, fishing, and farming. *Makahnas* were the spiritual leaders in ancient Chamorro society. They had powers because of their ability to communicate with the *ante* (spirits of ancestors). *Makahnas* worked on the behalf of their clients to influence supernatural forces. They could counteract the work of evil spirits and the curses of sorcerers. The *makahna* would spread salt on the intended victim and around his or her house to drive the evil spirits away. The *makahna* would also invoke ancestral spirits to help the client and counteract evil curses. The term *makahna* today means "the person who is cursed." In ancient Chamorro times it seems to have referred to the spiritual leader who was protecting the people who were cursed.

*Makahnas* were also sorcerers, who performed evil magic. *Makahnas* had the power to cause or cure sickness by spiritual means. The *makahna* needed something that had been in close association with the intended victim to perform his or her secret rites. Hair, feces, or spit would work. Most often a discarded betel nut quid was used. Through a curse, they could make people sick, or even kill them. They could cause a poor harvest, poor fishing, or bad luck. They went to the place of an *ante* to work evil spells. In modern times there was an old man who did not want the Marine Laboratory built by the University of Guam. He felt that the road would upset his ancestral spirits. He placed a curse on all those who were going ahead with the project. A bulldozer operator died of a heart attack, and the project was dropped until after the old man died. Was this a coincidence? Was this the effect of the old man's *ante*?

*Makahnas* were not priests. They did not work for the supernatural, but for their clients. One report claims that the devil gets into men and women who do not obey the *makahna*. Such a possessed person would rant and rave from 11 to 12 o'clock. His or her neighbors would admonish the person because he or she was mad. This embarrassment would cause the person to stay inside his or her house for days.

Other reports claim that the *makahnas* were forgotten until a favor was needed from the supernatural. Some reports claim that the *makahnas* had more influence. *Makahnas* were used because of their superior ability to communicate with the spirits of the dead. Like ordinary ancient Chamorros they invoked the help of the spirits by calling upon their ancestral skulls, which they kept in baskets. Some accounts state the *makahanas* kept the skulls of the powerful chiefs. *Makahnas* talked to the skulls. They gave the ancestral skulls offerings of food. Sometimes they would even bury the skulls for two or three days before the conjunction of the moon. Perhaps this was a threat to the ancestors to do as the *makahna* bid them.

The *makahnas* received presents for their services. The presents were probably betel nut, food, or money.

### *Makahna* Powers and Abilities

To identify offended ancestral spirits

To prescribe a means to make restitution to offended spirits

To transfer supernatural powers to others

To cast love spells (*atgimat* - enamor, cause to fall in love, bewitch)

To cause sickness or death

To produce rain

To cause a good harvest

To bring good luck, especially in fishing

To bring health and healing

To tell the future

In other parts of Micronesia foretelling the future or divination was accomplished by observing cloud formations, the flight of birds, or the edges of broken objects. The shamans would even look at the pattern of objects they cast on the ground.

In ancient Chamorro times, *suruhanus* were responsible for curing illnesses that had natural causes. They cured sickness by using medicines obtained from herbs and by massage. *Suruhanu* is a Spanish term; the ancient Chamorro word for this type of healer is not known. Today, *suruhanus* and *suruhanas* are believed by some to have the type of spiritual power that used to be associated with the *makahnas*.

In addition to the *makahnas*, clan heads probably contacted the ancestral spirits on formal matters. The ancestral spirits probably had titles that corresponded to their living titles. Contacting the spirit world was not the exclusive power of special practitioners. Ancient Chamorros believed they had the power to contact their ancestral spirits. They only sought the help of experts when their efforts were not getting satisfactory results.

# Ritual and Ceremonies

The purpose of ancient Chamorro ritual was to tap supernatural power. Individuals could call on the *ante* for help. In the early 1670s a report from a Spanish missionary stated, "The father saw a fish which the natives like very much, called *guatafi*, and without stopping to consider, was carried away by the old custom and began to invoke his *ante*, to gain their help in catching the fish." The *ante* could be an evil power too. According to reports of Padre Sanvitores, "A little girl was born on the island of Aguigan. It appeared to her father that the *ante* or demon threatened her, and was about to kill his child. The father begged it not to do so, even though it killed him instead. He told this to his wife, who a few days later found him dead in his bed." The ancient Chamorros believed that fishing, farming, and even life and death could be affected by the *ante*.

## Rituals

Ancient Chamorros anointed the skulls of their ancestors, kept the skulls safe in a basket in their homes, and offered the skulls food. By taking these actions and by fulfilling all of their family obligations, ancient Chamorros pleased their *antes*.

The ward of a skull had to protect it. Men gave special instructions to their family before they went to sea. No person was allowed to touch another person's ancestral skulls. Skulls were placed among the rafters in the house.

The ancient Chamorros believed that the *antes* were constantly at their sides, busy attending to their well-being. In a dangerous situation they called upon their dead relative, "Hu! hu! (the name or names of the relative whom they were invoking) I need your help now; if you ever loved your family, come and help me!" They repeated this as long as the danger lasted. Below are a list of the rituals associated with the ancestral skulls:

**Protecting and caring for the skull that symbolized the *ante*.**
The skulls were anointed with coconut oil; this duplicates the practice of anointing a person's living elders with coconut oil. It also duplicates the important custom of touching those who are close to you. The skulls were kept in a basket in the house.

**Communicating with the *ante* and invoking the *ante* to action.**

**Singing thanks and praises to the *ante* and recounting its accomplishments.**

**Making devotional offerings to the *ante*.**
The *ante* were offered food before a meal began. War booty was sacrificed to the *ante*. After a fishing trip, fish were offered to the *ante*.

**Making sacrifices to the *ante*.**
Complete silence was maintained when fishing. Long fasts were endured to please the *ante*.

# Ceremonies to Honor Ancestral Spirits

When a man returns from fishing, he first carries his fish up to the house, "then he removes the skulls from the little boxlike cases and sets them in front of the fish and while performing certain ceremonies, he offers them the flying fish that he has caught. He speaks to them very softly so that no other person can hear what he says. When he has caught a large fish, such as a blue marlin or a mahimahi, or a turtle, or a parbo, which they call *taga* [snapper: *tagagen saddok*; red snapper: *tagafe*] he places it on top of whatever he has caught. Then the relatives and closest neighbors are summoned and they make a fiesta for their skulls, drinking ground rice mixed with water or with grated coconut milk [this drink was called *atuli*]. They then make signs and perform ceremonies, as if inviting the old skull to eat. Then, they begin to sing very loudly, as if giving thanks to the fisherman. They tell him, 'You are much beloved, this head loves you very much. This skull loves you dearly because he has made you very lucky in fishing and he honors you so much.'" In 1602, Fray Juan Pobre de Zamora was the eyewitness to this ceremony on Luta (Rota).

The ancient Chamorros believed that an offended *ante* would tell a descendant that he or she and the skull had not been respected. Sometimes the *ante* would criticize them for letting guests come into the house where the skulls were kept. The *ante* would threaten to drown them. The ancient Chamorros felt the *ante* could capsize their canoes or cause their fishing or farming to fail.

When people were scolded and threatened by the *ante*, at night they ran about raving and shouting as if possessed. The neighbors reminded them that they had offended their ancestral spirits. The villagers held them in low esteem. They felt that the afflicted people deserved to be treated badly. The neighbors shamed the offenders and told them to go away. The neighbors told them to obey their *ante* and they would not have these problems. Thus, scolded by their friends and relatives, the offenders were so embarrassed that they would stay inside for more than ten days.

Feasts were provided to honor the ancient Chamorros' ancestors. The entire population of an area was invited. The historical traditions of ancestors were recounted through long stories. A special feast was held each year at Fouha Bay (the first bay north of Umatac). This was the legendary Chamorro "Garden of Eden." The ancient Chamorros held contests for amusement and to honor idols. They made offerings of seeds, nets, fishing hooks, and rice cakes to the ancestral spirits. After the ceremony, the ancient Chamorros kept the rice cake offerings as special blessed food for the sick.

The ancient Chamorros celebrated harvests, births, initiations into the men's house, marriages, and funerals. The funeral ceremonies were conducted to honor the newest ancestral spirits. It was mandatory that every Chamorro attend the funeral rites of all kinsmen. In all of these ancient Chamorro festivities, there were always singing or reciting of legends, and stories of the accomplishments of their ancestors. The wisest competed to see who could speak or sing the most couplets in long epic poems. The legend of Puntan, from whom the heavens and earth were created, was often sung. In all these activities the family, which included all of a person's kin, living and dead, was celebrated and reunited.

**10.1 Ancestor Worship**

# Taboos

The ancient Chamorros believed that certain acts would anger ancestral spirits. A taboo is a prohibition or ban on certain things or actions. For example, the *chamorri* (high caste) could not eat eel. *Chamorri* also could not eat freshwater fish. They could not eat any fish with large scales. You can see how these bans benefited the *manachang* (low caste), who were not permitted to even go near the ocean and were only allowed to fish in freshwater streams. They were probably given the large-scaled fish that the *chamorri* caught.

Another taboo forbid marrying anyone in the same clan. Incest was forbidden. Sexual intercourse was taboo between members of the *chamorri* and *manachang*, too. Ancient Chamorros fasted before some fishing expeditions. The entire community may have had to obey the taboos of the highest ranking lineage in a village.

103

The ancient Chamorros believed that if taboos were broken, misfortune would strike. For example, crop failure, drought, a typhoon, and illness were thought to be caused by someone who broke a taboo. The greatest taboo for ancient Chamorros was to fail to meet their kinship obligations.

# Icons

Ancestral skulls were the major symbol of the *ante*. They were kept in baskets or boxes in the rafters. The skulls were called **maranan uchan** (a miraculous thing for rain). The skulls were worn tied to the thighs of warriors on Luta (Rota).

Wooden figures with three heads were kept in ancient Chamorro homes. The ancient Chamorros painted and carved images on trees. Carved human figures stood at the head of their canoes. Drawings of their deceased relatives were made on pieces of bark.

One account claims the ancient Chamorros saved the dried hands of their ancestors.

Some archaeologists suspect that slingstones may have had a part in the ancient Chamorro ancestor veneration. Slingstones much too large for actual use have been found. Many of the ancient stories involved heroic deeds by giant ancestors. The huge slingstones were possibly used in ceremonies as proof that the giants existed. They could have been used as visual examples of just how big and strong their ancestors must have been. Some of the slingstones are over six inches long.

# *Taotaomo'na*

The belief in the *taotaomo'na* is a cultural survival of ancient Chamorro ancestor veneration. A **cultural survival** is an element of culture that remains long after it has lost its original function. The *taotaomo'na* are believed to be ancestral spirits or *manante* (plural of *ante*). Sometimes they are called *bihu* (ancient, grandfather, old man). Most of the *taotaomo'na* are thought to be the ancient chiefs of various districts. The present-day belief in the *taotaomo'na* is a survival of the ancient ancestor veneration practiced in the Mariana Islands.

Normally, *taotaomo'na* are described as invisible, but they can take a natural or a ghost-like form. Usually they are human, but they can take animal forms. *Taotaomo'na* are often described as giants but sometimes they are thought to be elf-like *duhendes*. They rarely show their faces. Oftentimes they are headless, or the face is a void. Most *taotaomona* are men, but some are women. Some are horrible looking. A common characteristic is an insisting gaze, which locks in on the person who witnesses their presence.

*Taotaomo'na* make sounds that only they can make. Their language sounds like a cobbler at work. It is similar to the sound of a stand of bamboo knocking, brushing, and hissing in the wind. Sometimes it is like two sticks being rubbed together to make a fire.

*Taotaomo'na* smell. Usually their smell is the heavy sweet smell of *ilangilang*, or flowering *fadang* (Federico palm or cycad), or the fresh smell of lemon, but sometimes their smell is unpleasant, like an unwashed toilet. They possess great strength and are oftentimes giants.

It is reported that *taotaomo'na* can be encountered anywhere day or night. Nevertheless, they usually are found in specific locations. They are believed to be guardians and spirits of the jungle and ancient *latte* (stone house supports) sites. Sometimes they are called *taotaohalomtano* (people of the jungle). There are reports that there were special ancestral places called *sulares* in ancient times. The spirits live in the jungle, in caves and crevices and in trees. Their favorite tree is the eerie-looking *nunu* (banyan or *Ficus prolixa*) tree. It has long aerial roots that hang from the limbs of the tree. These roots can be as thick as a tree trunk or as thin as hair. Sometimes *taotaomo'na* are found on the reefs and warn fishermen of their presence with phosphorescent or green, flickering lights.

The *taotaomo'na* are not mentioned by any of the early explorers or priests. Nevertheless, the *taotaomo'na* have their roots in ancient Chamorro culture. Despite the Christianization of the Chamorros, many believe in their ancestral spirits. After the Chamorro chiefs were killed by the Spanish, the people had to ask the dead chiefs' spirits for land-use privileges. From this practice the idea of the *taotaomo'na* developed. It is a continuation of the ancient Chamorros' respect for their ancestors. In most of the following account, the *taotaomo'na* will be examined through the eyes of a person who believes that the *taotaomo'na* is real.

*Taotaomo'na* are addressed to this day as

grandmother and grandfather. Literally, *taotaomo'na* means the people of before, or ancestor. The *taotaomo'na* is often described as headless because the ancestral skulls in ancient times were taken for worship. Perhaps they are headless because the Spanish forced the people to destroy their ancestral skulls. The superhuman strength of the *taotaomo'na* may come from the ancient Chamorro stories of ancestral heroes who had such strength.

## *Taotaomo'na* Behavior

The *taotaomo'na* are believed to own nature. They protect their territorial rights and conserve natural resources. *Taotaomo'na* who live near large trees keep the ground under them as clean as if the area had been swept by a broom. The *taotaomo'na* are upset by the willful destruction of the environment or by those who take more from the land or sea than their family needs. *Taotaomo'na* have a habit of taking fishing nets and food. Hunters will shoot an animal, but when they arrive at the spot where the deer or bat fell, they will find nothing. The *taotaomo'na* has already collected the kill. *Taotaomo'na* are reported to take the shape of a headless deer, a bird, a crab, or other animals.

People who do not ask the *taotaomo'na's* permission to enter the jungle will incur their wrath. Those who do not ask the *taotaomo'na's* permission to get water from the river, to fish or hunt, to eliminate body wastes, to pick fruit, or cut plants will be punished by the *taotaomo'na*.

The *taotaomo'na* can make a person sick or crazy. Oftentimes they leave brown, red, yellow, or purple marks on the intruder. Sometimes they leave teeth marks. The *taotaomo'na* often cause the illness *chetnot maipe* (a hot fever). Some people afflicted by the *taotaomo'na* have no apparent illness but just waste away. Physicians have been unable to diagnose these afflicted persons' illnesses and have been powerless to restore the victims' health. Those who have been kidnapped by the *taotaomo'na* often suffer from *chetnot manman*. In this condition they simply stare into space and cannot remember anything. *Suruhanus* (herb doctors) often are able to cure sicknesses caused by the *taotaomo'na*. They are able to diagnose and cure these illnesses because they have a special relationship with these ancestral spirits.

*Taotaomo'na* stir up damaging winds and cause the wind to moan and howl. Some are called *lamlamtaotao* (lightning people). Some *taotaomo'na* haunt people by making strange noises in the night or by pounding on the house. Oftentimes they are caught following someone, but when the person turns around, nothing is there. They have even been known to kidnap people. When those who have been kidnapped are found, they are usually dazed and cannot speak. Sometimes children are taken by a *taotaomo'na* disguised as their aunt or uncle.

Women and children are thought to be especially vulnerable to the *taotaomo'na*, especially pregnant women. They do not like the smell of breast milk or a pregnant woman. This may go back to the fact that women and children lived on their husband's or father's clan territory. This land was protected by the husband's or father's clan's ancestral spirits. The ancestral spirits of other people's clans were more likely to be hostile.

The *taotaomo'na* befriend some individuals. They are called *gai taotao* (possessed ones). The *taotaomo'na* give their friends supernatural strength. For example, they will help them lift a coconut log or a bridge beam. Nevertheless, no matter how strong the rapport with the *taotaomo'na*, a human can never control them. People can ask for help, but more often than not, they are the instrument of the *taotaomo'na*. People who have a **taotaomo'na ga'chong** or friend go to church, but always stand outside. When such a person dies, the *taotaomo'na* will try to attach itself to one of the person's close relatives.

10.2 *Taotaomo'na*

## How Believers Protect Themselves from the Wrath of the *Taotaomo'na*

Some *taotaomo'na* are obsessed with evil (*taotao tiamulek*). They are dedicated to causing problems for the unwary. The *taotaomo'na* seem to be more hostile than the ancient Chamorro *ante*. They are frequently believed to be the ancient chiefs. Perhaps they are angry because their skulls were not preserved and cared for. People can best protect themselves from the *taotaomo'na* by not offending them. It is not safe to invade the territory of other people's ancestral spirits. If you must enter their area, always show respect and ask permission. You should not be loud or sing. You should always explain why you need to infringe on their territory and how anything that you take will benefit more than just yourself.

Address the *taotaomo'na* as *guella yan guello* (grandmother and grandfather). This salutation is used before asking for permission to pass, eliminate, or to take something from the jungle or the sea. Ask permission each time you intend to breach their rights to the land. For example, "*Guella yan guello na fapus yu* (Grandmother and grandfather, allow me to pass)."

*Taotaomo'na* can be warded off with salt, anything red, fire, a white sheet, the sign of the cross, a crucifix, blessed palm fronds, prayers, or anything that is holy. They will sometimes disappear if they are scolded, or if a person does not show any weakness. Pregnant women should wear their husband's shirt, or mask their odor with some strong smell like onions or even burning rags, manure, or old tires.

Children dazed by the *taotaomo'na* can be helped by spanking them with an old lady's belt, or burning chicken feathers and dusting the child with the ashes. Oftentimes this will cause the child to vomit raw breadfruit peelings, shrimp, or parrotfish remains, which the *taotaomo'na* has been feeding them. Priests are often called on to break the spells of the *taotaomo'na*.

Offended *taotaomo'na* can be appeased if a sincere apology is given for trespassing or taking something that people did not ask permission to have or to use.

*Suruhanus* (herb doctors) are friends of *taotaomo'na* and are rewarded with special powers. They can communicate with the *taotaomo'na*, who tell them the causes of an illness. *Suruhanus* will often tell their patients that in order to get well they must apologize to the *taotaomo'na* they have displeased. In the case of *chetnot maipe*, the *suruhanus* prescribe an herb tea called *amot fresko*.

Nonbelievers are told that they can see the *taotaomo'na* if they put the "sleep" from a dog's eye into their eyes or look into the steam from cooking rice. Even people who are not sure about the existence of the *taotaomo'na* will ask permission to enter the jungle, because it does not hurt to play it safe.

The *taotaomo'na* belief emphasizes many of the ancient Chamorros' values. It is important to show respect for all relatives and especially dead relatives. Pregnant women must be careful and parents must always keep a close eye on their children. It is important to respect nature and take only what is needed. Humans' interdependence with nature and kinsmen, living and dead, must be honored or they will be punished. The idea of a *taotaomo'na ga'chong* is similar to the ancient belief that a person's *ante* is always standing by to help.

## Chamorrita giya Malesso

*Taotaomo'na* stories are usually told in the first person by the person who has had the experience with the *taotaomo'na*. Below is a story told by a teenage girl from Malesso. The experience took place during the Japanese occupation of Guam.

"I was about 14 at the time. I went to church for a special youth group meeting. This was a hard time and the meeting was the only fun we had in those days. I hoped to meet Jose Cruz, whom I really liked. He didn't show up and I was disappointed. When I left church, another fellow asked to walk me home. Since I had to walk past an area where there were soldiers staying, I wanted someone to walk with me. But I knew that if I allowed him to walk me home, my real boyfriend, Jose, would find out about it and get mad. So I decided to walk alone. It was a long walk; my family was staying out at our ranch.

"As I walked home, I felt that someone was following me, but when I looked behind me I could not see or hear anything. I was fearful that it was a soldier. I began to walk a little faster. But the faster I walked, the louder were the sounds from the person following me. Each time I looked back, nothing was there and I could not hear a thing. I was frightened, and thought that it must be the *taotaomo'na*. Finally, I wasn't just walking faster, I was running as fast as I could. I was praying to the Virgin Mary to protect me. I didn't stop running or praying even when I reached our house. I ran up the steps and into the house to our family altar, where we had some candles burning. I knelt down and thanked Mary for saving me. My family all began to tease me. They said, 'Look at Jesusa. It was not enough to just go to church and pray. She is trying to shame us by acting so holy.' They stopped the teasing when they saw how frightened I was, but they said it was just my imagination. They said nothing was following me.

"The next morning when we went out to our field to hoe the corn, the whole family was shocked. There were two rows of corn completely knocked down. Had this been done by the wind, it would have been all the rows knocked down. My father said, 'Maybe it was a wild pig or the carabao.' When we looked for tracks, we found human-like footprints, but they were two feet long and about 10 inches wide. Since then, my family has never doubted me, and I have never since forgotten to ask the *taotaomo'na's* permission to pass along the trail that leads to our ranch. My father said that the *taotaomo'na* did not intend to harm me, he was only making sure I made it home safe. He was just a little mad that I had not shown proper respect. I felt the only thing that saved me was my prayers, thank God."

## Gamson, Gatos, and Anufat

Some *taotaomo'na* have names like **Gamson** (octopus), **Gatos** (100), and **Anufat**. Gamson haunts the Pago Bay area. He smokes a cigar made of rolled coconut leaves, and is know for his great strength and prowess. One day a man from Talage

**10.3  Anufat**

107

came looking to fight him. Gamson invited the man to eat. He asked the visitor to get the fish for the meal. The man said, "I have a hook and line, but where will I get an *atupat* (slingstone) for a sinker?" Gamson laughed. He dove into deep water and came up with five fish, each over 18 inches long. The men then retired to Gamson's house to prepare the fish for cooking. Gamson said, "Would you get the coconut?" The man from Talage began to make a loop to keep his feet together as he climbed the tree. Gamson laughed and grabbed a tree and shook the coconuts down. The guest said, "I'll husk it and grate it; just show me your husking stake and *kamyo* (coconut grater)." Gamson laughed again. He grabbed the nut and squeezed it so hard the grated coconut oozed though the husk. As Gamson continued to prepare the meal, the visitor began to have second thoughts about fighting this man. Saying that he needed to move his bowels, he excused himself. Once out of sight, he ran from Pago all the way to Talage as fast as he could. In his rush he fell and left the imprint of his hand in the rock on the cliff. It can still be seen there.

Gamson haunts a *latte* site and a cave in a Pago area named after him. A group of people went coconut crab hunting one night. As they were searching for the *ayuyu*, four women entered a cave. They were attacked by Gamson. He stuck his spear into all of them. One of the women called her husband. When he came, Gamson stopped. Gamson swore he would have killed them, if the man had not been his *ga'chong*. This man had superhuman power. He had been given the strength of six men because Gamson was his *taotaomo'na ga'chong*.

Gatos travels with his soldiers. When they reach a river Gatos bridges it with his penis. His soldiers then march across. If someone urinates in his territory, he will get even by making them sick. He will touch them with his penis, and then they will be unable to urinate or unable to move their bowels.

Anufat is ugly, with big fangs. He has a hole in his side. The wound is stuffed with a growing *galak dankolo* (bird's nest fern, *Asplenium nidus*).

## White Lady

The belief in the white lady is found in Mexico and in Malaysia, as well as the Mariana Islands. In Mexico she has a beautiful body, but a face like a horse. In the stories on Guam the white lady is very beautiful. A sophisticated high class young man wanted to marry a beautiful *taotaomo'na* who lived in the woods with her cousins. She accepted his proposal. The young man's parents forbid the marriage. When the young man insisted, his mother killed him. The expectant bride still waits for him at the Maina bridge on Guam. She appears from time to time. She is most likely to be seen by men who resemble her dead lover. She is every man's dream girl. She wears white and has long black hair, which reaches to the ground. You can tell when she is near because she smells like *ilangilang*.

In a similar story from Agat she smells like fresh wild lemon. In some stories, she has white hair and long, flowing white robes.

In this story, some aspects of ancient Chamorro culture are revealed. Marriages between people of different social positions were forbidden. Since ancient Chamorro society was a matrilineage, children belonged to their mothers. There is a Chamorro proverb that states, "*Yanggen sina hao hu fanagu. Pues sina ha' lokkue' hu puno' hao* (You were born of me. Therefore, I have the right to kill you)."

## Duhendes

*Duhendes* are mischievous elves who live in the jungle. There is no mention of this belief among the early records on the ancient Chamorros. Even though "*duhendes*" is a Spanish word, some anthropologists think that the ancient Chamorros traditionally believed in these dwarfs or fairies. Similar elves are found in Pohnpeian (Ponapean) and Hawaiian folklore.

*Duhendes* are notorious for casting spells on children, shrinking them, and carrying them off into the jungle. The *duhendes* dance and use coconut shells to make music. Sometimes children who have been captured by the *duhendes* are unable to speak when they are found. Striking the child with an older woman's belt or calling a priest to pray for the child are believed to be the best ways to break these spells. The significance of the belt comes from an old custom of women wearing belts blessed by a priest. The burning of dung, or the application of urine from a male relative on the child could also break the spell.

# Origin Myths - No Gods or Goddesses, Just Venerated Ancestors

Every culture has myths about things they cannot understand. A **myth** is a traditional story about gods, goddesses, or heroes, and often offers an explanation for something in nature or in past events. These narrative tales explain the world view of the people. We can see the people's values in their myths. These values are that people's truth and reality. The myths of the ancient Chamorros reveal the values that we have studied. Their key value was the interdependence of humans and nature, of man and woman, and of relatives.

When early Roman Catholic priests asked the ancient Chamorros who made the heaven and earth, they got several answers. The Chamorros said, "We made the universe." The Spanish felt that this was a foolish answer. The priests did not realize that the ancient Chamorros were speaking about their ancestors. They also did not realize the interdependence the Chamorros felt with the universe, because it had been created from the body of one of their ancestors.

## Puntan Myth

Puntan and his sister, Fu'uña, were born of space and had neither a father nor a mother. They existed before the sky and earth. When it was Puntan's time to die, he instructed his sister to make a place for humans by using his chest and back to make the sky and earth, his eyes to make the sun and moon, and his eyebrows to make the rainbows. Puntan has been referred to as a god, but he is better understood as a venerated ancestor of really ancient origin. It is interesting that in Indian culture, Arjuna saw Krishna (god), and described him as having the moon and the sun for eyes.

Fray Antonio (1596) reported that the ancient Chamorros believed that they were born of a rock at Fouha bay. Every year the ancient Chamorros gathered there for a fiesta. The ancient Chamorros said that a woman gave birth to the land and to the sea, and to all that is visible. This does not necessarily contradict the Puntan Myth. In both cases a woman was creating the universe. When asked how a rock, not having eyes and not being able to eat, had given birth to men, they responded that it had given birth to two men and that one of them had become a woman. He also reported that ancestral spirits were worshipped in rocks or in whatever else strikes the Chamorros' fancy.

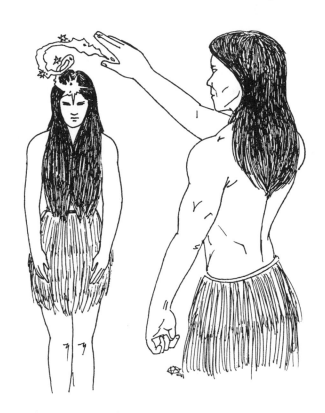

**10.4 Puntan instructs his sister Fu'uña.** Adapted from a Guam Department of Education illustration.

**10.5 Fu'uña Creates the Universe.** Adapted from a Guam Department of Education illustration.

Another version states that Fu'uña, the sister of Puntan, followed his instructions. She took the red earth of Guam and mixed it with water. Then she built a great rock called Laso de Fua. This rock divided into many smaller stones. These stones became the first people on earth. **Laso de Fua**, or "penis rock," at Fouha Bay can be seen from Fort Soledad near Umatac. Fouha Bay is the first bay north of Umatac. According to folklore, if you go to the northern part of Guam, you can see Puntan's body from the top of Mt. Santa Rosa if you look south.

**10.6  Fu'uña Creates Humans.** Adapted from a Guam Department of Education illustration.

# Guam's Adam

There is another account of how humans first came to the Mariana Islands. It is *not* an ancient Chamorro belief. Because of the reference to slaves, murder, blacksmithing, souls, hell, and a god, it seems to have been strongly influenced by the Spanish. Nevertheless, there is much in it that goes back to the ancient Chamorro fundamental truth that humans and nature are interdependent.

In a volcano (**Mt. Sasalaguan**) there lived a god named Chaife. He governed the winds, the waves, and fire. He created souls in his blacksmith shop to be his slaves. One day he was busy pounding out another soul into shape. Since he was in a hurry, he put too much wood in his oven. All of a sudden the whole place exploded in a huge eruption. Ash and stones were thrown into the air, and rivers of liquid fire began to pour down the sides of Mt. Sasalaguan.

Chaife was angry and began a search for any souls who might have escaped. He wanted to kill the lost soul.

One of the souls fell to the earth at Fouha Bay on Guam and turned to stone. The rock was near the ocean, and the waves caressed the rock's feet. Over time, the sun shone on the rock, and the rain and wind weathered it and it became a man. The man was so pleased with the beauty of Guam that he took the red earth and mixed it with water. From this clay he made sculptures of humans. Using what he had learned from Chaife, he made souls for the statues from the heat of the sun. He named these people the children of the earth.

Chaife found a child of the earth sitting by the shore on Guam. He assumed that it was his lost soul. He thought to himself, "I'm god of the wind, waves, and fire. Since the soul is on the beach, I will send a big wave to drown him." A huge wave came into the bay and covered the child of the earth. But the human soul was not killed because he turned into a fish and just swam away. Chaife did not know that he could not destroy the human because his soul came from the sun and Chaife did not control the sun.

In anger, Chaife set a great fire underneath the lagoon and boiled all the water away. But the fish did not die. When there was no water remaining, the fish turned into a *hilitai* (monitor lizard) and disappeared into the woods. Chaife turned up the fire and set the jungle on fire. As the blaze roared, Chaife could not believe his eyes. Out of the ashes the monitor lizard transformed itself into a bird that flew away.

Chaife's anger grew into a raging typhoon, for he controlled the wind. The typhoon dashed the bird against a cliff and broke its wing. But just as Chaife was about to pounce, the bird changed into a man. This child of the earth said to Chaife, "You can try with wind, waves, fire, and all your power, but you can never kill me. My soul comes from the sun." Chaife, outraged at this, said, "Your soul comes from Mt. Sasalaguan. I created your soul. You are my slave." The child of earth replied, "I'm not your slave. But you did a good job. Your soul is at Fouha Bay, and he is making souls from the heat of the sun. You see he made me, a soul from the sun, and the wisest cannot compete with me."

Chaife continued to look for his soul. But the soul wisely turned himself back into a rock, and he can still be seen today as a large rock tower at Fouha Bay.

# Myths Explain Nature

The ancient Chamorro values of subterfuge, tricks, joking, and ingenuity are best seen in the preceding Guam's Adam myth. All of these qualities were very valuable in the trying times of colonialism. The Guam's Adam myth also may reveal something about the origin of the ancient Chamorros. They may have come to the Mariana Islands to escape a volcanic eruption. However, there is a Mt. Sasalaguan on Guam. It is close to Malesso (Merizo). You can see the inter-dependence of man and nature in this myth. During the story, man was at times a rock, clay, a fish, a lizard, and a bird.

One of the purposes of myths is to explain things in nature. There is a tale of how the monitor lizard got its spots, and how the kingfisher got its colors. There are not only stories that explain the rock Laso de Fua, but others to explain Gapang Islet (Camel Rock), and the Palayi Islets just off Hagat (Agat). In all these myths ancient Chamorro values are revealed.

## How the Monitor Lizard Got Its Spots and the Rail Its Stripes

In the past, *hilitai* (monitor lizards) were black and could sing beautifully. The *hilitai* was so proud of its voice that it showed off by singing to all the other animals. The *totot* (Marianas Rose Crowned Fruit Dove) was jealous. The dove cried, "You may have a better voice than me, but my colors are prettier than yours!" This really upset the *hilitai*. He finally talked his friend the *ko'ko'* (Guam rail) into painting him. The rail agreed on the condition that the *hilitai* would paint him too. The rail painted little yellow dots all over the lizard. The *hilitai* was so impressed with the new look that he wanted to show-off in front of the other animals. The rail said, "Now wait a minute. What about painting me. You promised." The *hilitai* started painting white stripes above and below the rail's eye. He then painted thinner white

stripes on the rail's stomach. But the lizard never painted the wings and back. In a hurry to show off, he ran away. The rail was furious. When he caught the *hilitai*, he pecked him with his sharp beak. This split the *hilitai's* tongue in two. That is why monitor lizards cannot sing, and why they have a forked tongue and yellow dots on their back. And that is why the rail is striped only around the eye and on the stomach.

The importance of this story is not in the explanations for the characteristics of these animals. The real message is a core Chamorro value. People who do not meet their obligations will be punished.

The *ko'ko'* is found naturally only on the island of Guam. In an effort to preserve them, they are being introduced to Luta (Rota) and are even being raised on the U. S. mainland. The *totot* is Guam's Territorial bird. It is mostly green and has a reddish-purple cap, a light yellow and orange breast, and a bright yellow tail band.

**10.7 The monitor lizard before the rail gave him spots and a forked tongue.** Adapted from a Guam Department of Education illustration.

# Animism

Animism is the belief in the existence of a separate soul or spirit that can reside in anything. Living organisms or natural objects can be inhabited by these supernatural forces. The ancient Chamorros seem to have viewed these spirits as personal rather than impersonal spirits. They had human characteristics. An *ante* was believed to take up residence in a rock or anything else that took its fancy. For example, humans were believed to have been born from Laso de Fua, located near Umatac. In another myth the soul who escaped from Chaife turned into Laso de Fua. The most common story about a spirit inhabiting an animal is one about the legendary *utak* or *itak* (white-tailed tropic bird - *Phaethon lepturus*). It is one of the most beautiful birds in the world. They have a set of two black markings on each wing. The bird's most distinctive characteristic is the long, streaming feathers in its tail, which are longer than its body. *Utaks* feed on flying fish, other small fish, and squid. They can fly hundreds of miles in search of food. These beautiful birds can spend months at a time at sea. They nest on cliffs in the Mariana Islands. These birds are frequently seen at Two Lovers Point. Fishermen use them to help them locate schools of mahimahi. *Utaks* are noisy and they will sometimes circle a ship at sea and scream.

Sometimes an *utak* will visit a village at night. Only a few people ever hear an *utak*. Those who do hear them say they scream for several minutes over someone's house at night. Some people claim it will kill those who do not believe in it. When it screams over a house, it is an omen that someone inside will die soon, or that an unmarried girl in the house is pregnant. The latter belief is not ancient. An unwed mother was not considered shameful in ancient times. In ancient times men preferred to marry a pregnant woman, because the pregnancy was proof that she was fertile.

# SUMMARY

The ancient Chamorro religious philosophy was very practical and reasonable. It explained the creation of the universe. It explained the interdependence of humans and nature. The ancient Chamorro religious beliefs duplicated the values in their society. Ancient Chamorros knew that respect should be shown to relatives. They believed that you always had to be ready to meet your family obligations. The care of family members didn't end when a person died. Since the spirit of a person was believed to be eternal, it stood to reason that a dead person would continue to care for his or her descendants. The ancient Chamorros believed that their ancestral spirits would protect them from the *ante* that might try to harm them, and would help them in all their endeavors. Of course, this good treatment was dependent on their meeting all their obligations to their living relatives and dead ancestors. People could not expect help from the living nor the dead unless they met all of their family obligations. A violent death and a less pleasant afterlife awaited those who neglected their *ante*.

# Chapter 11
# Folklore

## INTRODUCTION

**Folklore** is traditional literature as expressed in folk tales, incantations, proverbs, riddles, songs, and prayers. Folklore has been described as a "mirror of a people." It explains nature and human nature, and serves as a means to give expression to our emotions. Folklore tells stories about proper behavior and reveals what a culture values. Folklore deals with the emotions of joy, grief, fear, jealousy, wonder, and triumph. It deals with the human characteristics of bravery, cowardice, greed, humor, grief, and love. Folklore also tells us about a people's dress, customs, economy, social structure, and environment.

Folk tales are divided into the categories of legends and myths. A **legend** is a story from the past that is popularly regarded as historical, although it cannot be verified. Many Chamorro legends are about the heroic feats of ancestors. A common theme is an aggressor who wants to prove he is the strongest. The aggressor always loses to his calm, nonaggressive opponent. As you can see, Chamorro legends usually have a moral lesson. A **myth** is a traditional story that reveals a people's world view, or explains a practice, belief, or natural phenomenon (happening). A myth is an explanatory tale that rationalizes religious beliefs and practices. For that reason the ancient Chamorro creation myths are not in this chapter. A people's myths are believed to be true stories by that people. Every society has myths about what it does not understand. Myths and legends can provide a special insight into a people's world view. Nikos Kazantzakis wrote, "Is there anything truer than truth? Yes, legend. This gives eternal meaning to the ephemeral truth." Chamorro myths and legends show how humanity and nature are interwoven and interdependent.

Folk tales reveal something about the culture of the ancient Chamorros. As you read a legend or myth, read "between the lines" to see the message behind the story. For example, the well-known legend of Sirena tells us that people should work before they play; that children should obey their parents; and that parents will be sorry if they curse their children. In many Chamorro legends, especially those during colonization, the hero does not win by strength, but rather by subterfuge and cleverness.

Ideally, folk tales should be heard and not read. Another limitation is that a translated story loses some of its power and spirit. The poetry and imagery is also often lost. Included in this chapter are a few of the folk tales of the Mariana Islands and a brief list of superstitions, proverbs, and songs from the Mariana Islands.

## FOLK TALES

## How Gadao Became Chief

Long ago Guam had a mountain twice as high as Mt. Lamlam. But about 1420 A.D. a great hero leveled the mountain. This was just one amazing deed that led to **Gadao** becoming chief of all of Guam.

Gadao was the *maga'lahi* of Inarajan. As time passed he became leader of all the southern villages. Umatac came under his leadership after a joint fishing trip with the men from Umatac. The men were spear fishing beyond the reef at Umatac. Each man carried a bamboo spear and a basket to carry home the fish. They had almost filled the baskets and were just diving for the last fish. Since men fasted before and during a fishing trip, they were hungry. The fish caught last would be eaten first when they returned to shore. On this last dive a huge shark harassed them. Gadao saved the lives of the fishermen by killing the shark. As the shark circled closer and closer, he patiently waited. Just as the shark came in with its huge jaws open wide, Gadao thrust his spear into the shark's throat.

The men returned home overjoyed that they were still alive. The village of Umatac felt obligated toward Gadao because he had saved the lives of their most important chiefs. In celebration, they had a great feast with the fish they had caught.

Gadao's fame spread all over the island. The leaders from each village met in a great council, during the rainy season that year. They all recognized the great strength and courage of

**11.1 Gadao and the Shark.** Adapted from a Guam Department of Education illustration.

Gadao. They decided that if he could perform three more heroic tasks, they would make him chief of the entire island. Gadao said that he accepted the challenge.

The challenge was to swim around the island 25 times without an aid of any kind. Next, he had to break a coconut tree into ten pieces. Finally, he had to raze the largest mountain on Guam.

In the middle of the rainy season he began. Gadao easily swam around the island 25 times in one hour. He rested one day and then grabbed a big coconut tree. He shook the tree so hard that coconuts flew for miles around. He shook it so hard that it broke up into ten pieces. After a few weeks he decided to level the mountain. First he uprooted a big tree. Then he broke off a huge limb. He used this as a digging stick and shovel. He tackled the mountain. After about two days he had dug down to a rock about half the size of Mt. Lamlam. He broke up the rock with the huge limb and threw the stones south to Umatac. The mountains around Umatac village were formed in this way.

Finally, he asked his sons to carry one rock to Agaña Bay. He wanted them to block the harbor against foreign invasion. The boys were told to be home before daylight. The boys carried the rock to the sea, but only got to the point on the reef between Piti and Asan. When they saw Venus, the morning star, they thought it was dawn. Not wanting to be late, they dropped the rock. It can still be seen on the reef, where they left it. Today people call it Camel Rock, but in Chamorro it is called **Gapang**, meaning "unfinished task." The morning star is called "*Dinague Laolao* (Fooled by the Twinkling Star)."

Now you know how Gadao became chief of Guam, how Gapang Rock got there, and how Venus got its name. For more on Gadao see the chapter on "Arts and Skills," under the subheading "Petroglyphs."

# Why Guam is Narrow in the Middle

Did you know that Guam would not be here today if a giant parrotfish (*Scaridae*) had not been stopped? The monster fish was determined to eat up Guam. Modern versions say the fish was punishing the people of Guam because they had sinned or because they had married outsiders. In the older versions, it is more likely that the cause was a broken taboo. For example, perhaps an ancient *maga'lahi* took a *manachang* lover or unknowingly married a distant relative of the same clan. These were strict taboos that would not have gone unpunished. A **taboo** is a rule, the violation of which means severe, automatic punishment.

Before the taboo was broken, the people were prosperous, happy, and content. After the taboo was broken, a great drought and famine came. The people pleaded with their *ante* (ancestral spirits or souls) to spare them. They pleaded with their ancestral skulls, which they called *maranan uchan* (a miraculous thing for rain). Still there was no relief.

To make matters worse, the huge parrotfish began to devour the island. Ordinary parrotfish have a beak especially designed to eat coral. If you ever try to spear a parrotfish, you can see this for yourself. When they swim away from you, they excrete the undigested rock as sand. Small parrotfish hide in caves along the reef face at night. At night a parrotfish secretes a slippery film over itself as camouflage. That is the reason the

11.2 **The people pleaded with their ancestral spirits to spare them.** Adapted from a Guam Department of Education illustration.

parrotfish is sometimes called *palakse'* (slippery) in Chamorro. If you catch this fish and cut the stomach open, you can see the coral rocks inside.

But this fish was not an ordinary parrotfish. It was more like the *atuhong* (large bump-head parrotfish). This huge fish was determined to destroy Guam. It intended to eat widthwise through the island, thereby dividing Guam into two islands. Then the fish intended to eat the island in half lengthwise, so there would be four islands. The fish planned to continue this process until there was nothing left of Guam. It was determined to destroy the entire island because a leader had broken a taboo.

All the men called on their ancestral spirits for help in catching the fish. Each day they went out to save the island. Meanwhile the fish ate at Agaña Bay, and then swam around and ate at Pago Bay. Every day the island got narrower and narrower in the middle.

The women of Agaña always bathed at Agaña Spring. One day they found lemon peels floating in the spring. The women of Pago were known to use lemon peels to scent their hair. The *maga'haga* (highest-ranking woman in a village) was the first to see the connection. The parrotfish had almost bored a tunnel through the island. At the rate the fish was going, Guam would soon be cut in half.

Since the men did not seem capable of stopping the fish, the *maga'haga* decided to take action. She directed the women to cut their hair. With the long strands of hair, they began to weave a strong, fine net. They laid the net in the water on the bottom of the spring. The women tied ropes to the circumference of the net. That evening when the fish came into the the spring to sleep, the women were ready. They surrounded the spring. Each woman had a rope attached to the net. When the fish was all settled, the *maga'haga* gave the order to heave and pull up the net.

The women caught the fish and saved the entire island. Some of the fish was eaten at a great feast. The rest of the huge fish was salted to preserve it. The women of Agaña shared the salted fish with all the other villages. This ended Guam's famine. Soon afterwards, the rains came and the crops grew. Once again the island of Guam became happy and prosperous, and the people were content.

Now you know why Guam is narrow in the middle and why women were held in such high esteem in ancient Guam. After all, it was the women and not the men who saved the island. In later versions of this legend, it was the Virgin Mary, instead of the women of Guam, who saved the island.

11.3 **Why Guam is Narrow in the Middle.** Adapted from a Guam Department of Education illustration.

# Alupang Island

Long ago there were two mighty chiefs. One was **Alu**, *maga'lahi* of Oka. He controlled the island of Guam from Asan to Dededo. The other *maga'lahi* was **Pang** of Inarajan. Pang heard that Alu was bragging about being the mightiest chief of all. Pang decided to see for himself. He sailed to Oka, which is in Tamuning. When he arrived he found that Alu was not home. Alu's wife said that her husband was catching fish for a morning meal.

Alu's son was at home that morning. He was a strapping boy with more strength than most men. He had caught two dozen sea crabs that morning. When one of the crabs escaped the pen and hid under a young coconut tree, he simply uprooted the tree and snatched up the crab. Pang was impressed by this show of strength.

Alu's wife offered Pang something to drink, but he refused. He said that he was not thirsty. When he still refused a drink even after she insisted, she realized that something was wrong. Alu's wife then inquired about the reason for Pang's visit. He said that he came to find out who was the mightiest man on Guam. He had heard people say that a man here named Alu thinks he is the mightiest man of all.

Alu's son heard this and rushed to Pang. He said, "I am the son of my father and you'll have to take me on first. Why bother my father if you cannot handle me?" Fortunately for the brave boy, his mother grabbed him around the waist and held him. She admonished him, "You behave yourself and don't anger our guest."

Alu was nearby and heard this commotion. He hurried home and asked, "What is going on?" Alu's son said, "This man wants to test your strength, but I told him he has to try me first."

Alu calmly said, "All in good time. First comes first, and I am hungry." He approached Pang and said, "If you don't mind, let's eat and then we will do whatever there is to be done. And for you, young man, fetch me a coconut."

His son grabbed a tree and shook the coconuts down. He then handed one of the coconuts to his father. Alu took the nut in both hands and squeezed it so hard that the grated coconut oozed through the husk. Pang was impressed, but not frightened. Pang refused to join Alu in the meal.

When Alu finished, he asked Pang, "What is your mission." Pang explained, "I have to know who is the mightiest." Alu said, "Well, let's take the mess away from the village." They walked toward Agaña. The two giants finally turned and faced each other and the fight began.

The fight was ferocious. The earth trembled, lightning flashed, and the noise was deafening. They battled all day. Their feet punched holes on the beach and on the reef. When darkness came, they were still going at it. Just before midnight Alu struck a fatal blow to the side of Pang's head. Pang flew back into the water. Alu then broke off a massive chunk of rock from Satpon Point (Hospital Point). He placed it on top of the fallen Pang. The lonely island off Oka-Tamuning in Agaña Bay is that grave marker. It is called Alupang Island in honor of the two great *maga'lahi* who fought this legendary battle. Even today you can still hear Alu's and Pang's spirits fighting when we have a thunder and lightning storm.

# *Puntan Patgon*

At the northernmost end of Hinapsan Beach in northern Guam, there is a giant footprint in the rock. It is about two-thirds of the way between Tarague Beach and Ritidian Point. The footprint has been there for centuries.

Long ago, in the time of the ancient Chamorros, Guam was inhabited by giants. On Apurguan Beach there lived the biggest and strongest of these giants. He was called **Masala**. As strong as he was of body, he was nevertheless weak. He let his mind be ruled by conceit and fear. He believed that it was not possible or morally right for anyone to exist who was stronger than he. Masala took great pride in being known as the strongest man in the world. He took too much pride in himself.

Fate, the trickster, decided that to this man should be born a son who would grow to be stronger than Masala. At first the father was proud to have begotten such a child. But when the child began to get more attention and praise than he did, it became intolerable. Masala knew that when his son came of age, he would go to the village of his mother's clan. Sons in those days did not remain in the villages to which they were born. The children belonged to the clan of their mother. In order to claim his family inheritance and land-use privileges, he would go to his clan's land at about the age of fourteen. The father was envious of the attention his son received. He also feared his son would some day fight for another village and he might have to face his son in battle.

The youngster, seeing the blazing anger in his father's face, fled from the spot in horror. He was hotly pursued by the enraged Masala. The boy ran as fast as he could, building up tremendous speed. He was running for his life and he knew it. The wind whistled in his wake. Knowing that he would not be safe on Guam, the boy ran toward Luta (Rota). That was where his mother was from. That was where his clan lived. When he reached the edge of the ocean, he pushed off with all his might, leaving his gigantic footprint in the rock. The leap carried him all the way to Luta. The footprint where he landed can still be seen in the rock on Luta's reef. In commemoration of this feat, the take-off point on Guam has been named Puntan Patgon (Child's Point).

**11.4 A father is jealous and frightened by his son's strength.** Adapted from a Guam Department of Education illustration.

Brooding over these bitter thoughts, Masala walked along a lonely beach one night. Up ahead he saw his three-year-old son chasing a crab. The boy was using a torch for a light. The crab ran into its hole at the base of a mature coconut tree. His son lay down and reached his arm down into the hole. With the other arm he held his torch. The father could see the tremendous strength of his son. His young muscles writhed like serpents in the flickering light of the torch. The father, trying to hide his anger, fear, and jealousy, said, "What are you up to now?" The boy answered, "Crab hunting, father, but this one, a huge fellow, has hidden itself among the roots of the tree. But I'll show you how to get it. Please hold my torch." The boy stood up and put his arms around the tree. Then he squatted and hugged the tree. With a thunderous grunt the boy uprooted the coconut tree, as if it were a weed.

The boy threw the tree aside and grabbed the huge crab. Triumphantly he held it up for his father to see. Instead of the smile of approval the boy expected, he saw a flash of anger on his father's face. The father realized that he must kill his son now. If he waited, the boy would soon be too strong for him.

**11.5 *Puntan Patgon*.** Adapted from a Guam Department of Education illustration.

# Okkodu: A Legend of the Mariana Islands

Years ago on the island of Guam there lived a young man from Orote Village named Okkodu. He was big, strong, and smart. Okkodu was noted for playing tricks on people. He was also a braggart and arrogant.

Once upon a time, the *maga'lahi* (high chief) of Songsong on the island of Luta (Rota) was seriously ill. To make matters even worse, a typhoon struck that lovely island. The people of Luta were without hope and were convinced that the beloved leader, Sunama, was dying. Suddenly,

117

their depression turned to joy when the Chamorros of Luta saw a *sakman* (oceangoing sailing canoe) approaching from the direction of Guam. The ease with which Okkodu sailed through the storm was viewed as a good omen by the people of Luta. They greeted him with open arms. When Okkodu found out how sick the *maga'lahi* was, he quickly devised a plan to take advantage of the situation. He promised the people of Luta that he would cure Sunama. The prankster insisted that the most beautiful girl on the island accompany him while he searched in the jungle for healing herbs.

After several days, Okkodu and the beautiful girl, Sosanbra, returned with the herbs. Okkodu, the trickster, told the people to make a tea by boiling the special herbs in water, but to hold off administering the medicine until he raised the sail on his sakman.

Okkodu sailed out into the harbor. Sosanbra, who was in love with Okkodu, was hiding under some mats on the floor of the outrigger canoe. When Okkodu was a safe distance away, he raised his sail. The *suruhana* (herb doctor) took the herb tea to Sunama. When the weak chief tasted the medicine, he immediately died. A chorus of mournful wails came from the women in the village. The men of Songsong began to beat their chests and cry out. A man yelled, "Okkodu! Okkodu! Our chief is dead. What do we do now?" Okkodu shouted back, "Bury him before he starts to stink!"

Although the men of Luta tried to catch and punish Okkodu, they were unsuccessful. Years later, Okkodu became a chief on Luta. An island-wide drought forced the people to dig wells in order to get fresh water. Okkodu challenged another high chief to a well-digging contest. For the first time in his life, Okkodu was defeated. The infamous braggart was so embarrassed by his defeat that he jumped from Luta's northernmost point into the sea. Okkodu left two stone-impressed footprints on the clifftop. According to legend, his body turned to stone and it can be seen in the water offshore. At low tide Okkodu's profile can be seen in the cliff face.

# SUPERSTITIONS

Ancient Chamorros probably did not have anything they regarded as a superstition in the sense we use the word today. They did not have the conflict that we have between the scientific and the spiritual realm. **Superstition** is a belief that many helpful and harmful supernatural forces exist, and that certain actions will anger or pacify them. People tend to be a little embarrassed about their superstitions, but almost everyone has at least one. For example, many Americans think that if you walk under a ladder, or if a black cat crosses your path, you will be unlucky. Some people carry a rabbit's foot for good luck. These superstitions rely on a magical force called luck.

Superstitions are often used to explain things in nature. For example, occasionally there are population explosions of red algae in the ocean. The Red Sea is named for this phenomenon. An Alabama college football team, the Crimson Tide, is named for this occurrence in the Gulf of Mexico. On Guam, this phenomenon is explained as the blood of Padre Sanvitores, whose body was dropped into Tumon Bay by Matapang and Hirao from their canoe in 1672. As you can see, there is a conflict between scientific reality and our day-to-day beliefs. In this case, the superstition is a belief that attempts to explain an event in nature. It demonstrates a false conception of causation.

Children who lose their baby teeth put them under their pillow. They do this so that they will receive money from the tooth fairy. Folklorists claim that this custom teaches children that their bodies are valuable and to take good care of their bodies. Not too many years ago children on Guam threw their baby teeth on the roofs of their houses. They chanted, "*Chaka, chaka, estaque i nifen-hu eata tulaika yan un oru* (Rat, rat, here is my dull tin tooth. Bring me a sharp gold tooth)." This custom taught children that it was important to have sound teeth with which to open things and crack betel nuts. In each of these cases the superstition was used to teach a lesson.

Some superstitions are a little extra encouragement to do something that we should do. For example, husbands were expected to kill a chicken and make fresh chicken soup for their wives who had just given birth. A good high-protein meal would help a breastfeeding mother. This practice would be good for the mother and the child.

Most superstitions are *not* taboos. A taboo is a rule, the violation of which means severe, automatic punishment. Breaking a taboo means that society or the supernatural will punish you. In the case of breaking a superstition, a person is usually not punished by society. For example, society does not punish people who walk under ladders. In the Mariana Islands many people believe that if you trespass in the jungle you will get sick. The punishment for those who do not follow a superstition is left up to a supernatural force, like luck or ancestral spirits.

In a sense, our reality is what we and a significant number of people around us believe to be true. Did George Washington chop down the cherry tree? No, not really, but many people believe it. Many people believe in ghosts even though they cannot be scientifically proven. Ghosts are not part of some people's 20th century reality, but for some, ghosts are just as real as other forces we cannot see, like the force of gravity. For some the *taotaomo'na*, *utak*, white lady, and *duhende* are real, and for others, they are superstitions.

Some of these beliefs go back to ancient times, like these taboos: Do not disobey the *makahna* or he will make you sick. Do not gaze on the body of your dead grandmother or you will go blind. Do not fish near a village where a woman has recently delivered a baby. Pregnant women should avoid areas associated with ancestral spirits or they will have a difficult delivery. Do not trespass, talk loudly, use bad words or do anything offensive in the jungle, or you will get *pukpuk maipe* (a swollen mouth or feet or some other part of your body). Do not resist the urge to pinch a child or the child will get sick. This custom is called *matgodai*. Other beliefs are clearly of more recent origin; for example: Behave during Lent or the *babwan kuresma* (wild boar) will chase naughty children.

Many superstitions are modern. Some have come to Guam through the process of cultural diffusion. **Cultural diffusion** is the process by which customs and discoveries are borrowed from other cultures. Cultural diffusion takes place when there is contact between cultures.

It is interesting to note the number of Chamorro superstitions that deal with women and children. This fact seems to demonstrate the ancient Chamorros' concern for the safety and well-being of women and children. It also reflects the old belief that they were more vulnerable to the *ante* (ancestral spirits) because women and children did not live on their clan's land. Girls moved to their husband's land when they married. Boys moved to their clan land when they reached puberty. For a full explanation of this, see the chapter on "Social Structure."

# PROVERBS AND SONGS

A **proverb** is an old and frequently repeated saying of advice or wisdom. Proverbs, like all folklore, mirror the beliefs and values of the people. For example, in American culture, the proberb "A rolling stone gathers no moss" reveals that Americans think it is important to be busy and to keep moving. Time is to not be wasted. Standing still means stagnation. Below are a few Chamorro proverbs and songs that Laura Thompson collected. The songs are *chamorritas*. The *chamorrita* is a Chamorro folk song sung in four-line stanzas. It has a single tune to which many different songs are created. Oftentimes it is made up as the singer goes along. The *chamorrita* usually has two couplets and a single tune. Usually, the second and fourth lines of the verse rhyme. For additional information on *chamorritas*, see the chapter on "Arts, Skill, and Education." Many of these proverbs and songs have roots in ancient Chamorro culture.

---

*Desde pa'go para mo'na u sen makkat*
    From now on life will be more difficult,
*i lina'la' sa' taigui i ante ni'*
    Lacking the one who
*muna'fanggagai sastansia todu.*
    Was the life of all . . .

---

*An humanao hao tumalaya*
    When you go net-fishing
*Chuchule' i talaya-mu,*
    Take along your net,
*Yan kontodu i guagua'-mu*
    And also your basket
*Ya un sisini i kinenne'-mu.*
    And fill it with the catch.

---

*An numa' piniti hao taotao*
    When you hurt somebody,
*Nangga ma na' piniti-mu;*
    Be expecting to be in pain;
*Maseha apmamam na tiempo,*
    For even if it takes time,
*Un apasi sa' dibi-mu.*
    Surely you'll pay for the pain you caused.

*Gaige i piniten nana*
  What sweet pain my mother must have had
*Anai hu chochochop sisu-ña:*
  To feel me sucking at her breast:
*Siempre guahu u pinitiyi*
  Surely she should feel for me
*Sa' guahu finañagu-ña.*
  Because she gave birth to me.

---

*Facho'cho ya un chocho*
  Work and you will eat.

---

*Maolekña manggagao ya ti ma na'i*
  It is better to ask and not be given than to
*ki ma na'i ya ti ma agradesi.*
  Give and not have it appreciated.

---

Source: *Guam and Its People*, by Laura Maud Thompson. The original text has been re-translated and put in modern orthography by Ann Rivera of the Guam Department of Education Bilingual and Bicultural Program.

*No hai muettu sin achaki.*
  There is no death without an illness.
*Taya' mina'lak sin hinemhum.*
  There is no brightness without darkness.
*Taya' tatautau sin anining.*
  There is no body without its shadow.
*Taya' finatai sin sina'pit.*
  There is no death without suffering.
*Taya' aksion sin rason.*
  There is no action without a reason.

Source: "Chamorro Proverbs," by Anthony J. Ramirez.

# SUMMARY

Folklore is traditional literature as expressed in folk tales, incantations, proverbs, riddles, songs, and prayers. It is the "mirror of a people." As students of culture examine folklore, they should try to understand what it reveals about the culture.

Folk tales are divided into the categories of legends and myths. A legend is a story from the past that is popularly regarded as historical, although it cannot be verified. A myth is a traditional story that reveals a people's world view, or explains a practice, belief, or natural phenomenon (happening).

Finally, a list of superstitions, proverbs, and songs from the Mariana Islands was presented. A superstition is a belief that many helpful and harmful supernatural forces exist and that certain actions will anger or pacify them. A proverb is an old and frequently repeated saying of advice or wisdom. A few of the proverbs and songs of Guam were presented. The *chamorrita* is a Chamorro folk song sung in four-line stanzas.

# Chapter 12
# Customs and Festivities

## INTRODUCTION

**Customs** are the habits and capabilities that are socially learned, performed, and transmitted. Sometimes customs guide day-to-day behavior. For example, the way we greet people or how we finalize an agreement are customs. Oftentimes customs are associated with a culture's institutions. Institutions were deliberately created by humans to help them function effectively and efficiently. For example, we have the institutions of marriage, kinship, government, religion, and school. An **institution** is a system of accepted rules that have grown up around a major social function.

Throughout our lives we perform customary rites of passage or life-crisis rites. **Rites of passage** are the formal behaviors that recognize a person's change from one social status to another. Typical rites of passage are those that accompany birth, the attainment of adult status, marriage, and death.

Around institutions and rites of passage, and even just day-to-day behavior, certain habits or practices develop. They are customs. Unlike the institutions they are associated with, customs are not created deliberately. They develop in an unconscious way. Humans work out behavior patterns on a trial-and-error basis. The good ones are passed on to each new generation as norms. A **norm** is a group-shared expectation of behavior. As we study ancient Chamorro customs, you will be expected to determine if the customs are associated with an institution, rite of passage, or day-to-day behavior.

Customs are sometimes called folkways. **Folkways** are the learned shared behavior common to a people. Over time some folkways or customs become mores. **Mores** are folkways or norms regarded as necessary for the welfare of society. Mores define what is right and wrong behavior. A violation of a **mor** (singular of mores) produces moral revulsion and justifies the use of sanctions against the violator. Violators of mores are punished. Most of our mores today are laws, but some mores are not. For example, there is no law against wearing a swimsuit to church. It is just not done. It is considered wrong. Throughout this section you will be expected to differentiate between ancient Chamorro folkways and mores.

Central to all ancient Chamorro customs is the principle of reciprocity. **Reciprocity** is the continuing process by which actions toward one party are returned. It was not just a simple matter of "you help me roll my log and I'll help you roll your log." That would be a payback. It is more like, "I cause; you cause." Reciprocity is an ongoing process. It begins a cycle of obligation that has no end. It weaves a pattern of interdependency for humans and their descendants. Reciprocity can be seen in most ancient Chamorro behavior. It takes the form of *chenchule'* (donation), *ayudu* (help), and *emmok* (revenge). In ancient Chamorro society gifts or assistance could be initially rejected. However, they could not be refused if the donator persisted, even though it would obligate the recipient. This ancient Chamorro process wove a web of interdependency. Below are a few examples:

If a sister or female cousin presented *ålas* (tortoiseshell money) to a Chamorro, he or she was obligated to give her land use or whatever else she wanted.

*Ika* was a funeral offering given to the family of a deceased person. Receiving *ika* obligated the family to reciprocate to the donor's family when they had a death in their family.

Master craftspersons could not refuse to teach an apprentice who gave him or her *ålas*. Nevertheless, the craftsperson could expect a gift for every single professional detail taught.

A person who neglected family obligations was condemned not to receive any aid. This was mortifying.

Insults to a chief had to be avenged by the entire community.

Culture forms a network or pattern of behaviors based on the society's structure of reality. Therefore, look for the ancient Chamorro basic values (discussed in the chapters on "Beliefs, Attitudes, and Values" and "Religion") in all of their customs.

# MARRIAGE

Every culture has its own marriage customs. There are rules that forbid some people to marry and rules that make it desirable for others to marry. Societies have rules of chastity or rules of license. Marriage is usually a legal contract defining the way in which man and wife should live together and the economic conditions of their union. Marriage is a public ceremony. It is important to the man and wife and their relatives. A marriage and its end through divorce or death is subject to fixed traditional rules.

Some cultures practice polygamy and others practice monogamy. **Polygamy** is the custom of having more than one spouse. A **spouse** is a husband or wife. Polygamy has two forms, polygyny and polyandry. **Polygyny** is the custom of having more than one wife at a time. **Polyandry** is the custom of having more than one husband at a time. **Monogamy** is the custom of having one spouse at a time.

The ancient Chamorros practiced monogamy. The ancient Chamorros practiced endogamy with regard to caste and exogamy with regard to clan. **Endogamy** is the custom of marrying within a specified social group. Castes are ranked social groups into which members are born and must remain for life. *Chamorri* (high caste) had to marry *chamorri*. *Manachang* (low caste) had to marry *manachang*. **Exogamy** is the custom of marrying out of a specified social group. The ancient Chamorros had to marry outside of their clan. A **clan** is a group of two or more family lines who are, or think they are, descended from a common ancestor.

Below are some of the rules that governed the institution of marriage in ancient Chamorro society:

Incest taboos stated that men could not marry their sisters, first cousins, nieces, or daughters, even if they were adopted, nor could they marry a clan member.

Chaste women could not marry.

Marriages were usually monogamous.

Widows and orphaned children were taken care of by their father's brother, unless the mother returned to her relatives.

A gift in *ålas* (tortoiseshell money) and/or labor was given to the bride's family.

Marriages were endogamous in regard to caste and exogamous in regard to clan.

The groom provided the house and utensils, which were called *guahayi* (dowry or enrichment).

If an ancient Chamorro man saved a male of higher rank, the rescued person was obligated to marry the rescuer's daughter or sister.

## Marriage Rites

The ancient Chamorros had a coming-out party for young people of marriageable age. It was a great celebration and feast.

When a couple decided to marry, the groom gave a gift to the bride's father. It was called *a'ok*. The father then entertained the groom and sent him a gift. In some cases the groom supplemented his gift by working for the bride's father. Sometimes this labor lasted as long as a year. It is important to note that in all cases the father's gift to the groom was only a token gift. It was not worth nearly as much as the groom's gift. For this reason some anthropologists have called the groom's gift a bride-price. They have reported that the groom bought the bride from her father. This was not the case. The bride did not become the property of the groom. After the marriage, the bride was free to leave her husband, even after there were children. *A'ok* was a non-refundable gift and not the purchase price for a slave.

After the presentation of a gift to the father, the wedding party went to the groom's home. There the groom gave a house and all the furnishings for it to the bride. This included baskets, mats, gourds, pottery, coconut graters, mortars, and pestles. After these two steps, the couple were married. The groom's gift to the bride was called the *guahayi* (dowry or enrichment). It belonged to her and, if the marriage ended, she could take all the furnishings. She could even destroy the house if she so desired.

Accounts from the 1800s give more details and seem to hold roughly to the pattern described in the older accounts. Boys usually married between the ages of 15 and 18. Girls generally married between the ages of 12 and 15. Even so, if girls married early, they seldom had children until at least 14. When a young man desired a bride, he asked his mother or another close female relative to ask for the girl's hand in marriage. The Chamorros had a subtle way of communicating this without speech. It was the custom to offer guests betel nut, leaf, and quicklime. If a woman offered the betel nut to the host, this meant that on behalf of her son she was asking for the host's daughter's hand in marriage. The betel nut was carried in a case called a *saluu*.

If the hosts did not want their daughter to marry this young man, they offered betel nut the moment the visitor arrived. This practice saved both parties the embarrassment of the proposal and the rejection. If the host accepted the betel nut, they then asked the purpose of the visit, as if they did not know. The female relative of the prospective groom then said, "I have come to ask for your daughter for my son (or grandson, or brother, or whatever the case)." The mother of the prospective bride replied that she could not promise anything without the advice of the grandmother. Actually, this was a stall to give the entire family a chance to discuss the proposal. The grandmother was then approached in the same manner. If the bride-to-be approved of the young man, the proposal was accepted during a second visit by the groom's mediating female relative.

From then on the suitor was obligated to assume the responsibility of his proposal. He demonstrated his skills in gardening, fishing, tree climbing, and canoe handling by working for his prospective bride's family. Young men considered excelling in these abilities a point of honor.

People invited to the wedding sent a *kottot* of rice. A *kottot* was a rectangular woven pandanus basket used to package a gift of rice. A few days before the wedding the relatives on both sides of the marriage ceremoniously beat and cleaned this rice. The soaked rice was crushed and coconut pulp was added to make a paste. This was then formed into pellets of rice for each guest. A portion of this was diluted in the sap of young coconuts (*manha*) in a wooden mortar to form a clear broth called *laulau*. Guests were allowed to take the wooden mortar home. On the day before the wedding, the female relatives cooked *lemmai* (breadfruit) and *hutu* (seeds from wild breadfruit, *dokdok*), root crops like *suni* (taro) and *dagu* (yam), and *guihan* (fish). The men gathered wood and constructed a *palapåla* (temporary shelter, or pavilion). It was thatched with coconut leaves.

On the eve of the marriage the families from both sides brought *chenchule'* (donations of food or money) to the young man's mother. Root crops, breadfruit, bananas, rice, fish, salt, and betel nut were taken to her. After betel nut was passed around, supper was served. A pandanus mat three feet wide and as long as the shelter was laid down. The food was set out at place settings. First, one group came into the shelter and collected their food. They took the food home to eat so the next group could be served. On and on, it went like that until all were fed. Finally, there were games and dancing, which lasted all night.

The next morning at daybreak most of the relatives of the groom went to the bride's house. Some had to stay and prepare food for later in the day. When they arrived at the house of the bride's father, they were served betel nut. The bride was given to the groom and they were officially married. Breakfast was served on pandanus mats in the *palapåla*. The groom's relatives were seated, first the females and then the males in order of their rank. Then the same was done for the bride's relatives. The mother of the bride and groom and the highest-ranking guests were served *hineksa' sinagan*, the largest pyramid-shaped rice cake (7 *gantas* of rice; by today's use of this term this would be 7 gallons; however, Freycinet reports it as 14 liters). This cake was placed on a platter called a *satghe*, which was supported by a litter. It took two men to carry it. The mother of the bride and the mother of the groom had the *hineksa' sinagan* presented to the eldest sisters of their husbands. They sent the gift to the eldest sisters of their husbands. The gift continued to circulate from one eldest sister to another until it reached the oldest female member of each family. She alone could serve the rice cake. She served it to all the relatives to whom it had been presented. Next, the second-ranked guests were presented *patcha*, which were smaller pyramid rice cakes. Each of these cakes contained two *gantas* of rice. Finally *hufot*, a small rice cake, was presented to the least-distinguished guests. It was circular and was two inches thick. It contained one-eighth liter of rice by Freycinet's estimate and was wrapped in a leaf.

After the breakfast with the bride's family the wedding guests went to the groom's house. A similar ceremony took place in which the bride's relatives were seated first and served according to rank. The *guahayi* then took place. The bride took possession of the house and all its furnishings.

# DIVORCE

Divorce was the wife's prerogative. If angered, she could have a divorce simply by leaving her husband's house. Women got the children and all the possessions in the house when there was a divorce. Usually she would return to the house of her parents or another close relative. Even during a separation the wife's relatives could pillage the husband's house. During the separation, the children would not acknowledge their father. The husband's relatives would often go to the wife and beg her to return. A man was strongly encouraged to treat his wife well. Since the husband depended on his relatives for a bride gift, his relatives often supported the wife. They had a real stake in the success of the marriage.

**12.1 Divorce Settlement**

If a husband committed adultery, the wife and her family had the right to kill her unfaithful husband. More frequently, the wife of an unfaithful husband and her friends adorned themselves as men and made fun of the guilty husband. The wife and her friends had the right to destroy the husband's garden and house, and the right to take his possessions.

If a wife committed adultery, the rules were very different. Although adultery was taboo for men and women, the penalties were less severe for a woman. A man was likely to pardon his wife, at the insistence of his relatives. Accounts vary on what a man could do. Some say that the aggrieved husband could not do anything to his wife. Nevertheless, the husband could kill his wife's lover. Other accounts say that a man was disgraced if he took his wife back. These accounts say he could banish his wife and deprive her of the house possessions, but not the children. If his wife

remarried, the children would look on the second husband as their father. The children belonged to the mother's clan and never the father's clan.

# CHILDBIRTH

Most cultures have taboos for pregnant women. Today most Chamorro superstitions revolve around childbirth. These prohibitions are intended to promote the prenatal care of the child and to protect the mother. For example, pregnant women should not have to do heavy work.

In ancient times the first time a woman was pregnant she visited her father or the *maga'lahi* (village chief). Her friends and relatives then brought her presents. When it was time to deliver, she went to the home of the relative where she would be most favored with gifts.

Women were expected not to complain during the delivery, regardless of the pain. During childbirth the women were clothed from the waist down with a mat. They were anointed with coconut oil and wore garlands of jasmine and flowers.

When labor started the *maga'haga* (highest-ranking woman in a village) was informed. Next, all the female relatives of the oldest branch of her husband's and her family were notified. They all had to come, including her aunts, and stay with her to help in the delivery. Other relatives of lower rank, like her sisters, cousins, and nieces, could come too.

The husband's sisters brought gourds of water to wash the newborn and the mother. The wife's brothers brought the food, which was supplied by her clan.

It was the husband's family's responsibility to protect the house. It was also their duty to make sure the house was in good repair and furnished with plenty of utensils and all other necessary articles.

Relations of all ages were expected to bring a *kottot* (rectangular woven pandanus basket used for presenting a gift of rice) of rice surmounted by fish. The only exceptions were the husband's sisters. They had already brought the gourds of water.

Deference was shown, if the father was of high rank, by sprinkling finely crushed rice on the steps of the house as a token of respect.

The food was shared in a feast to celebrate the birth of the child.

The baby was carried in a cradle made of woven pandanus, with a small board in the bottom. The basket was attached to a stick and could be carried over the shoulder when they traveled.

The father called the child *ninisho* (the one whom I begot). The father was referred to as *i lumilis* (the one who engendered or begot). The mother was referred to as *i fumagnago* (the one who gave birth or bore).

Ancient Chamorros belonged to their mother's clan. All over the world clans are often named after fish, plants (especially trees), or animals. The Chamorro family name "Ayuyu - (coconut crab)" and the fish names for some *taotaomo'nas* are probably survivals of old clan names. Children were given descriptive names as well. They were named for the talents or virtues of their ancestors or after useful objects. For example, one name was "Agad-gna," which meant "deft in the art of steering canoes." For a complete list of either action or descriptive Chamorro names see Anthony J. Ramirez, "Traditional Chamorro Surnames."

## Ancient Chamorro Names

**Male**

| | | | |
|---|---|---|---|
| Agua'lin | Hag'man | Osi | Sunamo |
| Ama | Hineti | Poyo | Taga |
| Ayhi | Hirao or Hurao | Quipuha | Toca |
| Ayihi | Mapuha | Signaro | Yay |
| Buyugo | Maripego | Sinaro | Yula' |
| Cha'fa'e | Mata'pang | Soom | **Female** |
| Chelef | Nufa | Soon | Mominasaria |
| Fataluerno | Nunn | Sunama | Sosanbra |
| Guiran | | | |

## Names for Skills, Virtues, or Faults

Agad-gna - deft in the art of steering canoes

Faulos-gna - fortunate navigator

Gof-higam - skilled handling an adze

Gof-sipek - skilled fisherman

Gof-tugtcha - skilled in throwing a lance

Massongsong - who settled village

Misgnon - patient

Nineti - ingenious

Tai-agnao - fearless

Tai-gualo - lazy

## *Taotaomo'na* or Legendary Names

| Female | Male | | |
|---|---|---|---|
| Fu'uña | Alu | Gamson (octopus) | Pang |
| Gonga | Anufat | Gatos (100) | Taga |
| | Chaife | Malaguana | Talage |
| | Gadao (grouper) | Mapappa | |
| | Masala | | |

## Tribe Names

Ruehan - Chamorros of west Saipan

Catau - Chamorros of east Saipan

Gani - Chamorros from the Mariana Islands north of Saipan. Literally, *gani* means "run around or stall." This name could refer to the fact that these people were forcibly moved by the Spanish from the northern islands to Inalajan and other Southern areas on Guam from 1699-1703.

# CHILDHOOD

The ties between a child and his or her parents and their relatives form the basis for kinship. Scientific explorers in the early 1800s said that "Family ties have always been very close in the Marianas; there is no country where the parents are more affectionate toward their children or where they take more pains to please and instruct them." The bond between parent and child is still very strong in Chamorro society.

When a child was born in ancient times, the child was recognized by the entire community through childbirth rituals and ceremonies. Friends and relatives became so taken with children that they were moved to pinch them, affectionately. This desire to pinch a baby is called *matgodai*. It was believed that this urge must be satisfied or an evil spell would be cast on the child. The spell was believed to cause sickness or even death.

Children were ranked in ancient Chamorro times. Older children had more privileges and more responsibilities. Below is a list of archaic terms used to describe this hierarchical relationship:

*i sologgnan inatnganan* : The youngest (as related to the elder).

*maga* : Oldest child (male or female) of a family. Boss.

*magtchaga* : Older sister or brother.

*sologgna* : Youngest brother or sister.

The ancient Chamorros loved their children and never spanked them. Instead, they scolded children, but with loving words. The child who misbehaved would be placed at the edge of the group. In order to let the child know this was not a permanent banishment, the parents would throw a pebble in the general direction of the child every few minutes. They did not hit the child. They just wanted to let the child know that they were still thinking about him or her. After a while, the parent would go over to the child and explain why the behavior was not acceptable, and why the child was being punished. After this, the child would be taken back to the group and given some special treat.

The ancient Chamorros not only sang praises of their ancestors at ceremonies, but also sang praises of their children.

**12.2 Discipline with Love**

## Guinahan Famagu'on

A sacred custom of the ancient Chamorros was called *guinahan famagu'on* (children's wealth). If an ancient Chamorro saved a child, the child's family was obligated to give the rescuer an almost priceless gift. It was the most valuable ancient Chamorro money. The *guinahan famagu'on* was composed of shell disks. They were not polished along the edges, nor were they of equal thickness. It was shaped like a long cone cut off at the apex. The diameter at the large end was six inches, but it tapered to only one inch at the small end. The *guinahan famagu'on* was worn for adornment at state occasions. It was worn like a collar around the neck, with the ends hanging down over the

chest. This ornament could only be purchased by the richest of men.

If this precious gift was refused, the rescuer became an in-law relative of the parents of the child. This option was probably best for those of lower status who rescued a child. Those who already had high status would have preferred the money.

The family of the rescued child was obligated to honor the requests of the rescuing family. Sometimes high-ranking rescuers would give their name to a child, if the parent consented.

Once again we see the great value that ancient Chamorros placed on children. In a society in which ancestor veneration was important, it was imperative that parents earn the respect of the younger generation.

## Adoption

Adoption was practiced among the ancient Chamorros. There were never orphans. In the case of the death of parents the children were taken by relatives or friends. If the parents were living, adoption had to be approved of by the *maga'lahi* (chief). He would consult with both families. These adoptions were for childless couples, or couples who needed a son or daughter to fill a status position or title.

Adopted children had all the rights and obligations of natural children with one exception. They could not take a titled position like lineage head if there was another relative who could fill that position. For example, it would have been rare for an adopted child to become *maga'lahi*.

## FUNERAL RITES

Funerals are rites of separation. They permit the living to express their grief over a death and provide for the social readjustment of the group. First a person is born, then comes of age, is married, achieves some status, and then dies. Each of these steps is recognized by ceremony. These events are called rites of passage. A **funeral** is the final rite of passage. Among the ancient Chamorros this final rite did not end a person's relationship to the deceased. The ancient Chamorros believed in the immortality of the soul. A death was the end of a person's relationship with the living person, and the beginning of his or her relationship to an ancestral spirit. The respect held for kin was extended after death by the practice of ancestor veneration or worship.

Ancient Chamorro funerals were elaborate. Of all the customs of the ancient Chamorros the funeral is described in the historical records better than any other. The problem with the descriptions lies in the fact that cultures are always undergoing change. Customs do not remain fixed. The following description of ancient Chamorro funerals is a composite of the funeral information provided by Fray Juan Antonio in 1596, Fray Juan Pobre de Zamora in 1602, Padre Sanvitores in 1670, the recollections of an old man, Don Luis de Torres, in the early 1800s, and the research of archaeologists.

# Dying

When a person was about to die, relatives gathered to hold a vigil until the death. Clan members even from other islands were informed. The dying person was carried to the home of a friend and was offered some raw fish. The assembled then ate from the same fish. During this period, all problems in the relationships between the living and the dying person were resolved. People did not want the deceased to die with any hard feelings.

# Death

When the person died, all relatives and friends were notified. The family of the deceased was expected to provide food for all those who had a right to participate in the funeral.

The body was laid out in the upper part of the house on a new pandanus mat. A basket was placed near the deceased's head. The *ante* (spirit) was invited to enter the basket. The *ante* was invited to remain at home. The *ante* was told that he or she was welcome and always had a place to stay or to visit. If the person died peacefully, it was believed he or she went to an underground paradise. It was full of good food and all the pleasures of life. If the person died violently or with suffering, this was a sign that the ancestral spirits had chosen not to protect that person. In some accounts this meant that people had to spend eternity away from their land. In other accounts, which show Spanish influence, they went to

*sasalaguan* (hell). This was a place of fire and torture.

The deceased's body was anointed with fragrant coconut oil and placed on a pandanus mat. The lips were painted with the red saliva from betel nut chewing. The funeral pandanus mat was decorated with flowers, palms, and shells. The deceased's eldest female relatives laid pieces of painted tree bark on top of the body. They sang a wailing song asking the deceased by name, "Why have you forsaken us? Why have you departed from our sight? Why have you deserted the women who loved you so? Why have you abandoned your lance and sling, your nets and your fishing boat? Why have you left the little basket in which you carried your betel nut wad? Why did you abandon your axe and knife?"

The singing began as soon as people started to arrive. The guests joined in the singing. The relatives embraced the corpse. The corpse was carried to relatives' houses on a board, so the soul could remain where it wished and know where it was welcome. When they returned, the guests were served a special food. Rice from the deceased's family and the *maga'lahi* was prepared for the guests and served with a drink to those who had sung. *Atuli*, a mixture of grated coconut, rice flour, and water was served. Some did not take the food because they were fasting. Some fasts continued until those fasting were actually wasting away and had become unrecognizable.

The demonstrations of grief were extreme. There was crying, wailing, the blowing of conch shells, and the rattling of shells tied to the ends of sticks. The mourning continued for six or eight or even more days. The length of the mourning depended on how much affection the mourner felt for the deceased and how close a relative the deceased was.

# Mementos

Mourners took locks of hair or even a hand from the deceased as something to remember. As a sign of love, some carried the dried hand of a relative in a little box. Sometime after burial, the skull of an important relative was taken as a token. Both the dried hands and the skulls were anointed with coconut oil. The deceased's mother cut off a lock of her child's hair. She marked the days after the death by tying a knot in a cord that she wore around her neck.

## Techa

A *techa* (prayer director) led the people in a chanted prayer or dirge. A **dirge** is a slow, sad song or piece of music at a funeral. One such *tinaitai* (prayer) from ancient times is presented below:

There is no life left for me; all that remains will be boredom and bitterness. The sun which warmed me has been eclipsed, the moon which lighted my path has darkened. The star which guided me has disappeared. I shall be buried in dense night and sunk in a sea of tears and bitterness.

The mourners passed the time with melancholy songs, gathered around a *palapåla* (shelter) that they set up on the grave or alongside it, adorning it with flowers, palms, seashells, and other things they valued. There were loud lamentations. The grief expressed was even greater for a *maga'lahi* (village chief), and was most extreme for the oldest female of a clan. In these two cases the ancient Chamorros covered their pathways with ropes of palm leaves, erected triumphal arches, destroyed coconut trees, burned houses, and dismantled canoes. They raised their shredded canoe sails before their houses as signs of their grief and suffering. Sorrowful songs, which praised the deceased, were sung well into the night. In such cases the *techa* would lead a deeply felt dirge like the one presented below:

In the future, life will be a burden to you, lacking him who was the life of everyone, lacking the sun of nobility, the moon that lighted you in the night of your ignorance, the star of all your achievements, the valor of your battles, the honor of your lineage, of your people, and of your land.

Another translation reads as follows:

From now on life will be more difficult lacking the one who was the life of all . . . lacking the sun, the moon, that illuminated the night of ignorance, the star of all good fortune, the bravery of all battles, the honor of his line, his village, and his country.

## Chenchule'

*Chenchule'* is a donation of money or food. All close relatives except widowers and widows were expected to give food or *ålas* (tortoiseshell money). This network formed a complex system of reciprocal gift giving. The gifts of food were presented by a man's wife. Unmarried male relatives had to get a sister or sister-in-law to make their presentations. Although widowers and widows were exempt, they often gave anyway. Widowers would get their sisters to make the presentations. On the opposite page is a diagram explaining this process. For simplicity, the deceased is an unmarried female.

From the diagram you can see that brothers on the husband's and the wife's side of the family donated food for the funeral feast. They had their wives make the presentations. Sisters on each side of the family donated *ålas*. They probably got this from their husbands. The husband and wife took some of this *ålas* and gave it back to their brothers who gave them the food. Again, they did this through their brothers' wives. This example is as simple as possible. It just includes brothers and sisters. Remember that parents, grandparents, cousins, nephews, and nieces were also involved.

The *ålas* did not have to be presented when the food was delivered. The ancient Chamorros knew the money was due and would be donated eventually. If a man was not too wealthy, the *ålas* given would be a *ghintos,* a fragment of a strand of *lukao hugua,* a string of button-sized tortoiseshell disks made into a long, pliable cylinder. It was worn as a necklace and went around the neck and extended to the waist. For the details on ancient Chamorro money, see the chapter on "Money."

The *chenchule',* which passed through many hands, demonstrates the interdependency of the kinship group. Ancient Chamorros needed relatives. The *chenchule'* helped maintain group solidarity.

## Burial

The burial did not take place until the corpse gave off a bad odor. The important people stayed around the body. Some ancient Chamorros sang and cried and talked to the dead person. Fray Juan Pobre de Zamora (1602) described a song as follows:

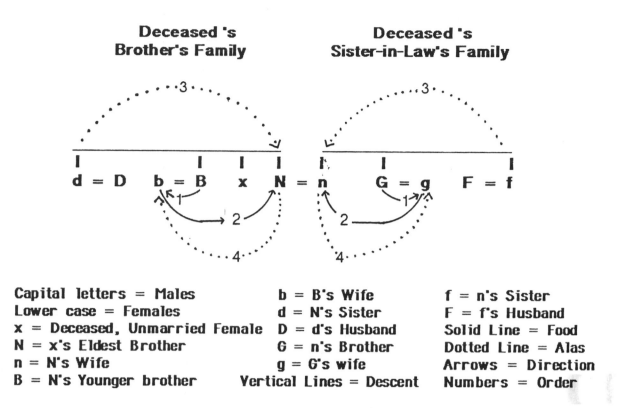

**Deceased 's Brother's Family**          **Deceased 's Sister-in-Law's Family**

| Capital letters = Males | b = B's Wife | f = n's Sister |
| Lower case = Females | d = N's Sister | F = f's Husband |
| x = Deceased, Unmarried Female | D = d's Husband | Solid Line = Food |
| N = x's Eldest Brother | G = n's Brother | Dotted Line = Alas |
| n = N's Wife | g = G's wife | Arrows = Direction |
| B = N's Younger brother | Vertical Lines = Descent | Numbers = Order |

12.3 Ancient Chamorro *Chenchule'*

In song, they tell the deceased that he will dwell among the stars and the sun and the moon, and that he will walk through the air, and that he will come to his home and eat rice. They praise him: as a great fisherman; for his strength; as an expert in the use of the lance and the sling; because he went out to the Spanish ship which passed there and returned with pieces of iron; because he built boats and gave fiestas to which he invited the populace; and because he had many turtle shells which they place in the grave and are highly valued.

The body was carried on a board or sometimes in a chair built on a scaffolding of palm and trees. A man's body was placed in front of his brother's house. If he did not have a brother, it would be placed in front of his sister's son's house. These men were a deceased man's heirs.

Spitting was always abhorred, but at a funeral it was unthinkable. Not only was it disrespectful, but *makahna* (shaman) could use a person's saliva to cast evil spells.

The grave was prepared. Usually the body was buried 12 to 39 inches below the surface. The body was wrapped in new pandanus mats. Some were buried with their feet toward the ocean. In some cases their heads were placed to the southeast and they were facing southwest. Some anthropologists have speculated that this was done so they were facing the direction from which their ancestors had migrated to the Mariana Islands. As more excavations are done by archaeologists, it is more and more difficult to generalize about the burials.

The deceased were buried with bones, spearheads, potsherds, fishhooks, adzes, and other artifacts. Some of these artifacts seem to have been broken before burial. There was a greater tendency to bury *chamorri* (high caste) with their possessions and even with tortoiseshell money. In Agaña and Tamuning on Guam, archaeologists have found evidence that some ancient Chamorros were buried in canoes.

The grave was filled and covered with beach sand. A new mat was placed on top. Posts were placed at the corners of the grave to support a platform on which more pandanus mats were placed. Tortoiseshell money called *ålas* was placed on these mats. This was *chenchule'*, which would be taken by the relatives. Possessions of the deceased, like canoe paddles, canoes, spears, fishnets, fishhooks, and knives, were at times placed on the grave. This let everyone know the skills that the dead person had in life.

If a person had been killed and his death was to be avenged, spears were stuck in the ground around the grave.

Usually bodies were buried underneath or near a house. Many burials have been uncovered in between the *latte* stone pillars of houses. The heirs of the deceased were most concerned with their newest ancestral spirit. They wanted the spirit to remain close to them.

Sometimes ancient Chamorro burials were in caves or earthenware urns called *sahayan*. The corpse was put in a squatting position and the urn was placed over it about three feet below the surface. Artifacts were placed with the body. This custom was similar to the practice in Southeast Asia and Indonesia. In those areas, after the body had decomposed, the bones were placed in urns.

Finally, the guests returned to the house of the deceased for a feast amidst their tears. This feast was provided by the dead person's family.

Drawings of the deceased were made on pieces of bark and wood and were kept in caves called *guma' alumsek*. Accounts from the early 1800s claim that the Chamorros mourned for a boy two months and six months for a girl. Females are viewed as more important in a **matrilineal** society.

The funeral was not an end. The once-living relative had become an ancestral spirit or *ante*. A relationship continued even after death. The survivors cared for the skulls of their important ancestors. They kept them in baskets and anointed them with coconut oil. When danger was near, they asked for their assistance. The ancient Chamorros asked their deceased relatives' help in matters of fishing, farming, and love. In return, the living would continue to respect their ancestors and not abuse the land they held in trust for the next generation.

# FESTIVITIES

Festivities were extremely important to the ancient Chamorros. The Chamorro word for a party, celebration, fiesta, festivity, holiday, or feast is *gupot*. Festivities served spiritual and social functions. Ceremonies expressed reverence for the forces of generation and fertility, but were also full of joy. Some festivities were just for family; others had political purposes. In all cases the festivities served to maintain unity within the family, the village, and even between villages. Usually there were sacred ceremonies during the festivities. In the ancient Chamorro religious and social ceremonies, a gift of food and hospitality strengthened bonds with family, neighbors, and ancestors. There were festivities for family get-togethers, childbirth, marriages, and funerals. There were celebrations for the launching of a new canoe. Festivities were probably associated with planting, first fruits, the first run of a certain kind of fish, harvesting, and other important times in the lives of the people. The capture of a turtle or a large fish like a marlin was a cause for celebration. Chamorro festivities always included huge quantities of food and hospitality. There were special festivities that involved an entire village or even villages within a district. Peace treaties were celebrated, too.

# Family

Families got together in ancient Chamorro times just as they do today. The *gupot* is a good way for a family to relax and enjoy the fruits of their work. In ancient times *gupti* was used to designate small family celebrations, while *gupot* was used for larger celebrations. The most important function of these get-togethers was to maintain family solidarity. Oftentimes a friend or even a stranger was welcomed by a family party. Marriages, births, and deaths were celebrated, and were considered a *gupot*, rather than a *gupti*. A good catch of fish or the success in any enterprise was a call for a celebration. For example, if a roof was thatched, a party followed. Besides the feasting and conversation, these informal parties included sports. A favorite pastime for the *chamorri* (upper caste) was a family outing in an outrigger canoe.

# Villages

A great deal of preparation went into village festivities. These events included feasting, ancestor veneration, music, conversation, and competition.

**12.4 Ancient Chamorro Family Outing**

population of their area. During these celebrations, they recounted their historical traditions through long stories.

At Fouha Bay, the "Chamorro Garden of Eden," they had a special feast each year. At Fouha Bay, the ancient Chamorros conducted contests to amuse themselves and to honor their idols. They offered seeds, nets, and hooks for fishing, and rice cakes to their ancestors' spirits. The rice-cake offerings were kept as a blessed food for the sick.

Festivities always included the singing or reciting of legends. They also did this to recognize the accomplishments of their ancestors. Those who were wisest competed to see who could speak or sing the most couplets. The legend of Puntan was typically sung. He was born of nothingness and instructed his sister to create the heaven and earth from his body.

## Music and Dancing

The ancient Chamorros enjoyed singing and dancing at their festivities. Dancing could go on all night before a wedding. Poets were held in great respect. Early Catholic priests reported that the Chamorros sang impressive pagan hymns. The most vivid accounts of dancing describe special feasts that the women held.

The women dressed in string skirts and adorned themselves in flowers. They wore shell necklaces and belts. These decorations included tortoiseshell money. A dozen or so women formed a circle and danced in place. They sang songs about their history with point and harmony of three voices (sopranos, contraltos, and falsettos). The tenor was sung by a chief who attended these entertainments. The songs were accompanied by hand movements. The right hand made semi-circular motions, while the left kept time by shaking a stick with shells attached to it. They accompanied this dancing and singing with rhythmic slapping.

In some of the ancient dances the women formed a circle and danced. A man would challenge a woman to dance. Relatives were not permitted to enter these contests. The female dancers declared the winner of the challenge.

Victories in battle were celebrated with satirical songs. They praised actions in battle, and poked fun at the defeated enemy.

The young people of a village paraded with banners attached to sticks.

Sometimes the feast would involve several villages and include 2,000-3,000 people. More common were the festivities for a particular village, which rarely included more than several hundred people. These festivities usually included the ceremonial exchange of gifts. A village often celebrated to repay others for a feast held in their honor.

## Feasting

A feast usually consisted of food provided by the host. Nevertheless, at times the guests brought food, too. In large ceremonies or family ceremonies it was a point of honor for wealthy people to send all near relatives a large portion of cooked rice. Rice seems to have been an important food. Although some accounts claim that rice was abundant, it seems likely that it was reserved for special occasions. The ancient Chamorros ate rice cakes, plain boiled rice, salted fish, as well as fresh seafood, coconuts, bananas, sugarcane, taro, and breadfruit, and they drank *atuli*, which was made of water, rice flour, and grated coconut. They did not have any intoxicating beverages.

## Ancestor Veneration

The ancient Chamorros honored their dead by providing feasts to which they invited the entire

131

**12.5 Festive Dancing**

Some music was competitive. The ancient Chamorros gambled on who could sing the most verses of a myth or a *chamorrita*. The most remarkable Chamorro art form remains the *chamorrita*. The *chamorrita* is a Chamorro folk song sung in four-line stanzas. The *chamorrita* has a tune for which many different songs are created. New words are improvised on the spot. Usually it has two couplets, and the second and fourth lines rhyme. It is permissible for the fourth line to be unrelated to the first in meaning. During competition a singer sang four lines. The opponent had to make up four lines to answer. Back and forth they created verses until one singer could no longer think of an appropriate response. The lines often teased a rival or a lover in good fun. Sometimes a group of singers sang in chorus or extemporaneously took turns singing. This bantering and joking often was about some important person. The following examples are not ancient; they were recorded by Gertrude Hornbostel in the early 1900s.

### *Chamorrita* Songs

*Ya malago' yu na hu tungo'*
  And I would like to know
*Manu nai gaige piniti-mu;*
  Where your love pain is;
*Kao i trongkon korason-mu,*
  Whether at the bottom of your heart,
*Pat i puntan babali-mu.*
  Or at the end of your lashes.

*An un kone' i haga-hu,*
  When you get my daughter
*Hagu siempre un facho;chu'i;*
  You will surely work to support her;
*Sa' an sakkan fina'cho'cho'-mu,*
  For when harvest time comes,
*Para hamyo en akannu'i.*
  You will both reap its abundance.

Source: *Archaeology of the Marianas Islands,* by Laura Maud Thompson. Published as Bernice P. Bishop Museum Bulletin 100 in 1932 by Bishop Museum Press. Used by permission. The original text has been retranslated and put in modern orthography by Ann Rivera of the Guam Bilingual and Bicultural Program.

# Competition

Friendly competition was an important part of ancient Chamorro festivities. These activities were carried out with much laughter and mocking. The contests were not only for amusement; like the ancient Greeks, the Chamorros used them as a means to honor their idols. The men met to dance, wrestle, throw spears and slingstones, run, jump, and demonstrate their strength and courage. They usually competed in a peaceful manner.

The ancient Chamorros hurled slingstones with great speed and amazing accuracy. The force was so great that the slingstone would actually stick in a coconut tree.

The ancient Chamorros demonstrated spear-throwing accuracy by hitting targets from 20, 30, 40, and even 50 paces away. A few warriors could throw spears even greater distances. While arrogantly jesting, some talented Chamorros actually caught spears that were thrown at them. Then they would taunt their opponent by saying, "You are mere children and should fight with children and not with me. Do you think I'm blind? Notice that I have good eyes."

Swimming games, racing, and jumping are mentioned in the historical record. One swimming game is described by explanation and the diagram on the next page:

C......................................A......................................$C^1$

Safe Area

D......................................B......................................$D^1$

The area between the two lines was safe. The object of the game was for player "A" to challenge player "B" or vice-versa. "A" cried, "*Anima!* (catch!)." "B" responded, "*Djuti ha.* (Come on then)." "A" replied, "*Mano djo?* (Where shall I go?)" "B" then said, "*Adjin ha* (Over there)." "B" pointed right or left. "A" then had to dive and come up beyond line D-$D^1$, out of safe territory. When "A" surfaced, "B" tried to catch him or her before the swimmer could return to safe territory. "B" could catch "A" on the surface or under the water. If "A" got back safely, he or she was then challenged by "B." Usually the game was played by many players along each line. The swimmers lined up on the two imaginary lines in teams of equal numbers. First one player challenged, and then another, so the competition was more or less continuous.

The young men wrestled for the entertainment of their leaders. This competition was strenuous and many took hard falls. After an opponent was pinned, his friend would relieve him by challenging the victor.

Sometimes the competition was between villages and sometimes it was between men's houses in the same village.

Children practiced their fighting skills by using mud slingstones and blunted spears. After the competition, they showed that there were no hard feelings. Injured players were comforted.

One game has been described in a *taotaomo'na* (ancestral spirit) story. The game was called *guauho.* Players formed a circle similar to that in the "mulberry bush" game. A *taotaomo'na*, after chasing a fisherman into a circle of *taotaomo'nas,* said, "*Guauho! Tuguanho! Pau lulumog, pau lansahi, pau acho, pau mati!* (Play *guauho*, play *guauho*, my partner! I can detect my partner by the smell of moss, seaweed, rock and low tide!)"

Competition was not limited to sports. As seen above, the gambling on the singing of *chamorritas* was also a very important type of competition. There was also *mari*. ***Mari*** is the old Chamorro word for debating contests. Some children were trained as debaters from the age of five. This intellectual competition often involved contests between villages.

**12.6 Festivities Included Competitive Sports**

These debates began as early as 8:00 a.m. The opposing sides gathered in separate, barn-like structures. A debater stood and argued, created ballads, and poked fun at the other group. When the debater was finished, a speaker from the other side began. About 2:00 p.m. they broke to eat. The host village provided most of the food.

Occasionally the debate broke down, and the two sides actually moved to a battlefield and skirmished with slings and spears. Usually even these encounters were settled peacefully.

There was some emphasis on competitive feasting. A man was praised at his funeral for the number and size of the feasts he had offered. Hospitality and the sharing of food were considered great virtues. Those who were most hospitable gained the greatest respect. Those who were blessed with good fortune felt obligated to share their wealth. In the case of ceremonial capture (*hotyong songsong*), a village captured a man or an entire work group from another village and held them for ransom. The captors showered the village who paid the ransom with more gifts than they demanded in ransom.

## Marlin Capture

When a man caught a large fish, he would fly a distinctive banner from the mast of his canoe. This would signal the people on shore to prepare for a celebration. When the fisherman arrived, the people who had assembled on shore greeted him with flowers and young palm leaves. The crowd carried the fisherman home in triumph. He presented the turtle or fish to his wife. She then sent it to her closest female relative of higher status. This woman, in turn, sent it to her closest female relative of higher rank. This passing of the turtle or fish continued until it could go no further.

The high-ranking woman at the end of the chain divided the fish or turtle. She sent the shares to all the women whose hands it had passed through on the way to her. It was like a long chain of sharing.

Later, the fisherman brought down his ancestral skulls. With his friends sitting in a circle he first offered the skulls food and thanked the *ante* (ancestral spirit) for the good catch of fish.

**12.7 An ancient Chamorro thanks his *ante* for a successful fishing expedition.**

134

# Turtle Capture

Tortoiseshell was used for money. It was called *ålas*. A turtle shell has 13 plates. If a group of men captured a turtle, the shares were passed through the chain of exchange like the fish above. Finally, each man's highest-ranking female relative gave shell plates from the turtle back to all the women whose hands it had passed through. These plates were not pierced. Tortoiseshell plates with holes placed in them had greater value. Only a special clansman could do this. These holes were made if a man captured a turtle by himself. If this was the first turtle a man had caught, each plate was pierced with a circular hole as large around as his wrist. The second time a person caught a turtle, each shell was pierced twice. One hole was like the first, and the second was as big around as a little finger. For the third turtle, three holes were pierced in each plate, and so on. Again, the turtle passed through all the female relatives to the highest, and then the shares were passed back.

It seems likely that the pieces of turtle removed from each plate were used to make the tortoiseshell money necklaces. Some accounts say that only one village in the Marianas had the privilege of making these necklaces. The name of the village was Fanutugan-ålas, on Tinian. It was their privilege to string the *ålas* necklaces. For a full account of ancient Chamorro ceremonial money, see the chapter on "Money."

# Conclusion

Festivities are still extremely important to Chamorros. Teenagers on Guam often cite barbecues as a favorite hobby. Family get-togethers on the beach or at home are a frequent occurrence. Life-crisis rituals for births, marriages, and funerals still include feasting and praying. Fiestas for a village patron saint are the most common major Chamorro festivity today. The hospitality of the past has continued to the present. Hospitality is extended to outsiders. Some villages adopt military squadrons. Oftentimes people are invited to the party just because they happen by. Just as in the past, festivities serve to maintain unity within the family and the village. Most festivities include music and dancing. Modern competition is seen in the display of huge amounts of delicious food and sometimes in gambling on cards. In the religious and social ceremonies, gifts of food and hospitality still strengthen the bonds within the family and among neighbors and friends.

# MISCELLANEOUS CUSTOMS

Just as in modern times, there were all sorts of customs in ancient Chamorro times. There were habits connected with every aspect of living.

# Friendship Bonds

Ancient Chamorros made pacts of eternal friendship. Friendship meant unconditional loyalty and mutual support. These ties were a sacred bond almost as close as kinship ties. Fray Juan Pobre de Zamora (1602) said, "Some ties are so close that when one goes to a friend's house, whether he is at home or not, the visitor will take whatever he wants from there, as if it were his own. In the same way, he freely takes from the produce of his land or of his palm trees, and even from among the things they value most . . . . So strong are the bonds among friends that they have a say in everything they do, or do not do." He continues this account by stating that the ancient Chamorro males hugged one another and walked arm and arm, but that homosexuality was unknown.

# Greetings, Gestures, and Etiquette

Etiquette refers to the rules for proper behavior. One of the most important rules in ancient Chamorro culture is revealed in the following proverb: "*Maulegña mangagao ja ti manae, ki manae ja ti ma agradesi* (It is better to ask for something and be refused than to be given something and refuse it)."

The ancient Chamorros were very courteous to one another. If they were wearing woven hats, they would remove the hat and share their betel nut, leaf, and quicklime. Men and women carried the makings for a good chew in small, well-made baskets. Betel nut was always offered as a token of friendship and esteem.

A visitor greeted his host with, "*Adjin-dyo* (Here I am)." This implied, here I am at your service. The master of the house replied, "*Attihau?* (Do you want me to pour some water on you?" This refers to the custom of washing a guest's feet. Most guests replied, "*Ti guailadji* (It is not necessary)." But if they wanted their feet washed they said, "*Adjan* (Here). "

If they met on a trail, they said, "Where are you going?" or "Where do you come from?" If they met a person of higher or equal rank, they offered to carry that person's burden. If that person was of lower rank, they offered to give him or her some of whatever they might be carrying.

The *manachang* (low caste) had to crouch before the *matao* (highest *chamorri*) but not the *acha'ot* (second-rate *chamorri*). The *chamorri* were the high caste.

A *matao* would have felt degraded if he or she continued to sit while in the presence of people of lower rank. *Matao* had to remain higher than people of lesser status.

When an ancient Chamorro passed the house of a person of equal status, the occupants asked the visitor to eat. The host always offered the guest betel nut. The juice from the betel nut was put in a bamboo container and was carefully disposed of later. The ancient Chamorros considered it rude to spit betel nut juice.

If guests wished to be very courteous, they passed their hands over the breast or stomach of the host. Today this custom seems to have been replaced by the custom of *mañgiñge*. This custom came from the Spanish. *Mañgiñge* is the holding of a respected elder's slightly raised hand and then bowing and touching the nose to the back of the elder's hand in order to show respect. It is not necessary to actually touch the nose to the hand, but it should be close. As this is done, the younger person says "*ñot*" to males and "*ñohra* " to women. The elder replies, "*Dos tia ayudi* (God bless you or Let God bless you in your way all the time)." Younger people were expected to greet elders like this. Children were also expected to not interfere in adult conversation.

In ancient times guests were given hot water with which to wash themselves. Cleanliness was valued by the ancient Chamorros. They bathed at least once a day. Honored guests are still anointed with coconut oil in many parts of Micronesia. The ancient Chamorros did this because it protected them from cool breezes, the sun, and insects. Even more important were the radiant glow and the fragrant smell left by the application of coconut oil. Hosts offered to wash their guests' feet.

Guests often brought a gift, but even if they did not, the guests were given a gift when they left. Those who gave the best gifts were most highly honored.

Business was always secondary to socializing. Business was taken care of off to the side of a group and usually at the end of a visit.

When a stranger arrived during the day, he had to report to the *maga'lahi* at once and ask for permission to stay in the village. If the stranger failed to do this, the stranger was arrested until the villagers found out what the visitor's purpose was. If the visit was peaceful, the visitor was given a cordial reception. If visitors came into a village at night, they had to go immediately to the canoe house. From there they could call or blow a conch shell to announce their presence. Normally, the shell would be hanging there. When people came, they asked the visitors to go to the chief and ask permission for the visit. After the visitors had secured permission, they could go anywhere in the village with safety.

According to Fray Antonio, who visited Guam in 1596, the ancient Chamorros joked among themselves and used some indecent gestures. Once a man was not invited to the wedding of one of his relatives through some mistake. He didn't say anything at the time. He waited until the morning of the wedding ceremony. He placed his fishing net, and then sent a friend to ask the bride and all his relatives for help. The wedding party was obligated to come and assist him and did so. The manner in which the fisherman reminded the wedding party of their oversight was considered proper and a great joke.

The ancient Chamorros had one expression of politeness that was considered sarcastic. For a hostess to say, "Be careful not to fall as you go down the stairs," was considered an insult against her whole family. The reason for this lies in the interdependence of the family. A person could not fall on a staircase that was properly maintained. At first this seems as if the hostess was insulting herself. But wives came from different clans than their husbands. The house belonged to her, but it had to be maintained by her husband's clan because it was on his family land.

The *manachang* (low caste) were not permitted to eat or drink at the houses of the nobles or even to

136

go near them. If they had business they would ask from a distance. A *manachang* had to bow in a crouching position when near a *chamorri* (high caste).

Even people of the same status did not normally invite anyone other than family members into their house. It was believed that the guest might jeopardize the safety of the ancestral skulls kept in the house or might offend the ancestral spirits. It was impolite to clear your throat in the presence of respected persons or even in the vicinity of a stranger's house.

The ancient Chamorros demonstrated affection for one another. They touched one another in greeting and were known to walk arm in arm. There are accounts that they rubbed each other's chests and stomachs. One account said that they did not kiss on the mouth even in passion. European kisses were referred to as *chiku bagbag* because of the noise. Other accounts state that the ancient Chamorros kissed on the face and bit each other hard on the arm as a show of affection. Leaving teeth marks was considered proof of affection.

Respect had to be shown to those of higher caste or class. Even within a caste special deference had to be shown to those who were ranked higher. Social consideration to relatives of the same rank depended upon age. The oldest person came first. Even younger children were expected to obey their older brother or sister.

A person's closest relatives were on the mother's side of the family. They were in the same clan. Women were given special deference. They were seated and served before men. A list of female relatives in order of decreasing respect is as follows: great-grandmother, grandmother, mother, great aunt, aunt, sister, first cousin once removed, first cousin, niece, and daughter. There were a few exceptions to this rule. For example, an unmarried aunt, daughter, or childless widow had lower status than a younger married female relative. This reminds us of just how important it was for women to have children and increase the strength of their clan. People outside of a person's clan were not considered relatives. The one exception was a man's wife. Through the marriage ceremony she became a member of his clan.

## Meals

The food was placed on plates of woven pandanus or banana leaves. It was placed on a pandanus mat that was between six and eight feet long and about two feet wide. Gourds, pottery, and coconut shells were used to hold liquids. It was considered bad manners to let the drinking vessel touch their mouths. Therefore, they drank by holding the vessel high and pouring the liquid from above. There was a beak on the vessel to facilitate this. Guests squatted down on their heels on each side of the mat. Early accounts say there were two meals a day. One was in the morning and the other in late afternoon. Later accounts say there was a meal at seven o'clock in the morning, a dinner at noon or one o'clock, and a supper at eight in the evening. Despite some evidence that the Chamorros ate moderately, it is also reported that the ancient Chamorros were great eaters and would eat throughout the day when they were hungry.

## Sleeping

People liked to lie in bed and talk. They spent nine or ten hours on their sleeping mats. In addition, people took naps when they were tired.

## Temperament

The ancient Chamorros were naturally kind to one another. Fray Juan Pobre de Zamora (1602) found so much love among the Chamorros and so little among Christians that he didn't know what to say. Ancient Chamorros were fond of tricks and jokes and were hurt if a person took offense at their jokes. They were fond of mockery and friendly, playful ridicule. They enjoyed festivities, dancing, singing, storytelling, and contests of strength and skill.

The ancient Chamorros were proud of their ability and genius.

They were rarely angered. Nevertheless, when the ancient Chamorros were angry they did not show it. They laughed instead. Generally there was peace within a village and between villages. Nevertheless, they were jealous and suspicious of people who lived in other districts. In their dealings with enemies they sought vengeance for all injuries. Although the affront might not be openly expressed, the grievance would be held until satisfied by revenge.

The ancient Chamorros had little regard for those who did not work. An old proverb states, *"Facho'cho ja yan cho'chu* (Work and you will eat)."

The ancient Chamorros were compassionate. This can be seen in their care for the sick and strangers. Food for the sick was prepared first. During a time of hardship, relatives provided food for the family of those in need. The relatives of sick men were given fish by returning fishermen.

# Betel Nut Chewing

Betel nut chewing is a custom that spread from India to Southeast Asia. From there it spread to the Philippines, Melanesia, Taiwan, and Micronesia. Betel nut comes from a type of palm tree botanists call *Areca atechu*. The pigeon-egg-sized nuts are covered by a fibrous husk. A cut through the nut reveals a sunburst of white in a field of wine red.

The ancient Chamorros chewed *pugua'* (betel nut) sprinkled with *åfok* (quicklime) and wrapped in a *pupulu* (pepper leaf). The entire quid was called *mama'on*.

Betel nut has no food value. It was and is chewed for the same reasons people today drink coffee or tea, or smoke cigarettes. Betel nut, like coffee, is a mild stimulant and is addictive. It is chewed when a person wishes to take a break, share, care, or relax.

As with tea or coffee, a great deal of social significance is still attached to betel nut. Although chewing betel nut lacks the formality of the Japanese tea ceremony, betel nut is associated with ritual behavior. When people meet, they share betel nut. In the past hosts and hostesses always offered betel nut.

# Hospitality

The ancient Chamorros received guests with great affection. Guests were treated with the same love and affection shown to family. Guests, whether friends, relatives, or strangers, were invited to share whatever the host had. If there was a shortage, the host and hostess did without. When there was plenty, they saw to it that the guests received the best. A special treat was made by pounding together rice and grated coconut and shaping the mixture into balls. This confection was considered a great gift. It was eaten in place of bread. A drink called *atuli* was made by diluting this confection with cold water. It was served in a pottery cup.

# Special Status of Women

No ancient Chamorro was expected to help a man in a quarrel, but the whole tribe would take the side of a woman. If you asked for help from a male relative, he came alone. If you made the plea to the highest ranking woman in your family, the whole family including in-laws had to help. This included help in making house repairs or constructing an entire new dwelling. Wealth, name, and titles were inherited through the female side of the family. Men did not become chiefs because their father was a chief. They inherited this status from their mother's brother. Women were consulted on all major decisions. Since decisions were made on the basis of consensus, the women exerted considerable influence.

# SUMMARY

Reciprocity was central to ancient Chamorro culture. This principle is evident in the custom of *chenchule'*, the interdependence of the ancient Chamorros in their social lives, their rites of passage ceremonies, and their festivities.

# Chapter 13
# Arts, Skills, and Education

## INTRODUCTION

The ancient Chamorro fishing and farming economy required many arts and skills. Women took care of the household labor. Occasionally they fished or even farmed. The women cooked, administered medicine, made the household utensils, and did all the weaving. They even wove the sails for canoes. Men did the fishing and farming, built houses and canoes, maintained roads, and carried heavy articles. The military and fishing were reserved for the *chamorri* (high caste). When the *acha'ot* (second-rank *chamorri*) did a good job, the *matao* (the highest *chamorri*) gave them presents. The *matao* owed the the *acha'ot* only food. *Manachang* (low caste) could not touch the sea or fight. For this reason, visitors to Guam were probably considered noblemen. The *manachang* had to take care of themselves. Their main job was to cultivate the *chamorri*'s land, help in the construction of large sheds for canoes, clear and repair roads, carry foodstuffs in battle, and gather the materials for construction projects.

## SKILLS

## Weaving

The ancient Chamorro women did most of the weaving. Their weaving included right angle and diagonal plaiting. The ancient Chamorros did not use looms. They wove mats, sails, hats, and baskets out of dried strips from textile pandanus leaves. The mats (*guafak*) were used as mattresses, blankets, funeral shrouds, clean surfaces for drying rice and serving food, and for wrapping gifts. Coconut or nipa fronds were used for thatch. Pandanus and coconut leaves were used for *finilak* (basketwork).

The *akgak* (*Pandanus tectorius*) leaf is best for weaving. The *akgak* tree differs from other pandanus trees like *pahong* and *kaffo'* because it begins to branch very close to the ground and has very long and wide leaves. Green leaves were cut near the base. The sharp spines on the edges and the stiff midrib were removed. The freshly cut leaves were boiled for two minutes and then scraped with a shell in order to remove the waxy powder on the leaves. The wet leaves were then dried in the sun. Next, they were rolled up and stored indoors for three days. After three days they were unrolled and cured in the sun for two weeks. During this time, they were brought in if it rained and were stored inside at night. The leaves were rolled up for storage. Before weaving the leaf, the weaver made the leaf pliable by drawing it across a shell tool called a *si'i*. Next, the weaver split the leaves into strips about one-half inch wide for mats. Narrower strips were used for a finer, almost cloth-like, texture.

The pandanus was woven into many types of baskets. A *kottot* was a rectangular basket. The *kottot* was used for the ceremonial presentation of gifts of rice. This was a type of *chenchule'*. Hand bags were called *tisage'*. *Alan mamao* was a betel nut box woven of pandanus leaves. It was about eight inches square, with two arcs that were used for handles. The *saluu*, used on festive occasions to hold betel nut, was delicately made and could be closed and used as a case. *Alan tchino* was a basket for storing provisions in the house. A *balakbagk* was a medium-sized bag with a lid. It was carried with a strap over the shoulder and rested at hip level. The *danglon* was made in a similar fashion, but was only ten inches long. The *hagug* was an enormous basket (three feet wide) in the shape of a case. Used to carry war provisions and food, it was carried on the back with straps. The *alan tugtug* baskets were divided into two compartments of equal size. A woven pandanus bag used to hold rice after the harvest was called *tataho*. A special baby cradle was also made of pandanus.

The ancient Chamorros had several kinds of mats. The mat for serving meals was called a *tefan*. Sleeping mats were called *guafak*. A *satghe* was a woven plate for rice cake.

In ancient times if a married man told his eldest ancestor that the house was not in good condition, all relatives were summoned to help contribute to the construction of a new dwelling or to make repairs. When a baby was about to be born, special care was taken to see that everything around the house was in good repair. Houses were thatched with coconut and nipa leaves. Coconut thatch lasted a year or two. Nipa thatch lasted for about five years. Nipa grows best in the brackish water near the sea or along river banks. The leaves look like coconut palm leaves but they are much sturdier. Nipa and pandanus leaves are sometimes sewn onto bamboo slats for thatching and sometimes last as long as eight years.

The best time for thatching a roof is in the dry season. First, the palm fronds are collected. Next, the fronds are split down the middle. This is easy to accomplish by taking the small leaflets at the end of the frond and separating them. The midrib will begin to split and then a person just walks down the center of the frond splitting the midrib as he or she goes. Each half of the leaf is woven by diagonal plaiting. The weaving stops about a foot and a half from the end of the frond. The thin end of the frond is cut off. After each half is woven, they are tied one on top of the other with the shiny side of the leaves facing up. The plaited and tied leaves are stacked to dry for two weeks. This drying period is necessary because it stiffens the leaves and helps them to hold their plaiting.

Neighbors were invited for a roof thatching. The roof thatching began at the eaves. The woven palm fronds were tied in place along the entire length of the house. Then another layer was tied on top, and so on, until they reached the gable of the house. Neighbors pitched in to help with such a big job. The house owner was obligated to provide refreshments. In this manner a tedious job was transformed into a joyful celebration.

Palm fronds were used to make hats and baskets for storing things. Young, almost yellow leaves are best for basket weaving. The center two or three leaves are too immature and won't last. Never cut the center frond, because it may kill the tree. The leaves are split and the midribs cut thin before weaving. Woven articles should be washed and dried in the sun for proper curing.

Baskets for holding produce were the most common type. Fishermen used a basket for a creel. An ordinary fish basket was called a *guagua'*. The type with a strap tied around the waist was called a *guagua' tumalaya*. A *che'op* was a basket that had straps and was carried on the back. *Åla* were ordinary baskets of medium or small size. Big baskets were called *pupung*. The *gueghe* was used to hold fish.

An *atupat* is woven from a strand of the coconut leaf. They are still used for cooking rice. The small, diamond-shaped cube is filled with rice grains. When the rice boils, it swells, filling the *atupat*. In the past this was a convenient way to package cooked rice for a traveler, hunter, fisherperson, warrior, or farmer.

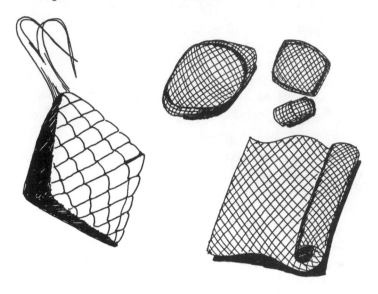

**13.1**   *Atupat*          *Akgak* **Woven Products**

The ancient Chamorros wove fish nets. Unfortunately, little is known about the methods and materials they used to make their nets. They probably used the bark from the *pagu* tree (wild hibiscus or *Hibiscus tiliaceus*) for this purpose. Bamboo awls have been used to weave these strands in the recent past. They were probably used in ancient times, too. The methods in which these fishing nets were used is discussed in the chapter on "Food."

# Rope Making

The best ancient Chamorro rope was made from the dried fibers of a coconut husk. The fibers were rolled on the thigh with the palm of the hand. As the fibers intertwined, more fibers were added to lengthen the strand. After the strands were anchored to a fixed point, they were twisted together into a sturdy rope. This rope is resistant to rotting. Knots tied in this type of rope hold very tightly, because of the loose fibers sticking out all over the rope. This rope was used to tie shell and stone blades on handles, to lash together houses and canoes, and to string *ålas* (tortoiseshell money).

Another rope is still made by peeling the bark off a *pagu* tree branch. The craftsperson uses his or her teeth to get the peeling started. The outer layer of the bark is separated from the white inner layer. Strands about half an inch wide are hung to dry. These fibers are twisted together to make rope. In the past, thin strands were used for fishing lines. One archaeologist made a 60-pound-test fishing line out of *pagu* fibers. These fibers were probably used for a string or grass skirt that ancient Chamorro women wore at festivals. Today, the fibers are twisted together on an apparatus called a *biradot*. This tool was introduced by the Spanish to make rope. Men usually make rope today, but in ancient times, women made the ropes, even for canoes.

# *Åfok* (Quicklime) Production

*Åfok* (quicklime) was made from reef coral. Coconut logs were stacked in a square. The center area was filled with firewood. A platform of coconut logs was laid on top to support a pile of coral rocks from the reef. The logs were set on fire. The heat broke down the calcium carbonate, or coral, into a white calcium hydroxide powder. After the fire was dead, the white power, *åfok*, was carefully scraped out from the ashes. *Åfok* was used for chewing with *pugua'* (betel nut). *Åfok* "cooks" the betel nut and *pupulu* (betel pepper leaf) as they are chewed. *Åfok* increases the mild narcotic effect of betel nut and makes a person's saliva turn red. The red saliva stains the teeth of the betel nut chewer. In the past, these stains were considered beautiful. *Åfok* was also mixed with coconut oil and red earth to make paint. One early account suggests that it was mixed with coconut oil to make a shiny caulking to seal the cracks between the timbers in ancient Chamorro houses. It was used to caulk canoes, too. Ancient Chamorro paint had a sheen. It made the utensils painted with it impervious to humidity.

## Coconut Oil

The ancient Chamorros grated coconut meat with a *kamyo* (coconut grater). The *kamyo* had a serrated shell blade attached to a wooden seat. The grated coconut meat was squeezed vigorously with both hands to extract the coconut milk. Six half coconut shells of water were added and mixed with the coconut meat and its milk. After the coconut meat and water mixture was squeezed, the coconut milk was transferred to a clay pot through a strainer. The strainer was made from *gunot*, the cloth-like fiber found at the base of palm fronds. The strainer was used to keep the white liquid and coconut meat separate. The coconut milk was boiled in a clay pot. After about an hour of boiling, the coconut oil rose to the top of the liquid. The oil was carefully skimmed off and placed in another clay pot and boiled for another half hour. Then the two tablespoons of coconut oil were left to cool.

Today coconut oil is used in making soap, shampoo, and tanning lotion. It is also used for cooking and making "filled milk" (milk made from vegetable oil rather than animal fat). In ancient times it was used as a fragrant, protective body lotion, in paint, and perhaps as a fuel for lamps.

## Salt Making

The ancient Chamorros probably let nature make their salt. There are many places on the east coast of Guam where waves wash up over terraces on the cliffs. The sea water trapped in natural depressions on these terraces evaporates, leaving salt. In the Malojloj area, about one-half of the way between Talofofo Bay and Pauliluc Bay, there is an area called Asiga (salt) Point. Chamorros who had access to salt probably traded it to others.

## Starting Fires

Some researchers have speculated that the ancient Chamorros used flint to start fires. It seems more likely that they used friction. Rubbing two sticks together generates a great deal of heat. This process of brushing two sticks together or using flint is called *yokyok*. When tender is added, and a person blows on it, a fire can be started.

## Measuring System of the Chamorros

The ancient Chamorro system of measurement was not recorded by early explorers. We must assume that their measurement was similar to that of other Micronesians and that only the terms have been replaced by Spanish words. Fractions played an important part in measuring. For example, a strand of string was used to measure the length of a dugout canoe. That length and fractions of that length were used for the booms, outriggers and all other parts of the canoe. In a similar fashion, the width of a house was commonly one-fourth the length.

# Counting System of the Chamorros

Today, Chamorros use the Spanish names for numbers when counting. Nevertheless, the ancient Chamorros had their own words for their decimal system of counting. It is interesting to note that slingstones were used for counting systems in the ancient Middle East. Slingstones of different sizes and materials stood for certain numbers. Slingstones in the Mariana Islands are made of many materials like clay, limestone, and marble. Local slingstones have been found from the size of bird eggs to the size of miniature (six-inch) footballs. There is no record of their being used for counting purposes, however. H. Costenoble found that the ancient Chamorro numbers are similar to those of other Pacific Island peoples, especially those in the southern Philippines.

## Measuring System

**Measurement of dry volume**
*chupa* = 1 cup
*ganta* = 8 cups = one-half gallon (also recorded as one gallon or even a liter)

**Measurement of length**
*dedo* = the length of the second joint of the index finger
*hemi* = the length from the tip of the index finger to the spread thumb
*kodu* = the length from the elbow to the end of a clenched fist
*kuatta* = the length from the end of the thumb to the end of the little finger when the hand is spread
*bara* = arm length from the shoulder to the end of the fingers
*brasa* = length from finger tip to finger tip, with both arms outstretched

## Number Similarities in Pacific Island Languages

|  | Mariana Is. | Philippines | | Indonesia | | Melanesia | Polynesia |
|---|---|---|---|---|---|---|---|
| No. | Chamorro | Iloko | Pampango | Napu | Batak | Fiji | Samoa |
| 1 | maisa | maisa | isa | isa | sada | dua | sa |
| 2 | hugua | dua | adua | dua | dua | rua | lua |
| 3 | tulo | tallo | atlu | talu | telu | tolu | tolu |
| 4 | fatfat | uppat | apat | iba | empat | va | fa |
| 5 | lima | lima | lima | lima | lima | lima | lima |
| 6 | gunum | innem | anam | ini | enem | ono | ono |
| 7 | fito | pito | pitu | pitu | pitu | vitu | fitu |
| 8 | gualo | walo | walu | walu | waluh | walu | walu |
| 9 | sigua | siam | siam | hio | siwah | thiwa | iwa |
| 10 | fulu | pulo | pulu | pulo | puluh | vulu | fulu |
| 100 | gatos | gasot | dinalan | atu | ratus | drau | lau |

H. Costenoble 's "The Family Tree of Chamorro." *Guam Recorder*, 4(2), 25. Used by permission of the Micronesia Area Research Center.

In English there is one form of numbers for counting everything. Other people, like the Japanese, have different forms for counting various things. They even have a separate form for counting books. In ancient Chamorro times there were four forms for numbers. There was a form for counting the days, months, and years, a form for measurement, a form for counting living things and a form for nonliving objects.

## Counting System for Nonliving Objects

| No. | Ancient Chamorro | Modern Chamorro Numbers (Similar to Spanish) |
|---|---|---|
| 1 | hachiyai | unu |
| 2 | huguiyai | dos |
| 3 | tolgiyai | tres |
| 4 | farfatai | kuatro |
| 5 | limiyai | sinko |
| 6 | gonmiyai | sais |
| 7 | fetguiyai | siete |
| 8 | gualguiyai | ocho |
| 9 | siguiyai | nuebi |
| 10 | manutai | dies |
| 11 | manutai nagai hachiyai | onse |
| 12 | manutai nagai huguiyai | dosse |
| 20 | huguiyai na fulu | bente |
| 21 | huguiyai na fulu nagai hachiyai | bente i unu |
| 30 | totquiyai na fulu | trenta |
| 40 | farfatai na fulu | kuarenta |
| 100 | gatus | siento |
| 200 | huguiyai na gatos | dos siento |
| 1000 | chalan | mit |
| 2000 | huguiyai na chalan | dos mit |
| 10,000 | manutai na chalan | dies mit |

Adapted from Janice J. Beaty's *Guam Today and Yesterday*. Agaña, Guam: Department of Education, 1968. Used by permission of the Guam Department of Education.

# Calendar of Chamorros

The ancient Chamorros measured the year from harvest to harvest. *Sakkan* (year) means "harvest." The year was divided into thirteen moons. Each moon seems to have been associated with something that was happening at that time of year. For example, Umatalaf was the time to catch red snappers (*gatafe*).

## Ancient Chamorro Calendar

January: *Tumaiguini* - "thus," or "in this way," or "like this."

February: *Maimo*

March: *Umatalaf* - " to go catch *gatafe* (red snapper)."

April: *Lumuhu* - "to go back, to return to the attack" - this may refer to the return of the year.

May: *Makmamao*

June: *Mananaf* or *Fananaf* - "the crawling time," "to go on all fours," or "to drag the body" - perhaps this refers to crabs, which go to the sea to breed.

July: *Semo*

August: *Tenhos* - "angry" - perhaps because of the unsettled weather associated with August. Some say it means "jealous."

September: *Lumamlam* or *Lamlam* - "lightning"

October: *Fanggualo'* or *Fa'gualo* - "planting time," or "time to hoe the field."

November: *Sumongsong* - "to put in the stopper" - perhaps because the heavy rains have stopped or "stop in a village" or "the time to mend nets."

December: *Umayanggan* - "troubled," "melancholy," - the season of slight but frequent showers.

*Umagahaf* or *Omagahaf* - "to get crayfish" - the moon to go catch freshwater shrimp or, some say, a kind of "sea crab."

# ARTS

# Debate

The ancient Chamorros held people who were good at debating in high esteem. They called this skill *mari*. Children were taught debating skills. Adults competed in intervillage debates. Each debater and his supporters gathered in barn-like structures, which faced each other. The debaters argued from early in the morning until around two in the afternoon. Then they broke for lunch. Sometimes the debates became fierce and actually led to ritual fighting. The contestants and their supporters retired to a field outside the village and threw slingstones at each other.

# Singing, Dancing, Poetry, and Storytelling

The ancient Chamorros enjoyed singing, dancing, and storytelling. Men and women who were gifted in creating poetry were highly respected. Storytelling was often in the form of poetic songs. Love, victory, ancestry, village, prayers, history, myths, and legends kindled their creative spirit.

Sopranos, contraltos, and falsettos sang in harmony. The men sang tenor. The women stood in a circle and danced. They kept time by shaking a stick that had shells attached to it, by rhythmic slapping, and by hand movements.

There are no early accounts of stick dancing. Chamorro stick dancing is practiced today. Since other Micronesian people have these dances, it seems likely that the ancient Chamorros had them, too.

There was competition in dancing between men and women. Since relatives could not compete, it seems likely that these dances were part of courtship. The women formed a circle and began to dance. A man challenged one of the women to a dance-off. The women in the circle declared who won the contest.

The most remarkable Chamorro art form remains the *chamorrita*. The *chamorrita* is a Chamorro folk song sung in four-line stanzas. It has a single tune to which many different songs are created. Oftentimes the *chamorrita* is made up as the singer goes along. So, it is the extemporaneous creation of poetry. These four-line poems are sung to another person, who is expected to answer the poems by singing back a response.

The ancient Chamorros gambled on who could sing the most verses of a *chamorrita*. During the competition, one singer sang four lines. The opponent made up four lines to answer.

The *chamorrita* usually has two **couplets** and a single tune. The second and fourth lines of the verse rhyme. It is permissible for the fourth line to be unrelated to the first in meaning. Sometimes a group of singers sang in chorus or extemporaneously took turns singing. This bantering and joking often was about some important person. Sometimes the first two lines were carried by a tenor, falsetto, or soprano, and the last two were sung in chorus. At other times an individual sang to another in falsetto.

In 1981 Pope John Paul visited Guam. The women of Luta (Rota) wove a huge pandanus mat for this celebration, which took place in Agaña. During the two-week period it took to weave the mat, the *manamko* (older women) sang *chamorritas* as they worked. The weaving and singing started in the morning and continued nonstop until lunch. After lunch they continued until time for supper. Every day the cycle continued. One woman sang four lines, then another answered, and so on, throughout the day. They improvised on the spot. Back and forth they created verses, never failing to think of an appropriate response. They often teased each other in good fun. The following examples of *chamorritas* were recorded by Gertrude Hornbostel over 50 years ago.

**13.2 *Chamorrita* Tune.** Adapted from *Archaeology of the Marianas Islands*, by Laura Maud Thompson. Published

## Chamorrita Songs

*Bendabat yan rimulinu*
    Changeable wind and whirlwind
*Nanalao, na freskon manglo';*
    O mother, what refreshing winds.
*Kada bes di hu konsidera,*
    Every time that I think about it,
*Kana yu' ha puno' anglo'.*
    It practically kills me.

---

*Basta neni nai tumanges,*
    Sweetheart, please stop crying,
*Sa'un na' tailaya mata-mu;*
    For your beautiful face will be marred;
*Po'lo palu gi lago'-mu,*
    Save some of your tears to cry,
*Para an matai si nana-mu.*
    Over your mother's death.

Source: *Archaeology of the Marianas Islands*, by Laura Maud Thompson. Published as Bernice P. Bishop Museum Bulletin 100 in 1932 by Bishop Museum Press. Used by permission. The original text has been retranslated and put in modern orthography by Ann Rivera of the Guam Bilingual and Bicultural Program.

Young people were taught to sing, dance, and make harmonious music. The *uritoi* (unmarried people) of a village were responsible for the creation of new songs (poetry) and dances. Some of their work was in a mysterious allegorical language called *fino' gualafon* (literally, full moon language). If the ancient Chamorros were like other Micronesians, songs and dances were considered property. They could be given as gifts. Sometimes one village gave another village the right to do a particular dance. Young people isolated themselves while they created new songs or poems, and while they choreographed the dance steps.

The *bilembao tuyan* is a musical stringed instrument. It has a single string and uses a coconut or a gourd held against the stomach for a sounding device. It is not recorded in any of the early accounts of the ancient Chamorros. It may have been introduced from the Philippines. Some say that the Spanish introduced it to the Chamorros from South America. This seems unlikely. This instrument is found even among the Zulus of South Africa. It seems likely that many people throughout the world have independently created this type of musical instrument. The music produced by the *bilembao tuyan* sounds very much like the music from Indonesia. It has a low-pitched, twangy sound, which is almost hypnotic. Those people who still play the *bilembao tuyan* are convinced the instrument is of ancient origin. They learned to play it from their parents or grandparents, who told them it was an ancient Chamorro tradition.

13.3 *Bilembao Tuyan*

*Bilembao tuyan*s are made from the *pagu* tree (wild hibiscus or *Hibiscus tiliaceus*). One report claims they were made of *palu maria* or *da'ok* (*Calophyllum inophyllum*). A bowed limb, *binadu*, was used. After the bark was peeled, it was about two to two and one-half inches in diameter, and eight to 15 feet long. The limb was rigged like a bow and arrow. Today, wire is used to string them. During Spanish times, pineapple fiber was used for a string. The side of the bow toward the string was planed off just a little. If the ancient Chamorros had *bilembao tuyan*s, they probably used *pagu* fiber or coconut fiber for strings.

In order to make this instrument, one half of a dried gourd or coconut shell is attached to the bow as a sounding device. The gourd or coconut shell is fastened to the bow so that the open side faces away from the bow. It is fastened on the side away from the string. Musicians who use the shorter bows place the sounding device midway along the bow. Those who use the longer bows place it about one third of the bow's length from the top. Some musicians use two half coconut shells for sounding devices.

A stick 15 inches long and about three-eighths of an inch in diameter is used to strike, pick, or draw across the single string. The other hand is used to run up and down the underneath side of the string above the sounding device. This varies the pitch of the sound produced by the stick. The open cavity of the gourd or coconut shell is held against the musician's stomach to improve the quality of the sounding device.

Although it is not mentioned in the early records, it seems likely that the *bilembao pachot* (Jew's harp) was also used in ancient times. It is a small musical instrument that is held between the teeth. It is played by striking a curved stick with the finger. It has a haunting, wailing sound similar to the *bilembao tuyan*. This instrument is found all over the world.

*Bilembao tuyan* and *bilembao pachot* are Chamorro names, but they are very similar to words used in the Philippines. When inventions are introduced to another culture, the foreign name is often adopted, too. But since the languages of the Philippines and Chamorro are Indonesian languages, it is hard to draw any firm conclusions on this matter.

Around 1760 the use of two kinds of flutes died out. One flute was called a *banai* (the name of a flute from the Philippines). The other was the *silag*. One of these was a nose flute. The flutes made a deep soft sound. One of the flutes was two and one-half feet long and as big around as the little finger. It was cut like a whistle. It had three holes on the upper side for each hand, and one hole on the lower side for each thumb. These instruments could have been ancient instruments, but we cannot be sure.

The ancient Chamorro music, singing, dancing, and poetry are also discussed in the chapter on "Customs."

# Visual Arts

Little is recorded about ancient Chamorro art. We can see great beauty in some of the finely worked shell artifacts and stone tools. Unfortunately, most ancient Chamorro art was in perishable materials like wood, and in the performing arts. Even the pottery has not survived in unbroken form. Early explorers have recorded that wooden statues were made. One account says that images of men with long hair tied in one or two knots at the crown were used as figureheads in ancient Chamorro canoes. Pictures of dead relatives were drawn on bark and pieces of wood and kept in caves. The cave where they were kept was called a *guma' alumsek*. None of the ancient Chamorro art has survived except for their drawings.

Throughout the Mariana Islands, drawings have been left on cave walls. Writings on or in stone are called **petroglyphs**. Sometimes they are of a single human figure. More frequently, the drawings seem to describe a great accomplishment or event. The ancient Chamorros' petroglyphs show weapons, animals, and environmental features. Nevertheless, they are mostly action-packed drawings of human figures. A few of the figures seem to resemble Chinese characters, which began as pictorial images.

Most of the petroglyphs are white, but some are black. The white drawings show up best in the dimly lit caves. The white pigment seems to have been painted on the cave walls with the fibrous end of a frayed stick or perhaps the end of several brush-like seeds found in the Mariana Islands. The white pigment seems to be quicklime or *åfok*. This fired and slaked coral is still chewed with betel nut. Every Chamorro is likely to have had an ample supply of this writing material at all times, because *pugua'* (betel nut), *pupulu* betel pepper leaf), and *åfok* were carried by most adults. Some of the white petroglyphs seem to be filled engravings.

The black drawings are frequently simpler in design. They were probably drawn with the sharp point of a charred stick. Through the passage of time, the charcoal has set into the porous limestone cave wall and cannot be easily rubbed off.

Archaeologists have determined the authenticity of these cave drawings. They have not determined how old they are.

Ancient Chamorro petroglyphs can be found on Guam in caves on the north coast, at Mergagan Point, at Inarajan Bay, and at Talofofo caves. Petroglyphs are found on Tinian in a cave in the Dumpke area. On Saipan, petroglyphs are found in the Laulau district on Magicienne Bay and in the Calavero area. Visitors to these caves should not touch the fragile drawings. These petroglyphs are one of our important contacts with the ancient Chamorros. Future generations deserve the privilege of seeing these treasures from the past.

Petroglyphs are found in the main Talofofo Cave and in the second cave on the left as you approach the "Eye of the Needle." At the "Eye of the Needle," there is a very small cave on the Talofofo River side of the natural bridge. It is necessary to use a flashlight to see this petroglyph. Some of the Talofofo Cave petroglyphs have been carved out of the cave wall and taken to the Bishop Museum in Honolulu where they are on permanent display.

a                                          b

**13.4 Ancient Chamorro Petroglyphs: (a) Laulau, Saipan; (b) Inarajan Bay.** Adapted from *Archaeology of the Marianas Islands*, by Laura Maud Thompson. Published as Bernice P. Bishop Museum Bulletin 100 in 1932 by Bishop Museum Press.

**13.5 Talofofo Cave Petroglyphs: (a) selected figures; (b) group of figures.** Adapted from *Archaeology of the Marianas Islands*, by Laura Maud Thompson. Published as Bernice P. Bishop Museum Bulletin 100 in 1932 by Bishop Museum Press.

The easiest ancient Chamorro petroglyphs to see are at Gadao's Cave, along the north shore of Inarajan Bay. A battle scene is inscribed on the wall. Two large stick figures appear to be in mortal combat. Legend claims that these figures are **Gadao** and **Malaguana**. Gadao was the *maga'lahi* (head chief) of Inarajan. Malaguana held the same position in Tumon. Each of these men thought that he was the smartest, wisest, and best looking. Malaguana had heard stories about Gadao's prowess. He went to Inarajan to prove that he was stronger than Gadao.

In the jungle outside of Inarajan, Malaguana came upon Gadao, who identified himself as Gadao's servant. He asked him where he could find Gadao. Malaguana said that he was going to show Gadao who was the strongest. Gadao said that he would take Malaguana to the man he sought, but first they should eat. He warned Malaguana about the awesome strength of the *maga'lahi* of Inarajan.

Anxious to demonstrate his great strength, Malaguana offered to gather the coconuts for the meal. He grabbed a nearby coconut tree and shook it so hard that all the coconuts fell down. Gadao, acting as if nothing unusual had happened, thanked Malaguana and took one of the brown coconuts. He squeezed it so hard that grated coconut meat oozed through the husk. Malaguana panicked. He thought that if Gadao's servant had all this strength, then the master must be much stronger. Using the excuse that he had a call of nature, Malaguana headed for his outrigger canoe.

Gadao swam after him. Malaguana said that he had to return to Tumon. Gadao said that he would help him row, but instead Gadao paddled toward Inarajan. Each man rowed with all his power. The canoe split in the middle. Malaguana's half flew to Tumon. Gadao's half dug a ditch so wide that it quickly filled with water and became the As Magas River. This explains why the As Magas river seems to have no source. Many claim that Gadao then went to his cave and recorded his clever victory over Malaguana. Old Chamorros claim that Gadao was proud, because he could claim victory without even fighting.

Other Chamorros claim that Gadao's Cave was formed when Gadao threw Malaguana into the rock wall along Inarajan Bay. They say that, after that fight, Gadao went into the cave and created

**13.6 Gadao's Cave Petroglyph.** The drawing is actually white on a light-yellowish-brown cave wall. Adapted from *Ancient Chamorro Kinship Organization*, by Lawrence J. Cunningham. Published by L. Joseph Press in 1984.

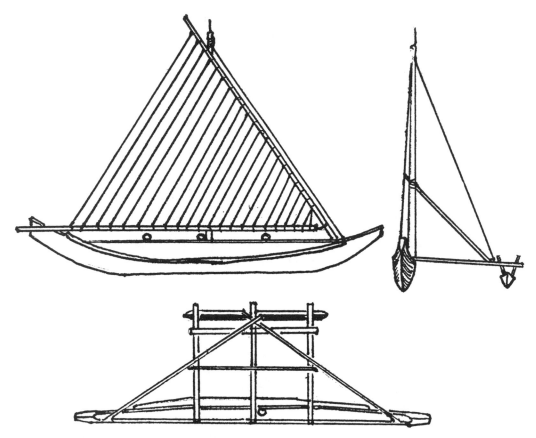

**13.7 A Sketch of the Chamorro Flying Proa made in 1742 by Commodore George Anson's British Expedition.** Adapted from *Canoes of Oceania*, by A. C. Haddon and James Hornell. Published as Bernice P. Bishop Museum Special Publication 27 in 1936 by Bishop Museum Press.

the petroglyphs that we see today. The drawings are supposed to illustrate his victory over Malaguana. The people of Inarajan still call bigshots "Gadao."

Humans know that some day they will die. This causes some people to want to leave a mark so that future generations will remember them. The stark, silent stickmen at Gadao's Cave still speak for the ancient Chamorros who created them.

# OUTRIGGER CANOES AND NAVIGATION

Early visitors were more impressed by the Chamorro sailing vessels than by any other aspect of their culture. Hundreds of Chamorro canoes came out to greet these foreign explorers. These famous European navigators described the Chamorro canoe as the best canoe of its type in the world. They called it the "flying proa." The ancient Chamorros called their oceangoing outrigger canoe a *sakman*. When they were ready to carry sail, it became a *ladjak* (sail). The next size smaller

was a *lelek*. Medium-sized canoes were *dudings*. The smallest canoe with a sail was called *duduli*. The same-sized craft without a sail was a *panga*. The small reef canoe was a *galaide'*.

The ancient Chamorro outrigger canoe had a very sophisticated design, and the ancient Chamorros had a successful navigation system, too. Laura Thompson, an anthropologist who studied Chamorro culture, claimed the outrigger canoe best expressed the spirit and creativity of the Chamorros. She felt the flying proa demonstrated that the ancient Chamorros were not just gatherers, farmers, and toolmakers, but also were spontaneous, gleeful, and playful.

A typical outrigger canoe was 26 to 28 feet long and less than two feet wide. War canoes ranged up to 40 feet in length. The long, deep, narrow hull served as a keel. A canoe this size would often have a crew of five to seven men or women. The smaller canoe hulls were made out of the trunk of a breadfruit tree (*dokdok* was preferred to *lemmai*). Usually they started with a single dugout tree trunk and built up the sides with planks. Split tree trunks were adzed down into smooth planks.

Most canoes were three to five feet deep. The planks were lashed together with coconut fiber rope and caulked. A coarse braid of coconut fiber rope was covered with a putty made of powered quicklime and coconut oil or boiled down breadfruit sap. This sap is a natural vegetable gum.

Canoes of 18 feet and longer were made of two dugout breadfruit tree trunks sewn together end to end. The outrigger booms, mast, and sail booms were probably made of bamboo. The float, made of breadfruit wood, was attached to the booms by wood rods, which were inserted into the float. The rods extended from the float to the booms in a V-shape. The float was about one-third to one-half the length of the canoe. The outrigger booms were not placed into holes in both sides of the canoe as shown in the original Anson illustration. Large holes like that would have weakened the canoe. Instead, only small holes were made in the hull for lashings, and the booms were tied on to the hull. The mast in the illustration would lean forward when under sail. Also, there was a deck built on the outrigger booms.

Although the ends of the hull were the same, the sides of the hull were different. The outrigger side was rounded. The lee side opposite the outrigger was flat to offer resistance to leeward drift. The thickness of the hull was about one inch at the gunwales and up to two inches thick at the keel.

The ends of the canoes curved upward. Cavendish, who visited the Mariana Islands in 1588, reported that there were figureheads on the ends of the canoes. The wooden busts had hair tied in one or two knots at the crown and resembled the Chamorros.

The canoes were either reddish brown or black. The paint was made from a mixture of coconut oil, quicklime, and red clay. Soot and charcoal from burnt coconut husks were added for black paint. Paint could also be made with *lemmai* sap. Both of these types of paint are very shiny and have a varnished look. The paint was applied with a pounded fragment of a coconut husk.

Outriggers kept the canoe from turning over easily and served as a weight to help balance the canoe against the force of the wind on the sails. The outrigger was constructed of a float suspended from poles extending outward on the windward side of the canoe. A platform for passengers and cargo was built over the outrigger

frame. No one has recorded that the ancient Chamorros had a lee platform like that of the Carolinian canoes. Nevertheless, since they had contact with the Carolinians and the lee platform is so useful, it seems likely that they had them, too.

A flying proa was fitted with a single lateen (triangular) sail. Magellan was so impressed by the Chamorro canoes that he named the Mariana Islands the Islands of Lateen Sails (Islas de los Latinas). Unfortunately, he later changed the name to the Islands of Thieves (Islas de los Ladrones) because a group of Chamorros took one of his small boats.

The lateen sail was supported on a mast, which was fitted into a socket at the middle of the length of the canoe. It was set just a little off center, favoring the outrigger side of the hull. The mast did not go to the bottom of the hull. It rested near the middle outrigger boom. The ropes for the rigging were called *talin gapu*. The sail was attached to a boom on each side. The uppermost boom fitted into a socket at the bow of the canoe. The mast served to hold the uppermost boom aloft. The mast leaned toward the bow.

The sails were made of finely woven pandanus leaves. They were called *guafak ladjak*. During rainy weather, the sails were lowered. When the sails were wet they became too heavy to use. A triangular-shaped sail allows a boat to sail very close to the wind. This means that the sailor will have to tack less when sailing to a windward destination. The narrow hull, which was rounded to the windward and flat to the lee side, also helped the ancient Chamorros sail very close to the wind without drifting off course.

Small sailing canoes were steered with a hand-held paddle. Along the reef they were even poled along. Larger canoes used a staff with a board attached at the far end for a rudder. Care had to be taken to keep the outrigger toward the wind. The pressure of wind on the sail tended to raise the float out of the water. If the outrigger was to leeward, the float would be driven under the water. This caused the canoe to capsize. The canoe on the Guam Seal is drawn incorrectly in this regard. The mast is on the wrong side of the sail. When the sails were trimmed perfectly, the outrigger float should skim along the surface. If the wind on the sails raised the float out of the water, the crew moved out along the booms to counteract that force.

When sailing to windward, a sailor had to be

**13.8 Guam Seal**

The flying proas were very fast. They could sail over 20 miles per hour. A four-day voyage to Manila is on record. This would mean the sailors averaged 12.5 knots.

The ancient Chamorros used the flying proa as the means to colonize the Mariana Islands. Besides adventuresome missions of discovery, the outrigger canoes were used for trading, deep-sea fishing, visiting, and war. The ancient Chamorros also used them for fun. They raced their canoes and used them for family outings.

In addition to the oceangoing *sakman*, the ancient Chamorros had a smaller reef canoe called a *galaide'*. Even though it was a sailing canoe, it was often just paddled or poled along. Usually, it carried three sailors, but could be handled by one person sitting in the middle. One person sat in the middle to bail and helped move the sail. One person sat at each end of the canoe and steered when his end became the stern. When one end of the canoe became the bow, the person positioned the boom in place.

Canoes could not be left in the water. Even though the canoes were painted, the water would eventually rot them. Nor could they be left in the sun. The sun would crack the wood and dry out the vegetable gum caulking. When the canoes were not in use, they were covered with coconut leaves, or placed in a shed, or in large boathouses. Some canoes were stored under the raised floor of *latte* houses. Canoes were hung under the elevated floor.

Sailing was the most hazardous activity of early humans. With all their skill in building canoes and developing a trustworthy navigation system, they could not always be sure of success. Uncontrollable forces, like wind, bad weather, currents, and hidden reefs could upset their plans. The ancient Chamorros believed that humans could increase their control over these mysterious elements and improve their luck by following rituals. Unfortunately, these rituals have been lost. Other Micronesians' sailing customs are still practiced. They observe strict measures to insure success. As the canoe is built, there are special ceremonies to satisfy supernatural forces. Besides careful observation of the signs that predict weather, there are also religious ceremonies prior to a voyage.

It is interesting to note how different ancient Chamorro and modern watercraft are. Today people try to overcome nature by building strong,

careful. Since the outrigger must be kept to windward in order to tack, the sail had to be moved to the other end of the canoe. So what had just been the bow became the stern with each tack. A helmsman was stationed at each end of the boat. These men, with the help of two others, moved the sail from end to end. The fifth man was responsible for bailing out the hull. While sailing, the crew also trimmed the sails.

Although families went sailing for pleasure, there is nothing in the historical record to indicate that women sailed canoes. Fathers began to teach their sons to sail at the age of four or five. Young men 14 years old knew how to sail. By the age of 16 or 18, they set out to sea alone. Some early explorers described the ancient Chamorros as the best seamen yet discovered.

sturdy boats. Sometimes the forces of nature are too strong, and modern boats are broken beyond repair. The ancient Chamorro outrigger canoe was designed in harmony with nature. It was lashed together. It could give instead of breaking. If it did break, it would do so at the lashed points, so it could easily be repaired, even at sea. Modern man tends to view nature as an enemy that must be conquered. The ancient Chamorros saw that they were part of nature and had to live in harmony with nature. Modern ecologists are beginning to realize this fundamental fact.

The ancient Chamorros had a navigation system that allowed them to sail out of the sight of land and return. Some men were named Faulos-gna, which translates as "fortunate navigator"; others were named Agad-gna (deft in the art of steering a canoe). The ancient Chamorros used the wind, waves, and stars to navigate. Birds, clouds, swells, and even phosphorescence in the water could lead them to a safe landfall. Thousands of years before Leif Ericson (1000) or Columbus (1492) sailed the Atlantic, the Chamorros were sailing in the open ocean waters of the Pacific. They probably reached the Mariana Islands around 2000 B.C. George Anson, a British explorer of the Mariana Islands in 1742, recognized just what an extraordinary invention the flying proa was. He admitted that any nation, no matter how skillful and intelligent, would be proud of such a technological accomplishment. These canoes sailed better and faster than any in the world at that time. They passed the other ships like a bird flying by.

# MEDICINE (*AMOT*)

Of all the ancient Chamorro arts and skills, medicine (*amot*) probably has survived the most intact. Today, there are still highly respected older men and women who practice traditional medicine. They are called **suruhanus** and **suruhanas**. *Suruhanu* is derived from the Spanish language. There is some mistrust between members of this profession. The greatest mistrust is between *suruhanus* and *suruhanas* rather than within those groups. They are usually trained by apprenticeship to an older relative of the same sex. Much of their knowledge is kept secret. They use herbs, magic, massage, and their personal power to cure the sick. They have very successful practices. Their success, like that of all doctors, depends on the scientific value of their treatments and the psychological confidence they give their patients.

Today, these healers usually accept gifts for their services; nevertheless, in the past, they were sometimes paid. There are more *suruhanas* than *suruhanus*, but each village in the Mariana Islands has at least one or two. Today their purpose is to promote good health within the community. In the past, the healers, who were mostly female, tended to specialize. Some were best for taking care of fevers, others set broken limbs, and some were midwives. Some men, called *kakahnas* or *makahnas*, used their power to cure or cause illness by spiritual means.

*Suruhanus* and *suruhanas* are thought to have a special calling for healing. Practitioners pass their healing knowledge on to a relative who seems to have the intelligence and the calling. A breach-born baby is believed to have a special aptitude for becoming a *suruhanu* or a *suruhana*. Breach births were believed to have been caused by the presence of a *taotaomo'na* (ancient ghost) when the baby was born, or because the mother saw a *taotaomo'na* while she was pregnant. The *suruhanus* possess a special relationship with the spirit world. They often have a *taotaomo'na ga'chong* (ancient ghost partner) who helps them cure their patients.

According to traditional healers, illness can be caused by spiritual means or by natural causes. The spiritual illness could be caused by evil spirits or by sorcery. In ancient times, it seems that men called *makahnas* or *kahkanas* cured the spiritual sicknesses, and female *suruhanas* cured the natural illnesses with herbs and massage. The women set broken bones. It was believed that the *makahnas* had the power to make people sick by calling on their supernatural powers. Today, *suruhanus* and *suruhanas* treat both types of illnesses, and use an integrated treatment of herbs, magic, massage, and their personal power.

An *ante* (ancestral spirit) or a *taotaomo'na* (ghost of an ancient ancestor) is believed capable of causing sickness or even death, if it has been offended. Women and children are thought to be at greatest risk. Trespassing or forgetting to ask permission to pick fruit, or go to the bathroom in the jungle, are said to upset the *taotaomo'nas*. The illnesses the *taotaomo'nas* cause are frequently a constriction of the throat, not being able to swallow, problems with breathing or urinating, loss of appetite, some fevers and chills (*chetnot maipe*), paralysis, craziness (*atmariao*), swelling (*pokpok*), marks on the body, and the inability to talk.

Modern *suruhanus* categorize illnesses as hot or cold sicknesses. Since this practice is similar to that of Mexican folk doctors, we cannot be sure that the ancient Chamorro *suruhanas* had this belief. According to this theory, if a disease is hot, cold medicine (*amot fresko*) is prescribed. *Gaso'so*, the soap plant, is an example of a cold medicine.

After a *suruhana* diagnoses the illness, fresh plants are collected to cure it. The medicinal value of plants is well known by pharmacists. Unfortunately, most of the plants on Guam have not been studied by scientists. Nevertheless, most experts are sure that the plants chosen at least contain many important vitamins. *Nunu* (banyan tree or *Ficus prolixa*) root sap has proven to stop the flow of blood when placed on a wound. Further research will probably confirm the medicinal value of many of the plants used by the *suruhanus*.

A *lusong* (stone mortar) and *lommok* (pestle) are still used to crush the plants. Often a tea is made by boiling the crushed *hagon* (leaf), the *hale'* (root), and the *lasas* (bark). Drops of the medicine are squeezed into the mouth of the patient or simply drunk.

Magical ashes from human sweat, white chicken feathers, and palm fronds are also used in treatments. Even the urine of a first-born male is used as medicine. Sometimes mystical body lotions are rubbed onto the body.

A massage is frequently used to relieve pain. In ancient times as many as four people would massage a patient by walking on the painful area. *Ugot* is the Chamorro word for this type of massage. *Suruhanus* and *suruhanas* squeezed a person's head with their thumbs, if the pain was in the head. The massages were very vigorous and pounding. Today some *suruhanus* and *suruhanas* actually hide rocks in their hands. Others use the innermost heart of the banana tree trunk as a small club to pound on a patient.

Some *suruhanas* give advice on what foods their patients should eat and what foods they should avoid.

In all cases the healer tells the patient what is wrong, and takes active scientific, magical, and religious steps to cure it. Healers, through these actions and because of their personal mystique, instill confidence in the patient. By having anxiety relieved, the patient is able to generate his or her own self-healing powers.

Family members are also very important in curing the sick. According to early accounts, they would not leave the side of the sick for even a moment day or night. Friends and relatives visited the sick and shared food with them.

# Cures for Natural Illnesses

### Headache (*malineg ulu*) caused by blood in the head

Soak a cloth in vinegar and place it on the patient's forehead; or massage the forehead with coconut oil; or tie a very young banana leaf or a *nonnak* leaf to the forehead.

### Headache (*malineg ulu*) caused by gas in the stomach

Drink a glass of water to which two tablespoons of vinegar and one tablespoon of sugar have been added; or squeeze *gaso'so'* leaves between the palms and drink a small amount.

### Headache and fever

Massage the whole body. Apply coconut oil. Give a dose of *amot pasmu* (medicine for pneumonia).

### Colds or pneumonia

Dose of *amot pasmu*:
3 *lodigao* (*Clerodendum inerme*) leaves
3 *akañghañg* (*Mucuna platyphylla*) leaves
3 *amot tumaga* (*Cassia sp.* or *Senna*) leaves
3 *gaso'so'* (*Columbrina asiatica*) leaves
2-1/2 *agao* (*Premna obtusifolia*) leaves
Pinch of salt
Boil in 1 *latandudu* (pint) of water.
If necessary, add *dadangsi ahgaga* (*Urena lobata*) root and *askuhijan adameluñg* root.

# Cures for Supernatural Illnesses

In Merizo there once was a missing girl. After a long search, she was found high in a tree. No one thought it was possible for her to climb this tree by herself. She wouldn't talk to anyone, and they could not get her down. As her brothers climbed for her, she climbed still higher. Her parents burned chicken feathers and palm shoots under the tree. When the smoke reached her, she allowed her brothers to take her down. Her eyes did not look natural, and she was afraid. She was cured only after her face and body were washed with the urine from one of her male relatives.

It is reported that the shock of being hit by an old woman's belt will often cure a child who has been frightened speechless. This sometimes works for *chetnot manman*, a condition in which a person stares blankly into space and cannot remember anything.

If the *taotaomo'na* causes *pokpok* (the swelling of the feet, mouth, or other parts of the body), *suruhanus* recommend applying the crushed leaves of *nonnak* (Hernandia sonora) and *gaso'so'* (Columbrina asiatica).

Finger-like marks on the body are thought to be caused by the *taotaomo'na*. These marks are red or brown. Sometimes they are like a bruise and start out yellow and turn purple. These marks can be prevented by rubbing onions and salt on the body. Cures for this condition include the application of urine on the mark. The urine should be from the patient's first-born male relative. The patient is also given two doses of *amot ginehi*, which is a tea consisting of the crushed leaves of *akañghañg* (Mucuna platyphylla), *dadangsi* (Urena lobata), *tumaga*, and *gaogao dankolo* (Tacca pinnatifida) and the ashes of burnt feathers and coconut leaf shoots.

Strong smelling substances, salt, religious amulets, and red-colored objects are used for keeping the *taotaomo'na* away.

Only a few examples of specific illnesses and cures have been presented here. More information on Chamorro medicine can be found in Patrick D. McMakin, "The Suruhanos: Traditional Curers on the Island of Guam. "*Micronesica* Vol. 14, No. 1, June 1978; or Laura M. Thompson' s *Guam and Its People*. New York: Princeton University Press, 1947. You may want to make some of the medicines, but you should not try them. They could be dangerous, if you get the wrong plant or the ingredients are not correctly prepared and mixed.

Folk medicines in other parts of the world have led to many modern medicines. For example, digitalis is a strong medicine used to stimulate the heart. It is made from the foxglove plant. Quinine is made from the bark of the cinchona tree. It is used in making drugs to treat malaria. Modern man learned of quinine's value from South American Indians. Resprine comes from folk medicine, too. Perhaps some day a full investigation will be done on the herbs used by the traditional healers of the Mariana Islands. The ancient Chamorros claimed they had a cure for every disease, prior to the time Europeans arrived. There is probably some truth to this. Only the healthy could have survived the long voyages to Guam. Unlike the area the Chamorros migrated from, Micronesia is malaria free. In Papua New Guinea, just 1,000 miles south of Guam, malaria is still the number one killer today.

# EDUCATION

The ancient Chamorros had an informal and effective educational system. Through education, they learned tradition, the use of tools and goods, and the way to exercise social power and responsibility. **Cultural transmission** is the process by which accumulated knowledge of one generation is passed on to other generations.

Children were not hurried to learn. Interested children simply observed and imitated the adult skills they were ready to learn. Children learned most things from their parents. Children were then given some guidance to improve their performance. There was no pressure and there were no classrooms. Early explorers have recorded that family ties were very close. A member of the Freycinet expedition said that ". . . there is no country where the parents are more affectionate toward their children, or where they take more pains to please and instruct them." Training was individualized, and the mimicking of adult behavior was play oriented.

Most ancient Chamorros had to learn some farming skills. Children's play probably included little garden plots. Early reports claim that boys played at war with darts and mud slingstones. Play built the strength and stamina children would need for adult work.

Observation of other Micronesian people shows that they are tolerant of children trying new things. Children in Yap play with machetes at a very young age and usually don't hurt themselves. The permissiveness of the parent builds confidence in the child that he or she is capable of handling adult work.

Boys imitated men's work and girls imitated women's work. Early accounts report that all healthy persons worked on farm plots. Children accompanied their parents to the field and were taught with love. Boys of four or five went sailing with their father and began to learn to sail. By the age of 14 they could sail as well as their fathers.

Traditions were passed from parents to children, too. Present day *bilembao tuyan* players report that they had no special training. They just watched and listened to their father or mother and just started practicing the skills. Wood carvers from Micronesia claim that they learned by watching their fathers. When they felt they were ready, they just started carving.

The *uritoi* were young people who formed clubs. The *uritoi* was an ancient Chamorro teenage peer group. A **peer group** is a group consisting of individuals who are approximately equal in such characteristics as age and social standing. The projects of the clubs allowed the members to learn, practice, and demonstrate their skills. For example, young men cleared trails and served as warriors. Social and vocational skills, which were learned in the home, were perfected in the clubs. Sex education took place in the clubs. Missionaries often criticized the practice of young men living with unmarried women in the *guma' uritao* (bachelor's house).

The primary means of any education is through language. In ancient Chamorro times, language was learned at home. Among the *uritoi*, language was experimented with and used in allegorical ways. They created songs that only the young could understand.

Specialized skills were secret in ancient Chamorro times. We can still see this practice among the *suruhanus* and *suruhanas* today. Secret clan histories, warfare, navigation, fishing, medicine, canoe building, magic, and spiritual matters were learned by apprenticeship. These types of special knowledge were the property of certain matrilineages. A mother's brother taught these skills to his sister's sons rather than his own sons. This type of knowledge was part of an ancient Chamorro's birthright. Mothers would teach secret knowledge to their daughters.

In order to obtain knowledge from non-relatives, the apprentice had to seek the favor of the teacher and pay for the expert's knowledge. Sometimes experts chose a particularly talented young person to teach, one who was capable, interested, and helpful. This practice made the parents financially obligated to the teacher.

Craftsmen were jealous and guarded their specialized skills. If *ålas* (tortoiseshell money) was offered to a master craftsperson for training, the expert could not refuse. But the craftsperson charged for each and every detail of his or her professional knowledge. Usually a young person would begin the quest for specialized knowledge by hanging around the professional. He or she would bring betel nut, run errands, and pick up after the teacher. If the expert thought the young person was worthy, and the student's lineage was willing to pay, instruction could begin. Usually, full instruction was not given until the teacher was very old. It is clear that knowledge was valued. People were willing to sacrifice and make payments to obtain it.

In rare cases a skilled craftsperson might teach a young person an important skill as a present. If the craftsperson's rank was above the rank of the child's parents and they consented, the craftsperson would give his own name to the child. This created a kind of alliance between the families.

Education is more than learning a series of skills for survival or even a profession. It is the means of preserving and changing culture. Education is the guardian of tradition, and the springboard for discovery and creation of new knowledge. Education through the extended family was the primary means by which ancient Chamorro children were socialized. **Socialization** is the process through which the individual learns to adjust to his society's rules and, as a result, becomes an accepted member of society.

The heart of any culture is found in its values. **Cultural values** are the assumptions shared by the members of a society as to what is right and wrong, good or bad, important or unimportant. Values are more important than simple skills. For example, it doesn't make a person less Chamorro to store things in a cardboard box rather than a coconut leaf basket. It does make a difference if a person stops respecting elders, people of higher status, or nature. When a society is ineffective in passing on its values, or its values are no longer clear, social disorganization will result. **Social disorganization** is a severe breakdown in the social order caused by failure to develop new behavioral guidelines needed to handle unique social situations.

Children learn their values by imitating the values of the adults they hold in high esteem. Most of this value training takes place at home. Ancient Chamorro values are discussed in the chapter on "Beliefs, Attitudes, and Values." In summary, the ancient Chamorros felt that once a child learned to share, he or she was well on the way to becoming a worthy adult.

# SUMMARY

The ancient Chamorros had many important arts and skills. In order to teach these arts and skills, they had an effective means of educating their young. Many of their most important skills, like tool making, stone work, the art of pottery making, farming, and fishing are covered in other chapters. Key skills described in this chapter are weaving, rope making, quicklime and salt production, and fire starting. The ancient Chamorros measured time by a lunar calendar. They had a system of measurement and counting.

Ancient Chamorro arts included debate, singing, dancing, poetry, storytelling, and cave drawing. The height of their performing arts was the *chamorrita*. The construction and navigation of oceangoing outrigger canoes were the most impressive aspects of the ancient Chamorros' material and technological cultures. Some ancient Chamorro medical knowledge is still being effectively used today.

Ancient Chamorro education was carried out by parents and skilled elders. Responsibility for getting an education was placed on the student.

# Chapter 14
# Social Structure

## INTRODUCTION

All around the world people organize to help satisfy their physical and mental needs. A hunting party, a **clan**, a tribe, a labor union, a corporation, or a nation is an organization that attempts to satisfy human needs. This includes physical and nonphysical needs. **Psychosocial needs** are those nonbiological needs of humans that have both psychological and social aspects. These needs must be satisfied if a person is to develop a well-integrated personality. **Social organization** regulates the way we behave. There are certain kinds of behaviors for people in the same gang, and a separate set of behaviors for outsiders. Relatives have very special bonds. The framework for these organizations is called **social structure**.

Like all aspects of culture, social structure is apt to change. Even so, there is one basic unit that is fundamental to all cultures' social structure. It is the family. Most **anthropologists** agree with this generalization, even though there have been efforts in some **societies** to break down the family's importance. For example, on a kibbutz (a collective farm or settlement in Israel) children visit their parents, but do not actually live with them. Even babies are kept away from their mothers in a nursery, except for specific times for feeding and playing. On some **communes** in China, children are separated from their parents a great deal of the time. Nevertheless, except for extreme cases, the family is still a fundamental unit of society.

**Society** is, broadly, the entire system of relationships existing among humans. Specifically, it is the largest group of people who share a unique way of life, occupy a definite territory, and think of themselves as a societal unit.

Let us look at the family. What is a family? How would you define family? Does your definition explain only your type of family system or does it apply to people everywhere? In other words, is your definition specific or general? Let us begin with a general definition of family. Then, we will look at **kinship** and the types of kinship systems in the world. Next, we will examine social **classes** and **castes**. With this basic understanding of social structure, we will examine our society today, and the society of the ancient Chamorros.

## FAMILY

## Nuclear Family

The **nuclear family** is a father, mother, and their children. The social structure of a family can be diagramed using symbols. A triangle represents a male. A circle represents a female. A shaded symbol represents **ego** (self, the person the diagram is about). When the gender of the person is not important, ego is represented by a shaded square. An equals sign is used to represent marriage. A vertical line is used to show that children come from their parents. The vertical line represents **descent**. Horizontal lines indicate that individuals are related as siblings (brothers and sisters). The first two letters of a relationship term are usually used to identify an individual. For example, a mother is "Mo," a brother is "Br," and a Husband is "Hu."

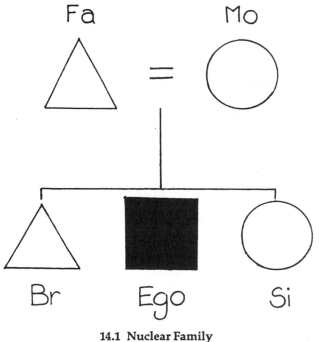

**14.1 Nuclear Family**

Since the nuclear family is found in all cultures throughout the world, it is **universal**. Wherever the nuclear family is found it has four functions:

1. Sexual: As husband and wife, a couple can enjoy legal sexual relations.

2. Reproductive: Married parents can have children recognized as legitimate by society.

3. Economic: The family cooperates to provide food, clothing and shelter for one another.

4. Education: Parents teach their children to walk and talk, and how to behave. In modern societies parents give part of this responsibility to the school. Parents must see that their children learn the means of survival and the ways of their people. Without this passing on of information a culture would die.

# Extended Family

An **extended family** is a family unit in which several generations of relatives live close to one another. The extended family includes all the relatives a person considers "close." Most people consider their grandfather (Gf), grandmother (Gm), uncle (Un), aunt (Au), cousins (Co), nephews (Ne), nieces (Ni), as well as mother, father, sister, and brother, "close" relatives.

There are two sides of the family, the father's side and the mother's side. The father's side of the family is called a **patrilineage**. The mother's side of the family is called a **matrilineage**.

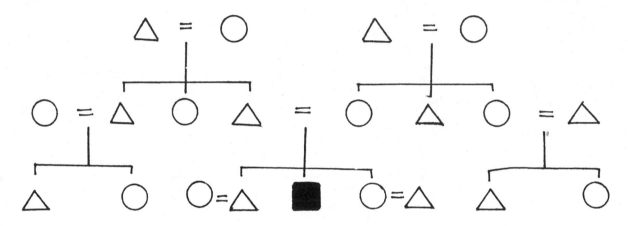

**14.2 Extended Family Diagram**

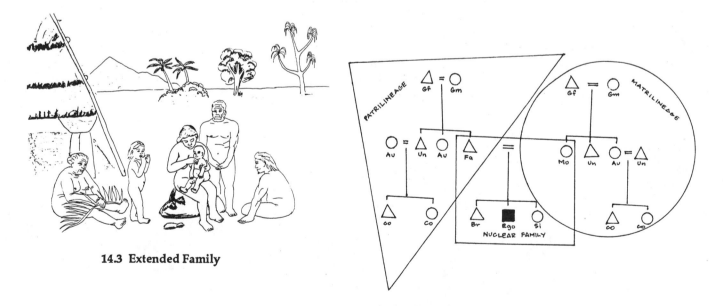

**14.3 Extended Family**

**14.4 Patrilineage, Matrilineage, & Nuclear Family**

In our society today we recognize both sides of our family as "close." But many cultures recognize only one side of their family as "close." Our kinship system is bilateral (both sides). Those societies that recognize only the father's side as "real" relatives are patrilineal. Those that recognize only the mother's side as "real" relatives are matrilineal.

Some relatives are "blood" relatives and others are relatives by marriage. Relatives who are descended from a common ancestor are "blood" relatives or **consanguineal** relatives. Relatives by marriage are **affinal** relatives.

On the "Consanguineal and Affinal Relatives" illustration a dot has been placed on all of ego's consanguineal or "blood" relatives. The relatives without dots are affinal relatives or relatives by marriage. Ego's affinal or marriage relatives are her husband (Hu); her mother's sister's husband (MoSiHu); her father's brother's wife (FaBrWi); her brother's wife (BrWi); and her sister's husband (SiHu).

In the diagram, ego's grandparents are the first generation. Ego's parents, aunts and uncles are the second generation. Ego's brothers, sisters, husband, brothers- and sisters-in-laws and cousins are all part of the same generation. In this chart they are the third generation. The fourth generation is composed of ego's children, nieces, nephews and, although not shown, her cousin's children.

The illustrations in this chapter are genealogical charts. **Genealogy** is literally the study of a person's genes, but it has come to mean the study of a person's descent. An individual who traces the descent of a person or families is a genealogist.

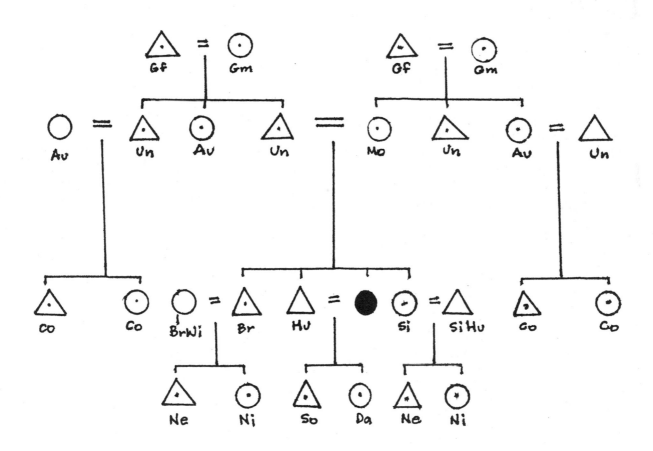

**14.5 Consanguineal and Affinal Relatives**

# KINSHIP

**Kinsmen** are a person's nuclear family and extended family. Kinship is the tie between children, their parents, and other relatives. Some of our kinsmen are related by "blood"; they are consanguineal relatives. Some of our kinsmen are related by marriage; they are affinal relatives. Some relatives may be both consanguineal and affinal. For example, if your mother's brother married your father's sister, that aunt would be a consanguineal aunt because she is your father's sister. She would be an affinal aunt because she married your mother's brother. We have some kinsmen that are not consanguineal; nor are they affinal. If a child is adopted, he or she will be treated just as if he or she was a consanguineal or "blood" relative.

We use kinship terms for some people who are not kinsmen. A priest is called father; a nun is called sister; a fellow union member is a brother or sister; and the *taotaomo'na* (ancestral ghost) is addressed as grandmother and grandfather. Godparents are another type of **fictional relative**. We use kinship terms for these people because we treat them as kinsmen.

Kinsmen, or relatives, have certain rights, duties, privileges, obligations, and responsibilities to one another. We are obligated to obey our parents, respect our grandparents, and help our brothers and sisters. Other people we treat in similar ways are often addressed with kinship terms. Most of our celebrations are concerned with kinship. When we gain new relatives by marriage, there is a ceremony and a celebration. When a new kinsman is born, we have a christening ceremony and add additional relatives through the custom of taking godparents. When we lose a kinsman, we have a funeral ceremony and a wake. From birth to death we are tied to our kinsman. We have important mutual responsibilities and privileges with our relatives.

## Kinship Systems

There are many ways to classify kinship systems. Often they are classified on the basis of cousin terminology. So that we can understand our modern kinship system and the kinship system of the ancient Chamorros, we must study **bilateral descent**, **patrilineal descent**, and **matrilineal descent**. Patrilineal relates to the tracing of descent through the father's line. Matrilineal relates to the tracing of descent through the mother. Bilateral descent traces kinship through both sides of the family more or less equally. Today, we feel related to our mother's and our father's relatives. Of course there must be some limit to this. Today most people in the United States do not consider people relatives beyond first cousins. Marriage is generally accepted between second cousins and more distant relatives. The Anglo-Saxons (the English language came from these people) in medieval times were obligated to assist relatives as distant as sixth cousins. Today, in the United States, it is hard to imagine being obligated to that many people. Chamorros are more concerned with relatives beyond the nuclear family than are most Americans. Although obligations extend beyond third cousins, marriage is usually accepted among relatives that distant.

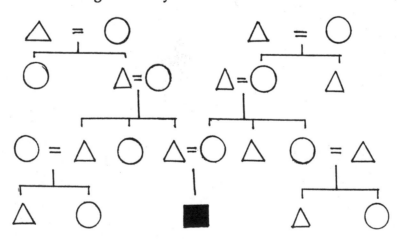

**14.6 Bilateral Descent**

160

Most cultures limit their relatives, not by generation, but by the side of the family they are on. In many cultures important relatives are either in the father's line, the patrilineal side; or in the mother's line, the matrilineal side. In a patrilineal society only the father's side of the family are considered relatives. In a matrilineal society the relatives of ego are limited to the mother's side of the family. People who do not group themselves bilaterally usually form clans. Clans are either matrilineal or patrilineal.

only the **matriclan, patriclan,** and the **avuncuclan** are found in known cultures. No known culture has an **amitaclan.** If such a culture existed, descent would be patrilineal and husbands would move to their wife's territory after marriage.

Clans have the problem of the in-marrying husband or wife, and must make a compromise. It is forbidden to marry a clan member, because all clan members, no matter how distant, are considered close relatives. A member of a clan must marry an outsider. **Exogamy** is the practice

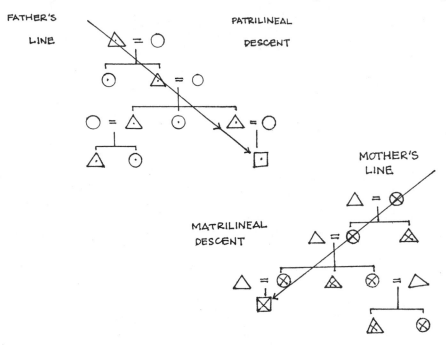

**14.7 Patrilineal and Matrilineal Descent**

# CLAN

A clan is a group of two or more **lineages** who are or think they are descended from a common ancestor. Usually clan members claim to be descended from a common mythological ancestor. Anthropologists do not always agree on the meaning of clan and often use the word in different ways. Today, most authorities agree that true clans must also be localized around either husbands or wives. The husband must move to his wife's family's territory, or the wife must move to the husband's territory. These two rules of residence, when combined with the two types of lineages (either patrilineal or matrilineal), mean there are theoretically four possible types of clans. Anthropologists must say theoretically because

of selecting a mate from outside one's own group. Tribal and clan exogamy are common. The outsider must give up his or her former clan membership after the marriage.

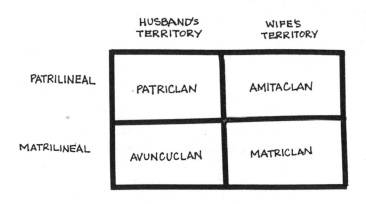

**14.8 Types of Clans**

In a patriclan and an avuncuclan, the wife must give up her clan membership and join her husband's clan. In matriclan societies, the husband must give up his clan and join his wife's clan. Children in the patriclan belong to the father's clan. In the matriclan the children belong to the mother's clan.

In the avuncuclan the children belong to the mother's clan, even though they are raised in their father's territory. In the avuncuclan, sons must return to their mother's clan land when they become young men. Often, sons will stay with their mother's brother after they come of age. Young women stay with their family until they marry. At the time of marriage, women move to their husband's territory. In the avuncuclan system, a woman's sons will have **only** land rights in the mother's brother's territory.

Clans are designed to meet the mental and physical needs of their members. Clans organize families into political and economic groups. Land is not owned by individual persons but by the clan. Land is controlled by the clan for the good of all the members. Family heads are the leaders in the clan. Clans organize families over many generations. Old clan members die, but new members are always being born. In this way the clan goes on and on.

Clans celebrate births, deaths, and other important events in the lives of their members. The clan members cooperate to meet their economic needs of food, clothing, and shelter. The clan members cooperate to give each other a sense of belonging. Clans usually look to their ancestors for spiritual uplifting.

Clan members stick together. The clan assumes responsibility for its members. If a clan member does something right or wrong, the entire clan shares in the praise or the blame. If a clan member is done a favor by an outsider, the entire clan is obligated to help repay the non-clan member. If a clan member is harmed, the entire clan will seek revenge.

The purpose of the clan is to be a person's everything. The clan determines who a person will marry, what kind of occupation a person will have, what the person's religion will be, and the amount of respect a person will receive inside and outside his or her clan.

How does the clan system work? A clan is like a modern corporation in some ways. There are rules of membership. You must be born into or adopted by a clan. Like a corporation, a clan organizes people to produce. A clan puts all of its resources together for the good of its members. Corporations have names and symbols, called trademarks. **W** is Westinghouse's trademark. The symbols for clans are called **totems**. Totems are usually an animal, a plant, or some force in nature. Some American Indian clans have the wolf for their totem. The clan name and symbol often influence the personality of the clan members. If this is true, would you rather meet a shark clansperson or a crab clansperson? What would the owl clan be noted for? Would wise people be limited to the owl clan? A clan's name and symbol have a limited effect on its members. There are still many personality types within a clan.

14.9 Halu'u Clan

In a clan and a corporation, individual members come and go, but the organization exists over many years. Corporations show great respect for their founders and so do clans. Clan ancestors are almost worshipped. Such extreme respect is called **veneration**. This respect usually means shark clansmen do not eat shark, or if they do it requires a special ceremony. As a person moves up the corporate ladder, promotions are celebrated. In a clan there are usually initiation ceremonies for members when they are old enough to marry.

Corporations have a system of rank from the president on down. Every person has a title or job description. In a clan there is a chief. Each lineage in the clan also has a less important chief or head-person. Each person in the clan has his specially ranked position. Usually, the older people get, the more respect they are given. Rank within a lineage is based on seniority. People respect those older than themselves and expect respect from the younger clan members.

The one big difference between a corporation and a clan is that the clan is never impersonal. Clan members are relatives; they depend on each other; they share and they care for one another.

In summary, clans are composed of two or more lineages who think they are descended from a common ancestor, and whose lineages follow a specific rule of residence. There are three known types of clan: patriclan, matriclan, and avuncuclan. In the patriclan, residence and lineage are dominated by the males. In the matriclan, residence and lineage are dominated by the females. In the avuncuclan, males control residence, but females dominate the lineage. Clans are like corporations. They organize people into effective work and ritual groups, have names, symbols, ranked positions, and rules of membership, and pattern the lives of their members. The clan kinship systems seem very foreign to people who recognize both sides of their family as equally important. Remember that many of the world's societies organize themselves in clans. In a clan, only the mother's or the father's relatives are considered family.

# SOCIAL CLASSES AND CASTES

Cultures often rank their members in general levels. These ranked levels are called **social classes**. Social classes are the categories of people grouped together because they are viewed as possessing similar levels of prestige. Social classes are based on the values of the group. In the United States there is an upper class, a middle class, and a lower class. Each of these levels is further divided into an upper and lower sublevel. What determines social class? It depends on what the culture values or thinks is important.

In the United States social class is determined by money to a large degree. Nevertheless, money is not the only factor. A person who makes money as a gambler has lower status than a person who makes the same amount of money as a businessperson. Occupation also determines class. Doctors are considered to be in a higher class than plumbers, even when the plumber earns more money. Family background is important, too. Families who have been important members of a community for many generations are considered to be in a higher class than those whose wealth and worth are more recent. The type of house and the area a person lives in usually reflects his or her social class. In the United States these are important factors in determining class.

The social classes in the United States are not typical of other cultures. Values among different cultures vary, so the people who receive respect and status also vary. In some cultures in which religion is very important, a poor holy man may be given extremely high status. In any culture, there is one constant fact about social class. Although it is unlikely, it is possible for an individual to change his or her social class.

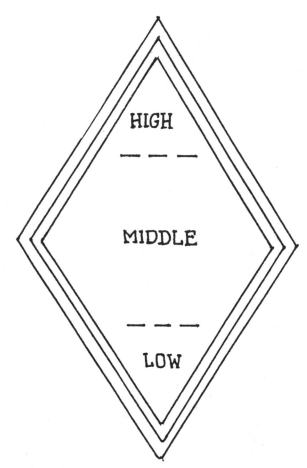

**14.10 Social Classes in the U.S.A.**

Without mobility (the ability to move), social classes become castes. A **caste system** is a social class system permitting virtually no upward social mobility and therefore preventing people from rising above the social level to which they were born. **Social mobility** is the changing of position within a class structure, usually as a result of an individual's own efforts. **Vertical mobility** is the movement between classes, either to a higher class (ascending) or a lower class (descending).

An individual is born into a caste and remains in that caste for life. Education and certain types of knowledge and jobs are limited to certain castes. People can never marry outside their caste.

**Endogamy** is the practice of selecting a mate from within one's own group. Each caste avoids the other castes. Members of different castes have contact with one another only when necessary. People are not encouraged to improve their caste. If a member of society is foolish enough to try to change caste, he or she is punished.

Most people remain in the social class of their parents. Nevertheless, most parents encourage their children to improve their position in society. Parents want their children to do better than they did. Parents are willing to make great sacrifices for their children's future. In the United States the key to improving social class is education. Only a few people move up in social class by marrying a rich person, winning a million dollar sweepstakes, or becoming a movie star. Most people move up the social ladder through education. If Cheryl's father is a manual laborer and she becomes a doctor, Cheryl will have moved up in social class. Mobility works the other way, too. A person can move down in societies with social classes. If Bill's mother is a doctor and he drops out of school, or becomes a "junkie" or an alcoholic, he will frequently lose social status.

**14.11 Education is the key to success.**

In summary, societies usually make social distinctions in the form of social classes or castes. In social classes openings are made for outsiders capable of living up to the standards of membership. These standards may include wealth, profession, occupational accomplishments, education, proper manners, or even an approved accent or vocabulary. Castes are permanent and there is no social mobility. People cannot marry outside their caste. People are born into a caste. There is no other way to gain membership in a caste. People from different castes tend to avoid one another socially. Castes have names and usually have exclusive rights to certain kinds of education, trades, professions and occupations.

# SOCIAL STRUCTURE TODAY

The nuclear family, consisting of a husband, wife, and their children, is the basic unit of family structure on Guam. Usually the nuclear family lives under one roof until the children get married and establish their nuclear families. Of course, there are many exceptions. Many households have more than one nuclear family. Some households include grandparents or other relatives. Even if the extended family does not live in the same house, they tend to live nearby. The extended family plays an important part in the lives of many people on Guam. However, the importance of family on Guam may not be as strong as it used to be. American culture emphasizes the importance of the individual. This encourages young couples to establish a residence separate from their parents. Most young couples do this if they can afford to.

Families on Guam are bilateral. They are not patrilineal or matrilineal. Both sides of the family are important and are considered relatives. Some may be closer to their father's relatives or their mother's relatives, but this is a matter of personal choice. It is not determined by social structure. Preference for father's relatives or mother's relatives may even vary among family members. Some may like their father's side of the family best, but others in the same family may like their mother's relatives best. Most people see both sides of the family as equally important.

Parents today tend to share decision making. Individual families vary, but in Chamorro families women usually take care of the money. This shows that women are considered important. Most of Guam's population is Roman Catholic. In the Roman Catholic wedding ceremony a veil is placed on the bride's head and the husband's shoulder. This symbolizes that there is only one head in the family and it is the husband. Despite the formal ceremony, many say that the husband is the head of the family, but the wife is the neck, and the head cannot move without the neck.

American social classes exist on Guam; nevertheless, there is an older class system. The American system involves all the people on Guam. The old system includes only Chamorros or others who have been on Guam several generations.

First, we will look at the American-style social classes on Guam. The lines for these social classes are not rigid, and it is difficult to classify many people. In general there are three classes: high, middle, and low. Usually, a person's class depends upon the amount of money his or her family has. Governors, admirals, generals, and rich people are considered high class on Guam. Middle class includes "white and blue collar workers." **White collar workers** are teachers and clerks or basically people who don't get dirty at work. **Blue collar workers** include the construction trades, farming, or a skilled job. Low class includes the unemployed and those people who do not hold skilled jobs.

People tend to be proud of themselves regardless of their class. Higher class people hold that status primarily because they earn more money or are better educated, and the society as a whole tends to value these things. They hold the jobs and positions society most respects. This does not always mean the job pays well. A priest does not make much money. Nevertheless, he is classified as middle class. If a priest becomes a Bishop he is considered high class. On Guam, as in the United States, the cleaner the job the more status it has. Even though most office workers earn less than an electrician, they hold a higher status.

On Guam it is easy to change social class. Usually this is accomplished by obtaining a job that has more status. A husband and wife who both work can increase family income and help raise the family's status. Usually, getting ahead means developing more valuable or respected skills. The key to this process is education. Education promotes upward social mobility. Most people on Guam remain in the social class of their parents; nevertheless, mobility, up or down, is possible.

Parents on Guam usually want their children to move up in status or at least maintain their family's status. Parents encourage their children to continue their education and "to make something out of themselves." Why do parents emphasize this so much?

Paralleling the American class system is an older Chamorro system that divides people into two classes. There are the *manakhilo* (high class) and the *manakpapa'* (low class). The *manakhilo* includes, generally, the wealthy families who have been important on Guam for many years. The *manakpapa'* includes everyone else.

Class lines are not strict on Guam. Most extended families have members in all social classes. Since these family ties are stronger than social class, you find the rich and the poor living side by side on Guam. This would be very unusual on the United States mainland.

The social structure of Guam has changed a great deal in recent years. Many functions of the family have been taken over by the government. An old-age home has been built on Tumon Bay. This was not needed in the past, because families took care of the elderly. In the past, if financial help or food was needed, a person's family would help. Today, some families in need rely on the government for assistance. The government is replacing the family in many ways.

# ANCIENT CHAMORRO SOCIAL STRUCTURE

The social structure of the ancient Chamorros will be divided into four sections: caste, clan, clubs and community organization. Caste and clan will be covered in this chapter. Clubs and community organization will be covered in the "Government" chapter.

## Castes

The ancient Chamorros organized themselves into two castes. The high caste was called *chamorri*. The low caste was *manachang* or *mamahlao*. As you would expect, there was no mobility between these groups. Caste membership was by birth. Marriage was impossible for people of different castes. The punishment for sexual contact between a *chamorri* and a *manachang* was severe. The *chamorri* could be put to death.

The ancient Chamorros also had social classes. Within the upper caste there were two distinct classes. The *matao* or *matua* were the higher class *chamorri*. *Matao* who broke society's rules were banished from their village and became *acha'ot* or *atcha'ot* or *achoti*. The *matao* and the *acha'ot* are classes and not castes, because there was social mobility between them. *Matao* who made serious mistakes were demoted to *acha'ot* status. *Acha'ot*, even several generations later, could regain the *matao* status by the payment of a large fine or a heroic action. Except for the *manachang* and the *acha'ot*, the whole tribe (village or district) was related.

*Acha'ot* had to wander from village to village until a village was found that would take them in. Sometimes a wealthy patron would give them the right to found a new village. Only men were exiled, because they were considered responsible for their wives' behavior. If an *acha'ot* was legally banished from a tribe, he could never return. But if he left voluntarily, before the trial, he could hope to return later. If an exiled man refused to leave the village, he was called *ma chatlamen*, a man who is detested. This shamed the entire village. Nevertheless, if he was pardoned, he could get his property back, too.

A few *matao* were able to make sure that they would never become *acha'ot*. This insurance was gained if a person built and furnished a house without any help from relatives. Those demoted to the *acha'ot* class most often regained their *matao* status through their courageous actions in battle. However, any outstanding accomplishment would work. An *acha'ot* who saved a lost fleet of *sakmans* (oceangoing outrigger canoes) would probably merit *matao* class again.

If an *acha'ot* could not regain his old position, his children were *acha'ot*. Perhaps this class was not too bad. Ancient Chamorro wives paid *ålas* (shell money) and food to the *maga'lahi* (ruler) for the privilege of being banished with their husbands. It was always a man who stood trial because he was responsible for his wife's behavior.

If a family had enough money, they could buy back their *matao* status. In a sense the *acha'ot* class was for those who could not pay their fines. More serious offenses were probably punished by death.

Early western explorers and missionaries noticed physical differences in the appearance of the *chamorri* and the *manachang*. The *chamorri* were described as having a light brown complexion and of being big and healthy. The *manachang* were described as having dark complexions and of being smaller and less healthy than the *chamorri*. Nevertheless, it was not these physical differences that determined caste. The difference between the castes, and the basic reason for their existence, involved land.

The *chamorri* owned land. The *manachang* did not own land. Consequently, they were at the mercy of the *chamorri*. They had to ask the *chamorri* for the privilege of using land.

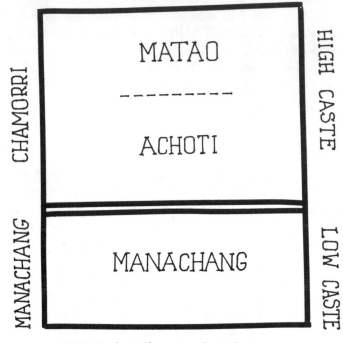

14.12 Ancient Chamorro Caste System

## *Manachang*

The *manachang* caste (low caste) cultivated the *chamorri's* land. For the privilege of using the land, they gave part of their produce to the *chamorri*. In addition to farming, the *manachang* did most of the undesirable work. They cleared and repaired trails. They transported building materials for houses and canoe sheds. Since they were not allowed to fight, they carried food and replacement weapons in battle. It was **taboo** for the *manachang* to go near the ocean. Their fishing was limited to freshwater streams. Even in their limited fishing, it was forbidden for them to use hooks, nets, or spears. They were allowed to club *asuli* (freshwater eels) or catch them by hand. It was taboo for the *chamorri* to eat eels, or fish that had tough scales.

# Chamorri

The *chamorri* were the high caste, but they did not lead a life of leisure. They worked and worked hard, but usually in the occupations that had a lot of prestige. The *matao* were assisted by the *acha'ot* in the following occupations: chief, warrior, fisherman, carpenter, *latte*-house builder, navigator, and money manufacturer. The *manachang* were forbidden to get the education necessary to practice these professions. The *chamorri* controlled the wealth and exchange, as well as the specialized occupations. Wealth was measured in terms of land and *ålas* (shell money). It was not below their dignity to farm. They even made their own household utensils. The *acha'ot* were given presents for assisting the *matao*.

## Inter-Caste Behavior

The *manachang* had to show proper respect to the *chamorri*. They had to avoid their houses. They could not talk freely with them, nor eat in their presence. In order to show respect they bowed low. A sexual union between castes was believed to result in the physical and moral weakening of the *chamorri*. The upper caste person was punished. A *chamorri* would consider it dishonorable if any *manachang* had eaten or drunk in his or her house. The *chamorri* scorned the *manachang*. It was a crime for them to approach the house of a member of the nobility, or draw near *chamorri*. If the *manachang* did not show a deep reverence for the *matao*, they would feel challenged. The *manachang* would be punished by death. The *manachang* did not have to show this reverence for the *acha'ot*. *Manachang* fretted over pleasing the *matao*.

**14.13** *Manachang* **Show Respect to** *Chamorri*

Respect was shown by acting in a *mamahlao* manner. It is difficult to translate *mamahlao* into English. It does not exactly mean ashamed. It is a respectful manner of behavior toward others. Age differences and rank differences demanded this type of behavior even within the *chamorri* caste. How do we show respect today? Can you think of similarities and differences between our actions today and in ancient Chamorro times?

The *manachang* and *chamorri* castes were dependent upon each other. The *chamorri* provided the land and the *manachang* a great deal of the labor. If *chamorri* were away from their houses, *manachang* could approach them. Under these circumstances the *chamorri* were obligated to give the *manachang* whatever they asked. Today in the Mariana Islands, when people come to ask a favor, they will often blow their car horns rather than approach the house. This show of respect may go back to ancient times. Other cultures often misinterpret this Chamorro custom. This is a good example of why it is important to study cultures. Can you think of other examples of cultural misunderstandings?

The relationship between the castes can best be understood by comparing it to the relationship between parents and children. Children are obligated to serve their parents, to obey them, to be loyal, and to respect them. The *manachang* caste acted toward the *chamorri* in the way children act toward their parents. The *chamorri* acted toward the *manachang* in the manner parents do toward their children. Parents are obligated to take care of their children, fulfill their proper requests, and protect them. The *manachang* were not slaves. They were never bought or sold. They were cared for and protected. They could ask favors of the *chamorri*. In return, the *chamorri* demanded respect, obedience, and tribute. The *manachang* were free to leave one *chamorri's* land and go to another village, if a *chamorri* there would grant them land-use privileges. *Chamorri* would have been slow to place too many hardships on the *manachang*. It would result in losing a useful servant, and would show that they were not kind. How are we like the ancient Chamorros today? How are we different?

American society emphasizes individual freedom. It is based on the belief that all people are created equal, although this principle is not always practiced. Americans tend to believe that they are just as good as the next person. With this attitude it is difficult to understand a caste system. Nevertheless, in a society where all members are ranked as to their importance, the caste system is logical. In such a society everyone has a place; there is no need to struggle to better oneself. Everyone is secure in his or her position. Do you see any similarities and differences between a caste system and the military?

There was some room in the caste system for individual ambition. War, competitive exchange and feasting, and skills such as navigating or *latte* building allowed for some individual initiative. The position of *makahna* (spiritual leader) probably allowed the most individual freedom. If we can judge by other Micronesian societies, *makahna* came from all castes and operated as a powerful check on the traditional rulers.

# Origin of Castes

**Ethnologists** (social scientists who study culture) differ in their explanation of castes in Micronesia. There are two main schools of thought. One favors the invasion theory; the other favors the evolution theory. The invasion theory explains castes by multiple migrations to the Mariana Islands. Perhaps an invading people conquered the original inhabitants, claimed all the land, and reduced the aborigines to a landless caste or a caste with the poorest land. Laura Thompson stated this theory first. Pedro Sanchez has offered a different twist to the multiple migration theory. He suggests that stragglers who voyaged to the Mariana Islands were incorporated into society by the aborigines. The newcomers were made the low caste. He bases this hypothesis on the historical evidence of the Carolinian settlement of Tamuning on Guam (see the "Trade" chapter).

The best spokesman for the evolutionary theory is William Alkire. He claims that, in a society that emphasizes rank, seniority and land control, a caste system is likely to evolve. He cannot see much evidence of separate migrations and certainly not separate "racial" origins. The prehistoric skeletons examined by archaeologists point to one type of people.

In the chapters on "Origin" and "Migration" we looked at this controversy. Let's review the facts.

1) The material cultural of the Mariana islands can be divided into two categories, **Latte** and **Pre-**latte **Periods**. The *Latte* Period type of pottery, *latte* stones, and slingstones were not used when the Mariana Islands were first settled.

2) The historical record describes the *chamorri* as big and healthy, with light brown skin color. The *manachang* are described as small, dark people.

Ethnologists use these facts to support both the invasion theory and the evolution theory.

The invasion theorists claim that the aborigines were conquered by the big, healthy, light brown, slingstone throwing, *latte*-building, and perhaps rice-growing *chamorri*.

The evolution theorists claim that the aborigines had plenty of land and status for the entire population in the beginning. Nevertheless, in a society where land, rank, and seniority were important, population increases led to a caste system. Perhaps the land fell into the hands of fewer and fewer clans. Warfare could cause one group to lose their land and status. Some clans could have failed to produce as many children as others. This would have made it difficult for them to maintain their land. Clans that produced many females may have gained land as part of their bride price. Clans with more males than females could have lost land to "buy" wives. Landless clans or clans with poor lands became dependent on the other clans. This resulted in the *chamorri* and *manachang* castes. The *latte*-stone houses were just a natural improvement over houses on wooden pillars. *Latte* were invented in the Mariana Islands and are not found anywhere else. The *manachang* were smaller and less healthy because, not being able to fish, they ate less protein. They were darker because they spent more time in the sun. The skeletal remains of the ancient Chamorros do not support the historical reports that there were two types of people in the Mariana Islands.

Alkire's evolutionary theory has gradually replaced Laura Thompson's invasion theory in most people's minds until recently.

Archaeologists at Pagat on Guam's northeast coast have found that the *latte* and pre-*latte* artifacts are separated by a layer of soil with no evidence of human inhabitation. Nevertheless, in other sites the transition between *latte* and pre-*latte* artifacts are gradual. At Ipao Beach separate settlements are found. The *latte* people lived near the present day Sampagita pavilion. The pre-*latte* people lived near the present day amphitheater. This may be explained by a general two- or three-foot uplift of Guam around 3,400 years ago. The village near the amphitheater was near the sea when the people lived there. The uplift changed that.

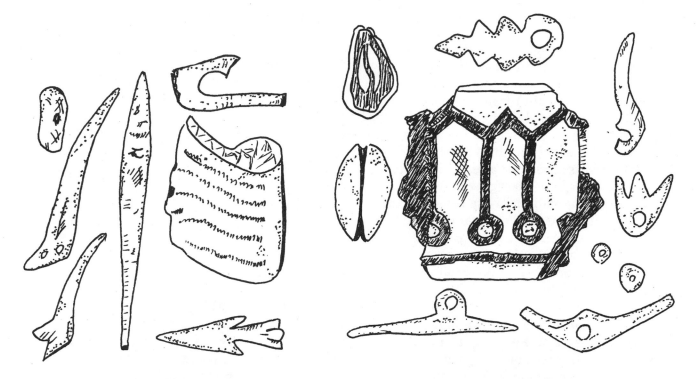

**Pre-*latte* Period**
**2000 B.C. - 800 A.D.**

**Latte Period**
**800 A.D. - 17th Century**

**14.14 Characteristic Artifiacts of Guam's Pre-Colonial Period:** Adapted from a sketch by Alejandro Lizama, Department of Parks and Recreation, Guam

**Latte Period**
**800 A.D. - 17th Century**

**Pre-*latte* Period**
**2000 B.C. - to 800 A.D.**

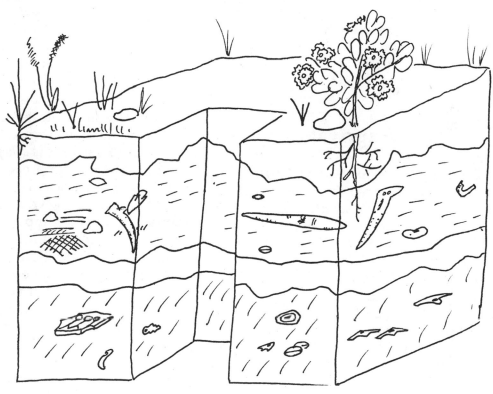

**14.15 Stratification**

169

Recent work in linguistics could support the invasion theory. Clay Carlson, of the University of Guam, claims that two languages (prior to Spanish colonization) may have combined to form the Chamorro language. Linguists can date the fusion of two languages by a process called glotto-chronology. If the date for the fusion of Chamorro is about the same as the shift from pre-*latte* to *latte* artifacts (800 A.D. -1100 A.D.), the invasion theory could gain its former acceptance. Meanwhile, the debate goes on. What do you think? Why?

The evolutionists agree that after 2,000 years in the Mariana Islands, the aborigines would have had a fairly large population for the resources that were available. It seems unlikely that the invaders could have outnumbered the aborigines. Of course, those who favor the invasion theory argue that the Spanish conquered the Chamorros of the Mariana Islands, the Incas of Peru and the Aztecs of Mexico with only a few better-armed men. In the Marianas this was possible because each village was a separate political unit. The invaders had to fight only one village at a time. In America, the Spanish conquered the Aztecs and the Incas by overthrowing the nobles. The invasion theory side argues that it does not take long for a society to change from outside influence. Look at what has happened to Guam under the rule of the United States. American culture through the schools, economy, and especially television, which invades a person's home, has had a tremendous effect on Chamorro culture in a very short period of time. How has this changed the language? How has this changed values?

## Caste Survivals?

The Spanish-Chamorro Wars (1672-1695) and the epidemics that followed the visits by Spanish ships depopulated the Mariana Islands. The Mariana Island population dropped from an estimated 24,000-40,000 in 1668 to 9,000 in 1690. This was a decrease of 62-78%. From 1698 until 1720 there was a 70% decline in the population caused by "sickness of the ship." These factors and colonization by the Spanish ended the old caste system. The Spanish moved the Chamorros from all the Mariana Islands to a few villages on Guam, Luta (Rota), and Saipan. This forced relocation disrupted the old caste system that was based on the control of land. Spaniards and Filipinos were appointed as government officials.

**Cultural survival** is an element of culture that remains long after it has lost its original function. Intermarriage between Spaniards and Chamorros created a new social structure. The *mestisu* became the new high class. They lived in town. The rest of the people lived in the country. Today, this division is sometimes referred to as *manggi Hagatña* for those people who lived in Agaña before World War II, and *manggi sengsong* for everyone else. The terms *manakhilo* for high class and *manakpapa'* for low class are also used to distinguish class differences. So, today there are classes but no castes on Guam.

# Clan
# Avuncuclan

According to one theory, the ancient Chamorros organized themselves into avuncuclans. Clans are either patrilineal or matrilineal. Avuncuclans are matrilineal. Matrilineal literally means "mother's line." *Achafnak* is the old Chamorro word for matrilineage. It comes from the root word *fañagu* (bear offspring, give birth) and the prefix *acha* (as, indicating equality). Literally, *achafnak* means "as same birth." It means relatives of the same womb. In the case of **lineages** the actual ancestress can usually be remembered. Several lineages who claim to be descended from a common ancestor form a clan. The ancestral father or mother of a clan is often mythological.

The diagram on the opposite page graphically shows two matrilineages who trace their ancestry to a mythological ancestress. The *achafnak* is shaded. Note that the *achafnak* is all those who can trace descent from a common female ancestress. This is the basis of a matrilineage.

Since ancestry was traced through females, women were very important in ancient Chamorro society. Family land, wealth, and name and the right of men to positions of leadership were passed through the female line or *achafnak* (matrilineage).

Usually a matrilineal society is localized around females. Under this system of social organization, husbands move to the wife's clan land upon marriage. The ancient Chamorros probably began with this type of matriclan organization. Through the years, however, the men gained additional power. The *achafnak* was localized around males. Wives moved to their husband's clan's land to live, and yet the men inherited land rights through the females or their matrilineage. The avuncuclan is a matrilineal society localized around male members rather than female members.

Young men probably made this move when they reached puberty (the age at which one becomes sexually mature).

Young men took up residence in the *uritao* (see "Social Clubs" in the chapter on "Government").

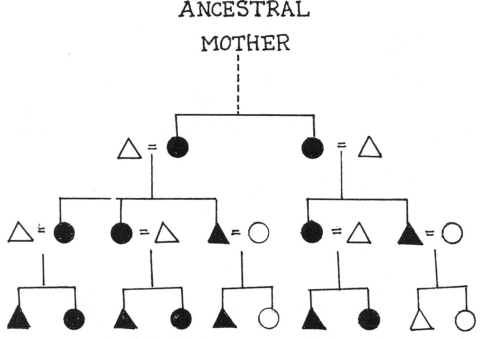

ANCESTRAL MOTHER

14.16 **Matrilineages:** *Achafnaks* Shaded

## Explanation

How can land be passed through the female line and be localized around males? Here is how it worked. Let us begin with the birth of a child. Children belonged to their mother and, in turn, to their matrilineage and clan. A clan was composed of several matrilineages descended from an ancestress.

Since the newborn child came from the mother's womb and in a direct line from the ancestral womb, the mother and the clan had rights over the child. Even today Chamorro mothers say, "*Yaki sina hao hu fañagu pus sina ha' lokkue' hu puno' hao* (I bore you and I have the right to kill you)."

Even though children belonged to their mother's clan, the mother had to join her husband's clan on his clan territory to live and raise their family. When a couple's daughters grew up, they, too, moved to their husband's clan's territory. When their sons grew up they moved to their mother's clan's territory. That was where they belonged, because that was their *achafnak's* land.

While living in the men's house or *uritao*, a young man was primarily under the supervision of his mother's brother. An uncle on the mother's side of the family was the most important man in the young man's life. This was the man from whom he would inherit position and land-use rights. Individuals did not normally own land. The land was owned collectively by the *achafnak* or clan. After spending several years in the *uritao*, and proving himself a capable and responsible member of his clan, the young man was ready to marry. Marriage had to be outside of his clan. It was taboo to marry a member of the same clan. Such a marriage would be considered **incestuous**, no matter how distant the clan relative. With the help of his clan, especially his lineage in the clan and his mother's brother, the young man would raise the bride price and build his house. If his clan was poor, he might work for his wife-to-be's family for several years instead of paying the bride price.

Once settled into his own home, or perhaps sharing his mother's brother's home if he was the youngest nephew, a young husband began to raise his family. Of course he had affection for his children, even though he knew that they belonged to his wife's clan. He also had affection for and a great deal of responsibility for his sister's children. Just as he had depended upon his mother's brother, so would his sister's son depend upon him.

Perhaps the avuncuclan system can best be seen graphically. Since clans usually had the names of animals, plants, or some force in nature, possible Chamorro clan names are used in this discussion. To make things simple, an assumption has been made that each ancient Chamorro district was controlled by one clan. Follow the "Mechanics of an Avuncuclan" diagram as you read the following scenario. The diagram will make the reading easier to understand.

A baby boy was born in Umatak. Umatak was controlled by the Lemmai avuncuclan. The father was a Lemmai. The baby boy was named Cheref. This was an Alu avuncuclan name. Cheref's mother named him that because she was an Alu. The Alu controlled the Malesso' district.

When Cheref became a young man he moved to his achafnak's Malesso' territory. He lived with the other Alu bachelors in the *uritao*. After learning advanced navigation and deep-sea fishing from his mother's brother and proving himself brave in battle, he felt ready to take a wife. All of the Alu,

especially those in his lineage, helped him build a house and contributed *ålas* (shell money) to pay his sweetheart's father the bride price. He was not really buying her; he was compensating her father for the loss of a hard-working daughter.

His bride was an Atdao from Inalahan. Inalahan was Ayuyu territory. Her father was an Ayuyu avuncuclan member, who married an Atdao woman. Cheref's wife's name was To'a. To'a and her brothers and sisters had Atdao names because they, like all children, belonged to their mother's avuncuclan.

Cheref and To'a had a good life and raised a fine son and daughter. The children, like their mother, were Atdaos. On his fourteenth birthday their son moved to the *uritao* (men's house) in Dano'. His mother's brother arranged for his initiation ceremony. He felt good to be in Atdao territory and was anxious to prove himself.

Cheref and To'a's daughter married a man from Hagåtña. Cheref received a large price for his daughter from his important son-in-law's clan. Cheref knew he would have to save the money to help pay the bride price for his sister's son. His sister, her husband, and their son were staying in Hagat. Cheref knew it would not be long before his nephew would be moving to Malesso' to take up residence in the Alu *uritao*.

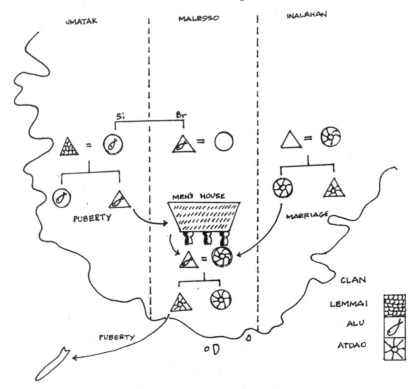

**14.17 Mechanics of an Avuncuclan**

# Authority

The avuncuclan system of social organization as practiced by the ancient Chamorros resulted in a balance of power between men and women. Under a patriclan, the men control everything. Under a matriclan, the women have the upper hand. Under the avuncuclan, wealth, land, and family name are passed through the females, but are administered by males who are advised by their female relatives.

Brother and sister relationships were very important. The brother was the ultimate authority over his sister's children. He administered the clan land on their behalf.

It is recorded that among the ancient Chamorros when people asked a man for help, they received his help alone. On the other hand, if they asked a woman for help, the entire family was obligated to help them. If a person had a quarrel with a man, it was personal, but quarrels with a woman involved the whole clan.

Married women actually became members of their husband's avuncuclan, despite the fact that a woman's children belonged to her *achafnak*.

Women were important in politics. The **avuncuclan** was the basis for government. Lineage heads, or perhaps clan heads in the *matao* class, formed a council in each village. These lineage heads were chiefs. The highest-ranking man was *maga'lahi*. The highest-ranking woman was *maga'haga*. Women could attend council meetings. Although men made the decisions, they never did so without consulting the women. For more details on this, see the chapter on "Government."

# Function

The avuncuclan controlled the distribution and use of land among its lineages. The lineages were the basic units within the clan. Each lineage unit received a fair share of the food distribution, and each lineage contributed to the projects of the clan. The clan, and especially the lineage, exercised control over the bride price and marriage. The clan supervised and cooperated in observing maturation celebrations for their young. The clan members cooperated in work efforts and in war. Although there was competition among lineages within a clan, the competition was usually on friendly terms. Serious conflict was rare, but could lead to a split in the clan. It could even cause a voyage to another land.

The importance of rank was seen inside and outside the clan. Outside the clan, castes and villages were ranked. *Hagatña* (Agaña) was the highest-ranking village. Clans were ranked and the lineages within the clan were ranked, too. Within the lineage, families were ranked in importance. The lineage and family ranking was based on the closeness of descent to the original avuncuclan ancestress. The first daughter of a first daughter of a first daughter, etc., would lead to the highest-ranking lineage and family in a clan.

The ranking of lineage was reflected in the quality and quantity of clan land, special titles, positions, rituals, and economic privileges, like the manufacture of *ålas* (shell money), that a lineage had. At all levels seniority was important. People were ranked by age. The older people were, the more respect they received.

In summary, from birth to death the individual was dependent upon his or her clan. Ancient Chamorros' rights, their position, and where they lived and worked were determined by their clan. The clan even had to approve the person they married. Above everything, a person's duty was to the clan. The clan was the ancient Chamorro's everything.

# Family

Authority in the family was officially vested in the father or oldest male living in a household. Nevertheless, the real power was held by the mother of the oldest female living in the household.

Usually, a family consisted of a husband, wife, and their children. Often, related nuclear families were clustered together in a housing compound on lineage land. A man's wife owned the house and all the utensils in it, even though it was built by his lineage on his clan's land. The house was really part of the bride price. Of course, the children belonged to the mother's clan or *achafnak*. A father did not have ultimate authority over his children. This did not mean that a father could not punish his children. He could discipline the children, so long as his wife agreed, which was usually the case. Since a father's real authority and responsibility were to his sister's children, this allowed him to be on friendlier and more relaxed terms with his own children.

Why did a wife have such tremendous authority in her husband's territory? She was free to return to her *achafnak* if she was not pleased with her husband. Not only could she leave but she could take the children and all the material goods in the house. If this happened, the husband lost not only a wife, but also a great deal of respect from his fellow clan members. They would not be anxious to help him pay another bride price. Also, many of the women from a wife's clan were probably married to men of her husband's clan. This meant that she would not be a complete stranger in his territory and could count on a lot of support from the other women.

The major duties of family members were to respect their elders and to help fulfill their family's reciprocal obligations. Most of these obligations centered on life-crisis rites. These included the celebration of birth, puberty, marriage and death. Ancient Chamorros could never afford to refuse a request from kin. People depended on the clan and the clan depended on them. Individual families, the lineage, and the clan often had a *gupot* (party, celebration, festivity, holiday, feast) to show their togetherness and to show their status. In all these celebrations the individual was obligated to do whatever was required. By helping others fulfill reciprocal obligations, an ancient Chamorro was always sure of receiving help when it was needed. These obligations may have been just a return of a favor or *chenchule'* (present, donation) or even *emmok* (revenge).

## Division of Labor

Labor in ancient Chamorro times was divided by caste, sex, and age. Except for the caste divisions, these categories were not strict. Every able-bodied person worked in the family garden plots. The day-to-day responsibilities of providing for food, clothing, and shelter were met by the family as a whole.

Children were given tasks to do that matched their abilities. Older children had more responsibilities than younger children. *Che'lu* (sibling, brother, sister) relationships were strong. Older children gave advice and direction to younger brothers and sisters. Girls spent a lot of time taking care of the younger family members. Children knew that they were members of their mother's clan. They knew that they would be dependent upon one another for their entire lives.

Boys generally helped their father in men's work. Boys helped carry the fish from the canoes to the village and they cleaned the fish. Girls helped their mother in women's work. Children seemed to have been eager to show their maturity by performing more and more adult tasks as they grew up. Most of their education was from their parents or mother's brother. Nevertheless, older children were tutored by experts in specialized fields such as carpentry, navigation, and medicine. Parents paid for this training. For more on ancient Chamorro education, see the chapter on "Arts and Skills."

Men were responsible for farming. This included not only the heavy work of clearing the land, but also planting, weeding, and harvesting the crops. Women helped the men in their farming tasks. Men hunted and fished, too. Men carried heavy loads and maintained paths. On special occasions men cooked, using the *chahan* (deep-pit cooking) method. Men were the warriors and did the fighting. Men were engaged in both intra- and inter-island trading. Men were also responsible for special trades such as canoe building, house building, and stone and shell tool making. Men held the positions of lineage chiefs, village chiefs, and *makahna* (spiritual leader).

Women took care of the house, the chores, and the day-to-day cooking. Women shared the farming responsibilities with men. Women did a great deal of the reef fishing and food gathering on the reef and on the land as well. Women plaited baskets and mats and made household utensils. They made what little clothing the family needed. Women also engaged in specialized tasks like plaiting canoe sails, making rope, making nets, manufacturing pottery and preparing and administering herb medicine. In ancient times, herb medicine was strictly a woman's job. Today, men practice this, too. They are called *suruhanus*. Women herb doctor's are called *suruhanas*.

Labor in ancient times was not strictly divided along male and female lines. Women could help in the farming; men could fish on the reef. Net fishing was often a family, lineage, or even village affair. Life was not all work and no play either. Families went sailing together just for the sheer enjoyment of it.

Caste divisions in labor were strict. *Manachang* never fished in the sea, nor did they go on trading voyages, nor fight in battle.

174

# Survival of the Avuncuclan

Is there any part of the old avuncuclan system of social organization that survives among Chamorros today? Today, Chamorros recognize both sides of their family as equally important relatives. The Spanish introduced this bilateral system. Nevertheless, there are still a few customs in the Mariana Islands that seem to be from the ancient Chamorro clan system.

## Matrilineal Reminders

Although men are still recognized as the head of the household, women still exert a great deal of influence. Today, women are usually the spiritual leaders of their families. They usually control the family money and guard the health of the family. Women usually take care of the household work and care for the children. Women often take care of the legal and business affairs of the family.

Until the 1950 Organic Act forbade the practice, some families took their mother's name for their last name or surname. This practice was not common. Most people adopted the Spanish practice of taking their mother's surname as a middle name and their father's surname as a last name.

Women in the Mariana Islands, especially in Guam, hold more positions of authority in government and business than would be expected in a mainland U.S.A. cultural setting. In 1990 one-third of the Guam senators were women.

The importance of women can be seen in the Chamorro wedding. Young men still usually do some service for the bride's family during their courtship. Often this will mean cutting firewood for a fiesta, or just mowing the lawn. The groom's family will pay most of the wedding expenses. All of this is reminiscent of the ancient bride price.

The importance of women and the responsibility given them is often seen in the custom of the oldest daughter taking care of her elderly parents.

## Reminders of Avunculocal Residence

The old practice of a wife moving to the husband's land and house can still be seen today.

The youngest son usually inherits the family house. Older males have already established their own homes. If there is a shortage of family land during *pattidu* (from the Spanish "partidos," custom of dividing the land), males will be given preference over females, just as was done in ancient times. It is assumed that a girl's husband will provide the land for her. If a young couple does not have enough money or land to establish a house of their own, they will usually move in with the groom's parents. This is usually the case even if the groom is stationed off-island in the military service. Not always, but usually, a bride will leave her family and live with her husband's family even if he is away. Just as in ancient times, it is the groom's responsibility to provide a house for his wife.

Most newly married couples establish a separate household, if they can. This is considered the most desirable practice, just as it was in ancient times. Nevertheless, there is a tendency for families to cluster their houses in an area or even on a single house lot, or at least in the same village. Recently this custom has been breaking down. Families are moving farther and farther apart. Many are leaving the Mariana Islands to live on the U.S. mainland This does not, in and of itself, mean that the Chamorro family is weakening. There is still a great deal of family solidarity, even when great distances are involved.

## Reminders of the Clan

In times of life crisis (birth, marriage, death) family members will gather from the far corners of the world. Families, today as in yesteryear, use life-crisis situations to reaffirm their ties. On a smaller scale the *gupot* (family party) is for the same purpose. These gatherings are reminiscent of the old lineage and clan celebrations.

Strong Chamorro lineage ties can be seen in the frequent cooperation among relatives. Families still help one another with *chenchule'* obligations. Most families before World War II operated as an economic unit. All family income was put together for the good of all. Widows and the elderly are still usually taken care of by the family. Just as in ancient times, families cooperate economically, religiously, and socially. This is especially true on Luta (Rota).

The old clan can be seen today in the village fiesta celebration. The whole village cooperates in the fiesta. This is an opportunity to demonstrate village pride. Clan rivalry can be seen in the village groups at schools, too. The village cliques have taken the place of the old *uritao*. The people of a village stick together. They protect one another. If necessary, they will fight for one another.

Intervillage sports on Guam are much more popular than school teams because the schools do not tap the old clan-oriented village pride. When a village team wins, they return home with horns blowing, just as ancient warriors shouted after returning from a victorious raid.

People are still loyal to their village even after they move away. This is especially true of women, who often leave their village upon marriage. They become members of their husband's village. They work in village and church projects and become a part of their new community, but there is still a strong sense of loyalty in their heart for their old village.

In ancient times, land use was controlled by the lineage heads. The strong kinship ties and their relation to the land can still be seen. The custom of asking the permission of the *taotaomo'na* (ancestral ghosts) for the use of land demonstrates this. The *taotaomo'na* is addressed as grandfather or grandmother. This respect for ancestors and asking their permission for land use definitely goes back to the days of ancestor veneration and the avuncuclan.

# SUMMARY

Social structure is the framework around which people organize themselves in order to satisfy their needs. A nuclear family is a mother and father and their children. Europeans traced descent patrilineally and ancient Chamorros matrilineally. Consanguineal relatives are "blood" relatives, while others are affinal kin, that is, relatives through marriage.

There are four types of clans: patriclan, matriclan, avuncuclan, and the theoretical amitaclan, which is not found in any culture. The purpose of a clan is to meet the mental and physical needs of its members. Clans are economic and political kinship groups.

There are high, middle, and low classes in the United States, and they are primarily based on wealth. Cultures rank their members in **hierarchical** order. If social mobility is forbidden, then social classes are called castes. The United States does not have castes. In ancient Guam there were three classes. The *matao* and the *acha'ot* classes made up the *chamorri* or nobility. The *manachang* was the low class. Since there was no social mobility between the *chamorri* and *manachang* classes, they were castes.

One theory states that the ancient Chamorros organized themselves into an avuncuclan. This type of clan follows a matrilineal descent pattern, but residence is in the husband's territory. Men, women, and children had various roles in ancient Chamorro society. Some aspects of the ancient Chamorro social system have survived to the present day.

# Chapter 15
# Government

## INTRODUCTION

Today we have a democratic form of government. We elect our leaders to represent and serve us. We have a government to protect us. We have a code of rules or laws by which we live. We follow these rules because they are right and just, and because it is in our best interest to do so.

Occasionally, we need to get rid of old laws or add new ones. In a dictatorial government, laws can be changed quickly. The ruler just declares a new law. In a democratic form of government, like ours, it takes time to change the law. Our legislature must pass a new law; then the chief executive (governor or president) must sign it.

Even after a law is passed and approved by the chief executive, it is still subject to judicial review. Laws can be declared unconstitutional by the courts. If we have a disagreement or problem, we have the written law and the court to settle our disputes. A jury of our peers decides many important legal matters in our judicial system.

This is the way our government works today. The democratic form of government we have today in the Mariana Islands was introduced from the United States, but our government's roots go back to Europe. We know a great deal about our government today, but what was the government like in ancient Chamorro times?

**Government** is the organization developed by officials to make and carry out decisions and conduct the general administration of public affairs. What kinds of decisions do the officials of government make? They set goals, allocate tax money, make laws, and make settlements.

The purpose of government is to organize and, to some extent, control the behavior of individuals within a given area. All governments are prepared to use force to control society when necessary. All governments operate over and control a certain amount of territory. The individuals within that land are subject to the laws of that government

Governments make laws, enforce laws and judge people. These functions of government can be in the hands of one man, like a king, or they can be shared by the legislative, executive, and judicial branches of government. In our society today the legislature makes the laws. The executive branch carries out the decisions of the legislative branch and enforces the laws. Judgments are made by the judicial branch of government. Some of their judgments are about criminal matters. Most of their work involves civil cases. The latter are cases that involve disagreements between two individuals or groups. Divorces and lawsuits are common types of civil cases.

Political order can be present without the existence of a country. Some researchers claim that the ancient Chamorros did not have a government. What these people mean is that the ancient Chamorros did not have written laws, a state, country, or nation. The territory controlled by ancient Chamorro government was limited to a village or several small villages grouped into a district. There might have been one or two exceptions to this general rule. Archaeologists believe that the huge *latte* stones on Tinian and on Luta (Rota) indicate that the ancient Chamorros had at least one powerful king. Legend claims that Taga controlled all or most of Tinian. According to legend, he abandoned his *latte*-stone building project on Luta to conquer Tinian. Spanish conquest seems to have interrupted the ancient Chamorros' development of a **monarchy**. A monarchy is a form of government in which a king rules the entire country.

The belief that the ancient Chamorros did not have a government can be seen in many early accounts. Garcia, who wrote about Padre Sanvitores's experiences in the Mariana Islands (1668-1672), made such an erroneous claim. He reported, "They have no laws whatsoever. Individual choice governs the behavior of each one. Transgressions are punished by war, if they are of the crowd, by public opinion if they are of the individual." The above statement is generally true of all societies even today. The ancient Chamorros did have laws and punishments for disobeying them. The ancient Chamorros had an organization designed to carry out decisions and to conduct the administration of public affairs.

# ORGANIZATION AND FUNCTION OF ANCIENT CHAMORRO GOVERNMENT

## Social Structure

In ancient times there was not a Chamorro nation. Instead, there were many Chamorro villages throughout the Mariana Islands. Occasionally, several small, closely related villages grouped themselves into a district. The village or district was the largest decision-making group in which differences were settled without war. The village was called *songsong*. This word may have been interchangeable with tribe. In Guam, according to various accounts about Padre Sanvitores's mission in the late 17th century, there were 180 villages with an average population of about 300 people each. Archaeologists today have verified that there were at least that many villages, and that village size ranged from 50 to 600 people. But were these villages all occupied at the same time? Luta had fifty villages with about 12,000 people, according to the report of Fray Juan Pobre (1602). Fr. Hezel, a modern researcher, estimates that the population of the entire Mariana Islands was probably not more than 40,000 people in 1668.

Each village and the surrounding territory was controlled by one **clan** or the combined territories of several clans. One reliable source states that except for the *manachang* and the *acha'ot* or *achoti*, the whole tribe (village or district) was related. The village was divided into **hamlets**. The hamlets were controlled by **lineages**. Each clan was composed of several **matrilineages** who claimed to be descended from common ancestors. A clan is a group of people who think they are descended from a common ancestor and who share a common territory. Since it is forbidden to marry a fellow clan member, outsiders who marry into a clan must give up their old clan membership. Among the Chamorros, clan membership was traced through the female line or matrilineage, but the land was administered by the male members of the matrilineage. Women, upon marriage, became members of their husbands' clans. For these reasons the ancient Chamorro clan has been classified as an **avuncuclan**. For the details on this ancient Chamorro kinship theory, see the chapter "Social Structure."

The avuncuclan was made up of matrilineages. The matrilineages were made up of **nuclear families**. The matrilineage was the basic unit in ancient Chamorro politics. Each matrilineage controlled a specified territory. The eldest male of each matrilineage controlled the use of the land and sea that was within his territory.

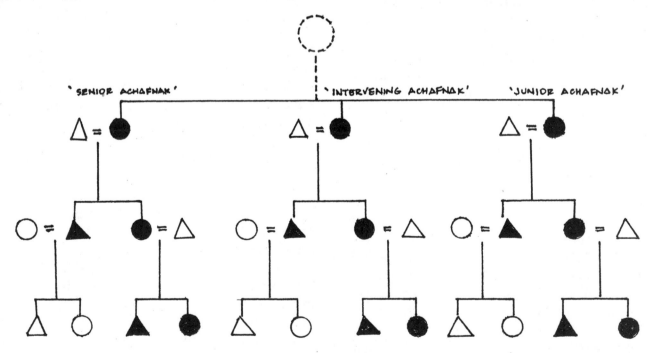

**15.1 Matrilineal structure of the avuncuclan: a diagram of three *achafnaks* descended from a common mythical ancestress. Avuncuclan members are shaded.** Adapted from *Ancient Chamorro Kinship Organization*, by Lawrence J. Cunningham. Published by L. Joseph Press.

Seniority was very important within the **lineage**. An individual had the power to boss lineage members who were younger. On the other hand, obedience and respect had to be shown to matrilineage members who were older.

Rank by seniority was very important on all levels of society. Within the clan, the matrilineage that was closest to the ancestral mother was oldest and, therefore, received the most respect. Within the matrilineage, the families were ranked by seniority, too. The ranking did not stop there. Within the family, the ancient Chamorros had specific terms for their eldest child and next-to-eldest and so on down to the youngest.

The importance of age can be seen throughout ancient Chamorro society. Generally, the older a person was, the more respect he or she got. Ranking was very important in all areas of ancient Chamorro life; because of rank, people knew just how they were to act toward everyone else. Within the clan, the more closely an individual was related to the ancestral mother, the more respect he or she received. This respect for seniority generally leads to ancestor **veneration**. Ancient Chamorro religion was based on the respect shown to ancestors. The easiest way to show that respect was to behave properly. The ancient Chamorros felt that if a people really cared about their family, they would act in a proper manner. One of the best ways to respect ancestors was to show respect to living elders.

Ranking went far beyond individuals within a clan. Clans were ranked too, as were villages. Clans and villages established rank by trading, competitive feasting, competitive gift giving, and warfare, and by the size of the village's population. In ancient times **Hagåtña** (Agaña) was the highest-ranked village, according to most early historical reports. There are some accounts that claim **Fuuña** and **Motac** were the highest ranking. **Hagåtña** did not rule the other villages, but the people of **Hagåtña** received the most respect.

Ranking also involved dividing people into two distinctive castes. **Castes** are social groups into which one is born and must remain for life. Individuals must marry a person in the same caste. Castes are always ranked. Higher castes have more privileges and fewer restrictions. The ancient Chamorros had two castes, the *chamorri* and the *manachang*. Of course, marriage was forbidden between members of the different ancient Chamorro castes.

*Chamorri* were property owners and skilled craftspersons and fisherpersons. *Manachang* were probably landless and dependent upon the *chamorri* for land-use privileges. They were mainly responsible for farming the *chamorri's* land. The *manachang* were restricted by many taboos. For example, they were not allowed to even touch the ocean. It was thought that if they did so it would contaminate the ocean and spoil the fishing. The *manachang* were not allowed to participate in battle directly. They could carry water and slingstones for the *chamorri*, who did the fighting. The relationship between the *manachang* and the *chamorri* was similar to a parent-child relationship. The *chamorri* were expected to protect and care for the *manachang*, and the *manachang* were expected to serve the *chamorri* and show them great respect.

The *manachang* caste did not exercise any direct power in the government of the ancient Chamorros. Nevertheless, they were free to choose their masters. Therefore, the *chamorri* were always faced with the threat that their *manachang* would leave. If the *chamorri* of a village made life unbearable, the *manachang* simply found another village to take them. The *manachang* were not slaves. They were not bought and sold. They were not serfs, because they were not tied to the land of their ancestors.

In general, the *chamorri* avoided marriage with commoners, dwelt in fine houses, monopolized fighting and overseas sailing, and demanded tribute and obedience.

Within the *chamorri*, there were two classes. The highest class was the *matao*. *Matao* who broke laws were forced to leave their village. They usually took their families with them and moved to another village that would accept them. From then on, they were known as *acha'ot* or *achoti*. Their children and their children's children remained *acha'ot*. Nevertheless, the *acha'ot* were not a separate caste like the *manachang*. Under special circumstances they could regain their *matao* status. If they acquired great wealth, they could buy back their *matao* status. If they had the power to do so, they could establish a new village by force of arms.

# Leadership

Leaders in ancient Chamorro society inherited position and wealth. Leadership rank was determined by lineage seniority and by the lineage's status in the clan. Further, it was determined by a clan's rank. The closer a person's lineage was to the ancestral clan mother, the higher his or her status. Of course, there was some consideration for ability and personality. Leaders had to be mentally competent.

Leaders were expected to put the interest of their followers before their own interests. Wealth, verbal skills, physical skills, bravery, and knowledge were greatly valued in leaders. Leaders were expected to be able to keep down internal rivalries and to promote peace in the village, to redistribute the wealth and see that all were adequately provided for. Being a fair and skillful trader was appreciated, too.

Since seniority was important, most men did not achieve high leadership positions until they were older. Leaders were elders. Leaders were given great respect in ancient Chamorro times, but they were expected to act humble. Leaders were supposed to be generous. There was a strong bond of loyalty between a leader and his followers. This bond was sacred and very similar to the bond in a family between parents and children. Leaders were expected to care for their followers just as a parent cares for his children. Followers were expected to give the leader their support just as children support their parents. This system is not surprising, because the political system of the ancient Chamorros came from its kinship system. Respect was shown for the chief by gifts of food and money, silence and humility in his presence, and recognition of his position.

Leadership was basically the function of the lineage heads or chiefs. What was the basis of the lineage chiefs' power? They administered the lineage land. Therefore, they controlled their family members economically. The lineage heads decided who could use certain pieces of land, they set family goals, directed economic activities, and settled disputes within the lineage.

The lineage chiefs in turn were ranked. The highest lineage chief was the clan chief. The clans were also ranked. The highest clan chief in an ancient Chamorro village was the paramount chief, or the *maga'lahi*. The female counterpart of the *maga'lahi* was the *maga'haga*. Although women were not openly active in the affairs of state, they were an important force behind the scenes. Men could not refuse the requests of female relatives. No serious matters were decided without their consultation.

Leadership was exercised in a similar manner in both the lower and upper caste of ancient Chamorro society. Nevertheless, the lower caste had no input into the village affairs. They were not members of the **village council**. Since the *manachang* were landless or occupied marginal lands (frequently interior lands), their economic subsistence depended upon the upper caste's giving them permission to use land. The only real political power they had was the right to leave a village in which they were not satisfied. Some books say they were like slaves or serfs. They were not bought and sold like slaves, nor were they tied to the land like serfs. It seems likely that *manachang* lineage heads could have exercised their right to move to the advantage of their lineage and, therefore, they had some measure of power.

# Village Council

The village council was composed of lineage heads of the upper-caste clan or clans in a village. The village council was a decision-making group composed of the highest-ranking men and women in a village. It seems that all *chamorri* could attend these meetings. Nevertheless, it does not seem likely that the *acha'ot* class were more than mere observers. Although they may have lived in a village for generations, they were still technically strangers, because the *acha'ot* had lost their *matao* status and had been forced to leave their clan land. The council's official members were composed of male and female *matao*.

Council decisions were made by consensus. **Consensus** means that decisions are made by general agreement. Matters coming before the council were discussed and rediscussed until all members held the same belief. In Chamorro there is an important term for this, "*todu manatungo'*." With this system it is not necessary to take a vote. When a vote is taken there are always winners and losers. Sometimes this creates hard feelings, which interfere with group cooperation. Group cooperation and the ability to operate as a strongly united family could be shattered by voting. When matters are settled by consensus, everyone in the council gets a chance to speak. Nevertheless, great deference (respect) was shown to those of higher rank. No individual person wanted to take sole responsibility for a decision. After a good deal of whispering and behind-the-scenes maneuvering by the women, some of the higher-ranking lineage chiefs would speak out. They probably would not speak their mind in the highly individualistic way **Westerners** (people originally from Europe) frequently do. Instead, they would attack the problem in a roundabout way, always emphasizing what was best for all. The *maga'lahi* never announced a decision until it was already agreed upon by the group. Could we use this approach today to avoid problems?

The council made all the important decisions on everything that concerned the well-being of the village. They made the final decision on matters of peace and war, treaties and alliances. Most land use was decided by the lineage heads. The council probably decided matters such as road work, community fishing projects, competitive gift giving, feasting, warfare, diplomacy, and holding a *gupot* (party). The purpose of a *gupot* was to reinforce the feeling of group **solidarity**. On the village level it was needed to maintain the strong sense of belonging that Micronesians have for their village. Village pride is an ancient Chamorro custom that certainly survives today. The council made judicial decisions when a *matao* was involved.

The council was composed of the chiefs (each *matao* lineage head), the *maga'lahi* (paramount chief), and all the *matao* women. The latter consisted of a very large majority. The *maga'lahi* had jurisdiction over the judgment of *manachang* and *acha'ot*. The council had jurisdiction over a *matao* who was accused of treason or cowardice, over those who traded outside the tribe without the permission of the *maga'lahi*, those who neglected to aid or were slow to aid their extended family, those who fought with illegal weapons (barbed spears), those who had a sexual relationship with a *manachang*, those who broke a fishing law, or those who disobeyed an order of the chief or a law of the land.

All of a criminal's relatives were embarrassed by a crime and they all came to demand reparations. If it was a serious crime, women who were related by marriage could air their grievances. The accused had a chance to state his innocence or explain why he should be excused for his actions. Only men were charged with crimes. A man was responsible for his wife's crimes. If the crime could be pardoned, a female relative (or several) put *ålas* (shell money) at the feet of the guilty man. He reciprocated by giving her fish, rice, taro, and yams. She then placed more *ålas* at his feet, and he reciprocated by giving her food. This continued until he could not continue, unless he was really wealthy. No IOU's were accepted.

The rich man who met the payments could withdraw honorably with his *ålas*. His accusers would have profited from the exchange and would go home with the food. The man who could not continue this exchange was condemned to suffer his punishment. This might be a fine or exile. The judgments were called *tadiu*. The close female relatives were the only ones who could present the *ålas*. The *ma uritaos* (girls who stayed in the men's house) could attend but did not have to attend as the married *matao* women did. They could not present *ålas*. Virgins were excluded from the council.

## Maga'lahi

The *maga'lahi* was the highest-ranking chief of the highest-ranking clan in a village. Literally, *maga'lahi* means "first-born son." The *maga'lahi* was a member of the *chamorri* caste and a member of a *matao* clan. The *maga'lahi* was the paramount village chief. He was a judge, and he controlled trade outside the village.

The *maga'lahi* came to hold his position by the right of his high birth. Because of his position in his family, he controlled certain land and resources that gave him wealth and power. A *maga'lahi* was expected to possess a great deal of traditional knowledge, to be clever, to be a good speech maker, to be strong, brave, and, perhaps most of all, generous. His generosity would prove that his interests were in the best interest of the people rather than himself. If he wished to raise his own status, he had to bring health, prosperity, and prestige to his village. Sometimes good fortune was accomplished through successful warfare. At other times it was through peaceful ceremonial exchange. A lot depended on the luck of good circumstances, which was interpreted as the spiritual blessing of a person's ancestors.

The *maga'lahi* was given great respect. His people were willing to go to war at the slightest insult to him. He led them in peace and war. He was the eldest male in the highest *matao* lineage in a village. The *acha'ot* clans and the *manachang* clans were dependent upon the *matao* clans' headmen for land-use privileges.

If two people quarrelled, they were expected to settle the quarrel on their own. Nevertheless, if it became violent, neighbors would intervene. If there were still problems, the *maga'lahi* would order them to stop. Oftentimes he would send his message by a child. The punishment for failure to obey an order of the *maga'lahi* was severe.

The *maga'lahi* had many duties. He was like a father figure to all members of the village. He presided over the village council. The *maga'lahi*, with the council, made the final decision on matters of peace and war, treaties and alliances, and all matters of general village well-being. He judged and fined or exiled *acha'ot* and *manachang* without the help of the council. In the case of a *matao* charged with a crime, the council assisted him in making a judgment.

As leader of the village council, the *maga'lahi's* primary role was to resolve conflicts and to make sure tradition was followed. He often acted as a judge and **mediator**. The guilt or innocence of an accused person was well known in ancient Chamorro society, for several reasons. A village was small, and the entire population knew what was going on. Also, loyalty was to elders rather than peers. Therefore, questioning by the *maga'lahi* usually found the truth of a matter pretty quickly.

The *maga'lahi* settled marriage disputes and approved adoptions. Economically the *maga'lahi* controlled commerce outside the village. He controlled the manufacture of *ålas* (shell money)

and *sakman* (large, open-ocean war and trading canoes). He controlled building, and held the most valuable land and fishing grounds. The *maga'lahi* served as the ceremonial head of village functions and received all visitors.

Succession to the position of *maga'lahi* was inherited. Since the ancient Chamorro society was **matrilineal**, a man became clan head through his mother. A *maga'lahi* who died was succeeded by his brothers in order of birth. If there was no younger living brother, then his eldest sister's eldest son or his mother's eldest sister's eldest son became chief.

When there were disagreements in regard to succession, ambitious brothers who were anxious to rule could establish their own villages, if they had the support to do so. The many villages that existed in ancient Guam suggest that clan fissioning (dividing) was a common occurrence.

## Maga'haga

There is considerable controversy over the meaning of *maga'haga*. Early accounts state that the *maga'haga* was the *maga'lahi's* wife. Laura Thompson suggests that the term means "first-born daughter," and you can infer that would make her the *maga'lahi's* sister. Nevertheless, that literal translation does not make much sense. Since

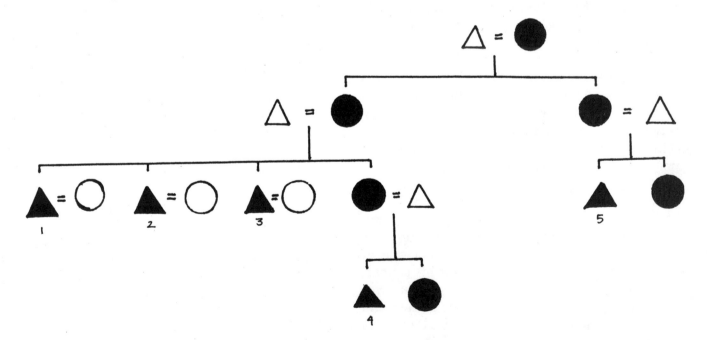

**15.2 Succession to chieftainship in a matrilineage. Numerals indicate order of succession. The matrilineage is shaded.** Adapted from *Ancient Chamorro Kinship Organization*, by Lawrence J. Cunningham. Published by L. Joseph Press.

residence was localized around males, wives became members of their husband's clan. Therefore, the *maga'lahi's* wife would become a clan member. Also, the *maga'lahi's* sister could not live on her brother's territory, because marriage was forbidden to members of the same clan. She would have to live in another village, on her husband's clan land. Further support for the belief that the *maga'haga* was the *maga'lahi's* wife can be seen in the word's use today. *Maga'lahi* is used for governor and *maga'haga* is used for the governor's wife or the "first lady." We can be sure that the *maga'haga* was the highest-ranking woman in her village.

## Spiritual Leaders

In ancient Chamorro society there were a few men who had special spiritual powers. A *makahna* was considered a person who had been given the power. In ancient times those with the most spiritual power were called *makahnas*. They were the ancient Chamorro religious leaders, because they performed religious rites, and they acted as mediators between the spiritual realm and humans. Although individuals could call upon ancestral spirits for help, the *makahna* was more skilled in this area. Today, we would call *makahnas* **shamans** rather than priests. A shaman is a religious leader who has special abilities to influence supernatural powers for his clients. On the other hand, a priest works for the supernatural power.

*Makahnas* were shaman who used magic for the purpose of curing the sick and guaranteeing success in warfare, fishing, and farming. They shared responsibility for the general welfare of the village. The *makahnas* insured good fishing and cured those possessed by evil spirits. In addition, *makahnas* were sorcerers, who practiced black magic. With dirt or spittle from a human being, they could cast a spell on that person. A side effect of this belief was very clean and sanitary villages. Ancient Chamorros could not risk spitting in the village or going to the bathroom just anywhere, because enemies could collect this refuse and, with the help of a *makahna*, use it against them.

The *makahna* did not perform his services for free. Those who sought the help of the *makahna* brought him gifts. Of course, successful *makahnas* received more gifts than those who were not good at making predictions and causing harm to enemies. This made it possible for a society based on rights and prestige by birth to recognize individual ability and merit in at least this area. Powerful *makahnas* probably came from both castes and all clans. The existence of the *makahnas* was an important factor in giving power and wealth to a person who might not otherwise enjoy it. The *makahna* position recognized the individual.

The *makahnas* were an important political force in ancient times. They served to provide the ancient Chamorro government with some needed checks and balances. Chiefs were hesitant to go against the wishes of the *makahna*. The *makahnas* were a prime force in keeping the Spanish-Chamorro Wars (1672-1695) going. On the other hand, a bothersome *makahna* could always be killed if the village council saw fit.

Today some of the supernatural powers of the *makahnas* are thought to be possessed by **suruhanus**. In ancient times it seems the *suruhanas* were women herb doctors. Today, there are men *suruhanus*, too. In addition to the practical skills in massage and herb medicine, modern *suruhanas* and *suruhanus* are generally believed to have been granted some special power by the *taotaomo'na* (ancestral spirits) or the Virgin Mary.

## Social Clubs

An important feature of community organization in ancient Chamorro society was the **uritao** or **guma' uritao**. This was a house of the bachelors. When young men reached puberty (sexual maturity), they left the home of their parents and resided in a dormitory for the young men of their clan. The Anson expedition (1742) reported that a vow was taken when a boy moved into the bachelors' house. There was probably a rite of passage for this step to manhood. Older married men also used this residence as a social center and a place to teach the younger men skills.

Since clan territory was localized around men and not women, wives had to move to their husbands' territory. Children belonged to their mother's clan. Therefore, young men had to leave their fathers' territory and return to the clan land of their mothers' brother. This move probably took place after a young man reached puberty. The bachelor would then live in the *uritao* until he got married and established his own household. Another reason for the move was that they believed that brothers and sisters should not live in the same house once they were sexually mature. The significance of the *uritao* goes far beyond its use as a bachelors' quarters.

The *uritao* was a social club for men. Most domestic activities were dominated by the women of the household. The men's house provided a place for men to gather and socialize with their friends. At the *uritao* men gathered to repair their nets and canoes or just to sit and talk while making coconut-fiber rope. Since married men also spent time at the *uritao*, it is also called a men's house.

15.3 *Guma' Uritao* or Men's House

Young men could get an education in the men's house by watching the older men work. If they really wanted to learn something special, they brought betel nut to an older man who had the knowledge they wished to learn. Most really important skills were kept secret. If a man was presented a piece of *ålas* (shell money), he was obligated to teach the donor some detail of his skill. A young man's mother's brother helped in these payments. In this way young men learned to be navigators, skilled canoe builders, and *latte*-house builders. The details of Chamorro education are presented in the chapter "Arts, Skills, and Education."

Perhaps the best-known aspect of the men's house was the sexual education young men received there. Early accounts by Europeans stress this function of the men's house because it seemed wrong and sinful to them. In ancient Chamorro times, men's social clubs acquired girls to serve the young men. The girls were obtained from another village. Gifts were given to the chosen girl's father. Having a daughter picked for the men's house was

considered an honor and was financially rewarding, too.

The girls chosen for the men's house were called *ma uritaos*. They served for a set time. Today, our values would consider this practice prostitution. Nevertheless, in ancient times girls chosen to serve in the men's house were given a great deal of respect. Mothers sang songs encouraging their daughters to visit the men's house. This practice raised a girl's parents' status and wealth. The *ma uritaos* had a better chance for a good marriage, too. Men preferred girls who served in the men's house over those who did not. There were several reasons for this. Children were considered important and were valued. Usually a woman left the men's house pregnant. Men preferred women who had proved that they could have children. Also, ancient Chamorro men did not wish to marry a virgin. This seems very strange in light of today's Christian values, but in those days it was an insult to marry a virgin. This was considered very embarrassing to a girl's parents. It demonstrated that their daughter was not very desirable.

15.4 A *ma uritao* is welcomed to the men's house.

The *uritao* was a place for the people to assemble. Most public ceremonies probably centered on a village's men's house. Important commercial transactions were probably taken care of at the *uritao*. The men's house was also used to house male visitors, and probably as a place to entertain them as well.

The young people in those days formed a

society called the *uritoi*. Its purpose was to learn the traditional songs and dances and to create new songs and dances. They even had a secret language called *fino' gualafon* for their love songs.

The men's house was used as a center for competitive sports, too. The young men competed in slingstone throwing, spear throwing, and wrestling.

Perhaps the most important purpose of the *uritao* was warfare. The young *chamorri* men were trained as warriors. Of course, the *manachang* were not part of the men's house organization. The men's house was an arsenal or storage place for weapons. It was also used to store war canoes. Even today many slingstones can be found in the waters around Guam. At the area known as Twin Reefs you can still find slingstones. There are no rivers in that part of Guam that could have deposited the slingstones there. The slingstones are not the type used as fishing sinkers. Those types of slingstones have grooves or holes for attaching them to fishing lines. Therefore, we must assume that this was the site of a great canoe battle.

Legazpi's voyage in 1565 records canoes full of warriors throwing slingstones in such great numbers and with such force that they had to clear the deck of men. They claimed that some of the slingstones were thrown with such force that they stuck in the sides of the ship. The war canoes were probably the pride of the *uritao*.

The social clubs were also used as a source of labor for village projects. The young men not only served the community by protecting it, but they cleared paths, built buildings, and completed any big community projects as well.

Less is known about the social clubs for women. It is possible that they met in their homes, while the males were at the men's house. We do know that occasionally they had festivities in which only women participated. Sometimes there were a few high-ranking men who participated in these meetings, too. The women's clubs were probably used as a source of labor for village projects.

Social clubs in ancient Chamorro times gave individuals a way to prove their worth and abilities. Since people were ranked in importance outside of the clubs, this was difficult. The symbolic standard of the *uritao* was the *tunas*. All the bachelors carried these carved five- or six-foot sticks with a *pagu* fiber tassel at the top. For more details on the *tunas*, see the chapter "Clothing."

In conclusion, the social club was an important part of ancient Chamorro community organization. For males the center of social activities was the *uritao* or men's house. It functioned as a meeting place, a dormitory for young men, and a school. The young men served as a labor pool for community projects and defended the village, too. There were social clubs for women.

**15.5 Bachelors carried carved sticks called *tunas*.**

15.6 Organization of Ancient Chamorro Government

# WARFARE AND DIPLOMACY

Warfare in ancient Chamorro times was a ritual. It was altogether different from the warfare practiced by modern people. The purpose of ancient Chamorro warfare was not to destroy the enemy, but only to demonstrate superiority over the enemy and thereby raise the rank and status of the victors. Consequently, warfare usually never amounted to more than a few deaths on either side. There were two major weapons used, the slingstone and the spear. After property was destroyed, houses were frequently burned, and sometimes a village's gardens were destroyed. For a complete description of ancient Chamorro warfare, see the chapter "Weapons."

Although wars were brief, they were frequent. The major cause of war was disagreement among acquaintances and even friends. Quarrels between individuals, especially if a woman was involved, resulted in a war. The same held true for an insult to a chief. Matters of honor were the prime cause of war in ancient Chamorro times. Of course, infringement of territorial land or fishing rights was cause for war too. Even these reasons were viewed as an insult to the rightful owner and, therefore, a matter of honor. Once a war began, although a settlement might be made, the injury would not soon be forgotten. Reciprocal behavior

was and is a strong motivation in all human relationships. Every action of a friend or enemy demanded a similar reaction. A present was given for a present received. If a life was taken, then a life must be taken in revenge. The kinship system kept this reciprocal behavior between opposing clans going on for generations. The original quarrel that started a war long ago might be forgotten. If a village was defeated in a war, the residents had to avenge those deaths later, when they were able to do so.

15.7 A Clan Plots Revenge

Warfare was encouraged by many as a means of raising village status. Individual warriors were anxious to prove themselves. *Acha'ot* class members saw war as a means to regain their *matao* status. Sometimes an ambitious man would establish a new village. Clan splitting is very common the world over. The large number of villages in ancient Chamorro society suggests that it was probably common in the Mariana Islands, too. New villages were probably immediately challenged from many sides. A people's success or failure in these clashes would establish their position in the ranking system between villages.

Diplomacy is the skill in handling disagreements between two groups without violence. The chief tool of the ancient Chamorro diplomat was the *gupot* (party). Mutual feasting, even competitive feasting, allowed for peaceful status competition. A *gupot* established solidarity on all levels of ancient Chamorro society, from the family to the lineage or the village, or in village alliances.

Alliances of villages, which were fairly close together, offered better mutual defense. Alliances were also needed to obtain wives. Men could not marry women from their own clan. Friendly clans were a potential source of brides. When the process broke down, the only satisfactory alternative was kidnapping. This may have been practiced in the Mariana Islands; it was in other areas of Micronesia. Nevertheless, more peaceful means were the rule.

Girls were obtained from other villages to serve in the men's houses. Although, in the case of brides and *ma uritaos*, payment was to the girl's parents, such transactions would not have been possible without inter-village cooperation. Also, a village would have been obligated to supply brides and *ma uritaos* to a village who had helped them out in these matters.

Alliances may have been needed for casual trading, although most natural resources were probably evenly distributed among the villages. This reduced the need for inter-village trade. There may have been some important trading between the inland areas and coastal areas, or between limestone area villages and savanna area villages. Perhaps the trading was based not on resource difference but on the fact that various areas were noted for some specific product. For example, one village might have made the best pottery and another village the best slingstones. In such cases it would have been to everyone's benefit to trade.

Probably, most of the trading was not of this direct sort. It seems more likely that reciprocal gift giving was more common. One village probably heaped gifts on another village. At some later date, in order to maintain their status, that village would have been expected to give gifts in return. If the gifts were of greater value, that village would have gained status and prestige.

*Hotyong songsong* was a ritual Chamorro diplomatic custom. It illustrates many of the important points made above. *Hotyong songsong* literally means "going out of the village." Actually, it was used to describe the ceremonial kidnapping of a group work leader from another village. The group work leader might have been the person in charge of a harvest or a canoe-building project. An arm band was placed on the captive to show his co-workers that this was a ceremonial capture and not an act of war. The group work leader was then held for ransom. Nevertheless, when the kidnappers released their prisoner, they gave gifts to their captive's village that greatly exceeded the ransom price. They also feasted the captive's village. The purpose of the *hotyong songsong* was to insure peace and harmony.

# RULES

All societies develop rules to live by. Usually these customs are formed through a consensus of public opinion. People feel that it is in their interest to follow these rules. Some rules are called folkways, others mores, and some laws.

**Folkways** are traditional social customs not considered vital to the society's welfare. Today, when we greet another person, we shake hands. This is our custom; we don't even realize why we do it. Researchers have found that this custom is meant to show that a person is not wielding a weapon. We observe many folkways every day. When a man enters a building, he removes his hat. It is considered impolite for a man to wear a hat indoors.

**Mores** are the morally binding customs of a particular group. Mores tell us what is right and wrong. Our conscience is full of mores. Society considers these rules necessary for group welfare. Society considers sex outside of marriage wrong, but sex between a parent and child or between brothers and sisters is strictly forbidden. The violation of social mores outrages society. A **taboo** is a mor (singular for mores), the violation of which involves severe, automatic punishment.

Laws are the customs and rules of society that are enforced by government. One of the main reasons we have government is to enforce the laws of the land. The law provides rules for orderly relationships between individuals and between individuals and groups. The law provides for the enforcement of order. Another function of the law is to provide a just settlement of disputes between individuals and for offenses against the community. The law adjusts to the changing conditions of life. Oftentimes this means developing new laws, dropping old laws, or reinterpreting old laws.

Today we have a legislature that makes laws. Nevertheless, most of our laws today are the result of long-standing customs, and that is the way it was for the ancient Chamorros. The ancient Chamorro laws were not written, but they served the same function. All the ancient Chamorro laws are not known. Early explorers and missionaries did record a few of the ancient Chamorro laws.

Back in the early 1800s Captain Luis Torres did ask about ancient Chamorro rules. A lot of his research was recorded by a French scientific expedition. Below is a list of ancient Chamorro rules governing caste, domestic relations, property, warfare, and reciprocity. This list is not complete, but it is presented to give you some idea of the laws of the ancient Chamorros.

# Caste Rules

Members of the two castes could not marry or even date. Only the high-caste person was punished for a violation of this rule.

Members of the lower caste were forbidden to go near the ocean.

Members of the high caste could not eat eels.

Members of the high caste could not eat tough-scaled fish.

Members of the lower caste could not perform the occupations reserved for the high caste.

Members of the lower caste could not own land.

Members of the lower caste were free to move and work the land of any high caste person who accepted them.

Members of the lower caste could not be warriors.

Members of the lower caste could fish in rivers, but were forbidden to use hooks or nets.

Members of the lower caste could not eat or drink in the presence of the high caste.

Members of the lower caste could not approach a noble or a noble's house without permission.

Members of the lower caste were expected to bow down before members of the high caste.

Members of the lower caste could not clear their throats in the presence of respected persons.

Members of the lower caste had to show a deep reverence for the *matao*, but not for the *acha'ot*.

**Endogamy** is the practice of selecting a mate from within one's own group. The ancient Chamorros practiced endogamy with regard to caste. Violations of any of these rules was believed to result in the physical and moral weakening of the *chamorri* (high caste). **Exogamy** is the practice of selecting a mate from outside one's own group. The ancient Chamorros practiced exogamy with regard to clan.

*Manachang* (lower caste) fretted over pleasing the *matao*. They would inquire to see if their service was satisfactory.

# Domestic Rules

Men could not marry their sisters, first cousins, nieces, or daughters, even if they were adopted, nor could they marry a clan member.

No one was free to commit adultery.

Women could obtain a divorce by leaving their husbands' house. Women got the children and the possessions in the house when there was a divorce.

A man was responsible for his wife's crime.

Inheritance of land went to a man's sisters' children.

Inheritance of personal possessions went to a man's wife, if there were children. If there were no children, the husband's relatives gave her the possessions and a gift of money called *fagahot* (literally an understanding person, one who comprehends things well; the Freycinet expedition records this word as "heritage").

Adopted children had the same rights, privileges and obligations as other children, except for succession to an office like *maga'lahi*.

# Property Rules

Land and sea resources cannot be used without asking permission from the owner.

One half of a catch of fish goes to the net's owner.

# Warfare Rules

No one was permitted to use barbed fishing spears unless trapped.

Warriors were to come from the *chamorri* caste and never the *manachang* caste.

War stopped when one side surrendered and offered to pay *âlas* (shell money) to the winners.

# Principle of Reciprocity

The principle of **reciprocity** or sharing was a primary feature of ancient Chamorro society. Human actions required reactions. For example, if a person gave a gift, the recipient felt obligated to the donor. On the other hand, if a person caused injury, the injured party was obligated to seek redress. Since the ancient Chamorros had a strong kinship system, this reciprocal action and reaction involved a person's family, lineage, clan and village. Reciprocity is mutual exchange. The value of reciprocity is the basis for the accepted behavior in the Chamorro customs of *chenchule'* (present, or donation, thing that is given away), *ika* (funeral gift), *ayudu* (help, assistance), *a'ok* (bride price or wedding gift), and *emmok* (revenge). The value of reciprocal behavior can also be seen in ancient Chamorro laws.

No one could refuse assistance or gifts, even though they knew acceptance would obligate them. Wealthy men usually tried to refuse assistance. But they could not refuse assistance from a relative.

If a female presented a relative with a piece of *ålas* (shell money), he or she could not refuse her request. A sister could even ask for a field. This practice was not abused.

People who did not meet their obligations were condemned not to receive assistance when in need. The punishment was not so much being denied the help, but the embarrassment this caused.

The value of reciprocal behavior was expressed on all levels of ancient Chamorro society; therefore, it is not surprising that the laws of the ancient Chamorros reflect that value.

# PUNISHMENT

**Social control** is the means by which a society secures conformity to its norms. A society has many ways of enforcing its rules or norms. A **norm** is a group-shared expectation of behavior. Society uses sanctions to reward those who follow the rules and punish those who break them. **Public opinion** is an expression of the moral judgment of the group. **Sanctions** are rewards or punishments used to secure conformity to norms. Rewards are positive sanctions. Punishments are negative sanctions.

Since everyone needs to be appreciated, we normally do what society considers proper. When we do what is right, we are praised. The ancient Chamorros were known to sing the praises of their properly behaved children.

Some people break the rules of society when they think it is in their best interest to do so. If they are caught, society will punish them. Of course, some rules are more important than others, so punishment varies. Some rules when broken are crimes; others are only **torts**. Some are **felonies**, others less serious are considered **misdemeanors**.

Some rules are even less significant. If a folkway is broken, the offender may receive only a frown. In some societies an offender's life can be taken for breaking a law. Punishment is society's way of settling a breach of the law.

Societies' laws vary considerably. In traditional Eskimo society, a person could receive the death penalty just for being uncooperative. Why? The whole group's survival depended upon cooperation. In that same society, a murder was considered a personal matter to be settled by relatives rather than by society as a whole. In our society today, it is wrong to take a life. The maximum penalty on Guam for this crime is life imprisonment. Nevertheless, our society gives medals for killing our country's enemies in time of war. Punishment varies from society to society and from circumstance to circumstance within a society. A few ancient Chamorro sanctions are described below.

## Ancestor Sanctions

The ancient Chamorros believed that people who followed the rules of society would be blessed by their *ante* (ancestral spirit). The *ante* punished descendents who did not follow the norms of society. Sickness, crop failure, bad luck, or even a violent death were expected to come to the person who did not follow the rules of society.

## Public Ridicule

The wife of an unfaithful husband and her friends adorned themselves as men and made fun of the guilty husband.

Public opinion affected not just the individual but the whole family. Ridicule was considered extremely embarrassing.

The greatest embarrassment was the denial of assistance. This could happen only to a person who had not met his or her kinship obligations.

## Death Penalty

A woman and her family had the right to kill an unfaithful husband. A man could kill his wife's lover but not his wife.

Death was the penalty for those who violated some fishing rights or had sex with a person not in their caste.

# Destruction of Property

The wife of an unfaithful husband and her friends had the right to destroy a man's garden and house, and take his possessions.

# Restitution

A person who wronged someone could right the wrong by repaying the person. Sometimes even a murderer could escape and then later make restitution to the family of the victim. Sometimes the relatives of the guilty party gave a turtle shell (tortoiseshell was used as money), rice, and a large fish to compensate the family of the deceased. It was not so much the gift as the sentiment behind it that was important.

# Fines

Crime was considered an insult to the *maga'lahi*. He could therefore levy fines against wrongdoers.

# Demotion and Ostracism

The *maga'lahi* and village council could reduce a *matao* to *acha'ot* status. *Acha'ot* implied the status of a stranger. The *acha'ot* was forced to leave the village and find a village that would accept him. Sometimes a wealthy patron gave him the right to found a new village.

If the exiled man's family wanted to accompany him, they had to pay the *maga'lahi*. The *acha'ot* class was composed of people whose ancestors had broken an important rule. This punishment was hereditary, not just for the individual but the whole family, including his children and his children's children. This punishment was severe in a rank-and status-conscious society.

If the *acha'ot* was legally banished from his tribe, he could never return. But if he left voluntarily, before a judgment, he could hope to return later. If an exiled man refused to leave the village after having been ordered to do so, he was called *ma chatlamen*, a man who is detested. This shamed the entire village. Nevertheless, if he was pardoned, he could get his title and his property back.

Banishments were reversible. Heroic deeds or vast accumulated wealth could allow a person to regain his family's former *matao* position. People who escaped before their trial could return to their village when things cooled down, especially if they were willing to make restitution. Nevertheless, banishment was more or less permanent.

At any trial a man's female relatives could beg for mercy if they offered a money gift to the *maga'lahi*. The rich were favored in other ways, too. Men who furnished their own house without aid from others received no punishment. If they built their own house, they were exempt from even becoming an *acha'ot*. The ancient Chamorros had a way to get around this loophole in the law. If the community really wanted to punish a man, they would give him a house, which by law he could not refuse; then, of course, he would be liable for punishment.

# War

Punishment for outsiders who broke the rules of society was death or the declaration war on their village.

Punishment in our society today is different than it was in the past. One of the main ways we punish people today is to lock them up in jails or prison. This was never used in ancient Chamorro times as a punishment.

# SUMMARY

Ancient Chamorro government was organized by village or district. Within the village, clan and lineage kinship groups were the basis of government. The highest-ranking male in a village was called a *maga'lahi*. He was the community leader. All the upper-caste *matao* formed a village council to decide village matters. Many of the council decisions were carried out by the *uritao*, or bachelors, who were the warriors and formed the work gangs. Leadership roles were usually inherited. The exception was the *makahna*, or spiritual leader, who relied on ability and served as a check on the *maga'lahi's* power. The ancient Chamorro government had rules and a system of punishment.

# Chapter 16
# Trade

## INTRODUCTION

**Trade** is the buying or selling or **bartering** of something useful or valuable. Useful or valuable articles are called **commodities**. Bartering is the exchange of one commodity for another. You have probably traded something to a friend for an article of his or hers you really liked. When you did this you were bartering. Bartering fills mutual needs. Traders give up something for a commodity or service they need and want more.

Today bartering is not very common. Trade usually means an exchange of **money** for economic goods or commodities. Money is a free medium of exchange. It solves the problem of not having something that is useful or valuable to your trading partner. During Spanish times in the Mariana Islands, tobacco and coins were used for money. Since people will accept money, it facilitates trading.

In ancient times and even during Spanish times, Chamorros used money mainly for ceremonial purposes. Most of the ancient Chamorros' *ålas* (shell money) was made from turtle shell. It was used more for giving than buying. *Chenchule'* (reciprocal gift-giving) obligations were settled with *ålas*. The ancient Chamorros did not use money in trading; they bartered.

Several categories of trade took place in ancient Chamorro times. There was **intra-island trade,** or trade within an island. There was also **inter-island trade,** or trade between different islands. This chapter covers trade within the Mariana Islands, trade within Micronesia and trade outside Micronesia. Under each of these categories the trade and types of goods traded will be discussed.

## INTRA-ISLAND TRADE

Trade within a Chamorro island was limited. In any society where most goods are shared within a village and where most villages control land that provides the same resources, there is little need for trade. Look at the map of an imaginary island titled Intra-island Trading Districts. Each clan controls some coastal land and some mountain land. On such an island there is not much need for trading resources.

In ancient times various areas may have been known for some special products and these were traded to other areas. On Guam, it is said that Inalajan (a correct spelling of Inarajan village) comes from *åla* (basket - usually made from coconut leaves). **Specialization** encourages trade. Some areas could have had better clay for pottery. They might have traded the raw clay or the finished pottery products.

During the *Latte* Period (after 845 A.D.) the population in the Mariana Islands increased greatly. Villages were built in the interior. These villages probably traded mountain resources like *dokdok* (wild breadfruit) timber and various wild foods like *gaddo'* (wild thorny yam) for seafoods. Although this seems likely, there is no evidence to prove it. It is known that trade outside the village was controlled by the village chief. So, there must have been some trade. The historical record claims that at least one interior village, Fena, had the first rights to fish for *mañahak* (juvenile rabbit fish) in Malesso (Merizo). Look at the Intra-island Trading Districts illustration; can you tell which products or resources each district would have to trade? Can you tell which things each district would need?

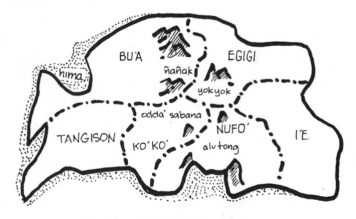

**16.1 Intra-island Trading Districts**

*hima* = tridacna clam used in making adzes.
*ñañak* = pumice used to make grindstones.
*odda' sabana* = clay used to make pottery.
*alutong* = basalt, a volcanic rock used to make mortars and pestles.
*yokyok* = flint used in starting fires.

On the larger islands like Guam and Saipan there is diversity in the land. On Guam the northern area is an uplifted limestone plateau. Generally, the southern area of Guam is volcanic, with some limestone on the southeast coast and on the ridge between Mt. Alifan and Mt. Lamlam. The people of northern Guam used tools made from *alutong* (basalt). Except at Mt. Santa Rosa, there is not much *alutong* found in northern Guam. High quality *alutong* is found in southern Guam. The northern clans on Guam must have traded with the southern villages for *alutong* or for the tools made from this volcanic rock. Geological differences in areas are often a basis for trade. One area is blessed with a useful commodity that other areas need, but do not have. So, trade is established. Trading is complementary. Each side gains something useful or valuable by the exchange. Trade cannot take place, however, unless there are communication and transportation links between people.

Within villages in the Mariana Islands there was a great deal of sharing rather than trading. Families shared fish, other sea resources, and the produce of the land. Services were also shared. People helped one another repair a roof or build a new house. Most of this sharing was within a person's lineage and clan. In some cases, men were forced to share with their female relatives. For example, the first fish caught in a fishing season were given to female relatives. This was probably true of the first of a harvest, too. Even the exchanges between the castes involved more reciprocal giving than trading. The *manachang* (low caste) were obligated to pay **tribute** to the *chamorri* (high caste). The *chamorri* probably reciprocated with gifts and certainly gave the *manachang* (low caste) the rights to use land.

The use of *ålas* (shell money) was ceremonial and not for regular commerce. *Ålas* paid in a bride price was often used to "buy" the bride's father's sister's son a wife. This payment was more accurately a gift. Wives were not owned. They were always free to break the marriage and return to their family. *Ålas* was used to pay the victors of a battle. Other ceremonial uses of money included money gifts, which often preceded requests for favors, and fines for improper behavior.

In summary, intra-island trading was limited because there were few resources not shared by all. Most exchange was reciprocal giving or ceremonial. There may have been some trade or

specialized commodities. Barter was the method used for what little trading there was. There are historical records that state that the village chief controlled trade outside the village.

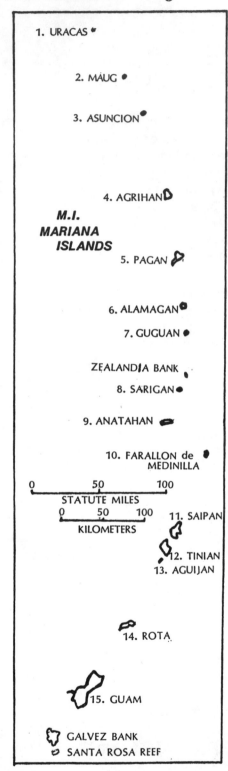

**16.2 Map of the Mariana Islands.** Adapted from *Guide to Place Names in the Trust Territory of the Pacific Islands*, compiled by E. H. Bryan, Jr. Published by Pacific Scientific Information Center, Bernice P. Bishop Museum, in 1971.

# INTER-MARIANA ISLANDS TRADE

There was a somewhat greater need for inter-island trade in the Mariana Islands because of geologic differences in the islands. Luta (Rota), Aguijan, and Tinian are uplifted limestone plateau islands. Although there are a few outcrops of *alutong* on Luta, for the most part these islands do not have good materials for making stone tools. Archaeological sites on Tinian have revealed large quantities of rocks from volcanic islands. These rocks were brought to Tinian for tool-making purposes. Limestone slingstones have been found on islands in the northern Marianas, which are entirely volcanic islands. Basalt mortars have been found on islands in the southern Marianas, which are limestone.

One account reports that one village on Tinian had the exclusive right to string *ålas* (tortoiseshell money). The village was named Fanutugan-ålas. Since people in all the Mariana Islands used *ålas* for money, there must have been considerable inter-island trade.

People on the limestone islands have trouble growing *pugua'* (betel nut), which grows especially well in damp areas near streams. The limestone soaks up most of the rainfall, and these islands have few streams of running water. There was probably *pugua'* trade between the Mariana Islands. The stained teeth that result from chewing *pugua'*, *pupulu* (betel pepper leaf) and *åfok* (quicklime) have been found in the prehistoric skeletons from these uplifted limestone islands. The *pugua'* trade to these islands continues today.

Trade between the Mariana Islands can be confirmed by examining some cultural evidence. The material **artifacts** are almost identical from island to island. The prehistoric tools or pottery from various Mariana Islands are not significantly different. The same Chamorro language was spoken throughout the Mariana Islands, too. Although there are differences in dialect between the islands, they are slight. If the speakers of a language are separated over time, the language will change in different ways. Over thousands of years this can lead to separate languages. This is the reason there are so many Austronesian languages. If there had not been regular contact between the Chamorros of the Mariana Islands, there would be greater differences in their tools and language. The contact was probably maintained by trade.

Transportation and communication are essential to trade. For this inter-island trade the ancient Chamorros used the *sakman* (oceangoing sailing canoe) for transportation. Westerners have tagged the *sakman* the "flying proa." Early European explorers were amazed at the skill and speed with which the ancient Chamorros handled their canoes.

# MICRONESIAN TRADE

There was some trade between the ancient Chamorros and the people of the Caroline Islands. Some Carolinians, who lived on **atolls**, had extensive trade networks and had the sailing knowledge that made it possible for them to sail to eastern Micronesia, New Guinea, and the Philippines. We know something about this trade because it has continued to the present day.

In 1721, a group from Faraulep set out for Ulithi. A storm drove them to Guam. The Carolinians were very afraid. They knew about the Spanish takeover of Guam because some Chamorros had escaped to the Caroline Islands. The Carolinians were told that the Spanish were cruel.

The fact that some Chamorros sailed to the Carolines to escape Spanish domination does not mean that they made regular trading voyages. The Mariana Islands had a great deal of diversity in resources in comparison with the atolls (low islands) of the Carolines. So, most of the trading voyages were probably made by the Carolinians.

In 1788, 1789 (some accounts say 1787 and 1788), and for a while almost yearly after 1804, there were purposeful voyages to the Mariana Islands. The Carolinians who made these voyages claimed that before the Spanish came to the Mariana Islands, these voyages had been on a regular basis. Canoes from Faraulep, Woleai, Ulithi, Ifaluk, and Satawal would group at Lamotrek. These islands are about 300 miles south of Guam. From Lamotrek a fleet of as many as eighteen canoes would proceed to West Fayu. From there, with the trade winds on their **starboard** side, they could make the Mariana Islands in a few days.

These voyages were made in April and the return was in May or early June. The weather is best during that part of the dry season. There are few calms, few storms and a steady **trade wind** breeze at that time of year.

These trading voyages led to some settlement of Carolinians in the Mariana Islands during the 1800s. Carolinians settled on Saipan and on Guam. The Carolinian settlement of Saipan began in 1815 or 1816.

In 1818, Kaoutao, a representative of the King of Lamotrek, visited Guam. He got permission for Carolinians to move to the Mariana Islands. Even though in 1816 the Carolinians lost at sea 120 canoes with 900 people, their home islands were still overpopulated. The Spanish granted them land and transportation to Saipan. The Carolinians agreed to live in perfect harmony with the Spanish and Chamorros.

After **a tsunami** (wave caused by an earthquake) washed over Satawal in 1849, more people left for Saipan. This same tsunami killed Josepha Lujan, a Chamorro from Agaña. She was walking by Talofofo Bay on Guam. The wave washed her out to sea when it receded.

On Guam, the Carolinians settled the eastern side of Agaña Bay. The settlement was called Maria Christina in Spanish, but the Carolinian name, Tamuning, is the name that has survived. These Carolinians provided the only reliable ocean transportation within the Mariana Islands for the Spanish.

Many Carolinians were taken to the Mariana Islands by recruiters or **blackbirders** to cut **copra** (dried meat of the coconut, which is used to make coconut oil) during Spanish times. Copra was an important trade item in Micronesia. In 1865 and 1869, a thousand Carolinians colonized the northern Marianas under encouragement of the Spanish to help the copra trade. Carolinians were relocated in the Mariana Islands by the Germans after a severe typhoon struck Woleai. The Germans controlled all the Mariana Islands, except Guam, and most of the rest of Micronesia from 1898 to 1914. They purchased this territory from Spain following the Spanish-American War. The Germans lost their Micronesian colonies to the Japanese in World War I.

Carolinians are still voyaging to the Mariana Islands. Their purposes today are pride in their traditions, as well as trade. There has been a cultural revival among the Carolinians. By making long sailing trips, they have demonstrated that they have not lost their old knowledge of navigation.

In 1970, Martin Raiuk, the Chief of Satawal, sent a canoe to Saipan. He did this to dramatize his people's claim to that island. After the Spanish-Chamorro Wars (1672-1695) and a series of epidemics around 1700, most of the Chamorros were moved to Guam, Luta, and Saipan. As the years went by, the population of Saipan dwindled, and the mission was closed in 1730. The people of the overpopulated, one-half square mile Satawal saw Saipan as a good place to move. They claim that Saipan means "empty place" in their language. It is said that Agrup, a Satawal chief, traded two women, two golden cowries, and four large coconut fiber ropes to the Spanish governor of the Mariana Islands for Saipan in 1815 or 1816. There is no official record of this transaction. The Carolinians of Puluwat claim that Agrup left two women on Guam because the trip had been too rough for them. The shells and ropes were a gift for the women's care, while the men continued on to Saipan.

Whatever the true case, Dr. Benusto Kaipat, a Carolinian leader in Saipan and Raiuk, thought a modern-day voyage would be a good way to protest the reintegration of the northern Mariana Islands with Guam. This movement was very unpopular with the people of Guam, too. Although the majority of northern Mariana Islanders voted for the reintegration, the people of Guam rejected it. Since 1970, the northern Mariana Islands have become a commonwealth of the United States. This movement was also opposed by many Carolinians on Saipan.

Since the 1970 voyage under the navigator Repunglug, the men of Satawal have made regular voyages to Saipan. They have done this to trade, for adventure, and to show their respect to their ancestors by visiting the grave of an important chief buried on the islet of Managaha. Carolinian pride in their ability and culture has been a strong motivating force for these voyages. Mau Piailug, a Satawal navigator, was chosen to guide the Polynesian Voyaging Society's Hawai'i to Tahiti voyage. Polynesians had to rely on the help of Carolinian navigators to make their 1976 canoe voyage from Hawai'i to Tahiti. No Hawaiians still knew how to navigate in the traditional ways. For the details on this trip, see "Hokule'a Follows the Stars to Tahiti" in the October 1976 *National Geographic*.

In 1972, a group of men from Puluwat atoll sailed to Guam on a trading voyage. They delivered a canoe to Henry Simpson, a Guam businessman, for $1,000 and return expenses. The sale was arranged by Carlos Viti, who later became a well-known photographer for the *Pacific Daily News*. This was the first time the men of Puluwat had sailed a traditional outrigger canoe to the Mariana Islands since 1905. Their navigator at first avoided Apra Harbor and landed at Nimitz Beach in Agat, because his old sailing instructions did not include the manmade Glass Breakwater near the mouth of Apra Harbor. After the voyage, their canoe was on display at the Inarajan Zoo. After the zoo went out of business, the canoe was moved to the Okura Hotel. Unfortunately, the canoe was destroyed beyond repair by Typhoon Pamela in 1976. Again, in 1991, the navigators from Puluwat sailed an outrigger canoe to Guam for a Micronesian cultural fair.

The atoll people of the Carolines were not the only Carolinians to voyage to the Mariana Islands. In the 1800s, men from the high island of Yap came to mine rock for stone money. The rock is called *acho' Yap* in Chamorro. It is not known if this trade was carried out in ancient times. In 1807, a lost canoe from Chuuk (Truk) came to Guam with 15 people aboard.

The trading that took place in the historical voyages was for tobacco, pipes, trade cloth, and, especially, metal products like hatchets, nails, machetes, and pots and pans. These are products which were not available in ancient times. The products the Carolinians offered in exchange probably have not changed much over the years. They traded lavalavas (fine textile skirts woven from banana stalk fibers), pandanus mats, shells of various types, coconut oil, coconut fiber rope, and wooden boxes (probably tackle boxes that float). During historical times, they also traded ocean-going outrigger canoes to the Spanish and Chamorros. After Spanish colonization, only small reef canoes were made by Chamorros. Since Carolinian money belts are similar to the *guini* and the *lukao hugua* tortoiseshell necklaces of the ancient Chamorros, these may have been used as a medium of exchange. Nevertheless, it is doubtful that the Carolinians would have desired turtle-shell products. There are many uninhabited atolls in their domain where sea turtles nest.

The atoll people of the Carolines probably wanted the resources found only on high islands. They may have traded for timber to make canoes; turmeric, a yellow cosmetic and spice; special types of food; and flintstone. These are the articles outer-island Carolinians trade for in Yap. The Yapese conquered these atolls and demanded tribute from them every year. These articles were probably desired from the Chamorros, too. Perhaps they also wanted pottery products from the Mariana Islands, since atolls do not have clay deposits. The Carolinians had great respect for the ancient Chamorros' military prowess and skill. In contrast, they expressed contempt for other Micronesians. Some Chamorros escaped to the Caroline Islands after the Spanish-Chamorro Wars (1672-1695).

In summary, the knowledge of traditional voyaging seen today, the historical record of this voyaging and trading, and the Carolinian names for many Mariana Islands suggest regular inter-island trading by the ancient Chamorros. Since the Chamorros had an abundance of resources, probably most traders came to them. The name **Guahan** (Guam, "we have") suggests that the people had plenty of everything. The inter-island trading in the Mariana Islands and the escape of some Chamorros to the Carolines during the Spanish-Chamorro Wars suggest the Chamorros made Micronesian trading voyages, too.

# EXTRA-MICRONESIAN TRADE

Trade outside of Micronesia was limited, but was not nonexistent. The ancient Chamorros' knowledge of geography included at least the non-Micronesian areas of New Guinea and the Philippines. The original settlers of the Mariana Islands probably maintained contact with their former home for some time. Metal was known in the Mariana Islands before the coming of the Spanish. This suggests some contact with the outside world, if not regular trade. The fact that metal was limited and in great demand indicated this contact was sporadic at best, and probably accidental. Some people of the islands of Southeast Asia had metal before contact with Europeans. People in western New Guinea had metal 3,000 years ago.

In 1648, a Chinese man by the name of Chaco or Choco came to Guam. He was shipwrecked in the Mariana Islands. He had been headed from Manila to Ternate in Indonesia. A storm blew him way off course. The Mariana Islands have been inhabited since 2000 B.C. Considering the unpredictable weather and the amount of voyaging and fishing the Chinese and Japanese did in those years, surely contact with the Mariana Islands was made in ancient times.

The red spondylus shell used to make ceremonial money necklaces for ancient Chamorro women is not found in the Mariana Islands. This shell is common in the Ryukyu Islands. This may suggest some trade. In the 1970s Carolinians sailed an outrigger canoe to a world "expo" on Oceanography, held on Okinawa. In 1988, Carolinians sailed their canoes all the way to Japan. Perhaps the people of the Ryukyus voyaged to Micronesia, or the Chamorros or Carolinians went to the Ryukyus in ancient times. This is one way to account for the red spondylus shell necklaces.

Beginning with Magellan's landing in the Mariana Islands in 1521, trade between Europeans and Chamorros became increasingly frequent. After 1668, when the Spanish established a permanent settlement on Guam, the trade became fairly regular. The Chamorros traded various types of food and drinking water for European metal and metal products. The Chamorros are often criticized in European records for placing rocks in their baskets of rice. Some see this as dishonesty, others as shrewdness. When you consider a basket of rice for a few nails, it is not difficult to see that the "cleverness" or "dishonesty" was practiced by the traders on both sides.

During historical times the Chamorros traveled to Manila. Dampier (1686) reports that a group of Chamorros made that trip in four days. This means that they averaged 13 knots (nautical miles per hour). Jesuit missionary reports confirm the fact that Chamorro proas went to the Philippines on Spanish business.

# SUMMARY

Trade is the buying, selling or bartering of something useful or valuable. The ancient Chamorros primarily conducted intra-island trade, but there was some inter-Mariana Island and Micronesian trade. Some evidence suggests that the ancient Chamorros participated in extra-Micronesian trade.

Trading is a bargain. Under ideal circumstances both sides "make out like bandits." If starving men can get food for a few nails, and those who have plenty of food can get metal tools that do a better job and last longer, both parties have benefited from the bartering. This is what trade is all about. It is exchange of valuable goods or commodities or services for mutual benefit.

# GLOSSARY

Chamorro words are italicized, except for the names of persons and places. In Chamorro, back "a's" and glottal stops are indicated by (å) and ('), respectively.

**aborigines** - the first or original inhabitants of a country or place.

**acculturation** - a process of cultural change, whereby one culture takes over elements from another culture.

*acha* - maul. Also a prefix as, indicating equality; it can also be used as an infix or suffix.

*achafnak* - relatives of the same womb; matrilineage.

*acha'on* - anvil.

*acha'ot* - second-ranked class in the *chamorri* (ancient Chamorro high caste). The working helpers of the *matao*. Also *achoti* and *atcha'ot*.

*acho'* - limestone and natural coral heads.

*acho' achuman* - a bait dispenser, composed of a spherical rock bound to half of a coconut shell, used to train fish and thereby make it easier to catch them.

*acho' atupat* - slingstone.

*acho' Yap* - a crypto-crystalline silica-type rock that was quarried and carved into Yapese stone money.

*achoti* - see *acha'ot*.

*achuman* - a small, tuna-like fish. Also salted herring. Also *hachuman* or *opelu*.

**adze** - a carpenter's tool for chipping and planing.

**affinal** - relatives by marriage.

*åfok* - quicklime, the white powder chewed with betel nut.

*aggon* - starchy foods such as rice, taro and breadfruit.

**agricultural** - a type of economy in which crops and animals are raised for food.

*akao* - a thrust hoe. Also a spade with a stone head.

*akgak* - a type of pandanus (used for weaving), *Pandanus tectorius*. Textile pandanus.

*åla* - ordinary woven baskets of medium or small size.

*ålas* - shell money.

**algae** - aquatic plants; although often one-celled they include seaweeds and kelps.

**alienation** - the feeling of estrangement from one's society and culture caused by a rapidly changing culture, which presents conflicting beliefs, values, and attitudes.

**Alu** - a legendary male chieftain from Oka who had superhuman strength.

*alutong* - basalt or volcanic rock.

**amitaclan** - a theoretical type of clan that traces descent through the male line localized around female rather than male members. Females would leave their home to live with their father's sister and continue to reside there after marriage. Males would move to their wife's land after marriage.

*amot fresko* - a cold medicine used for diseases diagnosed as "hot."

**ancestor worship** - the veneration of one's ancestors based on the belief that one's dead kinsmen can affect human life.

**ancestral spirits** - ghosts of relatives.

**ancient Chamorros** - precolonial Chamorros, Chamorros before the end of the Spanish-Chamorro War, 1695.

**animism** - a belief that everything in nature has a distinct and separate spirit or consciousness.

*aniti* - evil spirit.

*ante* - ancestral spirit, soul.

**anthropology** - the scientific study of humankind.

**anthropologist** - a professional who studies humankind.

**Anufat** - a male *taotaomo'na* with large fangs and a wound in his side.

**anvil** - a heavy block, on which things are pounded.

*a'ok* - wedding gifts (including labor) from the bridegroom's family to the bride's family.

**archaeological** - having to do with the scientific excavation of artifacts.

**archaeologist** - a professional who studies the remains of past cultures.

**archaeology** - the scientific study of the remains of past cultures.

**artifact** - object made by a human.

**assimilate** - the process through which one set of cultural traits is given up and new cultural traits are acquired.

*asuela* - chisel.

*asuli* - freshwater eel.

**atoll** - a low coral island with a reef surrounding a lagoon.

*atuli* - a special drink made of water, rice flour, and grated coconut.

**attitude** - a tendency to behave in a certain manner to a particular stimulus.

*atulai* - mackerel.

*atupat* - a sling for throwing slingstones. Also a diamond-shaped cube used to cook and carry cooked rice. It is woven from a strand of a coconut leaf.

**Australoid** - of or relating to a black race who are found in Australia and the Highlands of New Guinea.

**Austronesian** - relating to Malayo-Polynesian languages or the people who speak them. These languages are spoken by some people in Southeast Asia, Indonesia, Melanesia, the Philippines, Taiwan, Micronesia, and Polynesia.

**avuncuclan** - a clan which traces descent through the female line but is localized around male rather than female members. Males leave their home to live close to their mother's brother and continue to reside there after marriage. Females move to their husband's land when they marry.

**awl** - a pointed instrument for boring holes.

*ayudu* - help, aid, assist, succor, be of service, give aid.

*ayuyu* - coconut crab, *Birgus latro*. Also a Chamorro surname.

*babao* - a flag or banner carried into battle. Archaic. Also *babau*.

*babui* - pig.

*balakbak* - a shoulder bag used to hold slingstones.

*balate'* - sea cucumber.

**banks** - the relatively shallow ocean waters over submerged mountains, which are good fishing grounds.

**barter** - to directly trade goods and services.

**basalt** - black or dark gray volcanic rock.

*batangga* - the trolling method of fishing. Also *ma batsalla*.

*batto* - marlin.

*batya* - pandanus hat.

**bilateral descent** - the practice of tracing descent through both the mother's and father's side of the family.

*bilembao patchot* - Jew's harp.

*bilembao tuyan* - a single-stringed musical instrument with a coconut or gourd sounding box.

**blackbirder** - a person who kidnapped Pacific Islanders for use as plantation laborers.

**blue collar worker** - a skilled or unskilled person who works with his or her hands.

*boddek* - a disease, parkinsonian dementia.

*bongbong* - a bamboo tube used to carry water.

**caste** - a social group of a specified status into which a person is born and in which he or she remains for life.

**caste system** - a social class system that permits virtually no upward social mobility and prevents people from rising above the social level to which they were born.

**Caucasoid** - of or relating to the Indo-European, or white, race.

*chachachak* - knife.

*chahan* - method of cooking in an earthen oven. Also earthen oven.

**Chaife** - a male mythological character who tortured souls and who controlled the wind, the waves and fire.

*chamorri* - the highest caste in ancient Chamorro society, composed of the *matao* and *acha'ot*.

*chamorrita* - a Chamorro folk song sung in four-line stanzas. It is frequently extemporaneous poetry of a humorous, bantering nature.

**Chamorros** - the aborigines of the Mariana Islands and their descendants.

*champåda* - the competition for rank and status.

*changkocha* - boil meat. Also sterilize.

*che'lu* - sibling, brother, or sister.

*chenchule'* - a present of money or food that is given as a donation.

*chenchulu* - large drag fishing net.

*chetnot manman* - a condition in which a person stares blankly into space and cannot remember anything.

*chinahan* - food cooked in a deep-pit oven.

*chotda* - banana, *Musa paradisiaca* and *sapientum*

*chumenchulu* - a method of surrounding fish with a net.

**clan** - a group of people who think they are descended from a common ancestor and who share a common territory.

**class** - see social class.

**coir** - coconut fiber sennit or rope.

**commodity** - useful or valuable article.

**commune** - a rural community organized on the principle of sharing.

**competition** - a universal social process wherein people rival one another in an effort to obtain goals.

**consensus** - a decision-making process by general agreement.

**consanguineal** - "blood" relatives, or relatives of common ancestry.

**cooperation** - a universal social process wherein people work together toward the attainment of goals.

**copra** - the dried meat of the coconut. Oil is extracted from it and used in cooking and in soaps, shampoo, and suntan lotions.

**couplet** - two lines of verse that rhyme.

**crustaceans** - crabs, lobsters, and/or shrimp.

**cultivate** - to prepare the soil to help crops grow.

**cultural diffusion** - the process by which customs and discoveries are borrowed from other cultures.

**cultural survival** - an element of culture that remains long after it has lost its original function.

**cultural transmission** - the process by which knowledge is passed from one generation to the next.

**cultural values** - the assumptions shared by the members of a society as to what is right and wrong, good or bad, important or unimportant.

**culture** - the shared patterns of learned behavior that humans develop.

**customs**- the habits and capabilities that are socially learned, performed and transmitted.

*daddek* - a tiny coconut without meat or water.

*dagao* - a four-and-a-half-foot thrust hoe made from mangrove wood or ironwood.

*dagu* - winged yam, *Cyrtosperma chamissonis*.

*da'ok* - Maria or *palu maria*, *Calophyllum inophylum*.

**descent** - coming from an ancestor.

**dirge** - a slow, sad song or piece of music played and/or sung at a funeral.

*dokdok* - seeded breadfruit, *Artocarpus mariannensis*.

**domesticate** - to tame.

*duhendes* - mischievous elves who live in the jungle.

**echinoderms** - a category of sea animals that includes starfishes, sea urchins, and sea cucumbers.

**economy** - a system for the management and development of resources.

*edipok* - fishing with a pole and line in a tidal pool on the reef. Also fishing from a cliff into a tidal pool.

**ego** - self.

*emmok* - revenge.

**endogamy** - the custom of marrying within a specified social group.

*eskabeche* - fried fish cooked with vegetables.

*eskoplo* - adze. Archaic. Also *skopolo*.

**ethnobotanist** - scientist who studies the spread of various plants throughout the world.

**ethnocentric** - the view that a person's group is the most important group in the world.

**ethnologist** - scientist who studies ethnic groups.

**ethnology** - the scientific study of various ethnic groups.

*etokcha'* - spear fishing while skin diving.

**exogamy** - the custom of marrying out of a specified social group.

**extended family** - a family unit in which several generations of relatives live close together, or are bound closely in an emotional or economic manner.

*fadang* - federico palm and nuts, *Cycas circinalis*.

*fagahot* - a man's family's gift of shell money to which his childless widow was entitled. Heritage. Literally, "an understanding person, one who comprehends things well."

*fa'gualo* - planting time. *Fa'gualo* or *Fanggualo'* is October.

*fa'i* - rice growing in the field, *Oryza sativa*.

*fañagu* - bear offspring, give birth.

*fanihi* - fruit bat, *Pteropus mariannus*.

*fayao* - a large wooden pestle used from a standing position to husk rice or crush various foods.

**felony** - a serious criminal offense.

**fermentation** - a process whereby organic material is changed from a complex to a more simple state in which it can be preserved.

**fictional relative** - a person addressed by a kinship term who is not that person's blood or marriage relative, for example a "godfather," or a nun who is addressed as "sister."

*fino' gualafon* - an allegorical language in which songs were sung that only the young people could understand. Literally, "moonlight talk."

*fisga* - spear.

**flake** - a scale-like piece of rock with a sharp cutting edge.

**folklore** - the traditional literature as expressed in folk tales, incantations, proverbs, riddles, songs, and prayers.

**folkways** - the learned shared behavior common to a people.

**food gatherers** - an economic system in which food is collected rather than raised.

**Fouha Bay** - the first bay north of Umatac. The legendary birthplace of humankind.

*fruta* - all fruits that are eaten raw.

*fudfud* - a stick with palm tassels used to parry lance thrusts.

**funeral** - the final rite of passage ceremony.

*fusiños* - a thrust hoe with a metal blade.

**Fu'uña** - a female mythological character who was born of the air and who created the universe from the body parts of her deceased brother, Puntan. Also the ancient village at Fouha Bay. Some accounts state that at one time it was the highest-ranking village on Guam.

*gachai* - adze or axe. Also *guaddukon*.

*ga'chong* - partner or friend.

**Gadao** - a legendary male chieftain from Inalajan (Inarajan) of superhuman strength.

*gaddo'* - thorny wild yam, *Dioscorea esculenta*.

*gadi* - a fishing method in which palm leaves or a long net is used.

*gaga* - flying fish.

*gagu* - ironwood tree, *Casuarina equisetifolia*.

*galaide'* - a small canoe used mainly inside the reef.

**Gamson** - a male *taotaomo'na* reported to haunt the Pago Bay area. Literally, "octopus."

*gao* - node. A reduced form of *gahu*.

**Gapang** - Camel Rock. Literally, "unfinished task."

**Gatos** - a male *taotaomo'na* reported to make people sick. Literally, "one hundred."

**genealogist** - a person who studies the descent of persons or families.

**genealogy** - a report on the descent of a person, family, or group from an ancestor.

**generation** - a step in descent from parents to offspring.

**genetic drift** - gene frequency changes in small populations as the result of the chance preservation or extinction of particular genes.

**genus** - a category, smaller than family and larger than species, used by scientists to classify animals or plants with similar characteristics.

*ghintos* - a section of a *lukao hugua* money necklace.

*gigao* - a fish trap or fish weir. In ancient times it was a wedge-shaped barrier of rocks on the reef used to catch fish as the tide went out.

*gimen* - all drinks except alcoholic drinks.

**gods and goddeses** - remote beings who are believed to control the universe or various parts of it.

**government** - the organization developed by officials to make and carry out decisions and conduct the general administration of public affairs.

*guaddukon* - adze.

*guafak* - a pandanus mat. Various types were used as mattresses, blankets, funeral shrouds, a clean surface for drying rice and serving food, and for wrapping gifts.

*guagua'* - an ordinary woven fish basket.

*Guahan* - Chamorro name for Guam; literally, "we have."

*guahayi* - a dowry from the groom's family to the bride's family. Literally, "enrichment." Also *guadhadje*.

**Guamanian** - a Chamorro from Guam. Less frequently, it is used to describe someone born on Guam or who lives on Guam.

*guasa'* - method of poisoning or stupefying fish.

*guasa'on* - grindstone.

*guatafi* - red snapper.

*guesgues* - scraper.

*gugat* - fishing line.

*guinahan famagu'on* - child's wealth, an almost priceless piece of ancient Chamorro shell money.

*guini* - a tortoiseshell disk (approximately 3/8 inch in diameter) necklace used as money.

*guma'* - house.

*guma' alumsek* - a cave where the drawings, on bark, of a person's ancestors were kept.

*guma' uritao* - clubhouse for bachelors.

*gunot* - the fiber found on coconut trees where the leaves sprout from the trunk.

*gupot* - party, celebration, fiesta, festivity, holiday, feast.

**haft** - handle of a weapon or tool.

**Hagatña** - Agaña. Usually cited as the highest-ranking village on Guam.

*hagon* - leaf.

*haguet* - fishhook.

*ha'iguas* - coconut shell.

*hale'* - root.

*haligi* - the pillar part of a *latte* stone.

**hamlet** - a small village or part of a village.

**hierarchical** - relating to ranking in order.

**hierarchy** - a group of persons or things ranked in successive classes.

*higai* - coconut leaves.

*hilitai* - monitor lizards.

*hima* - giant clam, *Tridacna maxima* and *Tridacna squamosa*. This shell was used to make adzes.

*hineksa'* - cooked rice or rice cake.

**historian** - a professional who studies and writes history.

**history** - a chronological (in order of time) record and interpretation of the past.

**Hoabinhians** - early Southeast Asian people who may be the ancestors of the Micronesians and Polynesians.

*Homo erectus* - early humans; literally, "erect man."

*Homo sapiens* - human beings; literally, "thinking man."

**horticulturists** - people who cultivate the soil to produce food crops.

*hotyong songsong* - a ceremonial capture or kidnapping. Literally, "going out of the tribe."

*hoyu* - deep pit. Also deep pit of the kind used for an oven.

**humus** - decaying plants.

**hunter-gatherer** - a type of economic system in which people hunt animals and collect wild food plants.

*ika* - funeral gift from a family.

*ilangilang* - a fragrant tree, *Cananga ordorata*. Also *alangilang*.

*inafa'maolek* - interdependence, getting along. Literally, "making it good for each other."

**incestuous** - involving a forbidden sexual union between a couple who are closely related.

**indigenous** - having originated in and living naturally in a given territory.

**indigenous foods** - the foods found naturally in a place, the foods not introduced to a place by human beings.

**institution** - a system of norms that have grown up around a major social function.

**institutional order** - organized system that centers on a basic human need.

**inter-island trade** - trade between islands.

**intra-island trade** - trade within an island.

**invention** - the adoption by a society of a new way of doing something.

*kaffo'* - pandanus, *Pandanus fragrans*.

*kakahna* - a variation of *makahna*. In some accounts it is listed as a sorcerer, who could cure or make people sick by spiritual means.

*kalang* - pendant.

*kamyo* - a coconut grater. Also to grate coconut.

*katgaderu* - sinker.

*katgat* - fishing line.

*katna* - good fishing.

*ka'tokcha'* - fishing with a spear.

*kelaguen* - a type of food made of meat, salt, red pepper, and lemon juice.

**kiln** - oven for firing pottery.

**kinship** - the tie or bond between children, their parents and other relatives.

**kinsmen** - relatives.

**knot** - a nautical mile per hour.

*ko'ko'* - Guam rail, *Rallus owstoni*.

*kompaire* - a term of address used between parents and godparents.

*kotdet* - fishing line.

*kottot* - a rectangular woven pandanus basket used to package a gift of rice.

*kulales* - beads.

*kulo'* - triton trumpet shell used as a horn; *Charonia trinonis*.

*laggua* - a big parrotfish.

*lagua'* - small hand-fishing nets.

*lailai* - tortoiseshell plate used for money.

*lalagu* - a method of catching fish by hand.

*lalassas* - peeler.

**Lapita pottery** - a distinctive style of pottery, frequently made from red clay and tempered with shell or sand. It or similar types of pottery are found in Melanesia, Indonesia, the Philippines, Micronesia, and Polynesia.

**Laso de Fua** - a rock pillar at Fouha Bay associated with the Guam's Adam legend and the Puntan myth.

*lassas* - bark. Also skin, peel, crust or rind.

**lateen** - triangular shape.

*Latte* **Period** - the ancient Chamorro period of time from the 800s until the late 1600s.

*latte* **stones** - two-part stone supports for ancient Chamorro houses.

**legend** - an unverifiable story from the past that is popularly regarded as historical.

*lemmai* - breadfruit, *Artocarpus incisus*.

*lemon dichina* - limeberry, *Triphasia trifolia*.

**lineage** - all blood relatives who can trace their descent through either male relatives to a known ancestor or female relatives to a known ancestress.

202

**linguist** - a professional who studies the structure and modification of human speech.

**linguistics** - the scientific study of the structure and modification of human speech.

*litiku* - a disease, amyotropic lateral sclerosis.

*lommok* - pestle.

*lukao hugua* - a tortoiseshell disk (approximately 3/4 inch in diameter) necklace used as money.

*lulai* - fishing on a moonlit night with a hook and line.

*lusong* - mortar.

*ma batsalla* - the trolling method of fishing. Also *batangga*.

*ma chatlamen* - an exiled man who refuses to leave his village. Also a man who is detested.

*ma mongle* - a method of surrounding fish with a net. Also *chumenchulu*.

*ma uritao* - a girl chosen for the bachelors' house.

*maga'haga* - highest-ranking female in a village. Literally, "the daughter of the chief, or first-born daughter."

*maga'lahi* - highest ranking male in a village. Ruler, the highest rank of a state, as president, governor, major, magistrate, chief, chieftain. Literally, "first-born son."

**magic** - the use of supernatural power through chants or incantations.

*makahna* - shaman and/or sorcerer; ancient Chamorro spiritual leader.

*maku dudu* - a polished tortoiseshell plaque worn as an apron by wealthy women.

**Malaguaña** - a legendary male chieftain of superhuman strength from Tumon.

*mamahlao* - an attitude of deference and respect toward others. Also *manachang*.

*mama'on* - betel nut, sprinkled with quicklime, wrapped in a betel pepper leaf, and ready for chewing.

*manachang* - low caste. Literally, "flawed or imperfect." Also *mamahlao* or "*mangatchang*."

*managgam* - a method of blocking fish with a large net. Also *manhalla*.

*mañahak* - juvenile rabbit fish.

*manakhilo* - high class.

*manakpapa* - low class.

*maneska* - alcoholic drinks.

*mangga* - mango fruit, *Mangifera indica*.

*manggi Hagatña* - high-class people. It refers to the people whose family are from Agaña.

*manggi sengsong* - lower-class people. It refers to the people whose family are not from Agaña.

*mangle'* - mangrove tree, *Bruguiera gymnorrhiza* or *Rhizophora mucronata*.

*mango'* - turmeric or ginger used in cooking or for coloring; *Curcuma domestica*.

*manhalla* - a method of blocking fish with a large net. Also *managgam*.

*manñgiñge'* - the custom of holding a respected elder's slightly raised hand and then bowing and touching one's nose to the back of the elder's hand in order to show respect. The root word is *nginge'*.

*mannok* - chicken.

*maño'cho'* - a method of catching some types of parrotfish and wrasses by hand.

*maranan uchan* - ancestral skull. Literally, "a miraculous thing for rain."

*mari* - competitive debate.

**market economy** - an economy in which most of the output is produced for exchange, rather than for use by the immediate producers.

**"marmar"** - a crown of flowers. [Carolinian]

**Masala** - a legendary male chieftain from Apurguan whose son leaped to Luta (Rota).

*matao* - highest class in the *chamorri* (ancient Chamorro high caste). Also *matua*.

**matraclan** - a group of females living in close proximity with the unmarried males of their clan and the husbands and children of their married females.

**matrilineage** - mother's side of the family. All blood relatives who can trace their descent through female relatives to a known ancestress.

**matrilineal** - relating to the tracing of descent through the mother's side of the family.

**matrilineal descent** - a practice which traces descent through the mother's side of the family. Kinsmen are related to a person through females.

*mattiyu* - hammerstone.

**mediator** - a person who tries to get two parties to agree.

**Melanesia** - a geographical area in the Western Pacific north and east of Australia. It includes New Guinea, the Solomon Islands, the archipelago of Fiji, the Santa Cruz group, the Banks' Islands and Vanuatu, and New Caledonia with the Loyalty Islands. Literally, "black islands."

*mestisu* - a person of Spanish and Chamorro ancestry.

**Micronesia** - a geographical area in the Western Pacific east of the Philippines. It includes the Mariana Islands, the Caroline Islands (the Belau, Yap, Chuuk, Pohnpei, and Kosrae Islands), the Marshall Islands, and the Kiribati Islands. Literally, "small islands."

**midden** - soil that contains refuse, artifacts and other evidence of human inhabitation.

**misdemeanor** - a criminal offense, less serious than a felony.

*mitati* - a stone for grinding corn (sometimes spelled *metate*).

**mollusks** - shellfish like clams and single shelled animals. Octopus and squid are included in this category of animals.

**monarchy** - a form of government in which a king rules the entire country.

**money** - anything members of a community are willing to accept in payment for goods, services, or debts.

**Mongoloid** - of or relating to people whose origin is eastern Asia.

**monogamy** - the custom of having one spouse at a time.

**mor** - a folkway or norm regarded as necessary for the welfare of society.

**mores** - folkways or norms regarded as necessary for the welfare of society.

**mortar** - a thick bowl in which substances are pounded with a pestle.

**Motac** - the ancient village at Umatac Bay. Some accounts state that at one time it was the highest-ranking village on Guam.

**Mount Sasalaguan** - a mountain in Southern Guam (between Malesso and Inalajan). It is the mythological home of Chaife. *Sasalaguan* is translated as hell.

**Mount Tuyan** - a mountain in Barrigada. *Tuyan* is translated as stomach, belly, or abdomen.

**myth** - a traditional story that reveals a people's world view, or explains a practice or belief, or natural phenomenon (happening).

**mythology** - the supernatural stories of a people.

*na'lagu* - to cook in a pot.

*nanasu* - the small half-flower tree, the fruit of which is used as an eyewash.

*nasa* - a shrimp trap made of woven strips of bamboo.

**native** - born, living, and growing in a particular territory but not necessarily originating in that area.

**native foods** - foods introduced to an area by the original inhabitants.

**natural selection** - a process that causes individuals or groups best suited to their living conditions to survive and pass on their genetic qualities.

*na'yan nengkanno'* - foods used in making sauces.

**Negroid** - of or relating to African; black race.

**neolithic** - of or relating to the New Stone Age; literally, "new stone."

*nette* - swordgrass, *Miscanthus floridulus*.

*ngagsan* - a fish pond used to preserve fish for eating and bait.

*nginge'* - the custom of holding a respected elder's slightly raised hand and then bowing and touching one's nose to the back of the elder's hand in order to show respect. Also to sniff or smell (something).

*ngufa' guafak* - a sleeveless pandanus mat vest.

*nina* - godmother.

*ninu* - godfather.

*niyok* - coconut palm tree, *Cocos nucifera*.

**nomadic** - relating to those who roam from place to place.

**norm** - a group-shared expectation of behavior.

**nuclear family** - a married man and woman and their offspring.

*nunu* - banyan tree, *Ficus prolixa*.

**Nusantao** - a maritime people of Southeast Asia and their descendants who settled Western Micronesia.

**Oceania** - the Pacific Ocean islands of Melanesia, Micronesia, and Polynesia. Sometimes Australia is included.

*okkodon panglao* - a bamboo tube crab trap.  Also *okkodu*.

*okkodu* - bamboo tube crab trap.  Also *okkodon panglao*.

**Okkodu** - a legendary male chieftain who had superhuman strength and who tricked the people of Luta (Rota).

**omnivorous** - eating both plants and animals.

**overpopulation** - the condition of too many people in a given area for the resources and technology available.

*pagu* - wild Hibiscus tree, *Hibiscus tiliaceus*.  Its bark is used to make rope.

*pahong* - pandanus, *Pandanus dubius*.

*palakse'* - parrotfish.  Literally, "slippery."

*palapåla* - huts, shacks, or pavilions, usually of a temporary nature.

*palayi* - a type of fish poison.  Also Palayi Islets off Hagat (Agat) Village near the mouth of the Namu River.

**paleolithic** - of or relating to the Old Stone Age; literally, "old stone."

**Pang** - a legendary male chieftain from Inalajan (Inarajan) who had superhuman strength and fought Alu.

**patraclan** - a group of males living in close proximity with the unmarried females of their clan and the wives and children of their married males.

**patrilineage** - father's side of a family.  All "blood" relatives who can trace their descent through male relatives to a known ancestor.

**patrilineal** - relating to the tracing of descent through the father's side of the family.

**patrilineal descent** - a practice that traces descent through the father's side of the family.  Kinsmen are related to a person through males.

*pattidu* - division of family land among children.

**peer group** - a group consisting of individuals who are approximately equal in such characteristics as age and social standing.

**peskan sumulo'** - fishing by the light of a torch.

**pestle** - an instrument for pounding substances in a mortar.

**petroglyph** - writing on, or in stone.

*pi'ao* - bamboo, *Bambusa vulgaris*.

*pinipu* - perforated tortoiseshell plate used for money.

*pisao* - a fishing pole.

*pitor* - pottery used for cooking; pottery sauce pan.

**plankton** - small plant and animal organisms that float in water, and on which animal sea life is directly or indirectly dependent.

*platitos* - a leaf used as a plate, *Polyscias scutellaria*.

*poio* - hemispherical or spherical sinkers used in fishing.

*pokpok* - the swelling of the feet, mouth, or other part of the body.

*pokse'* - the bark fiber of the *pagu* tree, which was used to make rope, tassels, and clothing.

**polyandry** - the custom of having more than one husband at a time.

**polygamy** - the custom of having more than one spouse at a time.

**polygyny** - the custom of having more than one wife at a time.

**Polynesia** - a geographical area in the Pacifc Ocean from the Hawaiian Islands in the north, to Easter Island in the east, to New Zealand in the south.  Literally, "many islands."

*postre* - desserts like cakes, rolls or even ice cream.

*potseras* - bracelet.

**potsherd** - a pottery fragment.

**prehistoric** or **prehistorical** - relating to the time before written records.

**prehistory** - period before written records.

**Pre-*latte* Period** - the ancient Chamorro period from about 2000 B.C. until the 800s A.D.

**proverb** - an old and frequently repeated saying of advice or wisdom.

**psychosocial** - referring to nonbiological needs of humans that have both social and psychological aspects.

**public opinion** - an expression of the moral judgment of the group.

*pugua'* - betel nut, *Areca catechu*.

"puka" - a naturally formed shell disk with a hole in the center, used to make necklaces. Literally, "hole" in Polynesian languages.

*pulos* - a barbed harpoon.

pumice - a light, porous kind of lava used to sharpen some tools.

Puntan - a male mythological character who was born of the air and who had his sister Fu'uña create the universe from his body parts.

*pupulu* - betel pepper leaf, *Piper betle*.

*puteng* - a tree or its fruit, *Barringtonia asiatica*. The triangular-shaped fruits can be used for net floats. The seeds can be crushed and used as a fish poison.

*putot* - small mortar and pestle.

quarry - an open pit from which stone is obtained for building.

radiocarbon (C14) - an element that emits invisible rays that penetrate matter.

radiocarbon dating - a means of dating most organic material up to 70,000 years old. It is based on the fact that all things that have lived lose half of their C14 every 5,730 (+ or - 40) years.

reciprocity - the continuing process by which actions toward one party are returned.

religion - a system of beliefs in supernatural beings and worship.

rites of passage - the formal behavior that recognizes a person's change from one social status to another, for example from child to adult.

ritual - a ceremony performed in a particular way.

Rotanese - Chamorros from *Luta* (Rota).

*sahayan* - earthenware jar sometimes used as a burial urn.

*saibok* - to boil starchy foods.

*saina* - elder or parent.

Saipanese - Chamorros from Saipan or Chamorros and Carolinians from Saipan.

*sakman* - oceangoing outrigger sailing canoe.

*salape'* - money.

*saluu* - betel nut case used on festive occasions.

sanction - the means by which a society enforces its mores and folkways.

*sapblasos* - club.

*sasalaguan* - hell.

*sa'sime'* - raw fish.

satghe - a woven plate for serving rice cake. Also *sarghi*.

sennit - cord or string.

*se'se'* - knife.

shaman - a religious leader who has special abilities to influence supernatural powers for the benefit of his clients.

shovel incisor - a type of tooth characteristic of Mongoloids. A front tooth with vertical ridges on its back outside margins.

*si'i* - a shell tool used to make pandanus strips pliable for weaving.

slingstone - a football shaped rock about the size of a golf ball that is meant to be thrown from a sling.

slip - a smooth layer of wet clay put on a pot before firing.

social classes - categories of people grouped together because they are viewed as possessing similar levels of prestige.

social control - the means by which a society secures conformity to its norms.

social disorganization - a severe breakdown in the social order caused by failure to develop new behavioral guide-lines needed to handle unique social situations.

social mobility - the changing of position within a class structure.

social organization - the fixed way in which groups behave.

social sanction - the means by which a society enforces its mores and folkways.

social structure - the framework around which people organize themselves in order to satisfy their needs.

**socialization** - the process through which the individual learns to adjust to society's norms and thereby becomes a member of society.

**society** - a group of people sharing a common culture.

**solidarity** - unity based on mutual community interests.

*songsong* - village. Also Songsong, the major town on Luta (Rota).

**sorcerer** - a person who performs evil magic.

**sorcery** - the craft of evil magic.

**specialization** - the concentration of activities in a particular field.

**species** - a specific scientific classification of organisms capable of interbreeding.

**spouse** - a husband or wife.

**staple** - a basic part of a people's diet.

**starboard** - right side of a ship when facing forward.

**strata** - layers. Stratum - layer.

**stratigraphy** - the arrangement of strata.

**subsistence economy** - an economy in which most of the output is produced for use by the immediate producers or their friends and relatives.

*sulares* - ancestral places inhabited by *ante* or *aniti*. Also *solares*.

*sulo'* - torch fishing.

*suni* - taro, *Colocasia esculenta*.

**supernatural** - relating to an existence beyond the visible or observable; of or relating to God or a god, or spirit.

**superstition** - a belief that many helpful and harmful supernatural forces exist, and that certain actions will anger or pacify them.

*suruhanu/suruhana* - male/female herb doctor.

**swidden agriculture** - a slash and burn type of farming.

**taboo** - a rule, the violation of which means severe, automatic punishment.

*tadiu* - legal judgment.

*tagon nette* - swordgrass leaves sewn onto strips of bamboo to be used as shingles for a roof.

*tagon nipa* - nipa leaves sewn onto strips of bamboo to be used as shingles for a roof.

*tahu* - catching crabs with a flashlight.

*talac* - grooved fishing sinkers from conical to spherical shape.

*talåya* - a casting fishing net.

*tanum* - a thrust hoe used for planting taro and for opening coconuts.

*taotaomo'na* - ancestral spirits, ghosts, demons, disembodied souls or specters. Literally, "people of before."

*taotaomo'na gachong* - a *taotaomo'na* friend who gives a person special help.

*tasa* - the cap part of a *latte* stone.

*techa* - prayer director.

*tefan* - a pandanus sleeping mat.

*tekken* - a gill-fishing net.

**temper** - various types of sand mixed with clay to make pottery.

*ti'ao* - juvenile goatfish.

*tifi* - a small, triangular apron worn by women.

*tinaitai* - prayer.

**Tinianese** - Chamorros from Tinian.

*todu manatungo'* - consensus.

**tort** - a wrongful civil offense.

**tortoiseshell** - the shell of various turtles. It was used as money in ancient Chamorro times.

*totche* - high-protein foods like fish and meat.

**totem** - usually a plant or animal emblem of a clan.

**totemism** - a belief in kinship through common clan emblem affiliation.

*totot* - Marianas Rose Crown Fruit Dove, *Ptilinopus roseicapilla*. Guam's territorial bird. Also trustee of the land.

**trade** - the buying or selling or bartering of something useful or valuable.

**trade winds** - generally easterly winds in the tropical belt north and south of the equator.

**tribute** - a payment to another that acknowledges submission.

**tsunami** - a large sea wave caused by a submarine earthquake or volcanic eruption.

*tunas* - A long stick decorated with distinctive geometric carvings, colored orange, and topped with an 18-inch-long  tassel.  It was carried by bachelors.

*tunu* - roasting of food over embers.  Also *pehu*.

*tupu* - sugarcane, *Saccharum officinarum*.

*ugot* - a massage by walking on the body.

*umefohmo'* - a method of fishing in which fish are frightened from their hiding places into a basket of rocks.

**universal** - present or occurring everywhere.

*uritao* - a social group of young, single males.  Sometimes it is used as men's house or bachelors' quarters.  Also *urritao or ulitao*.

*uritoi* - a society or peer group of young people.

*utak* - white-tailed tropic bird.  Also *itak*.  The mythical bird that squawks around a house when an unmarried girl is pregnant.

**value** - a concept that culture sees as desirable.

**vegetarian** - a person who eats only plants.

**veneration** - looking on with great respect and reverence.

**vertical mobility** - movement between classes, either to a higher class (ascending) or to a lower class (descending).

**village council** - a decision-making group composed of the highest-ranking men and women in a village.

**wampum** - strung shells used as money by Native Americans.

**Westerner** - a person whose ancestors are from Western European cultures.

**white collar worker** - a person who has an office job or a job in which he or she can stay clean.

*yokyok* - rubbing two sticks together or using flint to start a fire.

**zoologist** - A professional who studies animals.

# BIBLIOGRAPHY

Abella, Domingo. "An Introduction to the Study of Philippine-Marianas Relations." *Guam Recorder*, n.s., 3 (2, 1973): 9-12.

Alkire, William H. *An Introduction to the Peoples and Cultures of Micronesia*, 2d ed. Menlo Park, California: Cummings Publishing Company, 1977.

Amesbury, Steven S., and Robert F. Myers. *Guide to the Coastal Resources of Guam*. Vol . I: *The Fishes*. University of Guam Marine Laboratory Contribution No. 173. Mangilao, Guam: University of Guam Press, 1982.

Amesbury, Steven S., Frank Cushing and Richard K. Sakamoto. *Guide to the Coastal Resources of Guam*. Vol . III: *Fishing on Guam*. University of Guam Marine Laboratory Contribution No. 225. Mangilao, Guam: University of Guam Press, 1986.

Amesbury, Steven S. "Whether Pigs Have Wings." *Agaña* (Guam) *Pacific Daily News*, 31 January 1988, sec. Islander, pp. 4-7.

Ansaldo, Marcelo. "Events that Transpired on June 15, 1668 on the Arrival of the Sanvitores Mission at Agaña Bay." Translated by Felicia Plaza. *Guam Recorder*, n.s.,1 (1971): 14-17.

Arago, Jacques Etienne Victor. *Narrative of a Voyage Round the World in the* Uranie *and* Physicienne *Corvettes Commanded by Captain Freycinet During the Years, 1817, 1818, 1819 and 1820*. London: Treuttel, and Wurtz, Treuttel, jun. and Richter, 1823.

Audleman, Al. "Legends of Guam." *Glimpses of Guam*, 1970, pp. 73-79.

Ballendorf, Dirk Anthony. "The Violent First Encounters." *Guam Recorder*, n.s., 4 (1, 1974): 37-40.

Barcinas, Jesus C. "The Legend of the Coconut." In *Coconut*, p. 11. Edited by Ruth Hembekides. Agaña, Guam: Department of Public Health and Welfare, n.d.

Barratt, Glynn. *Russian Exploration in the Mariana Islands, 1817-1828*. The Micronesian Archaeological Survey Report Series, no. 17. Saipan: CNMI Divsion of Historic Preservation, Department of Community and Cultural Affairs, 1984.

_____. *Carolinean [sic] Contacts with the Islands of the Marianas: The European Record*. The Micronesian Archaeological Survey Report Series, no. 25. Saipan: CNMI Divsion of Historic Preservation, Department of Community and Cultural Affairs, 1988a.

_____. *H.M.S. Centurion at Tinian, 1742: The Ethnographic and Historic Records*. The Micronesian Archaeological Survey Report Series, no. 26. Saipan: CNMI Divsion of Historic Preservation, Department of Community and Cultural Affairs, 1988b.

Barrett, Ward. *Mission in the Marianas: An Account of Father Diego Luis de Sanvitores and His Companions, 1669-1670*. Minneapolis: University of Minnesota Press, 1975.

Beaglehole, J. C. *The Exploration of the Pacific*, 3d ed. Stanford, California: Stanford University Press, 1966.

Beardsley, Charles. *Guam: Past and Present*. Tokyo: Charles E. Tuttle Company, 1964.

Beaty, Janice J. *Discovering Guam: A Guide to Its Towns, Trails and Tenants*. Tokyo: Tokyo News Service, Ltd. for Faith Book Store, Agaña, Guam, 1967.

_____. *Guam, Today and Yesterday*. Agaña, Guam: Department of Education, 1968.

Behrens, Larry. *Life on Guam: Limestone Forest*. Agaña, Guam: Department of Education, 1977.

Bellwood, P. S. "The Peopling of the Pacific." *Scientific American* (November 1974): 174-185.

_____. *Man's Conquest of the Pacific: The Prehistory of Southeast Asia and Oceania*. New York: Oxford University Press, 1979.

Bothmer, Judy. "Making Pots the Old Way." *Agaña* (Guam) *Pacific Daily News*, 15 June 1980, sec. Islander, pp. 10-11.

Bram, Joseph. *Language and Society*. New York: Random House, 1955.

Bryan, E. H. *Guide to Place Names in the Trust Territory of the Pacific Islands*. Honolulu, Hawaii: Pacific Scientific Information Center of the Bernice P. Bishop Museum, 1971a.

_____. "Notes on the Ancient Culture of Guam." *Guam Recorder*, n.s., 1,(1971b): 6-7.

Burney, James. *A Chronological History of the Discoveries of the Pacific Ocean*. 5 vols. London: Luke Hansard, 1803-1817; reprint ed., Bibliotheca Australiana no. 3. Amsterdam: N. Israel, 1967.

Butler, B.M. "Pots as Tools: The Marianas Case." *Micronesica*. Supplement No. 2 (October 1990): 33-46.

Calkin, F. "Prehistoric Pottery." *Agaña* (Guam) *Pacific Daily News*, 15 May 1976, sec. Islander, pp. 6-7.

Callahan, Raymond, *An Introduction to Education in American Society*. New York: Alfred A. Knopf, 1961.

Carano, Paul. "San Vitores – An Introduction." *Guam Recorder*, n.s., 1 (2 &3, 1972):    37-38.

_____. "Martyrdom of San Vitores." *Guam Recorder*, n.s., 1 (2 &3, 1972): 59-61.

_____. "Ancient Chamorro Leaders." *Guam Recorder*, n.s., 2 (4, 1972): 7-8.

_____. "Glimpses at the Historical Development of Representative Self-Government in Guam." *Guam Recorder*, n.s., 2 (4, 1972): 51-56.

_____. "British Privateers Visit Guam." *Guam Recorder*, n.s., 4, (3, 1974): 25-30.

_____. "The Ancient Chamorros." *Guam Recorder*, n.s., 6, (1, 1976): 3-13.

_____. "Martyrdom of Father San Vitores." In *San Vitores, His Life, Times, and Martyrdom*, pp. 67-75. Micronesia Area Research Center, Publication, no. 6. Edited by Emilie G. Johnston. Mangilao, Guam: Micronesia Area Research Center, 1977.

Carano, Paul and Pedro C. Sanchez. *A Complete History of Guam*. Rutland, Vermont: Charles E. Tuttle Company, 1964.

Chamorro-Buerba, Angel. *Cultural Hispanica en las Islas Mariana*. Fairbanks: University of Alaska, 1971.

Chamorro Language and Culture Program. *Legends of Guam*. Agaña, Guam: Department of Education, 1978.

Chamorro Language and Cultural Program. *Legends*. Agaña, Guam: Department of Education, 1985.

Chaney, Richard P. "Meta Organizational Aspects of Improving Social Life from the Native's Point of View." Paper presented at the meeting of the Society for Applied Anthropology, Reno, Nevada, March 1986.

Conklin, Harold C. "Ethnogenealogical Method." In *Explorations in Cultural Anthropology*, pp. 25-55. Editor Ward Hunt Goodenough. New York: McGraw-Hill, 1964.

Corey, Vicky. *Chronology of Ships Visiting Guam, 1521-1898*. Unpublished manuscript. Mangilao, Guam: University of Guam, n.d.

Corte, Don Felipe de la. "Memoirs of Don Felipe de la Corte's Eleven Years as Governor of Guam 1855-1866." *Guam Recorder*, n.s., 2 (4, 1972): 12-19.

Costenoble. H. "The Family Tree of Chamorro." *Guam Recorder*, n.s., 4 (2, 1974): 25-26.

Craib, John L. and Nancy L. Farrell. "On the Question of Prehistoric Rice Cultivation in the Mariana Islands." *Micronesica* 17 (1-2, December 1981): 1-9.

Crofts, George D. "Human Personality Develops: Gadao & Hildebrand." *Guam Recorder*, n.s., 4 (1, 1974): 25-26.

Crumrine, N. Ross. "Praying and Feasting: Modern Guamanian Fiestas." *Anthropos*, 77, (1982): 89-111.

Cunningham, Cheryl Napier, ed. *Know Your Land*. Agat, Guam: Agat Junior High School, 1975.

Cunningham, Lawrence J. "Guam's Birth." *Guam Recorder*, n.s., 6, (1, 1976): 23-27.

_____. *Origin and Migration of the Ancient Chamorros*. Mangilao GU: Teacher Corps, 1978.

_____. "Betel Mania." *Agaña* (Guam) *Pacific Daily News*, 22 February 1981, sec. Islander, p. 5.

_____. "Magellan: the Guam Visit." *Agaña* (Guam) *Pacific Daily News*, 1 March 1981, sec. Islander, pp. 8-9.

_____. "Search for Paradise." *Agaña* (Guam) *Pacific Daily News*, 15 March 1981, sec. Islander, pp. 8-9.

_____. "Martyrdom." *Agaña* (Guam) *Pacific Daily News*, 29 March1981, sec. Islander, pp. 8-9.

_____. "Writings on the Cave Wall." *Agaña* (Guam) *Pacific Daily News*, 17 May 1981, sec. Islander, p. 5.

_____. "Legacy of the Breadfruit." *Agaña* (Guam) *Pacific Daily News*, 14 June 1981, sec. Islander, pp. 8-9.

_____. "Return of the *Trinidad*." *Agaña* (Guam) *Pacific Daily News*, 14 March 1982, sec. Islander, pp. 7-9.

_____. "Legend of the Breadfruit." *Agaña* (Guam) *Pacific Daily News*, 20 February 1983, sec. Islander, pp. 7-9.

_____. *Ancient Chamorro Kinship Organization*. Agat, Guam: L. Joseph Press, 1984.

_____. "The Miracle of the Breadfruit." *Now*, (June 1985): 6-9.

_____. *The Development and Validation of a High School Textboook on the Ancient Chamorros of Guam*. Doctoral dissertation, University of Oregon, 1987.

Cunningham, Lawrence J., and M.D. Gall. "The Effects of Expository and Narrative Prose on Student Achievement and Attitudes Toward Textbooks." *The Journal of Experimental Education*, 58, (3, Spring 1990): 165-175.

Dampier, William. *A New Voyage Round the World*. New York: Dover Publications, Inc., 1968.

Del Valle, Teresa. "Tercentenary of the Evangelization of the Mariana Islands 1668-1968." *Guam Recorder*, n.s., 1, (1971): 21-24.

_____. *Social and Cultural Change in the Community of Umatac, Southern Guam*. Mangilao, Guam: Micronesian Area Research Center, 1979.

Diaz, Gaylord, and Dave Hotaling. *Life on Guam: Mangrove Flat*. Agaña, Guam: Department of Education, 1977.

Driver, Marjorie G. "Historical Documents from Mexico." *Guam Recorder*, n.s., 1 (1971): 18-19.

_____. "The Account of a Discalced Friar's Stay in the Islands of the Ladrones." *Guam Recorder*, n.s., 7 (1977): 19-21.

_____. "Notes and Documents: Fray Juan Pobre de Zamora and His Account of the Mariana Islands." *The Journal of Pacific History*, 18 (3), (July 1983): 198-216.

_____. "Notes and Documents: Fray Juan Pobre de Zamora Hitherto Unpublished Accounts of his Residence in the Mariana Islands." *The Journal of Pacific History*, 23, (1, April 1988): 85-94.

_____. *Cross, Sword, and Silver: The Nascent Spanish Colony in the Mariana Islands*. Mangilao, Guam: Micronesian Area Research Center, 1990a.

_____., ed. *The Guam Diary of Naturalist Antonio de Pineda y Ramirez*. Translated by Victor F. Mallada. Mangilao, Guam: Micronesian Area Research Center, 1990b.

Eldredge, L. G., and T. L. Tansy. *Inside the Reef*. Agaña, Guam: Pacific Graphics, 1975.

Elkins, Gail, Dave Hotaling and Richard H. Randall. *Life on Guam: Geology*. Agaña, Guam: Department of Education, 1977.

Eustaquio, Roque B. "Chamorro Funeral Ritual." Unpublished manuscript. Mangilao, Guam: University of Guam, 1976.

_____. *Islas: A Social Studies Workbook*. Barrigada, Guam: Marianas Red Publishing, 1989.

Falanruw, Margie Cushing. *Life on Guam: Beach Strand*. Agaña, Guam: Department of Education, 1977.

_____. *Life on Guam: Savanna, Old Fields, Roadsides*. Agaña, Guam: Department of Education, 1977.

Finney, Ben R., ed. *Pacific Navigation and Voyaging*. Wellington, New Zealand: The Polynesian Society, 1976.

Fischer, John L., and Ann M. Fischer. *The Eastern Carolines*. New Haven, Connecticut: Human Relations Area Files Press, 1957.

Franquez, Rita. "The Chamorro 'Hereafter'." Paper presented at the Guam Museum Symposium. Agaña, Guam: May 17, 1987.

Freeman, Lila L. "Island Legends: Sirene the Mermaid and the Crab and the Needlefish." *Guam Recorder*, n.s., 1 (2 &3, 1972): 63-64.

_____. "Island Legends: How the Young Maidens Saved Guam, The First Breadfruit Tree, & The Turtles and the Mountain Tunnel." *Guam Recorder*, n.s., 2 (4, 1972): 9-11.

Freycinet, Louis Claude Desousles de. *Voyage autour des monde execute sur los corvettes de S.M. l'Uranie et la Physicienne, pendant les annus 1817-1820*. 3 vols. Paris: Phillet aine, 1829-1837. (Mangilao, Guam: Micronesian Area Research Center Microfilm reel 58, unedited translation of Vol. 2: 228-515, New Haven, Connecticut: Yale University Human Relations Area Files MS 1410, 1943). (Los Angeles: Department of Special Collections, University Research Library, University of California, Los Angeles Q 115 F89v Atlas Sec.1 v.1 Plate 63: "Iles Mariannes: Usages Des Anciens Habitans. Peche.").

Fritz, Georg. "Die Chamorro: Eine Geschichte und Ethnographic de Marianen." *Ethnologisches Notizblatt*, Band 3, Left 3, pp. 25-100. Berlin, 1904. (Mangilao, Guam: Micronesian Area Research Center Microfilm reel 56, unedited translation, New Haven, Connecticut: Yale University Human Relations Area Files MS 1235, 1944?).

_____. *The Chamorro. A History and Ethnography of the Marianas*, 2nd ed. Edited by Scott Russell. Translated by Elfriede Craddock. Saipan, CNMI: Division of Historic Preservation, 1989.

Gall, M. D. *Handbook for Evaluating and Selecting Curriculum Materials*. Boston: Allyn & Bacon, 1981.

Garcia, Francisco. *Vida y matirio de el venerable Padre Diego de Sanvitores de la Compania de Jesus, primer apostol de la islas Marianas*. Madrid: Ivan Garcia Infanzon, 1683. Translated by Margaret Higgins. "First History of Guam." *Guam Recorder*, o.s., 13, 14, and 15 (September 1936 to July 1939).

Garrido, Maria T. "Why the Iguana Has a Double Tongue." *Guam Recorder*, n.s., 1 (2 &3, 1972): 65.

Geertz, Clifford. *The Interpretation of Cultures*. New York: Basic Books, Inc., 1973.

Geertz, Clifford. *Local Knowledge*. New York: Basic Books, Inc., 1983.

Gladwin, Thomas. *East is a Big Bird: Navigation and Logic on Puluwat Atoll*. Cambridge, Massachusetts: Harvard University Press, 1970.

Gomoll, Larry E., ed. *Plants of Guam*. Mangilao, Guam: College of Agriculture and Life, Sciences, 1979.

Goodenough, Ward H. "A Problem in Malayo-Polynesian Social Organization." In *Peoples and Cultures of the Pacific*, Andrew P. Vayda, ed. Garden City New York: The Natural History Press, 1968.

Grace, George W. "Classification of the Languages of the Pacific." In *Peoples and Cultures of the Pacific*, Andrew P. Vayda, ed. Garden City New York: The Natural History Press, 1968.

Graham, Robert B. "The Origins of the Chamorro People." *Micronesian Reporter*, 16, (3, 1972), 11-15.

_____. "Tinian: History of an Island." *Guam Recorder*, n.s., 4, (3, 1974): 13-18.

Graves, Michael W. "Archaeological Analysis of Ceramic Material from the Asan Drainage Corridor, Guam." Unpublished thesis, Behavioral Science Program, University of Guam, Mangilao, Guam, October 1983.

Guerrero, Jesus S. L. "Economic History of Guam." *Guam Recorder*, n.s., 2, (4, 1972): 68-71.

Guerrero, Sue, ed. *Superstitions: Myth or Reality*. Agaña, Guam: Department of Education, n.d.

Gunner, L. "Acho Yap." *Guam Recorder*, n.s., 1,(1971): 12-14.

Haddock, R. L. *A History of Health on Guam*. 2nd ed. Agaña, Guam: Department of Public Health and Social Services, 1973.

Haddon, A. C. and James Hornel. *Canoes of Oceania*. Honolulu: Bishop Museum Special Publications, 1975.

_____. "Functional, Structural, or Traditional?" *Guam Recorder*, n.s., 4,(2, 1974): 36-38.

Haviland, William A. *Cultural Anthropology*. New York. Holt, Rinehart and Winston, 1981.

Hedlund, S. E. *The Extent of Coral, Shell, and Algal Harvesting in Guam Waters*. University of Guam Marine Laboratory, Technical Report No. 37. Mangilao, Guam, 1977.

Hembekides, Ruth. *Coconut: Wonder Tree of the Pacific*. Nutrition Division, Department of Public Health and Welfare. Agaña, Guam, n.d.

Hernandez, Jose. "Conditions in Guam in 1690." Translated by W. C. Repetti. *Guam Recorder*, 1, (1971): 20-21.

Hezel, Francis X. *From Conquest to Colonization: Spain in the Mariana Islands 1690 - 1740*. Saipan, CNMI: Divsion of Historic Preservation, 1989.

Hezel, Francis X. and Charles Reafsnyder. *Micronesia Through the Years*. [Saipan: Trust Territory of the Pacific], n.d.

Hornbostel, Hans, and Gertrude Hornbostel. "Chamorro Locality Names." *Guam Recorder*, o.s., 2 (February 1926): 340; reprinted in *Guam Recorder*, n s., 1 (1971): 9.

_____. Unpublished field notes on the Mariana Islands, Bishop Museum, Honolulu. Cited by Laura Thompson, *Guam and Its People*, p. 99. 3d ed. Princeton: Princeton University Press, 1947, reprint ed., Westport, Connecticut: Greenwood Press, 1969.

Hornung, Ralph S. "Effects of Betel Nut Chewing." *Guam Recorder*, n.s., 1, (2 &3,1972): 72-73.

Howells, William. *The Pacific Islanders*. New York: Charles Scribner's Sons, 1973.

Hsu, Francis L. K., ed. *Kinship and Culture*. Chicago: Aldine Publishing Company, 1971.

Hynd, George W. "Religion and Magic Among the Ancient Chamorro." *Guam Recorder*, n.s., 4, (1, 1974): 23-24.

_____. "Taotaomona: A Functional Belief Among the Chamorro People." *Guam Recorder*, 5, (2, 1975): 16-17.

Ibanez del Carmen, Aniceto, and Francisco Resano. *Chronical of the Mariana Islands*. Translated by Marjorie G. Driver. Mangilao, Guam: Micronesian Area Research Center, 1976.

Johnston, Emilie G. "Chamorro Tools, Implements and Utensils." *Guam Recorder*, n.s., 1, (2 &3, 1972): 58-59.

_____. "A Review of the Literature on Native Medicine in Micronesia with Emphasis on Guam and the Mariana Islands." *Guam Recorder*, n.s., 5, (2, 1975): 60-65.

_____., ed. *San Vitores, His Life, Times, and Martyrdom*, Micronesia Area Research Center, Publication no. 6. Edited by Emilie G. Johnston. Mangilao, Guam: Micronesia Area Research Center, 1977.

Jones, R.S., and H. K. Larson. *A Key to the Families of Fishes as Recorded from Guam*. University of Guam Marine Laboratory, Technical Report No. 10. Mangilao, Guam, 1974.

Karolle, Bruce G. "A Geography of Guam Island." *Guam Recorder*, n.s., 3, (3, 1973): 16-25.

_____. *Atlas of Micronesia*. Agaña, Guam: Guam Publications Inc., 1988.

[Kesolei, Katherine]. *A History of Palau*. Vol. 1: *Traditional Palau, the First Europeans*. Koror, Palau: Palau Community Action Agency, 1976.

Key, Robert E., ed. *A Naturalist's Guide to Guam*. Agaña, Guam: Guam Science Teachers Association, 1968.

Kluckhohn, Clyde. *Mirror for Man*. New York: McGraw-Hill Book Company, 1949.

Knudson, K.E. "Social Complexity on Truk and in the Marianas: Lack of Correspondence between Anthropological Models and Historical Evidence." *Micronesica*. Supplement No. 2 (October 1990): 117-124.

Kotzebue, Otto van. *A Voyage of Discovery into the South Sea and Beering's Strait a North-east Passage undertaken in the Years 1815-1818*. 3 vols. Translated by H.E. Lloyd. London: Longman, Hurs, Rees, Orme, and Brown, 1821; reprint ed., Bibliotheca Australiana no. 19. Amsterdam: N. Israel, 1967.

Kroeber, A. L. "Kinship in the Philippines." In *Anthropological Papers of the American Museum of Natural History*, Vol. 19, part 3, pp. 73-84. New York: The American Museum of Natural History, 1919; photo-offset reprint ed., New Haven, Connecticut: Human Relations Area Files, 1955.

Kurashina, Hiro. *Prehistoric Settlement Patterns on Guam*. Paper presented at the meeting of the Society for American Archaeology, New Orleans, Louisiana (April 23-26, 1986).

Kurashina, Hiro, Darlene Moore, O. Kataoka, Russell N. Clayshulte, and Erwin R. Ray. "Prehistoric and Protohistoric Cultural Occurrences at Tarague, Guam." *Asian Perspectives*, 24, (1, 1981): 57-68.

Kurashina, H. and R. N. Clayshulte. Site Formation Processes and Cultural Sequence at Tarague, Guam. Manuscript submitted for publication. Mangilao, Guam: University of Guam, 1986.

[Ledesma, Andres de]. *Noticia de los Progressos de Nuestra Santa Fe, en las Islas Marianas, llamadas antes de las Ladrones*. Translated by Ward Barrett, *Mission in the Marianas, An Account of Father Luis de Sanvitores and his Companions 1669-1670*. Minneapolis: University of Minnesota Press, 1975.

"Legends of Guam." *Guam Recorder*, n.s., 3, (2, 1973): 15-16.

Le Gobien, Charles. *Histoire des islas Marianes, nouvellement converties a la religion Chrestienne, et de la mort glorieuse das primiers missionaires qui y ont preche la foy. Paris: N. Pepie, 1700*. Translated by Paul Daly C.P.S. *History of the Marianas Islands*. Guam, 1949. (Typewritten). Mangilao, Guam: Micronesian Area Research Center (photocopy).

Leon Guerrero, Victoria. "The Art of Amot." *Guam Recorder*, n.s., 3, (2, 1973): 34.

Lessa, William A. *Drake's Island of Thieves: Ethnological Sleuthing*. Honolulu: The University Press of Hawaii, 1975.

Lewis, David. *We, the Navigators*. Honolulu: The University Press of Hawaii, 1973.

Lizama, Alejandro, "Advanced Technology of the Ancients." *Agaña* (Guam) *Pacific Daily News*, 16 May 1976, sec. Islander, pp. 4-7.

Lizama, Alejandro, Marvin Montvel-Cohen, and Darlene Moore. "The As Nieves Quarry and Tatgua Site, Rota M.I." In *Latte: Occasional Papers in Anthropology and Historic Preservation*. Vol. 1 September 1981.

Lundsgaard, Henry P. "Pacific Island Tenure in a Nutshell." In *Land Tenure in Oceania*. Association for Social Anthropology in Oceania Monograph, no. 2, pp. 265-275. Edited by Henry Lundsgaard. Honolulu: University Press of Hawaii, 1974.

Marche, Antoine -Alfred. *The Mariana Islands*. Edited by Robert D. Craig. Translated by Sylvia E. Cheng. Mangilao, Guam: Micronesian Area Research Center, 1982.

McCoy, Michael. "A Renaissance in Carolinian-Marianas Voyaging." Edited by Ben R. Finney in *Pacific Navigation and Voyaging*. Wellington, New Zealand: The Polynesian Society, 1976.

McGrath, Thomas B. "A Man Determined." *Guam Recorder*, n.s., 1, (2 &3, 1972a): 43-45.

_____. "The Proas of the Marianas." *Guam Recorder*, n.s., 1, (2 &3, 1972b): 48-52.

_____. "Ilomaw: The Tough One." *Guam Recorder*, n.s., 8 (1978): 44.

McMakin, Patrick D. "The Suruhanos: Traditional Curers on the Island of Guam." *Micronesica* Vol. 14 (1, June 1978): 12-67.

Montvel-Cohen, Marvin, and Darlene Moore. *Latte: Occasional Papers in Anthropology and Historic Preservation.* Agaña, Guam: Department of Parks and Recreation, 1981.

Moore, Darlene. *Measuring Change in Marianas Pottery: The Sequence of Pottery Production at Tarague, Guam.* Unpublished master's thesis, Behavioral Science Program, University of Guam, Mangilao, Guam, 1983.

Moore, Philip H. *Life on Guam: Farm and Garden.* Agaña, Guam: Department of Education, 1977.

Morell, Virginia. "Wild Lessons." *International Wildlife*, 15 (6, Nov.-Dec., 1985): 47-50.

Morgan, William N. *Prehistoric Architecture in Micronesia.* Austin, Texas: University of Texas Press, 1988.

Munoz, Faye Untalan, "Pacific Islanders--A Perplexed, Neglected Minority." *Social Casework*, 1976, 57, 179-184.

_____. "Family Life Patterns of Pacific Islanders: The Insidious Displacement of Culture. Submitted as sub-chapter for *Psycho-social Development of Minority Group Children*, to be published by Brunner/Mazel, May 1977. Boulder, Colorado.

Murdock, George Peter. *Social Structure.* New York: Macmillan, 1949; paperback ed., New York: Free Press, 1965.

_____. "Genetic Classification of the Austronesian Languages: A Key to Oceanic Culture History." In *Peoples and Cultures of the Pacific*, Andrew p. Vayda, ed. Garden City, New York: The Natural History Press, 1968.

Nelli, Elizabeth. "Mirror of a People: Folktales and Social Studies." *Social Education.* (February 1985): 155-158.

Ngiruchelbad, Johana, and Lisa Saila. "Retaining Unity." *Agaña* (Guam) *Pacific Daily News*, 5 March 1989, sec. Islander, pp. 8-9.

Olive y Garcia, F. *The Mariana Islands: Random Notes Concerning Them.* Translated by Marjorie G. Driver. Micronesian Area Research Center Publication No. 10. Mangilao, Guam: Micronesian Area Research Center, 1984.

Oliver, Douglas L. *The Pacific Islands.* Honolulu: The University Press of Hawaii, 1961.

Osborne, D. *Chamorro Archaeology.* Unpublished manuscript. University of Washington, Seattle, n.d.

Peck, W. M., Ursula Atalig, and Gerald Calvo. "Offended Ancestors." *Agaña* (Guam) *Pacific Daily News*, 5 November 1989, sec. Islander, pp. 5-9.

Pietrusewsky, M. "The Physical Anthropology of Micronesia: A Brief Overview." *Micronesica.* Supplement No. 2 (October 1990): 317-322.

Plaza, Felicia. "Origin of the Word Chamorro." *Guam Recorder*, n.s., 1 (1, 1971): 4-5.

_____. "Companions of San Vitores." *Guam Recorder*, n.s.,1 (2 &3, 1972): 46-48.

_____. "The Lattes of the Marianas." *Guam Recorder*, n.s., 3 (1, 1973): 6-9.

Poignant, Roslyn. *Oceanic Mythology.* New York: Paul Hamlyn, 1967.

Radcliff-Brown, A. R. "The Study of Kinship Systems." *Journal of the Royal Anthropological Institute.* 71 (1941): 1-18.

Ramirez, Anthony J. "Chamorro Proverbs." In *40th Anniversary "Freedom to Be" of the Liberation of Guam.* Tamuning, Guam: Fiestan Guam Committee, 1984.

_____. "Chamorro Names." In *40th Anniversary "Freedom to Be"of the Liberation of Guam.* Tamuning, Guam: Fiestan Guam Committee, 1984.

Randall, Richard H., and Eldredge, R. G. *Life on Guam: Coral Reef.* Agaña, Guam: Department of Education, 1977.

Raulerson, Lynn. *Life on Guam: Freshwater.* Agaña, Guam: Department of Education, 1977.

Reinman, Fred. "Guam Prehistory." *Guam Recorder*, n.s., 1,(1973): 10-14.

_____. *An Archaeological Survey and Preliminary Test Excavations of the Island of Guam, Mariana Islands, 1964-66* (Micronesian Area Research Center, Miscellaneous Publication No. 1), Mangilao, Guam: University of Guam, 1977.

Repetti, W. C. "A Supplementary Note to the First History of Guam." *Guam Recorder*, o.s. 17 (1940): 91.

_____. "Another 17th Century Letter from Rota." *Guam Recorder*, o.s., 18 (1941a): 95.

_____. "The Uprising in Guam in 1684." *Guam Recorder*, o.s. 18 (1941b): 124.

_____. "Conditions in Guam in 1690." *Guam Recorder*, o.s.,18 (1941c): 230.

_____. "Relation of the Events in the Marianas Mission from June, 1681, to June 1682." *The Catholic Historical Review* , 31, (1946): 433.

_____. "An Early Church Census of Guam." *Guam Recorder*, n.s., 1 (2 &3,   1972): 69.

Ribadeneira, Marcelo. *Historia de las islas de archipelago Filipino y reinos de la Gran China, Tartaria, Cochinchina, Malaca, Siam, Cambodge y Japon.* Edicion, prologo y notas por el P. Juan R. de Legisima, O.F.M. Madrid: La Editorial Catolica, 1947. Translated in part (Capitulo xix) by Marjorie G. Driver. "The Account of a Discalced Friar's Stay in the Islands of the Ladrones." *Guam Recorder* n.s., 7 (1977): 19-21.

Risco, Alberto. *The Apostle of the Marianas.* Edited by Msgr. Oscar L. Calvo. Translated by Juan M. H. Ledesma, S.J. Agaña, Guam: Diocese of Agaña, 1970.

Rock, Tim. "Roots." *Agaña* (Guam) *Pacific Daily News*, 1 May 1988, sec. Islander,  pp. 4-7.

Roger, Woodes. *A Cruising Voyage Round the World.* New York: Dover Publications, Inc., 1970.

Safford, William E. "The Chamorro Calendar." *Guam Recorder*, n.s., 4 (2, 1974): 49.

Sanchez, Doanne. "Belembautuyan, Ancient and Vanishing Relic." *Agaña* (Guam) *Pacific Daily News*, 15  September 1985, sec. Islander,  pp. 6-7.

Sanchez, Pedro. *Guahan (Guam): The History of an Island and Its People.* Agaña, Guam: Sanchez Publishing House, 1988.

San Nicolas, Ruth. "Myths of Guam and Micronesia." *Agaña* (Guam) *Pacific Daily News*, 24 December 1989, sec. Islander,  pp. 4-7.

Sapir, E. *Time Perspective in Aboriginal American Culture, a Study in Methodology* (Department of Mines, Canada Geological Survey Memoir 90, Anthropological Series No. 13). Ottawa, Canada: Ottawa Government Printing, 1916. New York: Johnson Reprint Corp., 1968.

Scheffler, H. W. "Theory and Method in the Study of Kinship." *Reviews in Anthropology.* 12 (1, Winter, 1985): 34-40.

Schusky, Ernest L. *Manual for Kinship Analysis.* 2d ed. New York: Holt, Rinehart and Winston, 1972.

Searles, P. J. "The Queerest Stringed Instrument in the World." *Guam Recorder*, n.s. 2 (10): 20.

Sharp, Andrew. *Ancient Voyagers in Polynesia.* Berkeley, California: University of California Press, 1964.

Shutler, Richard Jr., and Mary Elizabeth Shutler. *Oceanic Prehistory.* Menlo Park, California: Cummings Publishing Company, 1975.

Solheim, W.G., II. "Thoughts on Land and Sea Peoples in Southeast Asia and their Possible Relationships to Initial Settlement of Micronesia." *Micronesica.* Supplement No. 2 (October 1990): 241-246.

Souder, Laura M., ed. *I Finaposta.* Agaña, Guam: Governor's Pre-White House Conference  on Libraries and Information Exhibition, 1978.

Souder, Paul. "The Latte: House of the Ancients." *Pacific Profiles.* October, 1964.

Spoehr, Alexander. "Saipan, the Ethnology of a War-Devastated Island." *Fieldiana: Anthropology*, 41, 1954.

_____. "Marianas Prehistory: Archaeolgical Survey and Excavations on Saipan, Tinian, and Rota." *Fieldiana: Anthropology*, 48, 1957.

_____. "Life of the Chamorros in the Marianas." *Guam Recorder*, n.s., 3 (2, 1973): 13-14.

Stephenson, F. A. "Talofofo Cave Writing." *Guam Recorder*, n.s., 1, (1971): 10-11.

Stephenson, Rebecca A., ed. *Freshwater Use Customs on Guam: an Exploratory Study.* Mangilao, Guam: University of Guam Water Resources Research Center Technical Report No. 8, April 1979.

Stewart, Edward C. *American Cultural Patterns: A Cross-Cultural Perspective.* Chicago: Intercultural Press, Inc., 1972.

Stojkovich, Jeanine O., and Barry D. Smith. *Survey of Edible Shellfish and Sea Urchins on the Reefs of Guam.* Aquatic and Wildlife Resources Division Department of Agriculture, Technical Report No. 2. Mangilao, Guam, 1978.

Stone, Benjamin, C. "The Flora of Guam." *Micronesica*, 6, 1970.

Strunka, J. V., ed. *A Model Competency Based Curriculum for Social Studies 7 - 12* (Teacher Corps Inservice Project). Agaña, Guam: University of Guam, College of Education, 1977.

Taitano, Carlos P., Remedios L.G. Perez,  Rosario T. Sablan, and Menna U. Cespedes. *Legend of Guam as Told by Old-time Guamanians.* Agaña, Guam: The Guam Tuberculosis and Health Association, n.d.

Takayama, J. & Tomoko E.  "Archaeology on Rota in the Marianas Islands:  Preliminary Report on the First Excavation of the Latte Site (m-1). *Reports of Pacific Archaeological Survey*, 1, 1971.

Thompson, Jim. "In the Beginning." *Glimpses of Guam*, 1968, pp. 1-7.

Thompson, Laura Maud. *Archaeology of the Marianas Islands*. Bernice Pauahi Bishop Museum Bulletin, 100. Honolulu:  Bishop Museum Press, 1932; reprint ed., New York:  Krauss Reprint, 1971.

_____. *Guam and Its People*, enl., with a Village Journal by Jesus C. Barcinas. 3d ed.  Princeton:  Princeton University Press, 1947; reprint ed., Westport, Connecticut:  Greenwood Press, 1969.

_____. *The Native Culture of the Marianas Islands*. Bernice Pauahi Bishop Museum  Bulletin, 185. Honolulu:  Bishop Museum Press, 1945; reprint ed. New York:  Krauss Reprint, 1971.

_____. "The Function of the Latte in the Marianas." *Journal of the Polynesian Society*, 195, (1940):  447-465.

Topping, Donald, Pedro M. Ogo, and Bernadita C. Dungca. *Chamorro-English Dictionary*. Pacific and Asian Linguistic Institute Language Texts:  Micronesia. Honolulu:  University Press of Hawaii, 1975.

Turner, C.G. "Origin and Affinity of the Prehistoric People of Guam:  A Dental Anthropological Assessment." *Micronesica*. Supplement No. 2 (October 1990): 403-416.

Underwood, Jane H. "The Native Origins of the Neo-Chamorros." *Guam Recorder*, n.s.,7 (1977):  25-29.

Underwood, Robert A. "What is a Family." *Agaña* (Guam) *Pacific Daily News*, 18 November 1979, sec. Islander, p. 10.

Van Peenen, Mavis Warner. *Chamorro Legends on the Island of Guam*. Micronesian Area Research Center, Publication, no. 4. Mangilao, Guam:  Micronesian Area Research Center, 1974.

Vayda, Andrew P., ed.  *Peoples and Cultures of the Pacific*. Garden City, New York:  The Natural History Press, 1968.

Wallace, Anthony F. C. "Handsome Lake and the Decline of the Iroquois Matriarchate." In *Kinship and Culture*, pp. 367-376. Edited by Francis L. K. Hsu. Chicago:  Aldine Publishing Company, 1971.

*World Book Encyclopaedia*, 1978 ed. S.v. "Races, Human," by Stanley M. Garn and illustrated by Neil O. Hardy.

Yawata, I. "Rice Cultivation of the Ancient Mariana Islanders." In *Plants and the Migrations of Pacific Peoples*, J. Barrau, ed. Honolulu:  Bishop Museum Press, 1963.

# INDEX

Page numbers in boldface refer to illustrations.

220

# About the Author

Lawrence J. Cunningham has been living in Agat (paradise), Guam, since 1968. Born in Pittsburgh, Pennsylvania, in 1943 and raised in Ashland, Kentucky, and Cincinnati, Ohio, he received a B. S. in Education (1965) and a M. Ed. (1967) from the University of Cincinnati. In 1987 he earned his Doctorate in Education from the University of Oregon. His major interest is in the research and development of curricular materials.

After teaching a year in Covington, Kentucky, Cunningham and his wife, Cheryl Faith Napier, decided to see the world. They have traveled throughout the United States, Micronesia, Japan, Southeast Asia, India, Nepal, and Africa.

Cunningham has taught a variety of Social Studies courses at Agat Junior High School, Inarajan Junior High School, and Oceanview High School on Guam. He has headed Oceanview High School's Accreditation Steering Committee and School Learning Improvement Plan Team, and has been the Social Studies Department Chairperson for all but three of his 23 years on Guam.

Cunningham has written many popular articles about the Mariana Islands' past for the *Pacific Daily News, American Pacific, New Pacific, Now,* and the *Guam Recorder.* He was winner of the *Espiriton Hurao* Award for Chamorro Publications in 1978. In 1984 his book *Ancient Chamorro Kinship Organization* was published. His research on the effects of expository and narrative prose on student achievement and attitudes toward textbooks has been published by *The Journal of Experimental Education* and in the 5th edition of *Educational Research* by Walter R. Borg and Meredith D. Gall.

Cunningham is also known as L. Joseph the woodcarver. His hardwood creations, which frequently depict local legends, have been the official gift of Guam to the heads of state of several countries, including the President of the United States.